Latter-Gay Saints

DATE DUE

Latter-Gay Saints

An Anthology of Gay Mormon Fiction

Edited and Introduced by Gerald S. Argetsinger

Co-edited by Jeff Laver and Johnny Townsend

LETHE PRESS
MAPLE SHADE NJ

Published May, 2013 by Lethe Press, 118 Heritage Ave,
    Maple Shade NJ 08052
lethepressbooks.com lethepress@aol.com

Book Design by Toby Johnson
Cover image: *Brother's Keeper II* by Trevor Southey
    trevorsoutheystudio.blogspot.com/

ISBN-13 978-1-59021-264-6
ISBN-10 1-59021-264-9
e-ISBN 978-1-59021-265-3

Library of Congress Cataloging-in-Publication Data

Latter-gay saints : an anthology of gay Mormon fiction / edited and introduced by Gerald S. Argetsinger ; co-edited by Jeff Laver and Johnny Townsend.
    pages cm
Includes bibliographical references.
    Summary: Contains twenty-five exemplary short works depicting a variety of perspectives of what it means to be both Mormon and gay. Some portray characters determined to reconcile their sexuality with the Mormon faith in accordance with its constantly evolving teachings and policies. The majority present the realities of gay/lesbian Mormons who have come to terms with their sexuality in a variety of alternative ways. Others are written from outside the Mormon community, commenting on often strange encounters with Mormons who are gay.
    ISBN-13: 978-1-59021-264-6
    ISBN-10: 1-59021-264-9
    ISBN-13: 978-1-59021-265-3
    1. Mormon gays--Fiction. 2. Homosexuality--Religious aspects--Church of Jesus Christ of Latter-day Saints--Fiction. I. Argetsinger, Gerald S., 1946- editor of compilation. II. Laver, Jeff, 1952- editor of compilation. III. Townsend, Johnny, editor of compilation.
    PN6071.H724L38 2013
    808.8'0353--dc23
                    2013010264

Contents

This is for Norm Burningham, Tom Graham, Neil Pitts, and Cary Jensen, all of whom know why.

—Jerry Argetsinger

Dedicated to Margo and the notion that, "Inasmuch as ye have done it unto one of the least of these…, ye have done it unto me."

—Jeff Laver

And dedicated to all people oppressed by religion "for their own good."

—Johnny Townsend

Introduction

Gerald S. Argetsinger

"What monk was there in the Monastery of my childhood who didn't hope one day to be with God? What do you say to me now, that we, the Children of Darkness, serve Him with no hope of ever being with Him?"

He looked broken suddenly.

"Pray there is some secret that we don't know," he whispered. He looked off as if he were in fact praying... "How can he not love us? I don't understand, but I am what I am, which is this, and you are the same." He looked at me, eyebrows rising gently again to underscore his wonder. "And we must serve Him. Otherwise we are lost."

—Anne Rice, *The Vampire Armand*

A community is defined, and its values disseminated, through its stories. For most gay Mormons, our stories have been hidden. Officially, they do not exist. No church publisher will print them and no church bookstore will accept them from outside sources. While individual stories have found their way into the pages of such alternative Mormon publications as *Sunstone Magazine* and *Dialogue: A Journal of Mormon Thought*, and into literary journals and Gay/Lesbian/Bi-Sexual/ Transgendered (GLBT) publications, they are few and far between and are usually discovered by accident. A quick internet search reveals several sites where gay Mormon themed erotica is posted, but fails to direct the serious reader to the stories that represent our lives. *Latter-Gay Saints* is the first anthology of our collective writings, the result of over five years work by the Gay Mormon Literature Project.

Several years ago I received notice from a major university press of a planned anthology that would examine how the Church of Jesus Christ of Latter-day Saints is depicted in popular culture. An editor contacted me asking if I would be willing to write a chapter on how the Mormon Church is portrayed in gay literature. I readily agreed: How much gay themed literature could there be that mentions the Mormon Church? My academic background and profession is film and theatre, so I knew of the Pulitzer Prize winners, Alan Drury's *Advise and Consent* (1959) and Tony Kushner's *Angels in America* (1993). I had directed Carol Lynn Pearson's *Facing East* (2006) and had seen Paul Rudd's Off Broadway comedy, *The Most*

Fabulous Story Ever Told (1999) in New York City. Levi Peterson's celebrated novel, *The Backslider* (1990), included the first transgendered Mormon character. Only two of those works were written by Mormon authors. Was it possible that non-Mormons were more interested in the notion of Mormonism and homosexuality than GLBT Mormons themselves? No sooner had I begun to assemble a respectable bibliography than I was notified that the planned book had been cancelled. But I was hooked, so I continued to collect copies of each and every work I could find that included a gay Mormon character and/or theme. It was like a treasure hunt. I never knew where the next story would be discovered. The next step was to organize the stories and report on the project and findings through conferences and publications. And thus the Gay Mormon Literature Project was born. At least ten papers have been presented and five articles published. The bibliography now includes nearly two hundred short stories, novels, and scripts.

Latter-Gay Saints brings together twenty-five exemplary short works from the Gay Mormon Literature Project. Each is unique, representing the individual perspective of its own creator. Stephen King explains, "The job of fiction is to find the truth inside the story's web of lies." (*On Writing*, p. 159) These stories present our truths of what it means to be both Mormon and gay. None of these stories purport to represent any "official position" of the Church of Jesus Christ of Latter-day Saints. But they do represent our lives, our hopes, our aspirations.

Some stories portray characters determined to reconcile their sexuality with the Mormon faith in accordance with its constantly evolving teachings and policies ranging from excommunication, to expulsion from church-owned universities, to encouraging parents to exclude GLBT relatives from family celebrations, and on to the current mantra "there is no sin in being 'same sex attracted,' only in acting on that attraction."

The majority of the stories represent the realities of gay/lesbian Mormons who have come to terms with their sexuality in a variety of alternative ways. Several are written from outside the Mormon community, commenting on often strange encounters with Mormons who are gay. One of the most important books for many gay men is *Boys Like Us: Gay Writers Tell Their Coming Out Stories* by Patrick Merla and Hetrick Martin (1997), which offers thirty essays that present an entire spectrum of the lives of gay men. These were offered without judgment or comment; they simply were what they were. Because of those personal stories men coming to terms with their sexuality are able to say to themselves, "I am not like those, but I am like these. There is a place for me the way I am. I can accept myself without trying to become something I am not." That is the value of *Latter-Gay Saints*: a broad representation of the experiences of gay Mormons is presented without judgment. Gay Mormons finally have a literature of their own; a place for each individual regardless of where they are on the spectrum of the Mormon Gay Community or on the spectrum of the Mormon Community at large. Our stories will show you the paths that have been walked by some of your brothers and sisters. They will help you to say, "I am this." Or, "I am not that." Perhaps even most importantly they may help you discover, "I want to become like this" or, "I do not want to become like that." What is certain is that they will help you to understand who you are and that you are not alone.

> Why couldn't we see they could live with us—Baptists and generals and pundits all—if we'd just stay in the closet? We can live with you if you'll just play dead.
>
> Paul Monette, *Last Watch of the Night*

Serendipitously, the day I sat down to write this introduction, the Mormon church announced a new website, the intent of which is explained as follows: "In an effort to encourage understanding and civil conversation about same-sex attraction, The Church of Jesus Christ of Latter-day Saints has launched the website Love One Another: A Discussion on Same-Sex Attraction" (www.mormonsandgays.org). As the stories in *Latter-Gay Saints* were collected before the launching of this website, it is clear that they are not intended to be a response in any way. However, the timing is perfect, or should I say *inspired*, because these stories contribute to the civil conversation and promote an understanding of GLBT Mormons.

Our stories are also of value for the broader GLBT community. They're a great read! Understandably, some individuals scoff at those who hope to reconcile their religious traditions with their homosexuality. But there *are* gay Mormons, and Jews, and Catholics, and Jehovah's Witnesses, and Muslims, and Hindus, ad nauseam. Reading works by those who "believe" reveals the similarities that people of faith, regardless of which faith, face in attempting to negotiate their religious heritage with their homosexuality. Our stories reveal that some find a way, while others do not, leaving their faith or having it ripped from them.

For those Mormons who are reading in order to understand a family member or friend; for those who are reading to find reasons to reject the notion of being Mormon and gay; for those reading to condemn the editors and writers of this volume in scathing blogs and commentaries; regardless of your motivation, you will find what you seek. You will also find stories to amaze and uplift your own faith. This collection does not attempt to define or describe a "Gay Mormon Agenda." There is no agenda. There are only individuals searching for answers to life's puzzles, some of whom will touch your souls, others who will not. That is as it should be.

I never gave you a chance to tell your story
Glenn Close, et al, *Albert Nobbs*

> There's this line that you can cross all you want as long as you have a reason for doing it. If it has a point and it has a story and it has genuine real character and emotion, then you can pretty much do whatever you

want. There is no line if you're being truthful. We learned that lesson a
long time ago.

> Trey Parker, *The Book of Mormon: The Testament of
> a Broadway Musical*

The first gay Mormon character was Senator Brigham Anderson in Drury's
Advise and Consent. The topic was so taboo in 1959 that even though the Mormon
Senator from Utah's homosexual affair was the pivotal event of the entire novel,
neither the word "homosexual" nor any of its counterparts appeared in the book.
The critical event of the story was exclusively implied. The movie version (1962)
directed by Otto Preminger actually exploited the fact that, for the first time in
film history, it took its audience into a gay bar. Drury's storyline required a senator
who was squeaky clean, intelligent, popular and above all respected. Depicting
Anderson as a Mormon fulfilled all the criteria. It also helped Drury because in
the late fifties, specifics about the religion were unknown, both to his readers and
apparently to Drury. Other than being labeled a "Mormon," everything about
Brigham Anderson and his religion is decidedly Catholic. It was over thirty years
until 1993 when Tony Kushner did the research required to depict a gay Mormon
accurately in *Angels in America*. Remarkably, both Drury and Kushner received
the Pulitzer Prize for their work.

The appearance of the first gay Mormons by a Mormon writer is even more
unusual. Richard Fullmer, a young gay man from Vernal, Utah, left his religious
community in the mid-1960's for the streets of San Francisco. At the time it was
still illegal to publish books with openly homosexual themes, but a few daring
writers braved prosecution and began to publish to the gay community. Fullmer
wanted to create gay characters who were comfortable with their homosexuality
and who found it to be life affirming, even uplifting. Writing under the name Dirk
Vanden, he created literary stories which included central Mormon characters. The
publisher did not believe gay fiction would sell without regular scenes of "hot gay
sex" and so added them to Vanden's books against his wishes. Today, Vanden's
All Trilogy: *I Want It All* (1969), *All the Way* (1970), and *All Is Well* (1971) are
considered seminal gay classics and Vanden is hailed as one of the pioneers of gay
fiction. Still writing today, we are proud to include "Gay Messiah" from his recent
award-winning novel, *All of Me* (2010). This is undoubtedly the most unusual story
in the collection. Consider that when Levi S. Peterson created a "Cowboy Jesus"
in his 1990 western novel, *The Backslider*, the Mormon reading audience was not
accepting. One can only imagine their response to a gay Messiah, even though he
is created from the author's belief in an all-loving god.

> Over fifty percent of Salt Lake City's homeless young men are gay.
> Salt Lake City Police Department, 2010

The experience of being young and homosexual is a central theme in gay Mormon literature. Mormonism is a religion that demands specific standards of behavior from its members. Beginning at age twelve, each young Mormon receives a personal copy of *For the Strength of Youth*, which outlines appropriate dress, speech, entertainment, internet, and sexual behavior. Regarding homosexuality it states, "Homosexual and lesbian behavior is a serious sin. If you find yourself struggling with same-gender attraction or you are being persuaded to participate in inappropriate behavior, seek counsel from your parents and bishop. They will help you." While every religion has the right to circumscribe acceptable behavior, there is a major problem with this particular advice. The Mormon Church is operated by a lay ministry. Mormon bishops are not trained in any area of psychological or social therapy. Homosexuality is probably the most taboo topic amongst Latter-day Saints. Since the church publishes only one brief pamphlet on the topic, *God Loveth His Children*, no parent is prepared for a gay son or daughter coming to them for help. The bishops are usually confused, while the parents panic. "From both adults and peers [Mormon youth] hear the deprecating epithets, the scornful aspersions, the biased misinformation about gays which cause them to feel contemptible. They struggle to understand their difference in an environment that demands conformity. They hide their feelings from the world, even from loved ones, and hate themselves for this deception." (Wayne Schow, *Remembering Brad*, p. 8) From the very beginnings of the realization that they might be gay, they believe that their very nature is evil. They are left to carry that burden of guilt which takes over every aspect of their lives. While gay youth are counseled that the rules of chastity are exactly the same for them as their straight counterparts, the leaders are unaware that heterosexuals do not have to brood continually about why they are the way they are. "Which is more immoral, being gay or being taught to hate yourself?" (Schow, p. 52) One does not convert to homosexuality as one would convert to Islam or to Mormonism. One merely *is* homosexual. One chooses to embrace one or another philosophy, whether political, social or religious. So why are those who *choose* so terrified of those who *are*? Neither they nor their children are in any danger of becoming that which they neither understand, embrace or are not.

The experiences of gay Mormon youth are explored in several stories. Rik Isensee's "The Summer My Cousin Turned Mormon" is a humorous look at a young man trying as hard as he can to go from normal teenage behavior to prescribed Mormon teenage behavior. His cousin discovers that he is struggling to follow the hilarious advice given in Mark E. Petersen's decades-old pamphlet "Steps in Overcoming Masturbation." Jonathan Langford's *No Going Back* tells of a Mormon teen trying desperately to become comfortable with his homosexuality. He attempts to follow church rules, but is still independent enough to push the boundaries. Jeff Laver's "Peter's Mirror" follows a Peruvian teen from the realization of his orientation through the events that ultimately lead to the understanding that he cannot be both Mormon and gay. The excerpt from Alan Michael Williams' *Ockham's Razor* takes the next step showing a young man as he tries to help his mother understand why he has chosen to accept his homosexuality over Mormon teachings. Finally, Hugo Olaiz's "The Birth of Tragedy" tells of a young man who turns to his gay brother for advice as he faces his own crisis of faith.

A remarkable number of gay youth serve two-year stints as Mormon missionaries. Many of them embark because their church leaders promised, "if you follow Church teachings, serve a mission and marry in the temple, you will overcome being gay." Missionary experiences are almost universally positive. They provide a unique coming of age experience that focuses on helping others. On the other hand, the intense immersion into spiritual service coupled with their continuing homosexual feelings lead to the realization that being gay is something that will never go away. Consequently, the missionary experience figures significantly in many of our stories. Potential missionaries are questioned extensively about any sexual experience including masturbation. The *LDS Mission President's Handbook* (2006, p.27) makes it clear that regardless of what is stated publicly, the official church position is that "homosexuality is a perversion." Young men who have engaged in heterosexual sex must demonstrate one year's abstinence, while those who have engaged in homosexual sex must demonstrate two years' abstinence before they are allowed to serve. It is not surprising that missionary interviews and even teenage masturbation experiences make up a part of both gay and straight stories. Steven Fales "Missionary Position" hilariously chronicles a young man's first experience with masturbation, his fight to control himself so he can serve a mission, and his ultimate failure to serve for two years without any kind of self-stimulation. As might be expected, an ancillary theme explains how that policy does little more than teach both straight and gay young men to lie and to hate themselves, to always feel the need to confess or hide their "weakness."

As I was searching for stories I was directed to a remarkable sequence of missionary experiences chronicled on the internet at www.nifty.org/nifty/gay/no-sex/mormon-missionaries. An extremely talented but unidentified writer had posted several stories based on his personal experiences both on and after his mission. I contacted the administrator of Nifty Gay, who was unable to make contact with the writer. However, the anonymous author identified only as "L" had chosen to merely ignore my request. Years later I experienced one of those unbelievable coincidences of life. I was presenting at a conference on the topic of the Gay Mormon Literature Project when someone came up behind me and whispered, "I am L." Ultimately we made friends and I received permission to include his Mission Training Center story, "MTC Interview" under his pseudonym, M. Larsen. He takes the Mormon worthiness interview one step further: What happens to the missionary who decides to come out to his leaders on his mission? After reading this story, you'll be turning to Nifty Gay for the rest of his collection. The final missionary story takes a different turn of events when a young man who cannot endure the burden of hiding his homosexuality takes his own life. Donna Banta's "The Call" spins this tragic event in a surprisingly different direction as she focuses on the mission president's response to the death.

He had lived with self-loathing too long to believe anyone could like him. His identity was under such siege that every encounter was a potential danger. The slightest abrasion could send him into a fury. His instinct was always to retreat, rejecting the source of pain before it could reject him. Any situation that rekindled his fears of being "nobody" were always terrifying.

— John Lahr, *Prick Up Your Ears*

Before a person can come out to others, he must go through the process of recognizing his own sexuality, coming to terms with it, and coming out to himself. Scott Singer's award-winning story "Lasting Impressions" is one man's journey to self-acceptance and ultimate love. The question changes from "Am I gay?" to "What kind of gay Mormon am I going to be?" which is the theme of the next section. John Bennion tackles "The Interview" after a young man has served his mission and has even become engaged to marry. He goes to his bishop to figure out what he'll do, now... and for the rest of his life. From there, things take a darker turn. Even though Brigham Young University denied for years there had ever been any electroshock therapy at BYU, the fact is that many gay Mormon young adults were subjected to physical torture in the name of trying to cure, or at least to modify the behavior of gay men. I have personal knowledge that this occurred because after my own mission I had a roommate at BYU who told me in detail about his participation in administering electroshock therapy to a group of gay men. One of the participants, John Cameron, has finally told his story in the play "14," so named because of the fourteen participants, two of whom killed themselves during the course of the treatment. In a related interview on August 22, 2006, Dallin H. Oaks of the Quorum of Twelve Apostles stated: "The aversive therapies that have been used in connection with same-sex attraction have contained some serious abuses that have been recognized over time within the professions. While we have no position about what the medical doctors do (except in very, very rare cases — abortion would be such an example), *we are conscious that there are abuses and we don't accept responsibility for those abuses.*" An esteemed lawyer, Oaks seems to be equivocating that although we admit that we have endorsed policies that led to abusive actions, we will not be held liable for the consequences of those policies.

"The Seduction of H. Lyman Winger" by Michael Fillerup presents a completely different slant on the worthiness interview. This time it is from the church leader's perspective. Not only is he trying to figure out if and how he can help the young gay adult coming to him for counsel, he is secretly concerned that his own daughter, a first year student at BYU, is a lesbian. Lyman constantly asks himself just where to draw the line, until a confrontation with his own issues and those of the man he is trying to counsel crash into each other. That moment of decision, the moment when the young Mormon gay decides that he cannot live as an active Mormon, is the theme of another story from a unique point of view. I fell in love with the stories of David Leavitt when I read his first novel, *The Lost Language of Cranes* (1986). He has since become one of the most highly respected literary gay writers in the world. As a non-Mormon writer, he comes face to face with a young Mormon taking his first step of rebellion in "The Term Paper Artist." The writer has returned home to Los Angeles to lick his wounds after a crushing blow to his last novel. To assuage his pain, he has taken to writing term papers for undergraduate students in exchange for personal favors. He is contacted by a young man, whom he discovers is Mormon, who wants him to write an essay that examines the Jack the Ripper mystery. Even though the Mormon student has never done anything seriously against his religion before, he has decided to buy a term paper and to submit to the writer's stipulations. The dichotomy between the Mormon's sense of right and wrong and his willingness to cross the line with a professional cheat ultimately leads to the unexpected redemption of both men.

Young men become middle-aged and face completely different sets of problems. Eric Samuelsen, one of the most popular of Mormon playwrights, presents a new play, *Duets*, that examines the toll taken when a gay Mormon gives in to his church leaders' encouragement to take a heterosexual wife. Bernard Cooper tells the amusing story of a gay man on a flight who is invited home to have dinner with a gay Mormon father together with his wife and children. The disastrous evening unfolds in "Hunters and Gatherers" as a small group of invited gay acquaintances try to figure out what is happening in this unbelievable Mormon household. The unspoken secret is that Cooper shows the actions of a gay man trying to live the principles of Evergreen, the Mormon version of Exodus and of reparative therapy for homosexuals. The religious families of gays are often so desperate to "heal" their gay family members that they become blind to the ridiculous strategies and practices of these reparative treatments. Robert Hodgson van Wagoner, who was awarded Utah Book of the Year for his gay-themed novel *Dancing Naked* (1999), continues with the theme of the married gay Mormon in his story "Strong Like Water." In it he takes the wife's point of view as she attempts to deal with the shock of discovering that her husband is having an affair with a man in the same week that she learns her mother has cancer. How does a person just hang on when their life is falling apart around them?

> We're not going anywhere because we don't come from anywhere. We're spontaneous events. We just appear in the middle of families. And we'll keep appearing. Even if the plague killed every homosexual on the planet, it wouldn't be extinction, because there's queer babies being born every minute. It's like magic.
>
> Clive Barker, *Sacrament*

One of the major themes of gay literature has been the AIDS story. Even though the AIDS epidemic hit the Mormon community the same as every other, AIDS is almost non-existent in our literature. One of the only exceptions is "Partying With

St. Roch" by Johnny Townsend, the most prolific of gay Mormon writers with almost two hundred short stories to his credit. Instead of focusing on the agonies of the plague, Townsend demonstrates the mature relationship that two men can have for one another. There is no sacrifice too large to make in the name of love.

The LDS Church has added three volumes of scripture to the Holy Bible. However, none of them have anything to say about homosexuality. Statements by church leaders have varied widely through the decades and are completely contradictory. So author Ken Shakin was surprised when he read D. Michael Quinn's *Same-Sex Dynamics Among Nineteenth-Century Americans: A Mormon Example* (1996), which unearths the only statement made by Joseph Smith, the founding prophet of the Church of Jesus Christ of Latter-day Saints, on what might be interpreted as homosexuality. Quinn comments on and quotes from B.H. Roberts' official *History of the Church*, 5:361(1948), "In fact, the Mormon prophet Joseph Smith enjoyed bedtime snuggling with male friends throughout his life. In an 1843 sermon, Smith preached that 'two who were vary friends indeed should lie down upon the same bed at night locked in each other's embrace talking of their love & should awake in the morning together. They could immediately renew their conversation of love even while rising from their bed." (Quinn, p. 87). The surprising statement intrigued Shakin who was in the process of writing gay-themed stories about the American West. In "Strange Bedfellows" he speculates on what might have happened if Smith's words were put into practice by nineteenth-century church members in the lonely isolation of frontier Colorado. As the young teen awaits his priesthood bedfellow, we turn to Levi S. Peterson's "The Dream," in which a present-day septuagenarian envisions himself strangely attired in a bright orange dress. Throughout the next day, as hard as he tries to put the dream behind him, he cannot get it out of his mind. How can a seventy-six-year-old man, married for over fifty years, suddenly question his sexuality?

> I think the idea only haunted him all the more. But it never stopped him from working, from pressing ahead, and it's that ability—to work through the self-doubts what any worthwhile human being feels—that is, so far as I can tell, the only thing what separates a meaningful life from a useless one.
>
> Caleb Carr, *The Angel of Darkness*

Today the LDS Church reports that church membership exceeds fourteen million members and is basking in the era when Mormonism seems to be enjoying a broader understanding and acceptance. To move this along, the Missionary Department initiated an advertising campaign, "And I'm A Mormon," to convince, perhaps even themselves, that there is diversity within the church. The most popular Broadway musical at the time of this writing is Trey Parker and Matt Stone's *The Book of Mormon* (which includes a gay Mormon missionary, both in the story and in the original Broadway cast). Senator Harry Reid and Presidential Candidate

Mitt Romney are prominent Mormons representing both political parties. There is no better proof that Mormons have entered the mainstream than three surprising contributions. Ron Oliver's horror story "Nestle's Revenge" assumes that the everyday gay reader knows exactly what it means to be a Mormon missionary. He imagines what might happen when our clean cut boys are invited into the home of a homicidal maniac. Julie Jensen's plays are produced throughout the world assuming that their audiences understand what it means when her characters talk about the attributes of her straight and lesbian Mormon characters, including those in her excerpt from *Wait!*. Marty Beaudet includes gay characters in the excerpt from his excellent thriller *By A Thread*, the very title of which refers to an apocryphal prophecy attributed to Joseph Smith that the U.S. Constitution will "hang by a thread and that the Priesthood will step in to save it."

> I believe that unarmed truth and unconditional love will have the final word.
>
> Martin Luther King, Jr.

We close with two very personal stories of Mormon families trying desperately to come to terms with their gay family members. Emily January Petersen presents the poignant story of a daughter learning that her father is gay. She loves him dearly and her primary fear is that she might lose him. Carol Lynn Pearson is the most beloved poet and playwright in the Mormon Church. She was famous within the church for her poetry and then became famous outside the church for her memoir, *Goodbye, I Love You* (1987), about the death of her gay ex-husband to AIDS. She is probably the first voice in the church in support of gays and lesbians. I am proud to have directed her play, *Facing East*, about parents trying to come to terms with the suicide of their gay son. Their deeply felt conversation pits the mother, speaking with the voice of the official Mormon position, shocked at the alternative perspective voiced by her church-leader husband. My stake in Rochester, NY presented *Facing East* to an overflow audience that concluded with a post-production discussion led by the Stake president of the church. In the closing minutes of the discussion, one woman stood up and wept as she said that she was going home to re-establish connections with her gay father whom she had abandoned.

Literature does have the power to heal and to change the hearts of those around us.

Tḥe Suɱɱer My Cousiṇ TurṇeᕷMorɱoṇ

Rik Isensee

My cousin Robby came to stay for two weeks every summer. I looked forward to these visits with mixed feelings. Being a year older and more rambunctious than I was, he would draw me into intrigues I was too timid to try on my own. Once we got into it, I allowed myself to be carried along by his enthusiasm and imagination. Robby embellished our explorations with tales of daring heroism in the face of untold dangers—gale-force winds, sinking ships, mountain rescues, or beating off pirates in the pursuit of treasure.

In reality, our gambits were never terribly outlandish: previous expeditions included sliding down grassy hillsides on pieces of cardboard to escape the dinosaurs (I got stickers in my butt); climbing up the ivy on the side of a small cliff to rescue a maiden (I broke my arm when the vines tore); slashing our way through underbrush to build the Panama Canal (the poison oak made my face puffy and my eyelids swelled shut. I looked like a radiation victim from a horror flick, and itched terribly for days in the most sensitive places).

Despite discomfort and occasional trauma, these escapades provoked only mild consternation in my mother, who would shake her head and wonder what had gotten into me, had I taken complete leave of my senses? But she never forbade us to go off on our adventures. She probably thought our exploration was a healthy challenge to my self-restraint, and she saw Robby as a fairly benign influence on my boyhood.

The summer I turned thirteen, however, everything changed. Robby was bigger, his voice had deepened, he was sprouting hair in ungodly places. My own body had barely begun its strange alterations, and I was both intrigued and repelled by the changes in his. The previous summer he had hinted at forbidden pleasures—smoking, sneaking a beer, messing around with some girl. I had looked forward to seeing him, although I was nervous about what sort of schemes he might lead me into now.

But rather than becoming even wilder, ready to go, he seemed oddly subdued. It was hard to draw him out. He was dismissive of any ideas I had of fun; he'd outgrown it all. Of course neither of us cared anymore about GI Joe or trains. But even swimming, horseback riding, or going "exploring," which in the past would have sent us racing out of the house, now evoked a sneer. I was crestfallen. How could I relate to him? And I was frankly angry with him for not leading me into illicit arenas—drunkenness, abandon, and sexuality—I was too reticent to explore on my own.

My mother would try to get us out of her hair, asking cheerfully, "So what are you boys up to today?" Not wanting to be scorned for my suggestions, I'd defer to Robby, who mostly shrugged.

"I don't know," I'd finally say. "Maybe just hang out." We'd drag ourselves to the mall and look over the newest releases at Tower Records, but nothing seemed to get us going again.

Then late one night, I heard this strange thumping noise and yelling coming from the den. We had a sofabed that Robby slept on, backed against my bedroom wall. I heard more thumping, and occasional yelps. I made out "Stop it! Stop that! No! No! No!"

Fearing an intruder had attacked him, I got out my baseball bat and was about to charge into his room, when I swore I heard him singing A Mighty Fortress is Our God.

I knocked on his door. "Robby?"

"What? What?"

"I heard some yelling. Are you all right?"

"It was nothing. I'm fine."

"Are you sure? Can I come in?"

"I'm fine. I'm fine. Go away."

"Did you have a nightmare?"

"I said I'm fine! Go away!"

My mother came out in the hall. "What's the matter?"

"Nothing. I think Robby had a nightmare."

"Is he all right? What are you doing with that baseball bat?"

"I thought I heard someone yelling, but he says he's fine."

"Well, okay. Goodnight, then."

I went back to my room and put the bat away. Something was up, and I had to get to the bottom of it.

The next morning Robby was his usual sullen self. I wanted to contrive some way of getting him out of the house so I could case his room. Not normally a sneak, I rationalized that I had the right to discover the source of my cousin's betrayal, as well as his puzzling behavior—for his own sake, if not mine.

After Mom left for work, I gave Robby a gift certificate for Macy's I'd gotten from our grandmother for my birthday, and said he could take my bike and get anything he wanted—I had enough clothes, anyway, and besides, I had to do some chores around the house, like washing the windows and scrubbing the kitchen floor. Not wanting to help me, he quickly agreed. I was surprised my ruse worked. Then I kicked myself for piling it on, since I'd committed myself to a hell of a lot of drudgery—but I wanted to make sure I got him out.

I watched him take a spin out of the driveway and coast down the hill. Then I got some Windex and paper towels and went into the den. I searched through some drawers, but he'd never really unpacked. His suitcase lay open with clothes piled on either side. As I rummaged through them, I wasn't sure what I was looking for—some girlie magazines, maybe, or a porn video—but I did not expect to find the Book of Mormon, which I spotted lying underneath the bed, along with *Overcoming Masturbation—A Ten-Point Guide to Self Control*, distributed by the LDS Church, plus a little calendar, in which day after day had been totally blackened with deep, dark ink.

I poured over this Mormon tract with fascination. "Masturbation is a sinful habit that is totally self-centered and secretive, and in no way expresses the proper use of the procreative power given to man to fulfill eternal purposes...This self-gratifying activity will cause one to lose his self-respect and feel guilty and depressed, which can in the extreme lead to further sinning."

It went on with a series of suggestions for overcoming this terrible habit:

1. Pray fervently and out loud when the temptations are the strongest.

2. Yell to stop those thoughts as loudly as you can, then recite a pre-chosen scripture or sing an inspirational hymn. (Ah ha! A Mighty Fortress, indeed.)

3. Take a small pocket calendar and if you have a lapse of self-control, color that day black. (I looked at his calendar, and smirked.)

4. If you are tempted to masturbate, think of having to bathe in a tub of worms, and eat several of them as you do the act! (Yum!)

5. A Book of Mormon, held firmly in hand, even in bed at night has proven helpful in extreme cases. (No doubt.)

6. Tie one hand to the bed frame, and wear several layers so you cannot easily touch your vital parts.

7. Never associate with other boys who have the same weakness. YOU MUST BREAK OFF THEIR FRIENDSHIP! Just to be in their presence will keep your problem foremost in your mind.

8. Do not admire yourself in the bathroom mirror. Leave the door open when you bathe, and never stay in the bath more than five minutes. THEN GET OUT OF THE BATHROOM!

9. Never read about your problem. KEEP THE PROBLEM OUT OF YOUR MIND BY NOT MENTIONING IT EVER, NOT EVEN IN YOUR PRAYERS! Keep it out of your mind!

10. Remember, Satan never gives up! You can win this fight! The joy and strength you will feel when you do will give your whole life a radiant and spiritual glow!

—

The previous summer, Robby asked me if I ever beat off. Looking back on it now, I realize it was probably an invitation. But at the time I'd never done it, and being the literal-minded boy that I was, it sounded a little painful. "No," I said, dubiously. Then to explain why I hadn't tried it, I told him, "I think if you have any tendency toward homosexuality, it might make it worse." Robby looked shocked, and quickly changed the subject. And although I wasn't especially attracted to him, I was enormously curious, and would gladly have participated with him that summer. Now it was too late. If I even hinted at it, I would no doubt be banished.

But what had happened to him? What caused this mysterious shift from the adventurous boy who'd try anything, to this sullen teen given to yelping and singing hymns to keep himself from self-abuse?

I quickly put everything back where I'd found it, and proceeded with my chores. My mother was amazed when she got home. "What's come over you?" she asked. The windows gleamed, the kitchen floor was spotless. "You poor thing, you must be bored out of your mind."

She didn't know the half of it. Robby came home and actually seemed somewhat cheered by the hooded 'Niners sweatshirt he bought at the mall. My mom took us out for pizza, then we went to see this movie called Sliding Doors, about a woman who misses her subway train, gets mugged, and goes home to her boring boyfriend; then she suddenly splits into what would have happened if she'd caught the train after all, got home in time to discover her boyfriend with another woman, and left him for the romantic stranger she'd met on the subway.

We chattered about this movie all the way home. In one split second, your whole life could change, and we played the "What if..." game trying to imagine what your life would be like if it went this way or that.

"Well, my life would have been infinitely worse off if I hadn't become a Mormon," Robby finally confessed. It was out in the open now, and though I dreaded the subsequent proselytizing, I asked him what had changed him.

He said he'd gotten into smoking pot and running around with a rough crowd, and if it hadn't been for this one girl in his class who had shown him the Book of Mormon, he's sure he would have become a juvenile delinquent. But now he had a purpose, to serve God, and all his bad habits had fallen away.

Except for one that I had some secret knowledge of, but of course I held my tongue. I wanted to catch him at it, maybe even do it with him, and was a little horrified by my own scheming.

That night, I lay in bed wide awake and totally turned on in anticipation of Robby giving in to temptation. Finally, I heard his tell-tale thumping, and then his husky voice barked out: "Eat worms! Eat worms!" I leapt out of bed, tore down the hall, and threw open his door.

"What? What are you doing!" he cried, squinting at the light, pulling the blankets over him. I grabbed at his covers, which he tried to hold on to, but since he had one wrist tied to the bed frame, I yanked them out of his grasp. His pajama pants (and the swimsuit he'd put on as an extra barrier) were shoved past his knees. He covered himself with the Book of Mormon. "Leave me alone!"

For a moment I hesitated. My God, what was I doing? I didn't mean to torment him, but to free us both from our self-imposed restraints. So I said "Look!" and parted the fly of my pajamas to show him my hard-on. He stared at me in astonishment. "Let's color this day black!"

My heart pounded as Robby considered my suggestion, and I prayed that he wouldn't scorn me. He leaned against the pillow, eyeing me with suspicion. Then the slightest grin turned the corner of his mouth as he put aside the Book of Mormon. He nodded toward the hand he had lashed to the couch. "Untie me, then."

So I did.

Lasting Impressions

Scott Singer

Back then?

Jeez... I was still in graduate school, working on my master's degree in music history at Bowling Green State University. I was still twenty-three years old and twenty-five pounds overweight. I was still married. I still even believed it when my bishop told me that if I went to the Lord's university, served a mission for the Church and got married in the temple, I wouldn't be gay any more. Well, I got my bachelor's degree from Brigham Young University, spent two years as an Elder tracting in Texas and married a Utah girl in the Manti Temple. I just hadn't admitted to myself that "I yam what I yam"—I am gay no matter what anyone promised. At that time I did not know my façade was already beginning to crumble. It was years before I recognized the significance of my weekend with Ben, Mike and Tim.

Once a month I'd take a break from my studies at BGSU and drive twenty miles north to attend the Toledo Ring of the International Brotherhood of Magicians. It was a chance to get away from the cloistered world of the university and spend some time with real people in the real world. No one there cared about the petty academic politics that consumed the music faculty. At magic club I could sit down with a doctor or a factory worker and practice the fine points of a "bottom deal." No one cared about the length of my hair or my politics, only about how I felt when Doug Henning fell through a trap door on live television. I was used to being the youngest guy there, but when three high school kids joined the club, I began to hang out primarily with them. We were more alike than I care to admit, my being fresh from BYU, naïve and still pretty much an innocent. Before long I found myself driving to Toledo every week to spend a few hours with them, not only talking about card tricks and magicians, but movies, music and girls.

I began to dread the summer when I would graduate and leave for whatever location offered my first real job. When Tim pointed out that his birthday fell in the middle of a three-day weekend in April, we decided to have one big farewell fling. First, we'd visit Abbott's Magic Factory in Colon, Michigan, and then drive another three hours north to Mike's family cabin at Houghton Lake. I packed an overnight bag, threw it and my sleeping bag into the trunk of our '68 Tempest, kissed my wife goodbye and headed north to pick up the guys. Tim and Mike were already waiting at Ben's house, so before we knew it, everything was loaded and we were off on our great adventure. Ben rode shotgun in the front seat. He was a bright Jewish seventeen-year-old, still teenage skinny, with the whisper of a mustache. A little bit the nerd, his wavy hair was always combed and he usually had small beads of sweat trying to escape the hairs on his upper lip. He considered himself the best magician of the three boys and was always trying to correct the others' mechanic's grip or shuffling technique. Mike sat behind Ben fumbling with a half-dollar as he told us about the latest escapade of his policeman brother. Mike was the most handsome of the lot, with long brown hair, dark eyes and fully developed shoulders. At sixteen, his back tapered in a perfect V and his tee shirt hung loosely over the top of his hip-hugging bell-bottoms. He wrestled at 145 pounds and, although clearly the strongest, was socially insecure and always sought my approval no matter what he did. I was glad that he sat on the passenger side because I could glance at him every time I looked over my shoulder. I even adjusted the mirror so I could see him better. I couldn't help myself! I loved the way he smiled.

Tim was turning sixteen, but he still looked like a kid compared with the other two guys. An army brat, he was the least involved of the three magically, but was, by far, the most street-wise. He entertained us by telling how the track team "initiated" a hotshot freshman on the bus coming home late after a race. This obnoxious kid was all mouth, but he placed dead last, so the older boys pretended to console him and got him to sit with them toward the back of the bus. Suddenly one of the seniors grabbed him from behind, jammed a jock in his mouth and held him while a couple of the other boys pulled down his sweats. Tim told us how he grabbed the kid's cock and held it up while two of the other guys wrapped white adhesive tape around his groin, taping up his ass and plastering down all of his pubic hair. "It took him almost two hours to cut himself out of the tape," Tim laughed, "and he didn't have a hair left on his balls. He walked bow-legged for a week!"

Soon we were bragging and sharing the latest jokes. "There was this salesman who came up to a farmhouse," started Ben. We convulsed with laughter as he finished, "The salesman drove away, yodeling back to the farmer, 'Got the ol' lady, too!'" That was about the time I asked if they'd ever played "Vagina." That's where you substitute "vagina" for a word in any well known title: "Funny Girl," for example, becomes "Funny Vagina." The guys caught on and we became giddy laughing at "A Clockwork Vagina," "The Diary of Anne Vagina," and "The Vagina That Came in From the Cold." When Tim suggested "Fiddler on the Vagina" we modified the rules and convulsed again at "Rebel Without a Penis" and "Joseph and the Amazing Technicolor Hard-on."

We snaked our way west on Route 86 through the hills of southern Michigan until we passed a sign that read, "Welcome to Colon—Magic Capital of the World." For magicians everywhere, a journey to Colon is like a pilgrimage to Mecca. Our boisterousness changed to silence as we drove through the village and saw the Abbott's Magic Company sign over a factory that looked like an embarrassed cliché out of some horror comics. The temple of magic looked like the old garage where my grandfather had repaired cars for almost four decades, excepting it was painted black and decorated with tacky skeletons in stick figure poses. "God, we're really here," said Mike almost prayerfully. Tim was already out of the car, "Last one in has sponge balls!"

Stepping inside Abbott's was like stepping back in time. There was no slick showroom, no glamour, only a bunch of old glass front cases filled to over-flowing with tricks and gimmicks. The walls were covered with framed 8 x 10, autographed glossies of scores of magicians. Walking in on the rough wooden floor, we passed an open area that was filled with stage illusions, The Mis-Made Girl, The Ultra-Thin Sawing a Lady in Half, and an exact duplicate of the French Guillotine designed for The Amazing Randi when he toured with rock star Alice Cooper. Our trance was broken when an old man came up behind the counter. He was wrinkled and disheveled, his shirt only half tucked into his polyester slacks. "What can I do for you boys?" he smiled as he squinted, trying to focus on us. "It's Duke Stern," whispered Ben. Then with more conviction, "That's right, isn't it? You're Duke Stern."

"Guilty as charged," he answered. "And you are…?"

"We drove up from Toledo," I answered. "I'm Brent Larsen."

"Brent," he said extending his hand. "I read the piece you wrote for *The Linking Ring*, the one about magic and music. I wish more of the boys would take your advice." He winked, knowing that I couldn't believe that he'd remembered my name from a single article, and then smiled broadly. "How would you boys like to see some magic?"

Suddenly the old factory was transformed into the most beautiful magic pavilion in the world. Duke Stern, almost blind, dazzled us for an hour and a half with the greatest magic we had ever seen. As we left, I realized he'd done his job, making our money magically vanish from our wallets, only to appear in the Abbott's cash register. We had given all we had and would have given more. At the last minute I remembered that we needed cash for the rest of the weekend. There were no ATM's then, so I covered everything with a single check, pocketed the boys' cash and we were on the road again, heading north to Mike's cabin up Highway 27.

Having experienced the priest in his Holy of Holies, the feeling in the car had changed. Every trick was remembered and dissected. Ben answered questions about Duke's life, reciting everything he could remember from the journal articles he'd read. The boys opened their new toys and occupied themselves with magic until it was too dark to see. No matter what else happened, the weekend was already more successful than we ever dreamed it could be.

The closer we got to the cabin the rougher and narrower the road became. When we passed a country store advertising Fresh Bait, Mike spoke up, "That's Acuff's. The cabin is just a couple more miles now. Turn right at the intersection." Jack pine lined the road, climbing straight into the night sky. "Indians used those trees for lodge poles," Mike explained, but shut up when Tim retorted, "Who the fuck cares?"

Ben raised his eyebrows and looked at Tim, "Underwear riding up?"

That was the first time I'd ever heard the boys act bitchy. I didn't say anything, but looked across at Ben. When our eyes met, he held my gaze for a moment and then turned away, looking out his side window.

"I'm sorry," Tim said, not sounding the least bit sincere. "It's just that I'm hungrier than a whore with her jaws wired." Silence. Suddenly he exploded, "Well, excu-u-se me!"

Mike came to the rescue, "Forget about it, Tim. I'm hungry, too."

"Hungry?" I said. "It's only an hour since we left McDonald's."

"There it is," said Mike. "Pull into that driveway on the left."

It wasn't exactly what I'd envisioned. Sitting in the middle of nowhere, surrounded by trees, sat a square frame cabin. Even in the moonlight I could see that the paint peeled off years ago. "When's the last time you were up here, Mike? Where's the lake?"

"The lake's about five miles back that way," he said. "There's usually somebody up here every weekend during the summer, but I guess we're the first ones here since Labor Day." We all grabbed our gear and followed Mike to the front porch, standing there while he fished the key out of his pocket and struggled to open the door.

The inside was better than the outside, but not much. There was one big room with a couple of support poles holding up the center beam. Along the right hand wall was a cupboard and a sink with a hand pump. A small kitchen table and four mis-matched chairs were near the counter. Along the left wall were two beds, one double, one single, and a lumpy sofa with a back that lay down to make a bed was in the opposite corner. The only other room was through a door in the back wall. It had a double bed and a chest of drawers and was obviously "for the grown ups," the kids being left to throw their sleeping bags wherever they could.

"Where's the bathroom?" asked Tim. "I gotta take a piss."

"Just find a tree outside. If ya gotta take a dump, there's an outhouse behind the cabin."

As Tim went out the door, Ben marched into the bedroom and threw his gear on the bed. "This is where I'm sleeping, Suckers," he announced. "Where's the fuckin' light switch?"

"Fuckin' light switch," I said. "Weren't you Mr. Clean back in the car?"

"We're fuckin' campin' now." Ben looked at me with what I guessed must be teenage defiance. I'd never been cast in the role of *adult* before and I wasn't quite sure what to do. "That's how guys talk when they fuckin' camp," he continued. "Get *fuckin'* used to it."

Our eyes locked. After what seemed to be an eternity, I clenched my teeth and threatened, "If some shit-assed high school pussy thinks he can fuckin' shock me, he's got another think comin'. Now if you wanna make sumthin' of it, let's get the fuck outside."

He stood there, not moving a muscle. Then, just as abruptly as he'd attacked, he broke into a broad smile, "Naw. I'm here to have fun." With that he turned and unrolled his sleeping bag, calling to Mike over his shoulder, "Just where the hell is the fuckin' light switch?"

"This place doesn't have electricity. All we've got is this one oil lamp and a couple of candles." Mike touched the wick with his lighter and a low light dimly filled the main room of the cabin as he placed a glass chimney over it. Tim walked back in as Mike continued, "There's not much oil here, though. We're gunna have to go back to Acuff's before he closes."

"And get something to eat!" exclaimed Tim.

"And get something to fuckin' eat," I corrected.

Tim looked at me a little surprised, then looked over at Ben. "I told you he wasn't a wimp. Now maybe I'll get what I *really* want for my birthday."

Ben smiled, "We can always hope."

I looked from one to the other. When I looked over at Mike, he busied himself with the lamp. "What's going on here, Tim? What do you want for your birthday?"

Tim grinned, "I want to get buzzed."

"Buzzed?"

"We want you to go down to Acuff's and pick up a case of beer," said Ben.

"Me?"

"You're the only one old enough and none of us look like your I.D., so you're elected."

"I've never bought beer in my life."

"I told you he was a tee-totaler!" laughed Tim. "A fuckin' Mormon tee-totaler!"

Ben continued, "It's just like buying Cokes, excepting you show them your driver's license when you pay for it. Think you can handle that, Big Bro?"

"What do you think about this, Mike? It's your cabin."

Mike stopped playing with the lamp and looked at me nervously. "Well, I've never…" His weak voice cracked a little and he started again, "I've never had any beer either. I'd like my first time to be with my buddies."

My mind raced. Mormons weren't supposed to drink beer. But I'd never wanted to be one of the guys more in my life, "What the hell! That's what buddies are for. Let's go get some fuckin' beer."

Ben chided, "Don't worry, we're all magicians. We know how to keep a secret." Suddenly he was all business. It was clear the three of them had planned this for a long time. "You'll have to go in by yourself. They know Mike, and he said that they got busted once, so they never sell beer if they even think it's going to be drunk by high school kids. Any brand is all right, just don't get any of that 'lite' shit."

"Here's our list of supplies," Tim said, adding lamp oil to his pre-written list.

Before I knew it I was in the car heading back to Acuff's and my first attempt to buy beer. I got the cold cuts, bread, chips and lamp oil as I cased the place, trying to get up my courage. My heart was pounding as I walked into the cooler and saw all the beer stacked there. I didn't know where to start. I had no idea there were so many different brands and packages. "Need some help in there?" I heard the guy call from behind the counter. "No," I yelled back. "I found it." I picked up a case of Bud and headed out. I couldn't figure out why, but it felt like the first time I bought condoms. I had been nervous and, even though I was married, I wasn't sure if Mormons were supposed to buy rubbers. I put the beer down on the counter, but when I reached over to get my basket of groceries, I slipped and spilled everything.

"You sure you're all right, son?" said the old man behind the counter. When I fumbled putting the chips on the counter he said, "I'm going to have to see some I.D. for that beer."

"Sure," I said, trying desperately to free my wallet from my back pocket. "Here it is."

He studied my Ohio driver's license and looked at me. "Thanks. I don't usually card guys your age, but you seemed so nervous I thought you might be underage anyway. You camping near here?"

"Up at Kosky's cabin," I said before I realized I really didn't want him to know.

"Didn't know they were here. Give my regards to John. He's the fireman, right?"

"No," I stammered. "He's the policeman."

The old man smiled, "That's right."

Picking up the beer I realized I'd just passed the old man's test. He piled my groceries on top of the case and I started to leave, "Thanks a lot. I'll probably see you tomorrow." I headed out the door, got everything loaded into the backseat and climbed in behind the wheel. I'd done it! I bought beer—and it hit me where it always hits when I try something that I'd previously considered wrong or dangerous: right in the groin. I'd sprung one of the hardest boners of my life.

Back at the cabin all three boys came running out to help carry in the groceries. "Way to go, Brent!" smiled Tim. "You not only got great suds, you got the kind of case that keeps 'em cold."

I smiled. I grabbed that case only because I thought the rectangular box would be easier to carry than bottles or six packs. We carried in everything and soon had chips and sandwich fixings spread all over the table and counter. Tim and Ben were already gulping down their first beers when they ceremoniously brought cans to Mike and me. We popped the tops and took tentative sips. Mike wrinkled up his nose at first, but then smiled, taking another small drink. Tim laughed, "Bottoms up, men! The first can you have to chug. That gets your buzz started. Then you can sip like old ladies if you want." They had no idea what a big deal this was for me. It was the first time I'd broken the Mormon health code since I tried smoking a cigarette in the eighth grade, but I was committed. I raised my beer, "This Bud's for you," and chugged the entire can. It wasn't much different than chugging a can of Coke, but it impressed the hell out of them. I didn't start feeling it until I was almost through my second beer and by then we were seated around the table, laughing and playing poker.

You'd think that four guys would be playing at least Penny Ante, but not so. Mike complained that he was lousy at cards and refused to play for money. So there we sat, playing poker for fun, using the poker chips we found in the bookcase. Mike and I grinned at each other as we shared our first buzz. "Damn, it's hot in here," he said, pulling off his tee shirt, exposing his wrestler's torso. There were tiny black hairs beginning to grow around his nipples and a treasure trail led down from his navel into his jeans.

"It sure is," I said, unbuttoning my shirt, pulling the tail out of my pants, and enjoying the comfortable warm feeling that was coming over me. Tim pulled off his shirt, too, as Ben went into the other room and emerged wearing only his tee shirt and boxers. He grabbed another round for each of us, sat down and picked up his cards. This was heaven. This was being with the guys, an experience I'd never shared because of my sheltered life. As we studied our hands, deciding how many cards we wanted to draw, Ben cleared his throat. "Could I ask you a personal question, Brent?"

"Shoot," I said, starting my third brew.

"Did you jerk off much when you were our age?"

Ben smiled and I looked at him, trying to figure out his angle. It was the kind of leading question I'd asked guys back when I was in high school, hoping to initiate sex with them. It had occurred to me that Ben might be gay, or curious, but he was a minor and I was trying to make a marriage work, so I never allowed my imagination to go there. Besides, I hadn't had sex with a guy since I talked to my bishop about trying to become straight. I looked at Tim and Mike, wondering if this was also part of their prearranged plan. "Sure, I masturbated in high school."

"So you admit you jerked off?"

"It's part of growing up," I answered.

"How's it compare to, you know, real sex?" asked Tim.

"Have any of you ever made it with a woman?" I asked. From the looks on their faces I knew they were all virgins. "Good for you. You've got your entire lives ahead of you for that." By now I knew that they were just curious teenage boys wanting to discuss sex with a guy who'd had experience. "Masturbating feels good, but all you're doing is getting your rocks off. Sex with a woman can be beautiful."

"How's it feel?" asked Mike.

"There's something about being naked, the feel of skin touching skin. Your entire body is involved and it's hot and wet and tight." I saw Ben reach down to rearrange his growing erection. His hand came back above the table as he picked up the cards to deal.

They asked a few more technical questions and then Tim stammered, "What about oral sex? Have you tried that?"

"To be honest, I can only give you a partial answer. I love having my cock sucked. It's one of my favorite things. But I've never been able to eat pussy. One time, when Susan was feeling really passionate, I kissed her breasts and then began to work my way down her stomach. I was tickling her vagina with my fingers, but when my lips reached her pubic hair that's all the farther I could go. There was no way I could put my mouth between her legs."

"That's not fair," Ben protested. "You like her to blow you."

"Fair has nothing to do with sex. A penis is on the outside where it's clean and dry. A vagina is on the inside, hot and wet with mucous. As far as I'm concerned it'd be like sticking your tongue in cow's nostril. A couple only does what they're comfortable with." I didn't tell them that the only blowjobs I'd ever had were from guys. Susan had kissed my penis a couple of times, but she wasn't going to blow me any more than I was going to eat her. "Remember the old joke: The difference between a man and a woman sucking cock is that the man wants to." It took a second for them to make the connection, but when they did, they laughed.

"Tell me about it," said Tim under his breath. When we all looked at him he explained, "There was this kid in my scout troop who'd suck your cock. I decided to try it, so I tented with him on a campout. At first I was really nervous, so he told me to just think about the things I thought of when I masturbated. I couldn't believe how great it felt, but when I was going to come I wanted him to stop. Instead, he grabbed my ass and sucked even harder. When I came, I exploded. It was the biggest load I'd ever had; everything came up but the kitchen sink. And he swallowed it! It almost made me sick. He tried to get me to blow him, but there was no way. I couldn't even look at the guy after that. Just thinking about it makes me feel weird."

"I know exactly what you mean," I said. "On the one hand it felt so great, but on the other hand, it was a guy."

Ben raised his eyebrows, "So you've been blown by a guy?"

"A few times when I was your age. It doesn't mean anything, does it, Tim?"

"Not to me, it doesn't," he said quietly.

We just sat there silently playing cards for a few minutes. Finally, Ben spoke, "So, Brent, when's the last time you jerked off?"

I didn't think he was trying to be a smart-ass, so I answered. "I'm a guy, aren't I? I've got a cock, haven't I? A couple of days ago in the shower."

They were stunned. It had never occurred to them. From their young perspective guys masturbated until they got married and then only fucked. Ben continued, "All married guys masturbate? Or, you masturbate?"

Was he trying to pin me down? I hadn't come out to myself yet; there was no way I was going to come out to them. I decided to get clinical. "Studies show that most men masturbate throughout their entire lives. The average college student masturbates four times a week; the average married man once every couple of months. Hell, even your grandfather masturbates. In fact, a lot of old men masturbate as often as teenagers. Don't get me wrong, sex with a woman is great, but it feels different than jerking off. Sometimes you just want to do it alone. Now if you'll excuse me, I've got to take a piss." I stood up and almost fell over. Sitting there I hadn't noticed how light-headed I'd become.

Tim laughed as I caught myself. "I think we could all do with a good piss."

I glanced over and noticed that Ben still had his erection, the head tucked under his waistband with his tee hanging loosely covering it. He smiled at me and shrugged. I smiled back and we were out the front door, lined up across the porch, our cocks in our hands arcing four streams of piss into the night air. "So, Mike, how do you like your first buzz?" Tim asked.

"It's great," he said, shaking the last drops off his cock and flipping it back into his pants. "How many beers are left?"

"There should be one more for each of us," Tim answered as we walked inside. "We can drink them while we get ready for bed." Tim went straight over to the sofa where he'd thrown his gear and took off his pants. For all his worldly experience, standing there in only his briefs, Tim looked like an uncorrupt kid. His basket was starting to fill, but he was still smooth, not even a trace of hair under his arms.

I took off my shirt and was just starting to pull off my Levi's when Tim exclaimed, "What kind of underwear are those, Brent?"

Sometimes I forgot how strange garments looked to other people, especially back then when they were one piece, patterned after the old Union Suits. They hung shapeless from my shoulders down to my knees. The top looked like a scoop neck tee shirt, but in back they had a vertical, buttoned-assflap like long johns.

"Haven't you seen those, before?" asked Ben. "Those are Mormon underwear."

Mike raised an eyebrow, "You wear uniform underwear?"

"Sometimes we call them Mormon Birth Control," I joked. "There's no way they can look sexy and we're supposed wear them twenty-four hours a day."

"Even when you have sex?" Tim asked incredulously.

"Not then, or when you shower, participate in sports, or… get drunk. But the rest of time we keep 'em on." I had pulled the neckband down over my shoulder and proceeded to peel out of them, standing there naked in the semi-darkness while I opened my pack to get out a pair of running shorts. I didn't want to wear a jock all night, so when I pulled on the shorts, it was all I was wearing.

"Here's your nightcap, gentlemen," Mike said as he handed around the last cans of beer. "What'll we drink to?"

Ben raised his beer, "Friends for life!"

"Friends for life!" we repeated and took long pulls.

"This is the greatest birthday ever," said Tim. "First Abbott's and Duke Stern, then sharing Buds with my buds."

"Don't get maudlin," Ben responded, walking towards him. He reached down, grabbed the elastic on Tim's briefs, pulled them out and poured beer into his shorts. Tim yelled in shock and the fight was on. Soon we were all laughing and running, emptying the last of the beer all over each other. Who'd have thought so little beer could make such a mess. Our hair has wet, our underwear was soaked through and we were slipping in puddles of beer on the floor in a four-way wrestling match, catch as catch can. Tim grabbed Ben's boxers and pulled them up, giving him a wedgie as he pulled away and grabbed Tim in a headlock. Mike rushed me and we fell over onto the bed. He grabbed me in one of his wrestling holds and the warm feel of his skin pressed against mine started to turn me on. I held my own, twisting out and grabbing him while I tried to hide the fact that I'd gotten a hard on. Suddenly Mike turned and I lost my balance, falling onto my back and pulling him down on top of me. There was no way Mike couldn't have felt my erection, as we lay there almost parallel. I expected him to react, to roll off and maybe continue to wrestle, but instead he just lay there with his head next to mine. As we lay there, I involuntarily flexed my penis. When he didn't move my erection flexed again. My mouth was right next to his ear, so I whispered, "Sorry about that."

That broke the spell. "It's all right," he said, and rolled over, ending the wrestling for us. Ben and Tim were also winding down. We all lay where we were, laughing. "I'm sticky all over," moaned Mike.

"The entire cabin is sticky all over," responded Ben. "Let's get cleaned up."

"I call first shower," yelled Tim. Then he stopped, his smile fading. "There is no shower, is there?" he said rhetorically.

"Not even a tub," said Mike. "All we have is the hand pump in the sink, and the water's ice cold."

We had no choice but to grab our towels and stand by the sink, naked and shivering, as we mopped the sticky beer out of our hair and off our bodies. Then we turned to the cabin and used our towels to mop up the counter, table and floor. Each of the guys had a change of underwear, but all I had were my garments. I didn't want to put them back on, so I climbed into my sleeping bag naked. We settled in to go to sleep, me on the double bed, Mike on the twin, Tim on the sofa and Ben in the bedroom. "G'night, guys," I said. "It's been real."

At first it got quiet, but suddenly, something was flying through the air. A pillow landed, plop, on Mike. He grabbed it, flung it at me, and the fight was on again. I jumped up, grabbed the pillow and swung it at Mike as I jumped onto his bed. Ben came barreling in, swinging his pillow as Tim came running over to reclaim his. We converged on Mike's bed, laughing and swinging, but when we landed, there was a loud "Crack!" His bed gave way; the mattress and coil spring crashed to the floor. This time the party was over. There was no way we could fix the bed in the dark, so Ben and Tim went back to their own sleeping bags and Mike threw his on the double bed alongside mine. Soon we were all trying to go to sleep.

As the minutes ticked by, I was aware that Ben and Tim were both breathing deeply, sound asleep. But I sensed that Mike was lying there next to me, awake. After a while I heard his soft voice, "Brent? Are you asleep?"

"I'm awake," I replied quietly.

"Could I ask you a question?"

"Sure."

"Are you normal if you don't masturbate?"

"You mean, never?" I asked, turning over to face him.

"I have a couple of times, but I never really got into it."

"Do you have wet dreams?"

"Like when you dream of something real sexy and wake up shooting your load? Yeah. Every week or so."

"There you have it," I assured him. "You don't need to masturbate."

"So it's all right if I don't jerk off?"

"Mike, you're normal. Every guy is unique. If you don't want to jerk off, forget about it."

He reached over and squeezed my shoulder. "Thanks, Brent." He didn't move, but his body relaxed and he snuggled his head into his pillow. When his breathing became slow and heavy, I rolled onto my back, staying close to him so his hand rested on my chest. I rubbed my own hand down my stomach and slowly began to pull at the erection that seemed to symbolize everything that happened since we arrived at Mike's cabin. I tried to force myself to think of Susan, but my mind was filled with men. As my heart beat faster and I began catching my breath, I half-feared and half-hoped that Mike would wake up, discovering me in mid-ejaculation. The last thing I remember was thinking of the irony that it was me who learned the most about himself that night. I drifted into sleep with Mike's hand still resting on me.

We slept late the next morning, but we were up by noon. I had a slight headache, but neither Tim nor Mike felt any worse for wear. Poor, Ben, though, was feeling the pains of an all-star hangover. He took four Excedrin and lay back down with a cold compress on his head. Even though we felt sorry for him, we couldn't help but tease, "What's the matter, Ben? Thought you were the big man, gunna teach us all how to hold our liquor!"

We spent the rest of the day lounging in the sun, swimming in the lake, and eating. That night we drove around until we found a movie theatre and caught the latest James Bond thriller, but back at the cabin, the guys were more interested in practicing magic than repeating the revelries of the night before. We drove back home on Sunday, basking in the warm glow of friendship that comes only through secret shared experiences. When we got to Ben's house, the three boys all grabbed their gear and we stood there, not wanting the time to end. Finally, we hugged awkwardly. I got back into my Tempest and headed home to Bowling Green and Susan. Two months later we were gone. My first job took us to Tennessee and a struggling music program deeply in need of better funding. I never saw Tim again and the last I heard from Mike was his impersonal high school graduation announcement. A couple of years later I got my final letter from Ben. The last I heard of him was when I received a form letter from the Michigan State Bar asking for a letter of recommendation on Ben's behalf. They were no longer part of my life, but the memory of my weekend with the guys never faded.

Twelve years later the Glass City Conjurers hired me to perform at their annual convention so I was back in Toledo. From the air, the city looked the same, but on the ground I became hopelessly lost. After stopping twice for directions, I finally found the Holiday Inn, checked into my room and went down to find old friends.

"Brent! Welcome back to Toledo," said the smiling face behind the registration table. I had no idea who the woman was that addressed me. It must have shown on my face, because she prompted, "I'm Marge... Harry's wife?"

"Oh, yes!" I smiled. "Nice to see you again."

"I have your registration packet right here," she said, handing me a large manila envelope. "You'll find Harry and the boys in the dealers' room."

I fumbled putting on my convention badge and headed in to dust off old memories. As I entered the dealers' room, I recalled when four boys walked into Abbott's. There were the usual scarves and posters, but this room was carpeted; there were bright lights and sterile motel colors. The early birds were already going from table to table examining the newest versions of the same old tricks. Someone caught my arm, "Brent! Remember me? Frank Towers."

"Sure I do," I said, shaking his hand. "Hey, Harry." I smiled as the old club president walked up. "I saw Marge at the registration table." We chatted for a bit, exchanging superficial details of our lives. Finally, I asked the question that had been gnawing at me ever since I'd been booked into Toledo, "Whatever happened to Ben, Mike and Tim? I haven't heard from them in years."

Harry looked as though he was going into a trance, "Tim joined the Air Force right out of high school. I don't know where he's stationed now."

"The Michigan Bar sent me a request for a letter of recommendation for Ben," I offered, "but that was years ago."

"Ben and his wife are living in Detroit," said Harry. "Mike still lives in town, though, but he hardly ever attends any magic meetings."

"Did you hear he's queer?" sneered Frank. My mouth must have dropped open, because he continued, "As a three dollar bill."

"Forget it, Frank," chided Harry. "I saw Mike a couple of weeks ago and asked if he was coming to the convention, but he said he was too busy."

"Is he in the phonebook?" I asked.

"Look under the name Crossland. He thought Koskey sounded too ethnic for an entrepreneur."

No wonder I hadn't been able to locate him. I almost ran to the lobby and found the pay phones. "You have reached 555-5267," the voice on the tape sounded the same as I remembered it. My heart was pounding as I waited for the recorded message to finish. "Mike, if you're there, pick up. This is Brent Larsen... Mike!"

I heard the phone click and he was on the line, "Brent? Where are you?"

"Mike! I'm in town for the magic convention!"

"I had no idea you'd be here. God, what's it been..."

"Twelve years! I can't wait to see you."

He hesitated. "I'm not into magic much anymore. I've changed a lot..."

"Haven't we all! I'll give you thirty minutes to get your ass to the Holiday Inn."

"Tell you what, Brent. I have to stop by the office for a while, but I can be there about ten. I'll meet you in the lobby."

Five hours later I was pacing, trying not to be rude to people who tried to stop to talk. Not wanting to look foolish, I sat down and tried to read a magazine, glancing repeatedly at the clock. At 9:56 p.m. he walked in, paused, caught my eye and headed towards me.

"My god, Mike, you look exactly the same!" I lied. The truth was, he looked better. He'd grown a couple of inches, but his stomach was still flat and his waist couldn't have been any bigger. We hugged in the masculine embrace of long lost friends.

"Brent! You look great! You've lost a little hair, but you've dropped, what, twenty pounds?"

"Almost thirty, but who's counting. Come up to my room, I've got some Bud on ice and a trunkful of things to talk about."

Up in my room, Mike sat in the upholstered chair that faced the bed where I sat.

"Friends for life," he smiled as he lifted his can of cold Budweiser.

"I thought I was the only one dumb enough to remember much of that weekend," I said as I drank to him.

He smiled. "Don't tell me that's the first beer you've had since that night."

"Not exactly," I said. But before I could continue he asked, "Is Susan with you? Do you have any kids?"

I held up my left hand displaying my naked ring finger. "Susan and I split up."

"I'm sorry," he said. "Shit! That sounds so stupid! I never know what to say when I hear someone got divorced."

I took a sip of beer. "Susan left me and the Church threw me out when I finally admitted that I'm gay."

Mike looked as though he'd been hit by a bucket of ice water. We just sat there and looked at each other. "You're gay," he stated quietly.

The corner of my lip curled up, "And from what Frank tells me, so are you—'queer as a three dollar bill,' I think is the way he put it."

Mike laughed, "That sounds like Frank, all right!" He shook his head in disbelief. "Brent Larsen is gay."

"Frankly, I thought of anyone, you are the one who should have figured it out. It was pretty obvious that I got turned on while we were wrestling."

"I remember that." He smiled coyly. "It made a real impression on me. I did wonder, but you were married and I was only a kid. I'm glad you didn't do anything that night, it would have freaked me out. I was really confused back then."

"We've got a lot to talk about, but it'll have to wait for a minute while I take a leak." I stood up and walked into the bathroom. I may have been pushing forty, but my cock still had a mind of its own and I wanted to rearrange my growing erection before it became too obvious. I flushed the toilet, ran some water and dried my hands. When I opened the door I caught something flying toward me out of the corner of my eye. I jerked up my hand just in time to block a flying pillow. What I hadn't noticed was Mike lunging at me under cover of the projectile. He grabbed me in one of his old wrestling holds and I lost my balance, falling back onto the bed with him on top of me, his body crushed against mine. He paused, just like he did in the cabin, and my erection flexed. "I think this is where we left off," I whispered into his ear.

He laughed, "You still make a great impression!" He rolled over and draped his arm across my chest, his hand on my shoulder. Our eyes locked, and the love I felt for him so many years ago came crashing down through time, engulfing the two of us. "That's exactly where we left off." He closed his eyes and pressed his lips to mine.

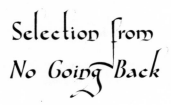

Selection from
No Going Back

Jonathan Langford

Christmas break. Paul was frustrated and upset. And, well, bored.

Christmas at Aunt Jean and Uncle George's had been okay. Paul always thought it was funny how Kyle, the youngest boy, would leap on top of him—from chairs, stairs, the arm of the couch—each time Paul got near. Hyper little rug rat. It was easy to imagine that Chad must have been like that back when he was a little kid.

Which brought his thoughts back to just how mad he was at his best friend.

Chad had tried to apologize to him at church last Sunday. Paul hadn't said anything, just stared at him.

Part of him said he was being unreasonable. It wasn't Chad's fault that he was freaked out by Paul being gay. He'd even tried to keep Paul from finding out. Which was well intended, in a stupid kind of way. Right now, though, Paul was just too upset to be around him.

I thought I had this really cool, tolerant friend. But I don't. He was just faking it.

Since church, they'd seen each other once, on Tuesday night when Paul and his mom had dropped off Christmas presents. The two exchanged cautious words, enough to keep anyone else from knowing they were fighting. Neither of them wanted to get the adults involved.

Unfortunately, that left Paul without anything to do or anyone to do it with, two days after Christmas.

On a sudden impulse, he pulled out Jared's number.

"Hi, Jared? Yeah, this is Paul. Nope, no disaster. Just regular Christmas stuff. Yeah, I got some cool stuff. Listen, you want to hang out today? Cool. Your house? Great." Paul took a look outside. "Weather doesn't look too bad right now. I'll bike over, okay?"

"So, how'd Christmas do you?"

"Pretty good," Paul answered. "Good stuff all around."

Only Jared was home, as it turned out. His parents were out visiting some relatives they saw only at this time of year. Jared had stayed home since, as he put it, he couldn't care less about the things they talked about and the relatives couldn't care less about him, so everyone was happier if he did his own thing while they were doing theirs. Paul could sympathize, kind of.

"Good stuff?" Jared asked. "Or good getting stuffed?"

"That too. We had this huge turkey… Oh, wait, you're still here, aren't you."

"Yuk, yuk. You're such a comedian. Except, actually, not."

As they were talking, Jared pulled out some pop, chips, crackers, and a leftover cheese ball. "Help yourself," he said. Paul opened up a Sprite, then tried the crackers and cheese.

" 'Sgood," he slurred, his mouth full. Jared laughed.

"So here it is, la casa de Jared. What brings you over this fine December day?"

"Well, my bicycle, to start with."

Jared raised an eyebrow. "Oh, please. Your sense of humor can't possibly be as desperate as that."

"I was sitting home bored," Paul confessed.

"So you came over here to see if I could entertain you?"

"Well, yeah."

"At least you're honest about it."

"So what were you doing before I came over?"

"Seeing if there's anything decent on the tube."

Paul rolled his eyes. "I could do that at home."

"Demanding, aren't you?"

"That's right. I'm the irritating little brother you're glad you never had, until now."

"Lucky me."

"Yes, you *are* lucky to be entertaining a superior being such as myself."

"Fine. I give up." They both laughed.

"So if TV isn't good enough for you, how do you want to waste time today?"

"Got any good movies?" Paul asked.

"Some action movies." A sly look. "Ones with hot guys."

"But is there decent character development?" As Jared stared at him, Paul giggled. "Okay, I don't care about character development either. Just so long as the guys are hot."

"And there's a lot of violence."

"Well, of course. That goes without saying."

They wound up watching *X-Men 2*, which had just come out on DVD. Aside from Logan, the cast of hot guys was somewhat lacking. Still, it was a lot of fun. Paul had seen the movie back in May when it was in the theaters, but it was great watching it again.

"So, enough hotties for you?" asked Jared. He'd gotten some more pop for both of them.

"Not really."

"Plenty of action, though."

"And character development." They both snickered.

"Not to mention that coming-out scene."

"Oh, yeah. Like, 'Have you ever tried not being a mutant?' That was classic."

"You know, the really disgusting thing is how the teenagers in these movies all have perfect hair and no zits." Paul paused. "Still, Logan was hot."

"Yeah, but we didn't see nearly enough of him. Not enough bare chest," Jared said with a grin.

Paul sighed in satisfaction. "You know, this is what I was talking about."

"Huh?"

"You asked one time what I get out of GSA. It's this kind of thing. Being able to sit around and talk about, you know, which guys I think are hot, just like it's normal. That kind of thing. I couldn't ever do that with Chad."

"Hmm?"

"My best friend." Paul frowned. "At least, I thought he was."

"Yeah?"

"Until last week."

With Jared's encouragement, Paul told the whole story. How he'd come out to Chad last spring. How Chad had freaked out at first, but then seemed to be okay with it. How they hadn't spent as much time doing stuff during soccer season but got together again afterward. And then the scene with Chad and his friends making fun of the GSA poster, and Paul's argument with Chad, and figuring out that Chad wasn't really as okay with everything as he'd been pretending.

After Paul finished, Jared was quiet for a moment. Finally he asked, "Dude, don't you think maybe you're being a little harsh with Chad, here?"

"What do you mean?"

"So, yeah, it sucks that he's not really okay with you being gay. But at least he cared enough about staying your friend that he went ahead and pretended."

Paul didn't say anything. The same thing had occurred to him, but he was still too upset to just let it go.

Jared cleared his throat. "So, what kind of guys do you like?"

Paul welcomed the change of subject. "You know, I really haven't thought about it. I mean, I know who I think is cute, but I haven't thought about body types." He thought a minute. "Guys who are fit. Muscular."

"Bodybuilders?"

"Not so much. Just ...fit. You know."

"Yeah." Jared snorted. "The kind of guys they put in underwear commercials." Paul blushed. "Yeah."

"There's this poster in my room... "

"What?"

Jared was blushing now. "I, um, had a poster made from a Calvin Klein ad. Not indecent or anything. Just, um, hot."

"Oh, this I gotta see." Paul started laughing.

"Fine. Just… you turd," Jared griped. But he got up anyway.

Paul followed Jared up to his room. The other boy opened the door with a flourish. "Here we are. My little fortress from the world."

"Nice." The room was larger than his, with what looked like a much bigger and more impressive music system, though Jared's computer was an older model than Paul's. The poster Jared had mentioned was very prominent—and, Paul had to admit, quite good.

"So, what do you think?"

"Nice."

"I've got a catalogue with a bunch more of those ads…" Jared was digging around in a stack of magazines. "Here."

Paul started thumbing through it, pausing every so often in appreciation. "You're right," he breathed. "Those guys are hot." He could tell from the tightness in his pants that his body agreed with him.

Finally Paul got to the end of the catalogue. He handed it back to Jared. "Wow. That was, um, really something. Especially that Mexican-looking dude."

"Yeah. He's hot."

"They all are." Paul adjusted his pants.

Jared looked at him kind of sideways. "You know, I can get some pictures online that are hotter than that." He paused. "You wanna see them?"

Paul knew he was crossing a line, but at the moment it didn't seem to matter that much. He knew most guys his age looked at porn sometimes, including some of the guys at church. In fact, he was pretty sure Chad had looked at porn once or twice. If he hadn't, it was only because there wasn't enough privacy in the family room where his parents kept the computer. "Sure," he said.

It had all happened so quickly.

Paul had been feeling mad at Chad and guilty about staying mad. He'd wanted something to distract him from how he was feeling. Jared had been a distraction. And then …and then …

Even after several days, Paul couldn't really believe what had happened. How easy it had been to wind up doing something that went so completely beyond anything he'd ever thought he'd do. Part of him kept insisting that it couldn't really have happened after all. Except that it had.

And what did you expect, when you agreed to look at porn with Jared? part of him asked. *Did you think it would stop at that?*

The answer, of course, was that he hadn't really thought about it at all. He'd been doing his best *not* to think about what was going on. That hadn't stopped it from happening, though.

The worst part was that even though he felt awful about it—and awful about himself for doing something like that—there was still a part of him that kept thinking about how great it had felt while it was happening and that wanted to do it again. Which made him hate himself even more.

———

Richard Mortensen had seen Paul Ficklin in a lot of different moods over the years. As the father of Paul's best friend—and, he believed, a kind of stand-in father at times—he'd seen Paul happy, silly, nervous, frightened, stubborn, angry, sad—many of the different moods common to boys as they grew up. Last July in this very office, he'd watched with concern as a scared but determined Paul had made sure his bishop knew about his feelings for other boys before accepting a calling of responsibility in his priesthood quorum. He'd seldom felt prouder of any young man than he'd felt of Paul that day.

Today, though, things weren't looking so good, judging by the expression on Paul's face. Richard had seen that particular mix of self-directed anger, embarrassment, and shame before. Not so much on Paul up to now, but on other boys he'd had in his office since becoming bishop.

Paul needed to confess something.

Sure enough, the first words out of his mouth, after Richard had closed the door and gestured him to sit, were, "I need to be released as teachers quorum president."

What do I do now? Richard asked within himself, as he always did. He'd learned never to proceed in situations like this without a prayer of that kind in his heart.

"Why?" he asked.

Paul dropped his eyes. "I'm not, uh, worthy anymore."

Bit by bit, the story came out. How Paul had started spending time with Jared, a junior he'd met in the gay-straight club at school, which Paul had started attending that fall. How he'd explained that he wouldn't ever be his boyfriend because he was Mormon. How Jared had seemed to accept that and was okay hanging out with Paul anyway. "He's a friend, you know? And he has this great sense of humor, and …well."

They'd been over at Jared's house, looking at some pictures of hot guys. "Just models, you know? Not like naked or anything." Then—

"Then he asked if I wanted to look at some porn. And I, um, said yes." And things had proceeded from there.

Richard sighed inwardly. He hated this next part, but he'd learned that he needed to get a clear idea of just how serious the problem was. The only way was by asking questions.

Had clothes come off? No.

Had hands gone underneath clothes? Um, yeah.

Had the other boy's hands touched Paul's sexual organs? Yes.

Had Paul's hands touched the other boy's sexual organs? No.

Had it happened again? Yes. A week later.

The same thing, or more? The same.

How long ago was this? A little over a week ago, the second time.

Richard remembered that the last couple of Sundays, Paul had assigned other boys to prepare the sacrament but hadn't helped himself. Now he knew why.

Had anything else happened since then, with this boy or anyone else? No.

Had he looked at pornography any other times? Once, a few days after the first time with Jared.

How did Paul feel about what had happened?

Ever since the conversation began, Paul had been looking down at his hands with a bleak expression on his face, but his voice had been steady. At this latest question, though, he closed his eyes and swallowed. Richard leaned forward.

"It was—I never felt anything like that before. Not even when I'm by myself and—anyway. And then it was all over, and I felt so awful. I, like, stood in the shower for a half-hour, just scrubbing, because I felt so dirty."

"But you did it again a week later."

"Yeah."

"Do you think it'll happen again?"

"I don't know." Paul opened his eyes and looked Richard in the eye for the first time since the questions had started. "I don't want it to happen, but I can't stop thinking about it. I've tried to pray, but I just feel so awful." He turned away again. "After the first time, I thought, I'm never gonna do that again. I was so sure. And then I went back a week later." Paul swallowed. "Yeah, I think it's gonna happen again."

Inside himself, Richard felt a great sense of frustration. Right now, he felt that if he had this—this Jared boy—in front of him, he'd be hard pressed not to physically attack him. *I wonder if this is what a father feels about the boy who knocked up his daughter?* he thought to himself. With difficulty, he kept his feelings from showing on his face. *It won't do any good if Paul thinks I'm angry at him.*

"Paul?"

"Yeah."

"Do you have faith in Jesus Christ? That he can help you?"

"I don't know," he whispered, and looked down again.

Richard contemplated the young man who sat before him. Paul's hands were shaking slightly, he realized. He hadn't noticed it before.

And suddenly in his mind's eye he saw a different scene. Paul, head still down, shaking the bishop's hand and walking out of his office. Paul going into the house where he and his mother lived. Paul opening the medicine cabinet in the bathroom, pouring pills from a bottle into his open hand, swallowing again and again—

The fleeting mental vision broke.

"Paul." He stood and held out his arms. "Come here."

Paul stood, but hesitated. Richard took a step toward him. With a gasp, Paul flung himself forward and clung to Richard as if he were a much younger boy.

"Paul," Richard said again, his arms wrapped around the boy's shoulders, which were shaking now with sobs. "Heavenly Father loves you. And so do I."

They stood there a long time, five minutes at least, while Richard's shirt grew damp with the boy's tears. Finally Paul released him and pulled away. "Thanks," he whispered.

Richard clasped an upper arm. "Hey, you. You're a good kid."

"I don't feel like it."

"That's Satan trying to get you to feel like you aren't worth anything. Like you can't change. Like you aren't worthy of God's love, or anyone else's." Richard cleared his throat. "There's a scripture I memorized back when I was about your age. 'For I am persuaded, that neither death, nor life, nor angels, nor principalities, nor powers, nor things present, nor things to come, nor height, nor depth, nor any other creature, shall be able to separate us from the love of God, which is in Christ Jesus our Lord.' That's what the missionary who interviewed me for baptism quoted when I told him I didn't think I could ever be good enough to be a member of the church."

"But you weren't gay."

Richard paused. How to handle this one? "I'm not completely sure you are, either."

"But—"

He held up his hand. "I don't doubt that you're attracted to other males. I'm not convinced, though, that it has to mean you're *gay*. I take gay to mean someone who's chosen to live a homosexual lifestyle, one that's not consistent with the gospel."

"But I—"

"You committed a sin. You made a mistake. You did something that naturally makes you feel bad, because you weren't living up to your own standards, God's standards. It made you feel rotten. Now Satan's jumped on that. He's trying to convince you that you're garbage because you made a mistake. He wants to convince you that you can't help acting that way. He wants you to think you're stuck. But you're not."

"I don't think I'm gonna stop feeling the way I do. About guys and stuff."

"I didn't say you would."

They were still standing. Richard gestured Paul to sit, then sat down himself. He no longer felt that same frightening sense that the boy might be on the edge of deciding life wasn't worth living anymore. Now all he had to do was convince Paul that being the way he was didn't mean he had to leave the church.

He began again. "Paul, God doesn't expect more from you than you're able to do. At this point, the only thing that's expected from you is the same thing that's expected of all young men in the church. Basically, that's to keep your hands and your body to yourself and do your best to train your thoughts and personal behavior not to go where they shouldn't." He softened his voice. "Do you have a testimony of the gospel?"

"I—I believe it's true." Paul looked down at his hands. "I've felt the Holy Ghost, sometimes. I think."

"Do you want to stay in the church?"

"Yes."

"Do you want to serve a mission, get married, have a family? I'm not talking about whether you think it can happen. What I'm asking is, do you *want* it?"

"Yes." The boy's voice was very quiet now.

Richard hesitated for a few seconds, then continued. "I don't know what you're going through. I've never been attracted to other men. But I do know that each of us encounters hard things in our lives. This thing you're struggling with is really tough. I don't know if you will ever be free of those feelings in this life. But I do know that being gay isn't part of your eternal character. Someday, whether in this life or the next, you can be married to a woman you love. You can have a family." He paused. "God can do this. Can you believe in him enough to give him a chance?"

Paul still looked hesitant, or maybe fearful. "I don't know if I can."

Richard thought some more. "There's another scripture I like. Let's see if I can find it … Here it is. Alma is talking to the Zoramites. 'But behold, if ye will awake and arouse your faculties, even to an experiment upon my words, and exercise a particle of faith, yea, even if ye can no more than desire to believe, let this desire work in you, even until ye believe in a manner that ye can give place for a portion of my words.' That's what I hear in what you're saying to me. You're not sure if you believe. You don't know if you can do it. But you *want* to believe. You *desire* to believe. My challenge to you, Paul, is to let that desire work within you, the way the scripture says. Do an experiment on the Lord's words, and on my words. Give them a try. I promise that God won't let you down. Will you do that?"

Slowly, hesitantly, Paul nodded.

"Okay." Richard took a deep breath. "So let's set some ground rules, some things you can do that will give you strength to make sure this doesn't happen again. Have you been reading your scriptures?"

"Most of the time."

"I want you to commit to reading your scriptures each day, at a regular time. Can you do that?"

"Yes."

"What about your prayers? Have you been saying them, each morning and evening?"

"Not always."

"I want you to commit to saying your prayers every day. Each morning, ask Heavenly Father specifically for his help in getting through the day. Each evening, report back to him about how things have gone. Can you do that?"

"Yes."

And now the tougher ones. "Paul, I think we need to make sure you don't ever find yourself in situations where this might happen again. How can you do that?"

"I don't know."

Richard shook his head. "I don't think it's a good idea for you to see this Jared person or keep going to this GSA group. But at the least, you definitely need to make sure you don't get into situations where you're alone with Jared or any other gay person."

Richard paused. He wanted to make sure Paul understood the reasons for these boundaries. "The impulses you've talked about—they're the product of opportunity and temptation. You may not be able to get rid of the temptation, at least not right away or all at once, but you *can* remove the opportunity. What you need to do is make sure that when those feelings come, you're not in a situation that makes it easy for you to act on them. No looking at porn, either alone or especially with someone else there. No intimate situations with other guys. No personal conversations, even, with someone you think might be same-sex attracted, unless another person is there as a chaperon. Can you do that?"

Paul swallowed. "Yes."

Richard looked at the youth sitting in front of him. Paul had made the commitments but didn't sound too happy. *He needs a lifeline,* he thought. *Something he can grab onto and hold onto when things get tough. Someone who can be there for him. He needs a dad, but I can't give him one.*

Richard guessed he would just have to do as a substitute.

"You have a cell phone, don't you?"

"Yeah."

"I want you to call me. Call me each day at"—he mentally flipped through his daily calendar—"3:30. Here's my number." He pulled out one of his business cards, circled the number, and handed it to Paul. "Call me, tell me how things are going. How your day is going. Even if it's just a minute. All right? Or I'll be calling you. Can you do that?"

"Yeah." Paul blushed and nodded, but he didn't seem angry or upset. *He really wants someone he can talk to about things,* Richard realized, *even if it's just the bishop.* Once again, as on numerous occasions over the years, Richard felt the temptation to seek out Barbara's ex-husband and smack him for leaving her to raise a boy pretty much on her own.

"Call me any other time as well, anytime day or night, if things start getting tough for you. If you start feeling bad about yourself, or if you feel like you might give in and make some bad choices. Or even if you just want to talk. Okay?"

"Okay."

Richard thought again for a moment. "Paul, there's one other thing I'd like to do before we leave today. Will you let me give you a blessing?"

"Yes."

Richard got out of his chair and put his hands on the boy's head. "Paul Eric Ficklin, by the authority of the holy Melchizedek priesthood which I hold, I lay my hands upon your head… "

As the words flowed, Richard could feel Paul relaxing under him. Somewhat to his own surprise, the main thrust of the blessing was admonishment to follow the counsel of his leaders—a reference, Richard assumed, to the things he'd just told the boy—with a promise of spiritual protection as he did so. Nothing about the larger issues of same-sex attraction or how Paul should lead his life in general. *Maybe just getting him past this is enough for right now.*

Soon the blessing was over. Paul stood, wiped tears from his face, seized Richard in a great hug, and then let him go. As the boy left the room, there was a tentative smile on his face—the first Richard had seen from him that afternoon.

It was Monday afternoon, and Chad was working on his algebra when the doorbell rang.

Paul was at the door. "Can I come in?"

"I thought you weren't talking to me right now," Chad answered, without moving from where he stood blocking the doorway. Part of him was happy to see his best friend. Another part was angry at the way Paul had lit into him that Friday before Christmas and even angrier at the way Paul had been avoiding him since then.

"Yeah, well, I'm sorry," Paul muttered, looking down. "I was wrong. And—well, I need some help with stuff."

Slowly, Chad opened the door all the way, then led the way up to his bedroom. Paul closed the bedroom door behind him and dropped onto a chair. Chad sat on the bed.

"So," Chad began. "Want to explain why you've been such a jerk the last couple of weeks?"

"Not really," Paul said, still looking away.

"Well, too bad, jerk-off."

Paul winced. "Yeah, well." He drew a deep breath. "At first, I was ticked off about all that stuff you and your friends were saying and 'cause you were pretending to be okay with me being gay when you really weren't. I still think you were being a real loser about that, by the way."

"And then?"

"I, uh, didn't want to hang out with you, because …I did something really stupid. And I didn't want to talk about it."

"This I gotta hear. Something stupid enough to make you not want to tell me about it?"

"I did stuff with Jared. That guy from GSA."

For a minute, Chad couldn't figure out what he meant. Then it all came clear. "Geez, Paul! What the fuh—I mean, why the hell did you do that?"

"Keep it down!" Paul yelped. Then, more quietly, he added, " 'Cause I was dumb. And horny."

Paul sat there looking at his best friend, who was staring back at him from his bed. He looked mad, which Paul had expected, but mostly he just seemed exasperated—as if Chad couldn't believe Paul had been so stupid.

Paul still couldn't believe it either.

Chad spoke. "So, you been to talk to my dad yet? Or does this favor you need have something to do with that?"

Paul stared at him. "Huh?"

"Come off it, Paul! We've been friends for seven years. Remember that time we stole those root beers when we were nine? Fifteen minutes later, you were going all guilty on me about it. You didn't last an hour before you were telling your mom. Got me into trouble too. I was mad at you for a week.

"I figure there's no way you won't tell my dad about this sooner or later. So the question is whether you told him already or decided to talk to me first." Chad paused. "Except that doesn't make sense either. There's no reason why you'd talk to me about this unless you had to. So I'm guessing you already talked to my dad." He peered at Paul suspiciously. "What's this favor you need from me?"

"You're right. I talked with your dad yesterday."

"And?"

"And he gave me some rules."

"Yeah? Like what?"

"I have to have someone else with me if I'm gonna be alone with any gay guys."

"Well, duh."

"What do you mean?"

Chad shrugged. "I kind of wondered about that. I mean, can you imagine my dad and mom letting me spend several hours alone with a girl, with no one else in the house? But you got together with that Jared guy whenever you wanted. You were sliding by."

Paul frowned. He hadn't thought about it that way before.

Chad continued. "So how does this affect me?"

"I really need to talk with Jared."

"Uh-uh. No way. I am not gonna stick around just so you can tell your ex-boyfriend why you're breaking up with him."

"It's not like that. I mean, he's really not my boyfriend."

"So basically your hormones got out of control and you jumped the guy?"

Paul could feel his face reddening even more. "More like I let him jump me."

"Geez, Paul, you're a dumb shit." Chad paused. "So if he's not your boyfriend, why do you have to talk to him about it at all?"

"Look, I just do, okay?"

Chad closed his eyes. "So when're you planning to deliver this bit of news to the fair Jared?"

"After school tomorrow. Either before or after the GSA meeting."

"Oh, great. You want me to go to this GSA thing, then hang around trying not to look like a homophobe while you tell this friend all about the new rules my dad said you have to follow."

"Look, I know you're not a homophobe. I'm sorry for saying it, okay?"

"I wouldn't be too sure about that. Right at the moment, I'm feeling pretty pissed at most of the gay people I know."

"Me, you mean."

"Well, yeah, you. Not to mention that pea-brain jerk-off Jared." Chad shook his head. "You're gonna owe me so bad for this."

"I know," Paul muttered.

—

Jared was having a good day. He'd been in a good mood generally, ever since Christmas.

Christmas vacation had been surprisingly good for him and his family. A few days after the holiday, to his great surprise, his dad had pulled him aside and talked with him about college. He'd told him they were still planning to support him at the University of Oregon if he did his best to earn good grades. "I know we haven't talked a lot, since …well," his dad had said, obviously uncomfortable. "I want you to know that you're still our son, and we'll support you in all the good things you want to do with your life." He'd looked away then. "I'm sorry. I've just had a hard time getting used to this." It wasn't a declaration of gay pride or even complete acceptance, but it was a sign that things were finally starting to get better—after Jared had pretty much given up hope that it would ever happen.

And then there was the stuff with Paul.

After Paul had come out at GSA, Jared hadn't seen him again before school let out for the break. So he was surprised when Paul called him up the Saturday after Christmas and asked if they could hang out. They'd talked for a while, then started looking at some mags and online pictures. Seeing how excited Paul was getting, Jared had made a snap decision and put his hand on Paul's back.

Things had progressed from there.

At one point Jared had stuck his hands down Paul's pants. He worried for a minute that he might have gone too far, but the other boy hadn't objected.

After it was all over, Paul had taken off pretty quickly. The next Saturday, though, he'd come over again, and pretty much the same thing had happened.

Since then, Jared had found himself thinking. His original idea had been to have some fun without going too far with the other boy. He didn't want a boyfriend right now, and he knew Paul wasn't up for one.

And that was all it had been the first time. Paul was cool, he was a good guy, he was cute. And he seemed to like what they'd been doing. The way Jared saw it, it wasn't like it was real sex. Just messing around.

The second time, though… Jared had felt something that second time, a kind of connection that hadn't been there before. Several times since then, he'd caught himself thinking about the other boy at odd moments.

Paul was cute. He was friendly, and he had a good sense of humor, without the extra layer of sarcasm Jared had found in a lot of the gay people he knew in GSA and elsewhere. Paul was…*nice*. Wholesome. Good natured. It was a combination, Jared was starting to realize, that he found a lot more attractive—at least in the case of Paul—than he ever would have guessed. He couldn't really explain it.

Jared was even starting to think maybe he could live with having a boyfriend he couldn't have sex with if the boyfriend was Paul. If it came to that. *After all,* he reminded himself, *it's not like I'm having sex with anyone right now anyway.*

Paul hadn't been at the first GSA meeting after Christmas break. Jared was surprised but didn't read too much into it. After all, Jared himself didn't come to all the meetings. He also hadn't expected to see the other boy this past weekend, since school had started up again and they hadn't talked about getting together. It had been a casual, one-time thing that happened to be repeated. It was only this past weekend that he'd started to realize he might want to find out if it could turn into something more than that.

And so Jared was hoping to see Paul at GSA today and maybe get a chance to talk to him afterward and see whether they might spend some more time hanging out together. That was where things stood when Jared spotted Paul and his friend standing outside the GSA room. Paul had an uncomfortable expression on his face, and his friend didn't look terribly friendly. "We need to talk," Paul said, and that was when things started going rapidly downhill.

Talking to the bishop had been hard. Talking to Chad had been embarrassing. But talking to Jared was turning out to be a lot worse than Paul had expected.

Seeing Jared walking toward the GSA room, Paul couldn't help but notice the smile on the other boy's face as he caught sight of Paul standing in the hallway. To Paul's surprise, he could feel his own breath speed up. Jared was—Paul had to admit—pretty good looking. A mental picture flashed in Paul's mind replaying what had happened the last couple of times they got together. His body definitely remembered and was reminding him of that fact.

Paul realized that Chad being there was a good idea for its own sake, not just so he could say he was following the bishop's rules. *Stupid teenage hormones.*

"So, Paul," Jared began. "Haven't seen you for awhile. You wanna introduce me to this guy?"

"This is my best friend, Chad. I told you about him."

"I guess you two are cool again."

"Yeah." Paul sucked in his breath. "We need to talk."

Jared was quiet for a long moment. "You wanna do this after GSA, or right now? We can skip out on the meeting."

"Right now would maybe be better, if that's okay with you."

"Okay."

They walked out into the courtyard. The minute they got there, Chad started. "Look, this all has nothing to do with me, okay? So I'll just go sit over there, and you two can talk about what you need to talk about, and I'll walk home with Paul afterward. Deal?" Without waiting for an answer, he walked over to a table about twenty feet away, then pulled out a textbook and started reading it, very obviously not looking their way.

"Well. I guess that tells us, doesn't it?"

"Yeah." There was an uncomfortable silence.

Paul drew a deep breath. "Jared. About the time we spent over Christmas." He swallowed. "I, uh, I crossed a line. A line I shouldn't have crossed."

Jared didn't say anything. Paul couldn't meet his eyes.

"I was… I, uh, talked to you that one time about the standards I'm supposed to keep. What we did was way beyond what I should have been doing. The porn and, um, the other stuff."

There was a pause. "Yeah. So, I guess that's good to know," Jared said finally. Paul couldn't tell anything from his expression.

"There's, uh, more. I kind of, um, talked with my bishop about it. My minister, you know?"

Jared closed his eyes. "And he doesn't want you hanging out with faggots like me anymore."

Paul winced. "Not exactly. But I'm, um, not supposed to be alone with any other gay guys."

"Shit. So now we need a chaperone just to get together and talk." He jerked his thumb over toward Chad. "That's why he's here, then?"

"Yeah."

"Well, that really sucks."

"It's—don't think—" Paul's words ran out then, as he realized he wasn't really sure what he was trying to say. He started again. "I still think you're a cool dude. This doesn't change that."

"And let's still be friends, that whole crap." Jared's voice sounded sarcastic and vaguely bitter. He glared over at Chad. "What happens to you if you don't go along with this?"

"It's not like that. I mean, yeah, I made an agreement with the bishop, but it was my choice really. It's a way that I can keep the promises I've made."

"Like that really makes me feel so much better, knowing you and your church think I'm some kind of chemical contaminant you have to be protected from."

"That's not it at all." Paul was now feeling thoroughly miserable.

"Sure feels like it."

"Look, I'm sorry if it makes you feel bad. That's really not what it's about, though. It's about making it easier for *me* to be sure I'm keeping my commitments." Paul laughed nervously. "I mean, it's not like we were boyfriends or anything."

Jared stared at him for a moment, then slapped one hand against a tree trunk. "Yeah. Of course. Well, thanks for letting me know, anyway, instead of just avoiding me like you've been doing the past two weeks." He picked up his backpack and headed toward the courtyard exit.

"Hey! Aren't you going to GSA?"

Jared paused. "Somehow, I just don't feel like going to a meeting right now about how we're all supposed to be happy being gay, or straight, or Mormon-in-the-closet, or whatever." He turned back toward the doors again. "See you, man. Hopefully not too soon, though." Then he was gone.

Paul stood staring after him for a minute, stunned.

"Well, looks like that went well." It was Chad.

"Not really."

"I was being ironic. Moron."

Paul looked at his watch. "Dang. I'm late for my call with your dad." He pulled out his cell phone and started pressing buttons.

"Dammit." Jared pounded a fist against his bedroom wall. "Dammit," he repeated.

Paul had warned him. Hell, he'd warned himself. *It's not like we're boyfriends.* No duh.

For one fleeting moment, the thought crossed his mind that really, this was all pretty ordinary stuff. Teenagers found out all the time that someone they liked didn't like them back. The fact that he and Paul were both boys didn't really have anything to do with it. *Yay for equal-opportunity disappointment.* Somehow it didn't make him feel any better.

("Adolescence")

Alan Williams

I'm giving my mom and my little brother Zeb a much-delayed visit. Their house in North Seattle is much bigger than needed for two people. My mom is planning to marry a man with four kids.

I pass the laundry room and she's folding Zeb's clothes.

"You know," she says. "I guess I wouldn't like it too much if someone insisted I be a lesbian."

This person is an alien clone. My real mother doesn't think about such things as lesbians. "Oh, really?" I say. "You know what the Church does, don't you? They try to convince gay people that it's in their best interests to be straight. In fact, they try to convince them that they're already straight. It's psychological torture, actually. There are—or, at least, there used to be—they probably don't still exist—but these facilities where men were strapped down and their genitals electrocuted to turn them off from gay porn. As if they can be zapped back to some kind of natural state."

"And what bogus site did you read that on?" she says, as she folds a shirt.

"It's documented. And what's worse is that most gay Mormon men don't even look at porn to begin with. They're already used to pushing their attractions out of their head. The worst part is that they subjected themselves to this torture willingly because they wanted to fit in with those they love. Their families. Their God."

"I think you should speak to our ward," Zeb says, materialized. He must have been listening from the family room and wanted to throw in his two cents. "To make our church a better church."

"That's a great idea," I say.

"Children don't need to hear about sex," my mom says. She drops a pile of folded shirts into a hamper and then begins on Zeb's jeans. "They internalize stuff like that. And people's genitals being electrocuted? Good grief."

"Okay, Mom. Suppose you were a Mormon psychologist and you were convinced that everyone in Heaven is straight."

She laughs. "Me? A psychologist?"

"Wouldn't you try electrocuting a deviant behavior away in your patients? It's called aversion therapy and it's still a practiced method used for many mental disorders. If used on a gay man, sure, he probably won't have sex with another man because every time he sees someone he thinks is attractive, his brain…well…I don't want to know how it feels. Needless to say, this isn't about sex, Mom. It's about people's lives, happiness and sanity. You said you wouldn't want to be a lesbian, so I'm clearing up your thoughts for you."

She continues to fold laundry.

"And what do you mean by children internalize stuff like that? Gayness doesn't rub off." I turn to Zeb. "You think girls are hot, don't you, bro?"

He doesn't answer, but my mom sees him blushing. "I caught him and the girl Chelsea next door," she says, "talking to each other through the woods. He was standing in our backyard and Chelsea was in hers, and they were yelling back and forth."

"That's hardly secretive," I say.

She shrugs. My brother is still blushing. Then he shrugs, too.

"Anyway," I say, "did you know that, statistically, if five percent of the population is gay, then a three-hundred member ward would have at least fifteen gay people in it? When people feel lost and alone, sometimes they commit suicide, which is not unheard of in the Mormon Church among young people. Shouldn't we bring issues to light that are leading young people to commit suicide?"

"Micah." She is exhausted by the subject already. "Children shouldn't hear about suicide. They internalize stuff like that." She sticks her tongue out at me, knowing she used the same irksome phrase. "Besides, sexual orientation can be discussed behind closed doors with one's bishop. Why would a person want the whole ward to know?"

"It's not about a single instance of gayness, Mom. It's about a general ignorance as to what being gay means. The fact that it's something made secret behind closed doors lends to the ongoing discrimination."

"It's not a secret," Zeb says, tapping my shoulder. "And there's no discrimination. I asked an Elder and he said that the Church accepts and loves gay people as much as everybody else. There's all kinds of stuff written for people who are gay in the Church. But then he asked me if I think I'm gay and I said, 'No, but my brother is.'"

I roll my eyes. "He was asking if you're gay so that he could report you to the bishop. The Church loves and accepts gay people so much, bro, that they want to make sure they make only the *right* choices."

Zeb stands there with a half-smile. He doesn't catch onto my sarcasm. "But, hey!" he says to our mom. "You know Brother Yesler? He's gay. Everybody knows about that."

I suppose there might be people in the Church open with their homosexuality these days. But that doesn't mean they can bring their partners to church, assuming they even have partners. I bet they're all celibate. They're like, look at me! I'm gay and Mormon and celibate! And I'm *miserable*!

"Micah," my mom says, like she somehow heard my evil thoughts. "A Sacrament meeting is a time for fellowship. Not a time for quarrelling in front of children about topics they wouldn't understand." Angry eyes turn toward Zeb. "Did you clean out your rabbit's cage, young man? How can you let that little animal suffer?"

He's startled by her tone.

"Yeah, Zeb. Only big animals should suffer."

He looks back and forth between us and sighs. He treads upstairs to his room.

"I don't want you talking about this stuff while your younger brother is around."

"And why not? Only meant for the bishop's office? Tried that. Didn't work."

"Actually," she says, "bishops tend to work with those therapists you mentioned. I have one. There's nothing wrong with seeing a therapist from time to time. There weren't any for you in Germany, though, because we were a small stake. I'm sure your testicles are happy they weren't shocked."

"Oh, that's fantastic, Mom. Glad to know."

"Your brother is twelve," she says. "Every child goes through a period when they want to– "

"Think on their own?"

"No, Micah. Break from the truth. Adolescence is a difficult period and he's just getting started."

"Am I an adolescent?"

"Well, technically not. But you still have adolescent tendencies."

"Are you talking about my being gay?"

She slaps a pair of jeans on the top of the washer and I nearly jump out of my skin! "Why do you always, *always* center on that?" she says. "Can't you talk about anything else?"

Processing…processing: no.

"That's the adolescent tendency I'm talking about. You barely visit and then when you do, you harass me about this one issue until you're positive I'm convinced. Is your sexuality the only thing that defines you, Micah?" Her frazzled hair has come loose from its band. "I certainly hope not. And you know…" She removes the band, puts it between her lips, gathers her hair and puts it back in the band. "Sometimes you have to agree to disagree. And when you're older, maybe you'll understand that."

"What I understand," I say, "is that disagreement disappears when it comes to your beliefs. But you started this, Mom. You told me you wouldn't want to be a lesbian and I can't understand why not because women are beautiful."

"Oh, you think so?" she says. "Men's penises are rather strange-looking. Especially your father's in the bathtub."

"Mother!"

"It floated like a buoy. It was the strangest thing."

"That's gross, Mom!"

Peter's Mirror

Jeff Laver

I was eight when my family decided to move to Lima, Peru. That was in 1997. My dad's company made him a good offer to take the position. However, I had mixed feelings. Dad had recently turned down a position in L.A., and I had been relieved. I did not want to leave my friends. But Peru was so exotic, even to an eight-year-old boy, that I couldn't help but feel a little excited. The idea of learning to speak another language intrigued me.

The school I attended there was primarily for the children of foreigners; half of the day was in English, the other half in Spanish, and while my friends at school were bi-lingual, the neighborhood kids didn't speak much English. Their well-to-do parents wanted to speak English to us, however, and they encouraged their kids to be friends with me and my siblings. Children learn languages more quickly than adults or adolescents, and I was excited to learn Spanish, so despite hearing both languages regularly, soon I was speaking almost exclusively in Spanish to everyone except my parents and during our half day of English at school. Oh, and sometimes at church. There were a couple of Utah families in our Mormon ward, and sometimes the missionaries were from the States. They loved to spend part of their day off at our house, and my mom loved to feed them. They too were bi-lingual, but they usually preferred to speak English to us. It was kind of awkward when one of the pair was a Latin who spoke little English, and the other a "Statesider," as I came to call us. Our Chilean neighbors next door would frequently remind us that, "We're Americans, too. South America is part of the Americas." I decided calling myself American was kind of like a Spaniard calling himself European.

Anyway, when one of the missionaries didn't speak English, we would try to include him or her by speaking Spanish, but occasionally the gringo side of the pair would refuse to utter a word of Spanish after crossing our threshold. My parents' Spanish got to be pretty good, but they always preferred English as long as it didn't mean excluding anyone. Sometimes when they would speak to me in English, though, I would answer in Spanish.

When I was thirteen, I reached puberty. I was fifteen when I developed my first crush on one of the missionaries, Elder Alonso, from Madrid. I thought he was wonderful. I loved doing "splits" with the missionaries while he was in our area. Mormon missionaries always go in pairs, but they frequently split up and take ward members with them to work. That way they can double their efforts and at the same time give the non-missionary member of the ward some of the "missionary experience." It was thought to be great preparation for those of us too young to serve full-time missions. There was a kid my age in the ward who was also from the States. Elder Young liked to take him because they would ogle attractive women and speak English together the whole time. I refused to speak English to Elder Young, partly because I knew that would get me "stuck" with Elder Alonso, which was exactly what I wanted.

Elder Alonso was a hard worker, but we would talk non-stop traveling between visits. Sometimes we'd laugh. Spaniards have a distinct accent which I loved, and I would frequently get tongue-tied trying to mimic it. Often Elder Alonso was frustrated with his companion. He tried to keep this frustration to himself but would occasionally have to unburden himself. Apparently, Elder Young had a bit of a mean streak. I had to admit, I had seen it myself. He would sometimes say the cruelest things to, or about, people, and would act like Elder Alonso wasn't even there when they were at our house.

One day I was talking to Elder Alonso, at a safe distance from the others, and making fun of Elder Young, "His Spanish is awful! How can you stand listening to him speak?"

"Be nice. I should have kept my complaints to myself. Now I've given you a bad impression of my companion."

"I already had a bad impression. He's a turd." I laughed. "Lisa says he's got a fat ass."

Lisa was my seventeen-year-old sister, who was very pretty and under strict orders from my parents to avoid the elders as much as possible. When they were around the house, Ana, our maid, kept a watchful eye, as did my mom.

Elder Alonso stifled a laugh. "You're awful. Did Lisa really say that?"

"No, but she said you're adorable."

"Did she?"

"No, I made that up, too."

He laughed. "Sometimes I think you're a bad influence."

"Who me? I'm only fifteen! Just a kid. You're nineteen, right?"

"Don't play innocent with me!"

I laughed. "You're the one who's supposed to be a good example. You're a missionary. I can be a shit if I feel like it."

Elder Alonso smiled. "All Mormons are supposed to be examples." Then he looked at me seriously. "I'm trying to be a good example and you're old enough to know better!"

"I know," I replied seriously, but then continued with a mischievous grin and a coy look, "And you are a good example. I really do look up to you."

If only you knew, I thought. I normally wasn't much of a smart aleck or trouble maker, but I had been trying, almost without realizing it, to flirt with Elder Alonso.

Although I was little when we had lived in Utah, I remember having kind of an idealized view of missionaries. There, we only had brief contact with them. Here, in the "real" mission field, we often got to know the missionaries quite well. Some of them were wonderful, and some of them were not. I could tell that my parents didn't even like Elder Young, but of course they would never say that. No speaking ill of the Lord's anointed, even though that rule only applied, in the strictest sense, to those called to positions of authority over us.

And then one day those Elders were both gone, transferred to other parts of the mission. We were used to that. A missionary was never in our area for more than a few months, and they weren't allowed to contact us. I was tempted to try to get Elder Alonso's email address, or try sending snail mail to him, but I never did. Until he went back to Spain it would have been against the rules for him to correspond with me or anyone else within the mission boundaries, so I knew he wouldn't reply. I also knew my crush wasn't reciprocated. It was clear we liked each other, but I doubt he suspected what I felt.

Around that time, while I was still fifteen, my affair with one of the neighbor boys progressed to mutual masturbation. Prior to that we had just caressed each other. None of it seemed like a sin to me until we kissed and gave each other blow-jobs when we were sixteen. At that point I briefly considered going to the local Bishop and confessing my sins, but decided I didn't feel that sinful, even then, in spite of what my church told me. For some reason I just didn't internalize much of the homophobia, or phobias about sex in general that surrounded me, and besides, I was having major doubts about Mormonism itself. Its story seemed like the stuff of myth and its claim to be the "one and only true church" seemed overreaching.

When the Bishop would call me in for the regular interviews that are expected in Mormonism, and would ask me if I had any sexual sins to confess, I would get a determined look and ask why he thought that was any of his business. He didn't know how to respond to that. After all, I was from Utah and was descended from Mormon pioneers. He was a convert to the church.

"I'm just doing what they tell me I'm supposed to do," he would always say. To which I would respond, "I'm far from perfect, but I'm a good, moral person."

It was true, I guess. Although I've often been guilty of thinking too highly of myself, I did spend part of most Saturdays volunteering for charities trying to help Peru's poor. I frequently volunteered at an orphanage. Sometimes I would read to the kids. Over the course of the year I tried to help collect toys so they would each get something for Christmas. Occasionally I would help with facility repairs. At first the nuns said I shouldn't stoop to such things, but I reminded them that Jesus had been a carpenter. I genuinely did feel that all people deserved the same respect that I did. I felt sorry for kids at school who were picked on, for homeless animals, and for the many people I saw who suffered real need.

"Human dignity is universal," I found myself chastising one of the gringo missionaries from Arizona when he spoke condescendingly of the Peruvians.

I suppose I was precocious. Sometimes I was also outspoken, judgmental and impatient.

I was also becoming a bit cynical. I was unusually introspective for someone my age. My gringo friends would quite often tease me, saying what a nerd I was because sometimes, rather than chasing around with them, I preferred to stay home and read novels or history books. I even found out some of the things about Mormon history that made church leaders cringe. I would go online, look up sources and have books shipped from the States. Among other things, I learned how Joseph Smith's accounts of his early visions seemed to evolve and change, and that his purchased, ancient papyri that were the purported source of part of "The Pearl of Great Price" had been found in Chicago and shown to have nothing to do with that version of Mormon scripture. In conversations with my parents I would kind of skirt around some of the things I was learning, saying something like, "Somebody at school told me such and such. Is that true?" I almost never lied, but I didn't want Mom and Dad to start censuring what I was reading. I soon realized that although my parents were both college graduates, and fairly well read, they knew virtually nothing about Mormonism beyond the orthodox version we learned at church. I didn't dwell on these topics since I didn't want to arouse their suspicions, but all this made me take official information from Salt Lake with a grain of salt. Was my church, at least partly, about control? I wondered. Was power such a thrill?

One day I asked our maid, "Ana, if you're dusting under my bed and find some books, would you please just leave them there?"

She winked at me, "Oh, I know what boys your age are like. I won't tell your mother."

"Ana, no, not those kinds of books! No magazines either. Come with me, I'll show you."

As she looked through the books she said, "No nasty pictures, but the words must be bad to make you want to hide them. I wish I could understand English."

"Ana, they're not what you think." I translated a few sentences for her, "They're history books, but they deal with history my parents would prefer not to know about."

She looked at me with a touch of sadness. Ana had been spoiling me since I was eight years old. My nerdiness and lack of macho qualities disturbed her. My mannerisms weren't effeminate, but I wasn't what she expected a maturing young man to be.

To reassure her, I smiled, "That kind of thing would be on my computer."

"Oh, you boys!" She gave me a conspiratorial look.

Ana was rather indulgent with my two younger brothers and me, but I knew she would be horrified if she discovered my true inclinations.

Although I was having doubts, I continued to search for religious truth. Once, while out in Lima, I saw a small dog attacked and killed by a larger one, while a crowd of men, women and children cheered. I tried to stop the incident, but people held me back. How could anyone enjoy such a spectacle? I was confused, and so angry that I yelled at the people. Most of them looked at me like I was crazy, but a couple of them gave me guilty looks. When I got home I ran to hug our dog and held her for a long time. I loved the scripture in Isaiah that says, "The wolf also shall dwell with the lamb, and the leopard shall lie down with the kid; and the calf and the young lion and the fatling together." I felt guilty that, sometimes, I would quickly scratch our dog's ears and hurry on when she wanted some real attention. I also liked Christ's words, "for every one that exalteth himself shall be abased and he that humbleth himself shall be exalted." I would remind myself that I wasn't superior to others, though I did wish the world could always be a gentle place.

Dad would only go to the States once a year with us, but Mom and we kids would usually go twice. I got very used to airplanes, airports and seeing people behaving badly. The people who annoyed me the most were often Peruvians who lived in the States. They were so hoity-toity now. Sometimes they would pretend not to understand Spanish and act superior around other Peruvians, and they were often rude and demanding with airport personnel and flight attendants. I once watched an exchange where a male flight attendant spoke to a woman in perfect Spanish because he was having a hard time understanding her English. She pretended not to understand him.

"American. Speak English," she insisted.

I had watched her husband earlier as he rudely demanded that a pregnant flight attendant lift his bags. She politely told him she couldn't do that. Later I heard him bragging in Spanish to a fellow passenger as he showed him pictures of his SUV, "In Peru we only drove a small car. It's too bad you don't have U.S. residency. I'm American now. Look at what I have," as he showed him pictures of his house and other things.

I've decided that, to a certain extent, "things" can help create pleasant surroundings, which do aid our happiness, but beyond pleasant surroundings, the accumulation of more and more stuff isn't the "stuff" of happiness.

It wasn't the desire for more things that drove me into prostitution. It was the thrill.

One day, when I was eighteen and in my last year of high school, I went over to a friend's house. I felt like chatting and she had told me earlier that she'd be there. It turned out that my friend's dad and the maid were the only ones home. He sent the maid to the kitchen and invited me into his den.

"You think you're a pretty boy, don't you?" he said.

"Excuse me?"

"Actually, you are."

"Thanks...I guess."

"Do you like to kiss the other boys?"

"What?"

"Do you want me to kiss you?"

I did.

Although I said nothing, he moved close and put his arms around me. His breath was intoxicating; I felt a thrill as our noses touched. The feel of his whiskers on my cheeks and lips almost made jelly of my legs. His lips on mine were ecstasy.

He began to unbutton my shirt.

"You want it, don't you?"

I nodded.

Soon my pants were around my ankles. His whiskers on my chest, stomach... he stood up and pointed to his crotch.

I went down.

He ejaculated on my face.

While I was wiping it off, he reached for his wallet, "You should work at 'The Sauna,'" he said as he threw some bills at me.

When I had finished fastening my pants and buttoning my shirt, I went to hug him.

He slapped me in the face.

It was all I could do to keep the tears from spilling out.

I ran home and never again set foot in that house. I determined not to allow myself to be humiliated like that ever again.

I did, however, go online and look up "The Sauna." It was a gay bath-house in Lima that offered "massage." I jotted down the address and stopped by one day after school. In a few months I would be going back to the States to begin my university studies. For now, rather than "Science" or "The Humanities," it would just be humanity, and male anatomy. Although I had hated the way the experience with my friend's father had ended, it had begun as an intoxicating thrill. I assumed few people would behave that way, and I intended to stop it if they did. It also seemed exciting that someone might want me enough to pay for it.

"You're a pretty, white boy, Pedro. You'll be popular. While you're here, we'll call you 'Kevin.' That sounds very North American. Feel free to let the clients hear you speak English."

At eighteen, I was the youngest "massage artist" at the place. There was one who was nineteen. The others were all in their twenties or early thirties.

I had been working out for months and had a decent body. We all had time to use the weight machines in the workout room which was used mainly by the employees, rarely by the customers. It was located in such a way that the clientele could easily see our "wares" as they wandered through the facility. They could check us out from different angles in the large mirrors on the walls. We only wore flip-flops and a skimpy towel, as did the clients. Our towels, however, were a different color and had "The Sauna" in big letters. We also carried a large bottle of lotion with us when we wandered around.

"¿Masaje?" we would say. Or "Massage?" if they seemed northern European or North American.

There were several private cubicles. If all they wanted was a massage they would pay the establishment and we would get a cut. If they wanted more, we would negotiate a price and give some of it to the business. We were free to give clients our numbers and arrange to meet them elsewhere on our own time. Several of us had regular customers and we functioned there as independent contractors.

In advertisements for "The Sauna" our availability was part of the bait used to entice customers. Of course the customers themselves were part of the bait, as they would offer each other the same services we did. For free. We were hired because of something alluring we offered that the average customer didn't.

I was fairly good-looking but was hired primarily for my blond hair and white skin, rare commodities in Peru. Two others looked European, but they weren't as fair as I. The nineteen-year-old had black hair and olive skin. His features were such that he could easily pass for a darker than average Spaniard, although his accent and word usage made it clear he was Peruvian. There was a gorgeous 27-year-old with chestnut hair and hazel eyes. He was very muscular and had what I, and apparently many others, felt was just the right amount of chest hair. He had spent time in Argentina and could imitate the Argentine accent quite convincingly, which made him slightly exotic. The three of us were particularly popular with Peruvians. The darker, more Indian or Mestizo looking workers often attracted North American or European clientele. It was all a rush for me. In addition to everything else, rebelling against my church felt almost liberating. I was familiar with Christian mythology stating that Mary Magdalene had been a prostitute, but at our church they had told us that couldn't possibly be true. It was stated that although we believed in repentance, Jesus would never choose a woman so fallen. Here I was, falling, in search of thrills. Had Jesus chosen a prostitute? I wondered. Why not? It was her body that had been for sale, not her soul. My colleagues all needed the money, but for some of them it was a rush too; at least some of the time. It wasn't unusual, however, for them to talk about doing things they didn't want to do, with people they didn't want to do them with. Sometimes it was just hard work; they couldn't afford to be as choosy as I was.

Of course many of the customers were only looking for other patrons. Sometimes, because they couldn't afford more than the entry fee they had paid at the door, or sometimes just because they didn't like the idea of paying for it. There were plenty of patrons for us, though.

Most of my customers seemed like very nice men. They treated me, and as far as I could tell, everyone else respectfully. I rejected the advances of those who seemed otherwise. Some of my customers became regulars. I would go to their home, or to a hotel if that wasn't an option. Sometimes it was because of their families. Other times because they didn't live in Lima, but visited frequently.

I even fell in love, a little bit, with some of them. There was one who told me that, growing up, he had always wanted to become a priest.

"Yeah, I even started at the seminary," he told me, "but my thoughts, and sometimes my actions, were too often focused on guys who turned me on. Like you." He caressed my cheek. "I realized I'm not cut out for celibacy."

I laughed. "I'm not either, but my religion only requires celibacy if you're gay. Church leaders have to be married."

"What religion are you?"

"Mormon, although obviously I don't live it. I've actually become pretty disenchanted."

"I did, too. Don't get me wrong, there are some very fine, wonderful priests and nuns, but besides the whole celibacy thing, I decided there's a lot of corruption in the Catholic Church. More than I could handle. I decided it was time to go my own way... But please, tell me a little more about yourself."

"You're not paying me to talk, are you?"

"Among other things."

"Well, that's enough about me. Let's get down to business."

Again I wondered about the seeming quest for power and control by the top leaders in my church.

In many ways my client-friend lived like a good priest. I found out a lot about him by going to his house earlier than the appointed time and talking to the maid. She wasn't a live-in maid and only came over three days a week. I soon began trying to schedule our appointments on days the maid would be there because I liked talking to her. When he arrived, he would send her home.

"You're here early."

"I like talking to your maid, she always offers me something to eat."

She had worked for his family when he was a boy, although she was only fourteen years older than he was. He paid her a good full-time salary, even though she only worked part time. She adored him. He had offered me more than I usually charged, but I told him to give it to someone who needed it.

The maid had figured out the nature of our relationship and even said to me one day, as she blushed deeply, "I'm glad you can give him an hour of happiness. He deserves it."

It turns out he had worked hard as an engineer. He had also invested his inheritance and made a fair amount of money, although he wasn't super rich. He lived in a nice, comfortable condo apartment in San Isidro, a good part of town, but could have afforded to live more extravagantly if he had wanted to. He donated lots of money and time to charity, including the orphanage where I volunteered. I never ran into him there, but heard the nuns mention his name frequently.

He continued to ask about me. I told him as little as I could get away with, but I did tell him I didn't need the extra money he had offered. When he asked me if I might want to consider moving in with him someday, I decided I had let things go too far. I liked him, respected him. Although I even loved him a little bit, it wasn't enough to change my life plans.

He offered, "You're what? Eighteen, I think you told me. I could help you go to university if you want to. If you need more preparation I could get that for you, although listening to you talk makes me think you're educated. You're obviously bright and seem like that's something that would interest you."

I just looked at him for a minute, then shook my head. "I don't know why I've been so evasive when you've asked about my life. That was stupid of me." I paused, "I'm not who you think I am. When you asked if Kevin was my real name, I told you it was Pedro Swayne, because that's what most people here call me. The name in my passport is Peter Justin Swayne. It's a U.S. passport." A confused expression was forming on his face, but he said nothing. I continued, "My family moved here when I was eight. We live in one of the best parts of La Molina. That's where I go to school, too. I'm in the IB program and will finish soon. Hopefully I'm prepared for university. In August I'm going to the States to study there."

His mouth was wide open. "Why...?"

"I don't know. Excitement? Rebellion? I told you I'm Mormon. I'm angry at the Church. My parents would die if they knew I go by 'The Sauna' or to see a client after I leave 'Sacred Heart Orphanage' on Saturdays."

He was stunned.

I continued, "All the money you've given me has gone to buy gifts for the children there." I smiled. "Maybe I should have taken it when you offered me more. I know 'Sacred Heart' is important to you. The nuns talk about you sometimes."

"So you're the gringo they've mentioned? I guess I never heard your name." His eyes were starting to water as he said, "Well, I was right about one thing. I always thought you seemed kind-hearted. I knew I was attracted by more than just your looks."

After a brief pause, I said, "I'm sorry."

"I'm a fool. I was beginning to fall in love with you."

"Then we're both fools." A tear ran down my cheek. "But I can't live with you."

He nodded.

I grabbed my cellphone as I wiped my cheek. "Let me give you Gonzalo's number. He works at 'The Sauna,' and won't waste the money you pay him. He's a good guy."

"I'll need a little time. I guess this is 'good-by.'"

"It's probably best. I'll miss you."

There was another client I particularly liked. As it turned out, he was from Alabama, and a Mormon!

We had started out speaking to each other in Spanish when we first met. He had been on a mission to Argentina. I noted his Anglo accent and asked if he was from the States.

"Where are you from?" he had asked me when we went into our cubicle.

"Utah, and you?"

"Alabama. Are you Mormon?"

"Yes."

"Me too."

"Imagine that! How many Mormons are there in Alabama? Three?"

"More like three hundred," he said with a grin. "Actually there are several thousand of us. Shouldn't people like us meet at BYU? How did you end up in a brothel in Peru?" He had a beautiful smile.

"Just a lark. I wanted to experience something completely different. I've never done drugs. Shouldn't I have some youthful indiscretion? I've lived here since I was eight, which is why I sound Peruvian. Soon, I'll be going back to Utah, to university. NOT BYU. I could ask you the same question. How did you end up in a bath-house in Peru?"

"Oh, just a bit of fun. I'm an airline pilot and come here about once a month. How old are you?" he asked.

"Eighteen."

"I thought you seemed a bit older."

"Eighteen will do though?"

"I guess... Why aren't you going to BYU?"

"You're kidding, right? I've had it up to here," putting my hand above my eyes, "with the Mormon Church."

"I went to BYU."

"You don't still go to church, do you?"

"Do you?"

"I'm trying to figure out how and when to break the news to my parents. They wanted me to go to BYU because they sense that I've lost my faith, and were hoping that being in that environment and being required to attend church might restore my childhood zeal. That's not going to happen. I know things about Mormonism they don't. Besides, I'm gay. Soon I need to say that to my parents and tell them I'm leaving the Church. I told them I wouldn't go to BYU and that this was a battle they couldn't win. They knew I was right."

"They could refuse to pay for your college."

"Yeah. They threatened that for about a second. But they don't want this to come between us. We really do love each other."

"How will they react when you tell them you're gay?"

"My dad will yell, my mom will cry. I'm dreading that conversation. I'm dreading the disappointment and sadness they will feel. But at the end of the day, we'll hug each other and they'll let me go. They know I'm at the age when they have to do that. They'll tell me to be celibate. I'll promise to practice safe sex. Of course I'll never tell them about this!"

The pilot and I began seeing each other regularly. He started coming to Peru more than once a month.

"Are you cheating on someone back home?" I once asked him.

"No, I'm alone."

"Why is that?"

I noticed a fleeting look of hurt in his eyes.

"I don't know. Relationships have never worked for me."

"I could show you around Lima sometime."

He didn't answer. We talked about the fact that we both had grandparents in Utah, and as we started having sex, we stared into each other's eyes.

As I was getting ready to leave his hotel and he handed me the money, he said, "Look, I do this because I'm not good at relationships."

"Then I guess it's time for you to go back to 'The Sauna' and find somebody new," I said as I closed the door behind me.

On the cab ride home I felt a mixture of sadness and anger. How dare he make me...How dare they let me...How could we allow these feelings to develop? He wasn't the love of my life or anything, but I had felt genuine affection for him. There was no point in letting it go any further. I found myself wondering about my future. Would I end up alone? Had his Mormonism somehow crippled him emotionally? Was I crippling myself? I vowed to move on with my life.

Some of my colleagues at the bath-house were self-serving and manipulative, but one of them, Gonzalo, was one of the sweetest people I've ever known. He was kind, considerate and gentle. One day after he attended to a client I noticed that he was in the locker room for a very long time. I went in and he was still in the shower with his back to the lockers.

"That's a very long shower," I said.

He turned around. His eyes were red and his expression quickly took the grin off my face. Of course his face was wet, he was in the shower, but I asked, "Have you been crying?"

He grimaced and nodded.

I handed him a towel, "Get dressed. We're leaving. I'm buying you dinner."

We got some churros and empanadas to go and walked around. He told me what had happened.

The customer had choked him for a second and then pushed him to his knees. He pulled his hair and told him to get down on all fours. He fucked him hard. When he was through, he dumped the contents of the used condom on his head, he handed him the money and then actually punched him in the stomach.

"Why didn't you stop him? You're strong, and if you'd needed help all you had to do was call out."

"I really need the money," he said. Then he tried to smile, "I did make him use a condom though."

I could barely contain my rage. If the guy had been there I would have beat the shit out of him.

When I went to bed that night, it took me a long time to fall asleep. I remembered hearing or reading somewhere, that sometimes when fighting evil, it's difficult not to become evil, and I remembered my rage. But no one should have to put up with abuse, and no one should need money that badly. I remembered that even Christ felt rage when he cleansed the temple.

Where does such evil come from? I wondered.

About the same time, my longtime affair with my neighborhood friend ended. He'd been my first kiss. We were the same age, and he said that now we were adults, and it was time to leave our adolescent experimentation behind. His dad had taken him to see a prostitute a couple of times, so he was experienced with women. "It's time to be a man. I'm only going to do it with women from now on!"

"Right!" I replied sarcastically, but I looked at him and could see that, for the moment at least, he meant what he was saying. I got serious. "To each his own. I'm a man. I'm an adult. I like other men."

"¿Vas a seguir con las mariconerías?"

"Yes. I'm a fag, and I thought maybe we had something special."

"You should try women."

"Latin machismo," I muttered as I left, not yet realizing that studly, U.S. style masculinity and bravado were just as intense, and even more of an act.

For me it was time to leave Peru. I was ready for the next stage, starting to realize that thrills alone aren't happiness. I was getting ready for the typical life of an ordinary, gay college student. At that point, I was beginning to feel like I had neither home nor religion.

I did, however, go to "The Sauna" a few more times before I left for the States.

The last time I was there, a Peruvian man in his forties came in. He spoke to everyone in heavily accented English and pretended not to speak much Spanish. I could tell by the little Spanish I did hear, though, that he was from Peru.

He swaggered around, leering at people, grabbing his crotch. "Sucky, sucky," he would say; then, "idiot" as he walked away.

I disliked him intensely.

He walked up to me, "You wan sum?"

This was going to be my last time here. "¿Masaje?" I replied with a shrug.

He motioned toward a private cubicle. Once we were inside he said, "You gimme blow-job."

I reached over and rubbed his shoulder.

"Stupeed white boy don't understand?" Then in very clear Spanish he said, "Suck it, stupid!" and started to push me down.

I straightened up. "¡Vete a la mierda!" I said as I slapped him in the face.

I started toward the door, but turned around, looked into his startled eyes, and said in very clear English, "By the way, your English sucks, stupid brown boy!"

On the way home, I felt very sad. I walked in the front door of my parents' house and caught a glimpse of myself in a mirror in the entry. As I rushed to my room, an intense feeling of guilt began to fill me. Tears welled up in my eyes. "Why? Why do we do this to each other?"

Things aren't always as they seem, but the evil is real.

As I showered I felt an intense longing, almost a homesickness, for another place. A different reality. Somewhere where no one took pleasure in cruelty. Where no one felt a need for control, for power. A world that didn't inspire thoughts of revenge. After my shower, I lay down, fell asleep and dreamed. I dreamt of heaven, wishing, but knowing, even in my dream, that heaven didn't exist on this fallen earth. We had to learn to live with our "knowledge of good and evil." Live with it, while dreaming, striving for Eden.

The Birth of Tragedy

Hugo Olaiz

For Neal Chandler, *il miglior fabbro*

"Is Mormonism still part of your *Weltanschauung*?" Aunt Doris asks me every time she sees me. She knows that at 2:15 on Sunday afternoons I'm blessing the sacrament like any other Mormon priest, even though I can be found Sunday mornings at St. James Episcopal helping administer the chalice—"the blood of our Lord Jesus Christ keep you in life everlasting"—and sometimes I even help lay out the cups and saucers for coffee hour. When I head from St. James to Sacramento Second Ward, it's like reversing the wedding at Cana—the wine becomes water, the priestly robes turn into dark suits, and the emaciated body of Christ, which at St. James is a wafer, miraculously rises to the texture of Wonder Bread. "That's the way our parents brought us up," I tell Aunt Doris for the millionth time. Dad is Mormon and Mom is Episcopalian, so my brother Steve and I were born Mormon-Episcopalians. Five years ago Steve decided he wanted to be only a Mormon, which Mom and Dad said was fine; but after his mission he moved in with his boyfriend Ramón, and now he says he's neither.

Aunt Doris forgives me for attending Sacramento Second because she knows that I attend Saturday rehearsals at the McHenry with the same devotion. The McHenry was built when Sacramento was a boom town and a certain Mrs. McHenry (a.k.a. the Merry Widow) couldn't think of a better way to immortalize her husband than by building a theater in his memory. Now the City of Sacramento owns the building and sponsors all McHenry Company productions. As the artistic director, Aunt Doris insists that we all call it an *amateur company* rather than community theater, and once she sued a reporter from the *Sacramento Bee* who described the company as "a troupe of loonies and bohemians who spend the weekends smoking pot." I got involved with the McHenry when I turned 12, and even though we do have plenty of loonies and bohemians (with Aunt Doris at the top of the list), the only pot I have seen so far is the cauldron we used in *Macbeth*.

There are some in the ward who think that Dad, as the family patriarch, shouldn't endorse my Episcopalian activities, but patriarchy is one of the many Mormon concepts that don't make sense to him. "I had a remarkable dream last night," Dad told Mom recently at the dinner table. "They released Keith, called Brother Marks in his stead, and the next thing we knew both our children had been officially kicked out of the Mormon Church." Keith Roberts is our bishop, and he'd rather get released than put me in the hot seat of the Mormon Inquisition. In our interviews he doesn't even mention the E word—it's all about feeling good when you go to church and living the gospel. But his first counselor, Brother Marks, is a different breed.

One could say that between St. James and Sacramento Second I have the best of both worlds. Every June it's a campout with the Boys Scouts, duty to God and country, and then in late July I go to cool places with the Episcopal youth group, which is strictly coed. We've done Yellowstone, the Grand Canyon, and once we even went to Baja. There's little conflict, because at St. James the year revolves around Advent, Christmas, Lent, and Easter, whereas at Sacramento Second there are no special Sundays except for conference.

Mom says it's good for me to grow up in a mixed household. "It's like ordering two main courses in a restaurant," she told me once. "When they bring them to the table you can smell them up close, get a taste of both of them, and then you'll know for certain which one better suits your appetite." She comes to Sacramento Second when Dad and I sing in the choir or give talks. When Brother Marks sees her at church, he always makes a point of shaking her hand with a smile calculated to show her how welcoming Mormons are, but when Mom isn't there things don't always run so smoothly. One Sunday he took Dad aside and asked him somberly if the rumor he had heard was true—"that your sister-in-law is a lesbian." "A *thespian*," Dad corrected him. That happened two years ago, and we're still laughing.

I started my career in the McHenry as the curtain boy, then I was promoted to the prompt box, and finally Aunt Doris put me in charge of the backdrops and stage furniture. A few months ago, when I turned seventeen, she endowed me with the additional title of *chauffeur*, which means that every Saturday before rehearsal I have to take her shopping. First we get her groceries, then we pass by Props and Frocks, and we always end up at the Salvation Army and other thrift stores that she insists on calling *vintage*. Last Saturday we were looking for helmets and swords, and at Props and Frocks we also got a wax head and some stage blood. Even though we have a tight budget, we buy stage blood because what we spend on blood we save in sweat. With stage blood the costumes don't need to be dry cleaned, and most of all we don't have to hear the building supervisor kvetch about tomato sauce stains on the stage floor. With Aunt Doris's passion for classic heroines, blood is one of our staples. Last year she played Blanche Dubois ("like a Parisian hooker," according to Steve). Two years ago she played Joan of Arc, for which she got a crew cut like Sigourney Weaver in *Aliens*. This year we're staging Hebbel's *Judith*, and who but Aunt Doris to cut off Holofernes' head and serve it to the audience on a silver platter.

Aunt Doris attended sacrament meeting with us for Steve's missionary homecoming, but afterwards she lamented that Mormon services are deprived of drama. "When the procession comes down the aisle, when you smell the incense and hear the bells—that's what I call celebration. Mormon services are the epitome of tedium." I told her that Dad and I attend the Mormon Church because we feel good about it. "And don't you see the problem with that?" she replied. "Mormonism is all about feeling warm and fuzzy, which might be a wonderful criterion when you're scarf shopping, but disastrous when you're choosing a religion. You need some Brechtian distancing, my dear. You need some *Verfremdungseffekt!*"

Steve met Ramón at Stanford, and sometimes on weekends they come visit. Last Thanksgiving it was the six of us for the first time; Ramón sat next to Aunt Doris, and Aunt Doris was trilling the R on *Ramón* as only a coloratura soprano would. "So, Rrrramón, who's your favorite playwright?" she asked him. Ramón said something about plays with religious themes—Antigone as a religious heroine, and Hochwälder's *Holy Experiment*. His reply pleased Aunt Doris immensely, because for her there's no language like German and no heroine like Antigone. "Why, of course," said Aunt Doris. "Tragedy is always born of a religious impulse. Have you read *Die Geburt der Tragödie*?" Steve told her she got it wrong—it wasn't Nietzsche who said that but Lévi-Strauss, and the three of them spent the rest of the evening discussing Carl Jung and the Thanksgiving turkey as a propitiatory sacrifice.

Last Sunday it finally happened. We released Keith Roberts with a vote of thanks and sustained Brother Marks in his stead. Marks didn't waste any time. Today just before rehearsal the ward clerk called me to set up an appointment for an interview, and I know perfectly well what's going to happen next. Marks is going to use the E word. Probably he'll quote Matthew: no one can serve two masters. Immediately after I hung up, I called Steve to tell him the news. Steve said, "This is the easiest decision you'll ever have to make in your life."

I hurried to the McHenry and found Aunt Doris off-stage—she had just killed Holofernes and was still carrying the wax head in one hand and a sword in the other. "This is so Oedipal," she said when I told her. "Don't you see? You'll have to kill your father so you can marry your mother." Then she began to recite from the lines she had learned when she played Queen Elizabeth in Schiller's *Mary Stuart:*

What mean the ties of blood, the laws of nations?
The Church can sever any bond of duty,
can sanctify betrayal and all crimes—
'tis this your priests have taught.

As she said it, she was still holding Holofernes' head by the hair, and those little drops of fake blood were falling on the floor like crazy.

Excerpts from

Missionary Position: A Coming-of-Age Tale (Part Two in The Mormon Boy Trilogy)

Steven Fales

This solo show is done in a very improvisational and conversational style. All the author's mission memorabilia comes from a large trunk that has been wheeled onstage.

In order to go on my mission I had to stop masturbating. Completely. Masturbation's a deal breaker! I found out about jacking off completely by accident. I was nineteen. Thirteen! It was another cold dry winter in the Mountain West and in the desert climate my skin would get itchy because of the hard water. My knuckles would crack and bleed. So I would put Vaseline Intensive Care all over my body. All over my body. And this one morning before school I think I got a little bit carried away because I was putting a little lotion on my male genitalia and it felt good. And so I put a little more lotion down there and it felt better. And my reproductive organ got bigger and harder. And three seconds later, I had an explosion of feeling rush through my body like a bolt of lightning. God had struck me down with pleasure! Holy Flip!

I dropped to my knees because whatever I just did to my private parts was bad and wrong. And I started praying with all the energy of my soul, begging God to forgive me. And I promised never to do it again as long as I lived.

So I wiped off the wall. And within a few months, I was doing it every single night. Then morning, noon, and night. In the shower before school. After school. And every night before bed. I could get so creative!

A month after I first had sex with myself, I was having a youth interview with the bishop in his closed office. It's the Mormon equivalent of confession. And the bishop (an insurance salesman by trade) asked me about self abuse. And I had to confess that I thought I might have done it. He was very disappointed in me.

And he told me not to take Mormon communion for a month! I was humiliated. Everyone would know. Why couldn't I be like all the other boys my age who didn't have a self abuse problem?

But now, at nineteen, well, I wasn't a twink anymore. I had to start making progress. I was white-knuckling it. Only masturbating once a week. But that wasn't nearly enough abstinence to qualify. So I asked my bishop (a new down-to-earth bishop who seemed approachable, a rancher by trade), "Bishop, now tell me truthfully. Please. What's the longest you've ever known anyone go without doing the M-word?"

He took his time as he very carefully thought about just what to say, and the consequences of what he would say, because whatever he said, would be counted as scripture, and would end up in a one-man show. So in his best Western drawl he very personally announced God's will and bluffed, "Six months."

Six months?! I couldn't even go six hours! But if he could, I could. I was going to try my hardest. I promised him I'd pull it off!

So as I played more basketball and thought about maggot-filled dead kittens, and promised to read *The Book of Mormon* once more cover to cover (without paying attention to the pictures of all the hot Nephite warriors on steroids), I filled out my missionary application. And on good faith, my rancher bishop sent it to the attorney stake president, who then sent it in to our prophet, seer, and revelator.

(Sings)
Hold to the rod, the iron rod;
'Tis strong, and bright, and true.
The iron rod is the word of God;
'Twill safely guide us through.

———

Here's my mission plaque...*And my mission call...*

Every male in my family has served a mission. *Everyone.* From Japan to Greece to Bolivia to exotic countries like Arkansas. "All my sons served an honorable full-time mission." That's very important to be able to say as a Mormon patriarch. Just ask my dad.

No one makes a dime on their mission. It's paid for out of your own savings or by sacrifices your family makes on your behalf. My dad, relieved that I'd survived super liberal Boston said, "I'd be honored to pay for the whole thing. I want the blessings."

My dad avoided the Vietnam draft by serving his conscripted monastic service. My dad even married the little sister of his favorite companion, my mother. She missed her high school graduation to attend her wedding. And exactly nine months later, I came out. I am a product in every conceivable way of the Mormon missionary position. Just ask my mom.

Oh! I almost forgot! Sisters can go on a non-obligatory mission when they become spinsters at age 21. But that's all I'm allowed to say about the lady missionaries (Sorry, lesbians!) since a woman's greatest calling is to be a wife and mother in Zion. Amen.

I thought my mission call would never arrive. It was a Saturday afternoon when it was discovered in the mailbox among the coupons. I grabbed a butter knife from the kitchen and ran to the living room with all kinds of butterflies fluttering and family hovering. The family camera was poised! But just before I ripped open the envelope, I had this horrifying thought. "What if I get sent state-side?" That's like riding the Mormon short bus! I rushed to the bathroom to pray:

"Oh, please, please, please, Lord. Don't waste all this charisma on North Dakota! I will die if I go to North Dakota! I don't have anything against the cold or Native Americans. I know the Lamanites need the Restored Gospel, too. But I promise to never masturbate again forever if you just don't send me to North Dakota. Send me somewhere I can truly use my talents and fashion sense like Milan or London or the Marais district in Paris? I know! If you have to send me stateside, send me to Manhattan...or Provincetown?"

I came out of the bathroom feeling much better.

I ripped it open and scanned the cover letter. It was signed by the prophet himself! *(Reads super fast)*

Dear Elder Fales:

You are hereby called to serve as a missionary of The Church of Jesus Christ of Latter-day Saints. You are assigned to labor in the Portugal Porto Mission...

Portugal! Yes! Where the heck's Portugal? Oh, yeah, that little green sliver-of-a-country stuck to the far left side of a bigger yellow country. Together they made up the Iberian Peninsula. Having memorized a particularly colorful globe in elementary school geography, the colors of the countries were still freeze-dried in my mind. Spain was yellow; Portugal was green. *(Continues reading)*

Greater blessings and more happiness than you have yet experienced await you as you humbly and prayerfully serve the Lord in this labor of love among his children.

I never would have guessed Portugal. If I had I would have dismissed it as some poor, has-been, third world country that nobody seemed to really care about. What did Portugal ever contribute to the world? Did they play any sports? What did their flag even look like? Sure they have the Azores. But we have Hawaii! If Spain was the jewel of Europe, Portugal is the arm pit!

My dad who served his mission to Denmark and hardly baptized anyone said, "Portugal's a very Catholic country. But at least they believe in God. Up north in godless Scandinavia they're Lutheran. They don't believe in anything. You're gonna do fine, son. If they believe in God, you can build on their common beliefs."

"Thanks, dad!"

Then I had a thought. The Explorers! Of course! The Portuguese were the first great navigators and colonizers in the Golden Age of global expansion. They were pioneers, too! And without their early seafaring technology, America would never have been discovered. And Mormonism would never have been invented! And the world would never be ready for the Second Coming of Christ like it is today thanks to us. You're welcome! It was amazing how my Mormon logic could fit Portugal and anything else perfectly into my Mormon world view. *Viva Portugal!* Maybe I was Portuguese in a past life...

My sister, "Weren't the Portuguese the first great slave traders?"

"Stop it! That's all in the past."

My cousin, "I heard they're all dark and swarthy Moors!"

"No. They have blondes. And Sephardic Jews."

My brother, "Didn't they used to be communist?"

"Shut up! That ended in 1975. They're not communist now!"

My Mom was so excited, "Portugal! You're just gonna love South America. And Spanish is such a special language!"

"They say Spanish is the language for talking to God; but She answers in Portuguese."

———

After getting all the necessary immunization shots, and having my wisdom teeth pulled. And after getting my patriarchal blessing from an authorized Mormon psychic that foretold my future—including how many kids I would have and how many solo shows I would write. And after my farewell talk in my home ward, where Liza flew in and wowed the congregation with a solo—and then a duet with me. The big day finally arrived for me to go to the MTC, the Missionary Training Center in Provo, Utah—next door to BYU and the Provo Temple!

The MTC campus is an enclosed fortress surrounded by spiritual barbed wire and an invisible force field of virtue. Flags from every nation proudly wave at the entrance proclaiming: "The World Is Our Campus!" The MTC is spiritual boot camp for God's Army. We had over 50,000 troops at any given time around the world preaching the same meticulously manicured Restored Gospel message in almost every language since the confounding of the languages at the Tower of Babel! From Vietnamese to Afrikaans—even American Sign Language.

When my family dropped me off there was an orientation for us where we watched an inspiring, sentimental propaganda film where we cried. Then hugged. Then wept again. We were parting for two years. I would only get to write home once a week on P-days, Preparation Days. We didn't have email back then. No phone calls except on Christmas and Mother's Day. No television, radio, newspapers, magazines, or movies. No secular music. Only Grammy Award-winning Mormon Tabernacle Choir....

—

As companions we studied, prayed, ate together. We never left each other's side—except to go to the bathroom. And even then! We could hug each other all we wanted. And we did! But we could only shake hands with the opposite sex. "Lock your hearts, Elders!" At the MTC we slept in bunk beds. Lights were out by ten. Ten thirty at the latest!

Elder Jock: "Goodnight, Elder."

Elder Nerd: "Goodnight, Elder."

Elder Jock: "Wasn't that 20-elder dog pile in our garments in the hallway crazy?"

Elder Nerd: "Yeah, it sure was fun. Especially all the blue-darting!"

Elder Jock: "I love the all-you-can-eat food in the cafeteria!"

Elder Nerd: "Yeah, me, too! And I get so much studying done in those long lines."

Elder Jock: "And all the care-packages from home! Hey, do you think Elder Fales is a faggot?"

Elder Nerd: "Nah. They don't let faggots go on missions. He's swishy 'cause he's soulful."

Elder Jock: "He wouldn't dog pile. And he's always writing in his journal when we play volleyball. I think it's weird he's always singing."

Elder Nerd: "Didn't you see the picture of his girlfriend he keeps showing everyone?"

Elder Jock: "Oh, yeah, I forgot. She's a babe. Okay, he's a stud."

Elder Nerd: "Hey, Elder. Did you really give up your position on the BYU football team to serve a mission?"

Elder Jock: "Yeah. Tight End. But my dad's buying me a new truck when I get back, though, so I guess it's okay."

Elder Nerd: "That's cool. Real cool. Love you, Elder."

Elder Jock: "Love you more, Elder."

Elder Nerd: "You need a back rub, Elder?"

Elder Jock: "No. Not tonight. But thanks, Elder."

Elder Nerd: "Okay. See you in the morning. I sure hope we don't have another earthquake. Last night I could've sworn our whole bunk bed was shaking…"

—

So inevitably Elder Barrett and I did something we could have been sent home for. As Zone Leaders we had a car and one day we couldn't take it anymore and we left the mission boundaries and drove to the border of Spain! And walked around and talked. We were so wicked!

Barrett: "Hey, Fales."

Fales: "Yeah?"
Barrett: "Did you see that?"
Fales: "No. What?"
Barrett: "The mini-skirt that just walked by."
Fales: "Oh."
Barrett: "Sometimes I get so distracted."
Fales: "Yeah. I noticed."
Barrett: "You have?"
Fales: "'Does the rain in Spain stay mainly in the plain?'"
Barrett: "Isn't that a hymn?"
Fales: "Sorta."
Barrett: "You know, they almost didn't let me go on a mission because… I'd gone all the way with my old girlfriend."
Fales: "Oh?"
Barrett: "They made me wait almost two years without…"
Fales: "What?"
Barrett: "Sex."
Fales: "Really. What's it like?"
Barrett: "It feels so— You'll find out when you get married. But make sure you get married quick, because once you've had a taste it's so hard not to… You know, you're the best comp I've had in that girls just don't seem to faze you."
Fales: "They honestly don't."
Barrett: "Really?"
Fales: "I mean, they're nice and all."
Barrett: "Well, they sure notice you. They convert just for your smile. They always ask me if your teeth are real."
Fales: "They're not."
Barrett: "What?"
Fales: *(Smiling)* "Just kidding."
Barrett: "Well, they're beautiful. Like you."
Fales: *(Surprised)* "Thanks."
Barrett: "Don't worry, Fales. Someday you'll find the right slot, and it'll all fall into place. You know what I mean?"
Fales: "Yeah. I hope so."
Barrett: "Spain's a dive."
Fales: "Yeah. Spanish is so barbaric…"
Barrett: "Hey, let's go home and wrestle!"
Fales: "I don't know about that."
Barrett: "I'll teach you. Hey, Fales. *(Pause)* I hope we stay friends long after our missions. You've really shown me what a mission is. Thanks."

Everyone cried when Elder Barrett was transferred. He yelled from the train, "*Fique Firme!*" "Firm in the Faith!" Barrett gave me this tie when he left. I wore it the rest of my mission. *(Softly hums "How Firm a Foundation.")*

———

I went almost my entire mission without masturbating. I had a few slips towards the end. When I blew, there were chunks. But other than that, I finished my mission and returned home with honor. Just ask my dad. (I went into such acute mission withdrawal that I baptized his Brazilian neighbors!)

MTC Interview

M. Larsen

This is my second Sunday in the Missionary Training Center. I am sitting with my companion, Elder Daley, outside the branch president's office. President MacIntyre serves as our priesthood leader during our stay in the MTC—the equivalent of a bishop, back in our home wards. I have requested an interview with him.

I haven't told Elder Daley why I need to talk with President MacIntyre. But the very fact that I haven't told him must make Elder Daley suspect that I'm here to do more than simply ask President MacIntyre's permission to make a phone call home. On our district's first evening here in the MTC, President MacIntyre warned us that missionaries who enter the MTC with unconfessed transgressions offend the Spirit and therefore have no protection against the buffetings of Satan. "If there's anything you should have talked about with your bishop and stake president before you came here, come see me immediately. For your own sake, get your life in order."

President MacIntyre's assistants are sitting with us. They, too, are missionaries in training, but they've already been in the MTC for nearly two months. They are eager to leave for the mission field. One is going to Ecuador, the other to Bolivia. Elder Daley and I have been called to Colombia. The assistants and Elder Daley talk excitedly amongst themselves, swapping horror stories they've heard about daily life in South America: dysentery, supersized cockroaches, hospitable church members who serve cow's hooves for dinner. They can hardly wait for the adventure to begin.

My attention drifts in and out of their conversation. I feel slightly sick. It's like hunger pangs, but with a sharper edge. In my mind's eye, I see ulcers bursting open like roses along the inside of my stomach lining. What's taking President MacIntyre so long?

Elder Daley laments that he has so much time left in the MTC. Six weeks, he says; I'm gonna go crazy. The assistants are empathetic. They've been where we are now, they know how we feel. The time'll fly, they assure Elder Daley. By the time you get your travel papers, you won't be able to believe it's been two months already.

Time passes differently in the MTC. Everyone says it. The days are like weeks, and the weeks are like days. How else could things have developed so quickly between Elder Braithwaite and me? Sometimes it feels like we met just yesterday, but at other times it feels like we've known each other for weeks. In fact, we met a week and a half ago. Elder Braithwaite doesn't know I'm seeing President MacIntyre. We haven't talked since—

President MacIntyre steps out of his office, apologizes for the delay. Instinctively, we all stand. President MacIntyre is as old as our fathers. He served in the military for most of his adult life, and it shows; his mere presence commands respect. He shakes Elder Daley's hand, claps his other hand on Elder Daley's shoulder, asks how he's adjusting to missionary life. Fine, President, I'm doing great; the language is tough, but I'm working on it. The President nods approvingly. Keep up the good work, Elder Daley.

My palms are slick with sweat. I wipe them off on my pants leg before shaking hands with President MacIntyre. He acknowledges me in a solemn voice—"Elder Mitchell"—and then pins me with a piercing look, as if reading my soul. I try to meet his gaze, but after a couple seconds, I fold.

He already knows, I'm sure of it. He probably had me pegged from the first evening we met. Who do I think I've been kidding? Probably every missionary in my district knows.

President MacIntyre guides me towards the office, a hand on my shoulder. "Wait here, Elder Daley," he tells my companion.

"Sure thing, President."

And now it begins. I'm going to be sent home from my mission early—before it really even got started. I'm going to have to explain to my parents. I'll probably be excommunicated. They won't let me back into BYU.

President MacIntyre closes the office door behind us. This looks like the office of every other priesthood leader I've ever interviewed with throughout my life: a large wooden desk, bare except for a desk calendar and a set of scriptures; a high-backed swivel chair behind the desk for President MacIntyre; a lower, harder chair in front of the desk for me; a painting of the Savior and a photo of the First Presidency on the wall.

I'm already regretting having asked for this interview. But this has to be done. It's the only way out of the mess I've gotten myself into.

"Let's kneel for a word of prayer, Elder Mitchell." This is a touch I've never encountered before in an interview with a priesthood leader. We kneel together on the floor. President MacIntyre prays. "Father in Heaven, we thank thee for the weighty privilege and responsibility which thou hast placed upon us in calling us to thy holy work. We pray thy Spirit to be with us during this interview, that Elder Mitchell will be able to open his soul, and that I will be able to know how best to guide and assist him. In the name of our beloved Master, thy Son, Jesus Christ, amen."

I add a silent prayer of my own: I need you, Heavenly Father. My life is about to fall to pieces. But I'm doing this because I want to be right with you. I'm doing what I should have done long before now. I want to get help. I want to put these urges behind me for once and for all.

President MacIntyre sits behind his desk, facing me— the usual position. Like every other Latter-day Saint, I've been having regular interviews with my bishop since I turned twelve. The interviews became more frequent as I approached my mission. In the space of a year, I had to be cleared for ordination to the Melchizedek priesthood, then for missionary service, then for my first temple recommend. Each interview has been basically the same: small talk about how things are going in my life, then a list of probing questions to test my faith and moral worthiness. The interview is an opportunity for me to confess my sins—or to lie, as the case may be.

I should definitely have come clean long ago. If I had, things wouldn't have gotten so far out of control.

President MacIntyre's expression is solemn. He gets straight to the point, no small talk. "What's on your mind, Elder Mitchell?"

Here we go. Just spit it out. Get it into the air.

I can't bring myself to look President MacIntyre directly in the eyes, so I focus on the wall beyond his shoulder. The First Presidency return my gaze, three elderly men in business suits. "I have something I need to confess to you."

You're stalling. You know what you need to say, you've worked it over in your mind a hundred times. Just say it.

"I had inappropriate relations with a missionary in my district."

His expression undergoes no change whatsoever. "You mean sexual relations?"

The moment he says "sexual relations," I go cold inside. I need to make him realize that things didn't go that far—that I'm still clean, at least in that sense. At the same time, though, I have no illusions about how far things might have gone if we hadn't been interrupted, or if I had agreed to meet Elder Braithwaite that night the way he wanted. Did Elder Braithwaite and I have sexual relations? Not exactly. Did I want to have sexual relations with Elder Braithwaite? Oh yes.

"It wasn't actually sex." I try to sound contrite as I say this. I don't want to seem like I'm making excuses or trying to minimize my guilt. But I can tell that's exactly how it's coming out. I trail off helplessly.

President MacIntyre leans forward, clasps his hands on the desktop. "Elder Mitchell, as branch president, I'm both a judge in Israel and a shepherd of the Lord's flock. I need to know exactly what happened so I can decide what judgment needs to be applied, and so I can know how to help you." He pauses to let me soak this in. "Who did you have relations with?"

I had harbored a hope—a miniscule hope—that he might not ask that. But of course he has to.

"Elder Braithwaite," I tell him.

Elder Braithwaite and I became friends on our second day in the MTC. He was the elder in our district most like me: studious, pensive, a little shy, a perfectionist, high-stressed. He laughed a lot to release his nervous energy. He had a sharp mind—he'd worked as a computer technician before his mission—but languages

*were not his forte, and he lagged behind everyone else in our fast-paced Spanish
class. His frustration at falling behind paralyzed him, causing him to lag even
further behind. I coached him outside class, usually while we were standing in line
at the cafeteria with the rest of our district. Together we'd go over the vocabulary
or verb forms from our last class session; I'd calm him down when he began to get
high-strung. "I don't know what I'd do if you weren't here," he told me once. His
words embarrassed me but also sent a thrill up my scalp.*

"Where did it happen?" President MacIntyre asked.

"In my room."

*I share my dorm room with Elders Daley, Gundersen, and Holt. Elder
Braithwaite and his companion, Elder Saunders, have the next room over to
themselves.*

"When?"

"Two days ago. Friday."

"When, Friday?" My short answers are irritating him. He wants more
information. "How did it happen?"

*Our district has gym from 1:00 to 2:00, four days a week. I hate gym. As soon
as warm-up exercises are over and everyone breaks up to run, or lift weights,
or play basketball or volleyball, I and a handful of other chess club types hide
out on the stairs, where the instructor can't see us, killing time. On Friday, Elder
Braithwaite came to the stairs looking for me. "This is lame," he said, with his
usual nervous laugh. "Let's sneak out and go back to the dorm. I want to write
some letters." I hesitated. What about our companions? No problem. Elder
Braithwaite had already gotten Elder Saunders to agree to a split: Elder Saunders
would temporarily be companions with my companion, Elder Daley. Exchanging
companions like this was against MTC rules. But we knew it was done in the
mission field, which is how I rationalized that it would be all right.*

"We came back early from gym class—we did an unauthorized split."

*Sneaking out of gym was remarkably easy; the instructor was nowhere in
sight. If I'd known it could be so easily done, I would have done it before.*

"Who suggested that you do a split? You or Elder Braithwaite?"

"He did."

Does that sound like I'm evading responsibility?

"Why did you go to your room?" From the way he emphasizes *your*, I can
tell President MacIntyre means: Why did you go to your room and not Elder
Braithwaite's?

*Mission rules require us always to be in the same room with our companion,
unless one of us is in the bathroom. Elder Braithwaite suggested we go to his room.
This was only natural, given that we had returned to the dorms so he could write
letters. But going into his room with him, alone, felt unsafe to me. I had the idea
I'd be better able to resist temptation if we were in my room. That makes no sense,
of course, in retrospect. Perhaps I was trying to fool myself into believing that I
wanted to resist temptation.*

"He was going to write letters, and I was going to read, so I suggested we go to my room. That way I could lie down on my own bed and read."

"And then?"

I was propped up in bed, pretending to read, listening to Elder Braithwaite's pen scratching away behind me, where he sat at my desk. Scratch. Pause. Scratch. Pause. The pauses became longer. Then the scratching stopped altogether. The sound of air hissing out of the radiator seemed very loud.

"After a few minutes, he came over and sat on the bed. He said he couldn't keep his mind on his writing. He asked me what I was reading, so I showed him. And then he lay down on the bed next to me to read, too."

"What were you reading?"

"A book about Colombia my parents gave me."

Elder Braithwaite had asked the same question. "Contraband," I told him. Missionaries weren't supposed to have books aside from the scriptures and other Church publications. He laughed. I passed him the book. He started flipping through it. When he came to a part he wanted to read more thoroughly, he kicked off his shoes and moved around into the same half-lying, half-sitting position I was in. I had to scoot over towards the wall to make room for him. We had never been so physically close to one another before.

President MacIntyre nods to himself a little, as if he finds my answer satisfactory. It occurs to me to wonder what he imagined I might have been reading. "What happened next?"

Elder Braithwaite leafed through the book. Occasionally he'd say something— "Wow," or "I didn't know this"—and I would have to lean up close to him in order to see what he was responding to. I could smell his deodorant, the conditioner in his hair. I remembered the rule from the Missionary Handbook that said missionaries should sleep in the same room but not in the same bed. In my mind, different voices clamored for attention. This is dangerous. Don't be silly, Elder Braithwaite's just being friendly. Nothing can go wrong as long as you keep your own abnormal feelings under control. Just enjoy the moment. See where it might go. Not that it's going to go anywhere. You'd better hope it doesn't go anywhere. But wouldn't it be wild if... And then it happened.

I steel myself to continue. "We were lying next to each other on the bed, looking at the book together. And then he pushed his leg up close against mine."

He did it slowly, casually, as if he wasn't thinking about it. But there was no mistaking what he was doing. I looked at him, surprised, thrilled, frightened. He locked eyes with me. I resisted the impulse to turn away. My heart was racing. Without breaking eye contact, Elder Braithwaite closed the book and laid it aside. He put one hand on my shoulder, close to the neck, so that his thumb brushed my bare skin. I took a deep, shivering breath. He brought his face towards mine.

"And then we kissed—"

"Who initiated the kiss?"

"Um—" I don't see what difference that makes. "He did."

I have kissed one girl in my entire life, and the experience left me wondering what all the fuss is about. Elder Braithwaite's kiss was something from another world altogether. Instincts I never knew I had erupted from somewhere deep inside me. I found myself trying to devour Elder Braithwaite's lips, then breaking free to work my mouth along the side of his face, up to his ear, and down his neck until the fabric of his t-shirt kept me from going any farther. We clasped each other tightly. Elder Braithwaite pulled his neck free of my lips so we could resume kissing. After a while he put his tongue cautiously into my mouth. The idea of french-kissing had always repulsed me, so I was surprised to find how much the act excited me.

President MacIntyre's face is stone. "What else did you do besides kiss?"

"We... stroked each other."

"Where?"

"All over. Hair... face... arms... chest... back..."

"On top of your clothes, or underneath?"

"On top, at first. Then later, he put his hand under my shirt, and after that, I put my hands on his back."

The flesh-on-flesh contact when he touched my stomach made the muscles contract involuntarily. Elder Braithwaite slid his hand slowly up my torso to the center of my chest. I wished he would touch my nipples, but after pressing against my breastbone for a few seconds, he retreated, pulling his hand out from under my shirt. He embraced me tightly again, rolled over on top of me. I could feel his erection pushing against my own. I closed my eyes and tipped my head back, whimpering a little. Elder Braithwaite buried his face in my neck. I reached up under his shirt, dragged my hands up the length of his back. We moved our bodies back and forth, struggling to find the same rhythm.

"Did either of you touch the other below the waist?"

"No. I mean, well, not with our hands. He lay down on top of me, so we were touching below the waist, you know, that way."

"So at no point did either of you directly touch or handle the other's genitals?"

I shake my head.

"Did either of you ejaculate?"

"Things didn't go that far," I mumble, humiliated. "The other elders came back."

Loud voices came down the hall towards the bedroom, one of them clearly Elder Gundersen's. I panicked, but Elder Braithwaite kept his cool. Swiftly but calmly, he returned to his seat at the desk. He got there just as someone's key rattled in the doorknob. I grabbed my book, opened to a page at random, and set the book on my lap to conceal my erection. My heart thundered. It hit me what an extraordinarily dangerous, foolhardy thing Elder Braithwaite and I had done.

"Did the other elders see you and Elder Braithwaite?"

"No. Elder Braithwaite got up before they opened the door. And then he left..."

The elders burst into the room, high on adrenaline. Elder Braithwaite gathered up his things and accompanied Elder Saunders back to their room. Elder Daley laughed good-naturedly when he saw me with the book. "Don't you get enough of that in class?" I couldn't think of a rejoinder, just smiled. When the elders stripped down to hit the showers, I made a point of focusing on the book so I wouldn't see them naked, even out of the corner of my eye. Soon I could hear the elders bantering loudly with each other in the showers down the hall. Still lying on my bed, I closed my eyes and offered a silent but fervent prayer of thanks that Elder Braithwaite and I hadn't been caught. Never again, I vowed. I swear it.

"But then he came back a few minutes later, while the others were showering, and told me to meet him that night, after everyone was asleep."

"Meet him where?"

"In one of the private showers in the bathroom."

The bathroom on our dorm floor has both communal and private showers. I would prefer to use a private shower, to avoid being surrounded by naked male bodies. But I've never seen anyone else using the private showers, and I don't want to be conspicuous. Instead I get up a half hour early, so I can use the communal showers, but alone. Elder Braithwaite, too, had noticed that no one uses the private showers. That's why he thought to have us meet there. It would be dry, and with the curtain drawn, someone getting up late at night to use the toilet wouldn't see us.

"Did you meet him?"

"No."

I promised to meet him, but only so he would leave the room before the other elders came back from the shower. I had no intention of keeping that promise. It wasn't even a temptation now. He planted a quick kiss on my lips before he left. He was beaming. "I never imagined this would happen in the MTC," he told me.

"Why didn't you meet him?"

"I knew that what we'd done was wrong."

Lights out was 10:30; Elder Braithwaite had told me to meet him at 11:30. At 11:26, by Elder Holt's digital alarm clock, I heard a door shut quietly somewhere nearby. I lay in bed, my hands clasped chastely across my chest, on top of the blanket. At 11:44, someone came and stood outside our door. I was afraid he would knock, or whisper my name. But he just stood there for a while. Then he went away.

"Did he say anything to you the next day?"

"He asked me what happened."

"What did you say?"

"I told him I'd fallen asleep."

He managed to separate me from the others as our district was walking from our dorm to the cafeteria for breakfast. He was troubled. I acted sheepish, laughed it off: Couldn't stay awake, zonked right out, feel so stupid. Tonight. Same time. I'll be there, I promise. I hurried to catch up with the others. I steered clear of Elder Braithwaite for the rest of the day, and he didn't try to pull me aside again. We didn't study together like we always did. He laughed as usual with the other elders, but every now and then he shot me a worried glance—"anxious" would be a better description. That night, I waited to hear if Elder Braithwaite would go to the bathroom to wait for me. He didn't.

"Does Elder Braithwaite know you're confessing this to me?"

"No."

Surely he must be afraid of that, though.

"Why are you confessing this to me, Elder Mitchell?"

"Because... I know that what we did was a serious sin. And I need to get right with the Lord."

President MacIntyre regards me somberly. "Elder Mitchell, have you ever had homosexual relations? Before this, I mean?"

"Not before this. Never."

My physical development had always lagged behind my peers', so at first I didn't think anything of the fact that I wasn't interested in girls the way other boys my age were. It took me a while to realize that I was, in fact, experiencing the same new feelings my peers were. I just wasn't having those feelings for the right sex.

"Have you associated in the past with homosexual individuals?"

"No. Not that I know of, anyway."

"Have you ever used pornography?"

"No."

I've had to answer this question in past interviews. My answer's an honest one, assuming that clothing catalogues, National Geographic *magazine, and classical art don't count as pornography even when used as such.*

"Do you now or have you in the past had problems with masturbation?"

"No."

This is a bald-faced lie, one I've told in every interview I've had with a priesthood leader since I was fifteen. I tell the lie to President MacIntyre instinctively. Immediately I consider backtracking and coming clean, but he pushes on before I have time.

"Did you date before your mission?"

"Yes."

I dated only because my parents pressured me to. I've always assumed that they insisted so much because they thought I was shy. Now it occurs to me to wonder if they had a different worry.

"Were you sexually attracted to the young women you dated?"

"Yes."

At BYU, the year before my mission, I dated a girl from one of my classes. She was my first girlfriend, and the only girl I've ever kissed. That distinction is due to her being the most aggressive girl I've dated. She asked me out, not the other way around. It was she who put her hand in mine, who lifted my arm into place around her shoulders, who initiated the first kiss. Crossing these borders for the first time excited me sexually, and that in turn gave me hope that I could put homosexual temptation safely behind me. The summer before my mission, she moved back home to Washington state and become engaged to a returned missionary there.

"Did thinking about young women cause you to become sexually aroused—to have an erection?"

"Yes."

I suddenly understand why he's pursuing this line of questioning.

President MacIntyre settles back in his chair; I can tell the questions are over. His demeanor is more sympathetic now. "Elder Mitchell, a mission is a very stressful time. You're separated from your family and your friends. You're cut off from romantic contact with the opposite sex. It's natural to feel lonely. And when people are in a same-sex environment, that can do… strange things to their emotions. It can happen in the military, for instance. Perfectly normal men will experience a certain… inclination to seek sexual solace from other men. It's wrong to act on that inclination, of course. The prophets teach us that homosexual acts are a grievous sin, because they pervert the sacred powers of procreation. But the inclination to… perform such acts is normal under the kind of circumstances that you find yourself in right now."

This isn't going to be as bad as I thought. My life may not be ruined after all.

"What I'm saying is this, Elder Mitchell. What you and Elder Braithwaite did was wrong, and you know that. The fact that you came to confess so promptly indicates a repentant spirit on your part. And you are to be commended for that."

He pauses.

"But actually, Elder Mitchell, it doesn't seem to me that you have anything to repent of. Things between you and Elder Braithwaite went farther than they should have, but not as far as they might have. And more importantly, I don't see that you're really responsible for what's happened here. You were taken advantage of by a predator. From what you've described to me, it sounds like Elder Braithwaite has experience in setting up this kind of situation. He poses an extremely serious danger to others, and he should never have been cleared for missionary service. He needs to be shipped home immediately."

My face is hot with relief, but my stomach sinks. President MacIntyre is blind. I am not the innocent I have apparently convinced him I am. Elder Braithwaite is no predator.

"I want you to put this behind you, Elder Mitchell. Don't think about it. Don't dwell on it. Never talk to anyone about it. It's over. You're going to stay in the MTC, you're going to learn to teach the gospel, and you're going to serve an honorable mission for the Lord."

I have no doubt what the truly honorable thing to do at this moment is. But I also have no doubt what will happen to me if I fail to take advantage of the out President MacIntyre is holding open for me.

I say nothing. I nod and look appropriately humble.

"One more thing, Elder Mitchell. It's something I heard one of the Twelve preach in general priesthood conference some years ago."

I am a model of rapt attention.

"If someone ever tries to take advantage of you like that again, you floor him if you have to. Understood?"

I understand.

The interview is over. As President MacIntyre escorts me out the door, he makes a point of squeezing my shoulder and affectionately slapping my back. "Elder Daley," he booms—the elders waiting outside leap to their feet—"you take good care of your companion. He's a fine man."

"Yes, President."

I can tell from the surprised glance Elder Daley gives me that he indeed believed I was here to confess a pre-mission transgression. He expected I'd be sent home. If I were really the fine man President MacIntyre declares me to be, I would be going home.

"Remember what I said to you, Elder Mitchell," President MacIntyre tells me. I nod, unable to speak.

Maybe President MacIntyre's right. It was Elder Braithwaite who suggested we go back to the dorm. It was Elder Braithwaite who came and sat down on the bed. He was the one who put his leg up against mine. He was the one who initiated the kiss. Not me.

As Elder Daley and I turn to go, President MacIntyre says in a low voice to the assistants, "Find Elder Braithwaite and his companion, and have them come see me immediately."

I know better than to believe my own rationalizations. This is my last chance to do the right thing instead of the safe thing.

I keep walking. Behind me, I hear President MacIntyre return to his office and shut the door. Elder Daley and I will return to our room. We'll go to gospel study class, dinner, tonight's devotional. While we do that, Elder Braithwaite will be packing. By the time we return from the devotional, he will be gone. I will never see him again.

Which is the greater sin? What I did with *Elder Braithwaite? Or what I did* to *Elder Braithwaite? I have two years of missionary service—and a whole lifetime after that—to wonder.*

This is my second Sunday in the Missionary Training Center.

The Call

Donna Banta

Detective Lieutenant Matt Ryan
Abbottsville, California
Friday, June 13, 2008. 4:15 PM

My cell phone pulsed an eerie jolt through my system. Instinct told me another shoe was about to fall.

"Ryan here."

"It's Davis. We've got a Mormon missionary dangling behind the LDS mission home."

There was the shoe. I let loose a long exhale, then asked, "Suicide?"

"Looks like a lynching."

"Be there in five."

I turned my car around and scrolled down my cell phone menu to Sergeant Stella Romano.

"We have a possible lynching over at the LDS mission home," I told her.

"The place on Lancaster?"

"That's the one."

"Okay Ryan, I'm on my way."

Minutes later, I pulled up to the flat stucco building. Its plaque read, *LDS Mission Home.* I panned the curtained windows. Not a stir. Then I saw Davis waving his arms. I jogged his way.

"Where are all the missionaries?" I asked him.

"Ordered inside for safety's sake."

I looked back at the curtains. "Who's in charge over there?"

"Guy named Watson." Davis pointed me over some yellow police tape.

"Elder Holland," I said to the corpse.

"You know him?" Davis asked.

"Met him yesterday."

The boy hung from a branch by an electrical cord noose. His left eye was blackened, possibly by somebody with a strong left hook. Silver duct tape covered his mouth, bound his hands behind his back and his legs at the ankle. *Fag Hater* was spelled out in white spray paint on the back of his navy suit coat.

"Who found him?"

"Neighborhood kids," said Davis.

I studied the hands behind his back. The tips of his pale fingers peeked out beneath the duct tape. I pulled out my pad to take notes. Instead I drew a five point star on the page. I gazed up at the victim, then beyond to the mission home. It looked like a hate crime.

The notion rattled through my brain like an empty freight car. I retraced the star on my pad.

Approaching voices startled me from my thoughts. First the crime lab bookends, Gatz and Mosely. After that, Romano in a turquoise tee and black skinny jeans.

"Whoa Nellie," said Mosely.

Gatz aimed his camera.

Romano looked up at the victim. "How's this for a crazy coincidence?"

"On top of that I actually met the kid last night."

"Where?" Romano said.

"He and his partner were on my block so I invited them in."

I studied the poor kid's beaten face. Christ, I wished I hadn't chased him off yesterday.

"Elder Holland was a very intense young man," I said to Romano. Then I turned to Gatz and Mosely. "Solve this one for us."

Romano and I headed for the mission home's door. It opened before I knocked. A grumpy version of Clark Kent gave me the once over.

Held up my badge. "Lieutenant Ryan, Homicide, this is Sergeant Romano."

"Come in Lieutenant, Sergeant. I'm Elder Anderson, President Watson's assistant."

We entered into a small lobby. Two Polynesian hulks sat stuffed behind tiny desks.

"You boys Tongan?" I asked.

They brightened. "Why yes, how did you know?"

"How did you know that?" Romano echoed.

Elder Anderson interrupted before I could reply. "President Watson will see you now."

Downcast eyes on the Tongans told me they reported to Anderson. Romano and I told them goodbye, then followed Elder Anderson through a door marked *Mission President.*

The president shook our hands, excused Elder Anderson, and offered us each a seat across from his massive mahogany desk. He settled into an executive chair that was conspicuously higher than ours, nodded briefly at Romano, and eyed me silently, apparently hoping to command my respect.

"Here's a copy of our records on Elder Nathan Holland," he said finally, and slid a manila folder across the chocolate lacquer. "It's yours to keep."

I opened to a snapshot of a somber looking Elder Holland with a plastic nametag on his lapel. I pocketed the photo and turned to his personal information. "From Murray, Utah, the seventh of ten children."

I looked up at President Watson. He did not elaborate.

"His companion was Elder Sloat," I continued.

"Elder Sloat's here if you want to talk to him, Lieutenant."

I clicked my pen closed, then open. "Had Elder Holland fallen out of sorts with anyone? Another missionary, perhaps?"

"Certainly not," Watson snapped, then drew a breath. "Lieutenant Ryan, this was obviously a hate crime. We Mormons have been persecuted for nearly two centuries."

The president's expression seemed to convey that I was among these persecutors.

"President Watson, I actually met Elders Holland and Sloat yesterday evening. They were on my block."

Watson nodded. "Excellent. I've challenged all of our missionaries to increase their hours of tracting door to door in search of investigators."

I copied the terms "tracting" and "investigators" into my notes then looked up and met his eyes. "Holland impressed me as a rather stern and unyielding young man."

"Are you implying that Elder Holland invited this act of violence, Lieutenant?"

"I just think it's possible that he may have offended some people. If you know of any, I'd like to talk to them."

"Lieutenant, I assure you that there is nothing about our missionaries' conduct that could possibly offend anybody. It's our stand on moral issues that some people object to. For example, our defense of traditional marriage prompted thousands to stage protests at our temples recently. We live in constant fear for our missionaries' safety."

"Perhaps you're confusing persecution with a differing opinion," said Romano.

The president shot her a startled glare then turned back to me. "Is there anything else, Lieutenant?"

"For now, no. We'd like to talk to Elder Holland's companion first."

Watson depressed a button on his phone. "Elder Anderson will take you to Elder Sloat."

Anderson materialized at once, and escorted us past pictures of old men in conservative suits. Their benign eyes followed us down the narrow hall to Sloat's room. The boy's face had paled to the color of fresh snow and his robin's egg eyes were rimmed in red. He sat on the edge of a twin bed; Romano and I sank onto the one opposite. Anderson disappeared, but left the door ajar.

I held up my badge for him to see. "Elder Sloat, we meet again."

"Mr. Ryan," he replied.

"It's Lieutenant Ryan actually, and this is my partner, Sergeant Romano."

Sloat nodded mournfully at Romano. "Nice to meet you, ma'am."

I pulled out my notepad. "When did you last see Elder Holland, the deceased?"

"Deceased," he whispered, and shut his eyes. A tear sprang onto his cheek. "About ten last night, at the apartment. I was tired, he wanted to stay up and read."

I paused my pen. "You don't live here?"

"Only as of today."

I pointed at the closetful of clothes. "Those yours?"

"Yes."

"How'd they get here?"

He shrugged. "I found them here when I checked in."

"So last night Elder Holland wanted to read?"

"He went to the machine for a pop. I turned in. I woke up this morning and he was gone. His bed hadn't been slept in. I looked everywhere. I finally came here and told President Watson he was missing." He drew a jagged breath. "I should have gone to the machine with him."

"Don't beat yourself up," said Romano.

I pocketed my pad and pen, leaned toward him and rested my elbows on each of my knees. "Elder Sloat, Elder Holland seemed rather aggressive in his approach. At least he was with me last night when you were at my house."

"I know, I'm sorry about that, Lieutenant."

"Oh no, that's fine. I was just curious. Had he offended anyone? A contact, a potential convert, maybe even another missionary?"

"He could get under people's skin. But I was usually able to smooth things over. That was my job. Smoothing things over."

I smiled. "Yes, I believe I saw you in action last night. Do you have many contacts? People you're teaching about your church?"

He smirked. "None. Mormons aren't too popular right now, what with Prop 8 and all. Other than tracting door to door, the only interaction we have is with people where we shop and eat, also at St. Paul's. We volunteer in the soup kitchen there."

My stomach growled. I checked my watch. It was already half past five and I had more stops to make. I pulled a business card from my pocket.

"Elder, I have to go, but these are the numbers where you can reach me."

He took the card and slipped it in his shirt pocket without looking at it.

"I'd like to know where you and Elder Holland shopped and ate recently, also the people you interacted with at St. Paul's." I turned to Romano. "Sergeant, can you stay behind and get that information?"

She smiled at Elder Sloat. "Sure."

I nodded my goodbye and left to find Anderson in the hallway.

"Elder Anderson, I'd like to see the victim's apartment."

He sped toward Watson's door. I ambled behind, hands in my pockets.

The president emerged from his office. "You may follow me to the apartment, Lieutenant."

"Thank you. Has anyone been there since Elder Sloat reported Elder Holland missing?"

President Watson's face clouded. "Elder Sloat collected his belongings."

"Elder Sloat packed his clothes?"

President Watson nodded. "Shall we go, Lieutenant?"

I hopped in my car and started the ignition. Either Sloat or Watson had lied to me just now. Instinct told me both had. I drove behind Watson's shiny new Buick toward the southern edge of town. Our surroundings grew seedier with each block. I followed the president into a small lot and parked next to his Buick. We climbed to the second level of a dive called "The Manor." President Watson unlocked the bolt on the apartment door and motioned me inside.

A garage sale couch and chair. Then an orange kitchen that boasted a Formica dining set and a lopsided ceiling fan.

"This was the safest residence you could provide?" I asked.

He blinked. "We're careful with the members' money."

Sounded good. Only I figured his mahogany desk cost a pretty penny. Also his new Buick. I poked my head in the moldy bath, then checked out the bedroom. The closet was half full. There were athletic shoes on the floor and next to them a laundry basket filled with navy sweats and a set of Mormon underwear. A tidy row of shirts hung on the rack above. An image of Holland's pale fingers peeking out of the duct tape swam through my brain.

I turned to find Watson directly behind me, almost invading my personal space. Investigating felt awkward with him on my tail.

"President, I'd appreciate it if you'd leave Elder Holland's things as they are for the next day or so."

He agreed. We shook hands and parted ways in the parking lot.

I climbed into the car and cruised to the nearest corner. Al's Tavern on one side, 24 Hour Donuts on the other. I bet on the donuts.

A tiny bell atop the door prompted a raven-haired knockout to look up from her apple fritters. I read the embroidery on her blouse and took out my badge.

"Hi Cindy, I'm Lieutenant Ryan."

"Can I see that?"

"Sure."

She took my badge and ran her fingers over the seal.

"Ma'am, I'd like to ask you some questions if you don't mind."

Cindy reached up, opened my coat, slipped the badge back into the inside pocket, and smoothed my lapel in place. "Ask away, Lieutenant."

I kept my expression even. "Did the Mormon missionaries ever come in here?"

"Mormons? No. I don't get Mormons on my shift."

"Not even him?" I slid Elder Holland's snapshot across the counter toward her.

"He's a Mormon?" Her cheeks reddened.

I had to wonder what would make this girl blush. "Do you know him?"

"No. But they do across the street."

I jabbed backwards with my thumb. "You mean Al's Tavern?"

"I've seen him go in some nights, usually a little after ten o'clock."

"Did you see him leave as well?"

"I saw them leave. Him and another man."

"The same man or different men?"

"Same man. A fine looking one too." She pointed to Holland's picture. "This guy was always in sweat pants. He must have relied solely on his charm. Sort of like you, huh Lieutenant?"

I half laughed. "Indeed. Cindy, did you see which direction they went?"

"The hunky one drove a red Volkswagon Golf. They'd get into his car and head that way." She pointed in the opposite direction of The Manor apartments.

"Don't suppose you caught the license plate?"

Her full lips formed a bemused smile. "No, Lieutenant. I'm not one to check out a guy's license plate. But the car was a new model."

"Thank you, that's helpful." I put the picture back into my pocket.

"I prefer older models, know what I mean?"

I smiled back at her. "Yes, I believe I do. Do you think you could you identify the other man?"

"Sure. Especially if it's worth my while."

I laughed. "And how would I make it worth your while?"

"I've got a legal situation pending."

"Could you be more specific?"

"Just a misunderstanding between me and a certain judge. I have a little online business. Sort of a social network. It's a tough economy. If a girl wants to pay the rent she's got to sell more than just donuts."

Why wasn't I surprised? "There might be something we can arrange. When did you last see the missionary?"

"As a matter of fact, last night. Only he didn't leave with his friend. He stumbled out alone and took off in the direction of that shitty apartment complex next door. Looked like someone had roughed him up."

I handed her my pen and pad. "Cindy, will you write your full name and contact information for me?"

"You bet. Call any time. I'm always open."

She leaned over the counter to write, at an angle that afforded me a full view of her ample breasts. I refocused on the stack of paper coffee cups on the shelf behind her. She closed my pad and reached to return it to my pocket. I swiped it from her with a wink.

"I wrote down all my information, Lieutenant. You'll be sure to look me up now, won't you?"

"Thanks, Cindy."

"My name's not really Cindy, Lieutenant."

I smiled at her reflection in the glass door.

Had to admit, I was grateful for the attention from such a beautiful girl, even a hooker. But at my age I took my flattery where I could get it.

I crossed the street to the tavern and walked into a packed room. Ted Nugent competed with the crowd via a rusty old jukebox. I looked around for a man who might have been Holland's hook-up. But after nearly thirty years of police work, I had yet to develop even a hint of "gaydar." Instead I found Al behind his bar.

"Lieutenant, always a pleasure."

"Hi Al, how's it going?"

"You ought to come by more often. We're ten times more fun than The Swizzle Stick."

"Yeah, well, maybe that's because they've got a cop that hangs out there."

He let out a snort of laughter. "Could very well be. Fix you a drink?" Even when Al smiled his eyes remained mirthless.

"Nope. I'm still on duty." I gave him Holland's mission photo. "Ever seen him in here?"

"Sure, Ryan. We let the Mormons drink for free."

"Witness says he meets a man here."

"This ain't no gay bar," said a voice behind me. I turned toward it.

I'll be damned. Charlie Vernon. And in a shirt that covered his entire gut.

"You come here to meet women, Vernon?" I asked.

I turned back to Al. He handed back the picture.

"Kid came in last night around ten, only in sweats and without the nametag. I poured him a ginger ale. That's it, Ryan."

As usual, the bare minimum from Al. I returned the photo to my coat pocket, quit the bar and found my car.

The competing events of the day were tumbling around in my brain. I needed to sort things out, gain some perspective. I headed for the best place to regain my inner focus, The Swizzle Stick.

—

I bolted upright and felt around me. Mattress, crumpled sheets. Peeked over the side of the bed. Pillows and blanket were on the floor. My head throbbed.

I got up, threw the pillows and blanket on the bed and covered them with the bedspread. One chore completed. Across the hall in Alice's room, her old stuffed bear awaited her return. I stopped in the bathroom and did the minimum. Nobody here to care what I smelled like. Then I headed for the kitchen in my bare feet and boxer shorts. Opened the dishwasher for a glass. Shit. It still hadn't been run. I wandered through the dining then living room. Last night's scotch still sat on the coffee table where I'd left it. I peeked out the curtain to see the newspaper on my front step. Fetching it would require pants, or at least a robe. But then it was early on a Saturday; maybe everyone was still asleep. If I was fast enough… Mrs.

Calloway walked down her drive and began pruning her hedge across the street. I jerked away from the window, sank into my old easy chair, and finished the scotch.

A shower revived me enough to dress and go out for the paper. I unfolded it to a picture of Elder Holland on the front page. The accompanying article spun his death as a hate crime and quoted President Watson.

I collected my gun from the shelf by my TV and put it in my holster. Then I pulled out my cell and called Romano.

Half a ring then, "Ryan, where the hell are you? I've been waiting here at your desk for twenty minutes."

"Jesus, you're already at the station?"

"You said first thing."

"Okay, be there in five."

I went out the backdoor to find that I'd left the car unlocked in the drive. Careless. I spotted my next-door neighbor's bike stashed alongside his house and made a mental note to remind him to lock it up. I hopped in my driver's seat and clicked my seatbelt in place. Then I started the ignition and used the control on my door to tweak my side mirror. I looked over at the neighbor's bike. Didn't it used to be blue? Probably not. The events of the past twenty-four hours gave me reason to believe I was finally losing my mind. I released the emergency brake, set the car in reverse, pressed my foot down on the gas, and looked up to see a face in my rear view mirror.

"What the FUCK?" I slammed on the brake and reached for my gun. Then I exhaled when the recognition settled.

"Sorry I scared you, Lieutenant," said Elder Sloat.

I shoved my gearshift into park and looked back at Sloat in the mirror. Except for the red-rimmed eyes he was a ghost.

"I knocked on your door, Lieutenant. You didn't answer. Then I heard your shower running, knew you'd be a while, so I crawled into your backseat, laid down and hid. My bike's over there behind that bush."

"So that's *your* bike." I now noticed that the neighbor's overgrown oleander obscured it from street view.

"Yes sir. I left the mission home without permission. I'm sure they're looking for me."

I unfastened my seatbelt and turned to face him. "Is there something you want to get off your chest?"

"Elder Holland snuck out that night. He came home at around ten-thirty with a black eye."

"Any idea where he'd been?"

Sloat nodded. "Yes sir. I'm fairly certain he was at this bar up the street from us called Al's."

I pulled out my pad. "You mean Al's Tavern?"

"Yes. He'd been going there at night for a while. I even followed him once. I watched him go in, then I waited outside and saw him leave twenty or so minutes later with a guy."

"Could you identify this guy if you saw him again?"

"Oh sure. I recognized him. He was an investigator we'd tracted out in those new condos off of Broadway."

"What was this investigator's name?"

His face clouded. "Mitch, or Rich, maybe. It was at least two months ago."

"No last name?"

"I don't think he told us. He invited us in for a few minutes, we gave him the spiel like we tried to give you, then he said he had to leave for work. He gave Elder Holland his e-mail and told him to contact him to set up another appointment."

"Which he obviously did."

Sloat sighed. "Elder Holland always used the computer at the public library, never at the mission home. He probably set up an e-mail account the mission presidency didn't know about."

"The church monitors your e-mail?"

"They monitor everything, Lieutenant."

I looked into the poor kid's pale, red-rimmed eyes. My heart went out to him. "This is a brave thing you're doing, son, coming to me like this."

He shrugged.

I turned back to my pad. "Do you remember which condo the investigator lived in?"

"Only that it was by the pool."

"Okay. That's helpful. Also the fact that you can identify him. Any idea how many times they met?"

"I don't know, half a dozen. I tried not to notice. I figured it wasn't hurting anyone, and I didn't want him to get in trouble. Also, because I'd broken the rules too, with a girl in my last area." He looked at me woefully. "It's kind of hard for twenty-year-old guys to go two whole years without thinking about sex."

I smiled. "It would be hard for old men too."

He nodded. "Anyhow, then Elder Holland came home with his eye bashed in, and I was scared, for him and me. I told him I was going to President Watson. I begged him to come too but he refused."

"When did you see him last?"

"Yesterday morning, in our apartment, right before I went to President Watson. He was sitting on his bed in his sweats." Elder Sloat paused to shake his head. "He wasn't cut out for a mission. But when you're from a big Utah family..."

A mental image of sweats in the laundry basket distracted me from the conversation for a moment. "I'm sorry. You were saying about Utah?"

"Elder Holland was descended from prophets. It was his obligation to serve."

I copied "obligation" into my notes. "What did you tell President Watson yesterday morning?"

"Everything. He chewed me out but good, like it was all my fault. Then he sent me to help the Tongans in the office. A couple of hours later, news of the murder came out. President Watson fed me that story about the pop machine. I went along 'cause I was in shock. Also 'cause I didn't want to be sent home. Then I felt like crap. I was tired of all the lying and covering up. First for myself, then for Holland, then for Watson. Now I will be sent home. Dad will be furious, mom will cry, my girlfriend will dump me, my friends too probably. But at least I won't have to lie anymore. Lying tears you apart."

"Son, what's your first name?"

"Mike."

"Mike, you want to fasten your seatbelt? I'm going to take you downtown so you can issue a formal statement. Also so Forensics can collect a DNA sample from you."

He clicked his belt in place. I did the same with mine.

"After that do I have to go back to the mission home?"

I started the ignition and backed out of my drive. "No. Where do you want to go?"

"Home to Burbank. They're going to send me there anyway. Only I should return the bike."

"I'll see they get the bike back, Mike. Do you have enough for bus fare home?"

"I've got everything I need here in my backpack, Lieutenant."

"We'll check the schedule and do our best to get you to the station in time. But you may have to come back to Abbottsville if there's a trial, Mike."

"But not to the mission home?"

I smiled at his reflection in the rear view mirror. "No, Mike, we'll put you up in a motel."

As we drove to headquarters, I thought of all the things I wanted to say to the kid. I wanted to tell him again how brave he was for coming to me with the truth. I wanted him to know that I thought President Watson was a lying, cowardly, pompous, self-important prick. I wanted to say that there's a huge society of unreligious people with high moral standards, and plenty of religious people without any morals at all. But instinct told me my opinion on those subjects wouldn't resonate with him. Also I was here to learn, not the other way around.

"Mike, there's something that's bothering me. Why do you think Elder Holland went to Al's Tavern to meet his friend? I mean, I know they couldn't have met at your apartment. But that crowd at Al's isn't exactly gay-friendly, and there's a donut shop across the street. Seems like that would have been the safer bet."

"I don't know about the gay-friendly part, Lieutenant. But I do know that for a Mormon, going to a bar is a wildly exotic idea. My guess is he thought that if he was going to hook-up with his boyfriend, why not go all the way and do it in a bar? I don't know. Repression does weird stuff to people, know what I mean, Lieutenant?"

"I think you're onto something."

I left Mike in the charge of a junior officer, then scrolled down my cell for the number to the coroner's office. Instinct told me what he would say. Even so, it still surprised the hell out of me. That's the thing about instincts. They warn but they don't explain.

I set out to look for Romano. I found her cooling her heels behind my desk, pushing the chair to swivel one way, then the other.

"Pretty fun, huh?" I said. "It goes back and forth too."

"Finally!" she cried, and jumped to her feet. "What took you so long?"

I smiled down at her. "Elder Sloat paid me a visit this morning."

"You talked to Sloat?"

"Yes, but before I tell you about it, I'd better stop by the little boys' room."

The scotch, both last night's and this morning's, had announced its presence immediately after I'd climbed from the car.

"Hurry, will you? Your lipstick looks fine," she called after me.

———

"Unbelievable," Romano said, as we arrived at the LDS Mission Home. "What made him think he could get away with it?"

"He's a self-righteous prick, that's what."

I parked and we got out of the car. A black and white pulled up next to me. I rapped on the passenger side. The officer rolled down his window.

"This won't take long," I told him.

Romano and I walked through the front door. A Tongan jumped out of his chair. We strode past him and into Watson's office.

The president looked up from his desk. "It's customary to call, or at least knock, Lieutenant."

Without waiting for an invitation, we took our seats across from him.

I folded my arms across my chest, stretched out my legs and crossed them at the ankle. "I've got a question for you, President."

"Do you?"

"I do. But first I should tell you that, other than the eye, the coroner found no marks on Elder Holland's body. No head wound and no blood or skin under his fingernails to indicate a struggle. His clothes were clean, his shoes polished, and his hair washed."

"So?" Watson asked, his expression smug.

"So for starters it wasn't a hate crime," said Romano.

Watson heaved a disgusted sigh. "Young lady, what else could it be? The boy was punched in the eye, bound in duct tape and hung from a tree right here on church property."

"You may address the young lady as Sergeant," I fired back at him, then in a quieter tone added, "and Elder Sloat told me the truth about Elder Holland's eye, just as he told you yesterday morning. Only unlike you, I did not advise him to lie to the police. He's at headquarters now, issuing a sworn statement."

"After that he's heading back home to Burbank," Romano added. "He asked us to tell you goodbye for him."

Watson's face reddened. "*What?* He can't do that! He hasn't been released from his mission yet."

Jesus, this guy was an even bigger prick than I thought.

"Hate to tell you this president, but the former Elder Mike Sloat is a legal adult who is not under arrest and can go and come as he pleases." I turned to my partner. "That reminds me, I promised I'd return his bike. Romano, will you make a note of that?"

"Will do," she replied.

I refocused on Watson. "As for the hanging, I think I can explain how that happened. Elder Holland was a tortured soul. I found him a tad offensive when I met him Thursday evening. Since then, I've learned that he was a closeted gay man who'd been slipping out for trysts at a local bar. The guilt he carried home on his nightly returns must have been staggering. But when Elder Sloat decided to come to you, Holland knew he now faced the unthinkable. He was going to be sent home from his mission in disgrace. Elder Holland was descended from prophets. It was his obligation to serve."

I paused to take in President Watson's appearance. His lips had parted, his complexion paled, and he showed no sign of forming a response. Amazing how quickly the truth could puncture hubris.

"In his mind, he had one way out," I continued. "To demonstrate his belief, he showered, shined his shoes, and got into his missionary suit. Then he hung himself in his apartment, probably from the lopsided fan in his kitchen."

"You can't prove that," he half whispered.

"Sure we can. We've got some real smart guys in our crime lab. Once they obtain the necessary DNA samples, they'll determine who hung Holland's clean corpse in that field behind the mission home, then bound him in duct tape."

Watson frowned.

"So President, here's my question. I've seen lots of murders disguised as suicides, but never a suicide disguised as a murder. Why on earth would you do that?"

The president stared over my head as he spoke. "A gay Mormon commits suicide. That's just what you people want to hear, isn't it? Even more reason to whine about Prop 8 and label us as bigots. Fire up more creeps to picket our temples. Sometimes, for the sake of fairness, we have to—" He pulled out his handkerchief and mopped his face.

I eyed him silently. His rigid jaw had collapsed and his chair no longer seemed conspicuously higher than ours.

"What now, Lieutenant?" he asked.

"There are a couple of uniformed officers out front. They'll take you downtown for questioning. After that, it's unclear. It might not even be our case."

I stood and buttoned my coat. Romano rose as well.

"This is no longer a homicide investigation," I told him.

The Interview

John Bennion

Tom looked at the sweat shining in the palms of his hands. Wiping them on his slacks, he opened the door into the stake president's office. A man behind a desk placed a paper onto a stack, stretched his chin upward, unbuttoned his top button, and pulled his shirt open at the collar. He glanced at Tom over his glasses. "You here to see President Williams?"

"Temple recommend," said Tom. He touched his pocket.

The man nodded toward the door marked "High Council." "They're still going strong." He stood and leaned across his desk, his hand extended. "I'm Brother Clark."

Tom shook Brother Clark's hand. "Tom Mathews," he said and sat in a chair against the wall.

Brother Clark glanced at the clock. "Shouldn't be much longer." He leaned back in his chair. "Actually, they've been improving. Their meetings only go over a half-hour now." He lifted another paper from the stack on his left. "They've got too much work to do."

Tom rubbed the place above his right temple where the hair was thinning. Then he stood and walked to the bulletin board. There was a calendar with a picture of the Provo Temple at night. Next to it was a pink Happiness-Is-Family-Home-Evening sign.

"You're getting married, right?"

"Yes," said Tom. "How did you guess?"

"I was here when President Williams got your call." He wrote something on a paper. "When's the happy day?"

"The first of next month." Tom walked back to his chair and sat down again, pulling at his pant legs where his garments were creeping up.

Brother Clark took off his glasses and stretched back, his hands behind his head. "He said something about this being the one he'd been waiting for. He likes to see good marriages happen. Used to be your bishop, didn't he?"

"Before my mission." Tom put his hand to his front shirt pocket and took out his recommend. "I was his priests' quorum assistant once." He looked at his new bishop's signature. Underneath was the blank for the stake president's.

"They don't make them much better than him." Brother Clark pointed a thumb toward the meeting room.

Tom nodded, frowning. "Dad said he's aged quite a bit."

"Especially since he's been stake president," Brother Clark said. "I've watched a lot of people come in here. They talk to him; then they leave and go on with their lives. They don't see him drag himself home after a night of interviews." Brother Clark stood to reach more papers from a file cabinet. "The worst on him are the young people. I mean the ones just back from their missions. They come in looking like they've just walked out of a seminary filmstrip, but later I read in the paper, 'Marriage to be performed in the home of the parents of the bride.' I wish they could see how he looks after they leave."

Tom rose and walked to the door leading out. "I'm a little thirsty," he said, feeling Brother Clark's eyes on his back as he shut the door behind him. Out in the hall he bent over the fountain, then turned to look into his former ward's trophy case. The dustier awards had his and his friends' names engraved on them. "100% Attendance—1964." Bishop Williams had given Tom and another priest that one. "Aspen Valley Woodlore Contest—1st Place." "Stake Basketball Champions." These too, had been won under Bishop Williams's direction. Next to the trophies was a colored map of the world with pins stuck where missionaries were. None were in France, his old mission. He tried to find Fontainbleau but it wasn't on the map.

He walked down the hall to the priests' old classroom. The sun had shone through the east window, pleasantly warm on Sunday mornings. Bishop Williams had planned camping trips with the quorum in this room and told stories from his mission. Tom had anticipated his own.

Bishop Williams taught them about the gospel, waving his arms and laughing, scrawling words and pictures across the blackboard, making his quorum stand and repeat memorized verses. "The first principles and ordinances of the gospel are: first, Faith in the Lord Jesus Christ; second, Repentance...."

Tom turned back toward the office, pushed into the restroom, and washed and dried his hands. He watched himself in the mirror, then flicked off the light. The fan died with a rattle.

He looked out through the front door at his car; he could leave now and avoid facing his old friend. Standing by the water fountain, he touched his stomach where it was tight and took a deep breath. Then he shook his head and turned back to the office.

He waited at the door, listening. Finally he heard voices and went in. George Peterson, a high councilman, turned when the door opened. "Tom!" He reached for the younger man's hand, drawing him close with his other hand on Tom's back. "It's been awhile; we were happy to hear the good news." Tom nodded and returned the handshake quickly. He turned away to look through the door into the high council room, seeing the stake president still talking to several brethren, smiling and gesturing. He had always reminded Tom of John Wayne, that is until he spoke; Bob Williams's voice was much deeper and he didn't have a drawl. Tom looked at the lines in his face, at the shoulders sloping more than Tom remembered. President Williams looked out through the doorway and beckoned Tom in.

"This is Tom Mathews, one of the best ever to come up through the Aaronic Priesthood. Tom, this is Brother Gilger, Brother Christensen...," President Williams said, nodding to the other men. "Tom's decided to settle down and start a family." He beamed at the others. Tom smiled briefly, then moved back, waiting until the president was finished. They walked together past the clerk into the president's office.

The older man closed the door and they stood facing each other. He put his large hands on Tom's shoulders. "You're looking good. It was a joy to hear your news." Tom hesitated, then laid both hands nervously on the president's arms.

"Well now," President Williams sat behind his desk, "let's have the whole story. How did you meet—" he looked at a piece of paper on his desk—"Carolyn?"

"At the institute at school."

"University of Denver?"

"Right. Carolyn and I were in the same class, and the teacher asked us to be on this committee together."

"Oh, a little match-making, eh?" Tom didn't smile. The president looked at him. "Well, you know this can't be final until I pass judgment. That's what we agreed, wasn't it?" He smiled across at Tom.

The young man nodded, holding his hands tight against his knees. He looked straight at President Williams, silently. The smile faded from President Williams's face. He leaned forward, lifted a pen from his desk and turned it in his fingers.

"We kind of lost touch with you clear out in Denver."

Tom nodded.

"You worked for your dad's old partner out there, didn't you? Ah...what was his name?"

"Monte Daniels."

"Oh, yes. Lived in our stake awhile." The president leaned back, talking easier now. "Cement contractor, isn't he?"

"I tied iron for him."

"Then when you came back you met your fiancée?"

"Yes."

The president folded his hands across his middle. There was silence. He stuck his finger into his collar and pulled on it, then leaned forward again. "Something wrong about the wedding?"

"Yes."

The clock whirred.

"You want to talk?"

"Yes."

Silence. The president rubbed his forehead. "You have cold feet, Tom?"

"No."

President Williams turned his chair to one side. "Did you get involved?"

Tom was quiet.

"You know you can be forgiven for that if you have." The president turned suddenly to Tom. "Did you get sexually involved?"

Tom shook his head. "No."

Brother Clark's chair squeaked in the outer room.

"I don't think I can do it." Tom looked at his hands.

"Get married?"

"Yes." Tom looked up. "You asked me if I'd slept with Carolyn. I wish I had."

"What? What did you say?"

"I wish I had. If I'd done that, I could repent. And then go on. It'd be over then. But I can't repent of what I am."

"What you are? I don't—." The older man pushed his hand along the side of his face and up through his hair. "Maybe if you'll just tell me exactly what's happened." He put his hands together on the desk.

"It started on my mission," said Tom.

"What did?"

Tom opened his mouth then shut it.

"Something happened on your mission?"

Tom let his breath go out. "I had a junior companion once who wasn't—ah—. He didn't get up on time, didn't study, didn't like to go out. Homesick." Tom looked up at President Williams and back at the corner of the desk. "I talked him out of going home every week for a month. Every night I prayed that he would stay. I don't even know why I did it." Tom felt his face and ears grow hot. "We fasted one Sunday. After church we went up on this hill outside of town. I prayed, then he prayed. He stayed on his knees a long time and then started telling me how he was going to work harder and a lot of things like that." Tom looked up. "It made me feel glad," he said, his voice thick.

"I imagine it would," said President Williams frowning.

"That night after prayer, I lay in bed. I just kept looking at him. When I thought he was asleep, I got out of bed and prayed again. Then I went over and stood by his bed and—" Tom looked at his hands.

"Go on."

"It was creepy. I got this idea of blessing him. Of putting my hands on him and blessing him. So I knelt down and I did." Tom's voice was shaking but he didn't take his eyes off the president.

President Williams spoke slowly. "You loved your companion and had been through quite an experience with him. Don't misinterpret what happened. I don't see—"

"What was wrong was how I felt. I was warm all over and I couldn't move my hands. I just kept—"

"Touching him," the president finally said.

"Yes. I touched him."

"Where did you touch him?" the president asked, looking out the window.

"On the chest." Tom put both his hands on his own chest.

"He didn't wake up?"

"I almost hoped he would, but that night I thought he was asleep. I found out the next day I was wrong. Even now I can't understand why he lay there awake and didn't move away from me. Anyway, the next day while he was studying, I walked up behind him and put my hands on his shoulders. He jumped up and shouted, 'Don't ever do that again!' That week I was transferred to the mission home."

"Are you sure you were transferred because of what happened?"

"I think so. When I first got there, the mission president gave me a long interview. No questions. Just talked. About how nice it was to come home at night to a wife and children. He told me about the pleasure of seeing his wife pregnant with their first child. 'It was the greatest thrill of my life,' he said."

President Williams rubbed his eyes.

"At the end he was really serious. He said that some elders get weird ideas and are sent home early. He said that it's a waste because if they'd just control themselves until the end of their missions, even if they did have powerful tendencies, they could marry a good woman and that would settle them."

"Maybe he was jumping to a conclusion about you."

"No he wasn't," Tom said quickly.

"Maybe you're jumping to a conclusion about yourself."

"No." Tom moved forward on his seat. "After I was in the mission home, I started thinking, fitting some things together."

"Like what?"

"Once before my mission, a bunch of us were riding around after M.I.A. We ended up parking on the hill outside of town. I was sitting next to Stacy Bingham and I knew she wanted me to kiss her, so I did." Tom frowned. "It wasn't anything like I thought it would be."

"You didn't like it?"

"I pushed her away. She said she wanted to go home."

The president smiled, then stopped. Tom hurried on. "Another time was when I was much younger, you remember, when we lived next to Sweeny Hansen." Tom's face was red and he watched the president as he talked. "One day I was playing out back and Sweeny was working in his garden. He stopped to urinate and saw me watching through the fence. He came over laughing, didn't do his pants up. He said something. I can't remember now, but I can still see him standing there. I could never stop thinking about it."

President Williams looked at Tom a moment, and then spoke slowly. "I don't want to minimize what you've said, but you've confessed to me, and a lot of young men are confused about themselves as they grow up. It passes."

"Bishop, I'm thirty years old."

They both waited. "Have there been other experiences then?" President Williams asked.

"Yes."

Tom was silent.

"Like what?"

The president waited. "You need to tell me." He turned in his chair. "Does Carolyn know any of this?"

"No. I tried a few times but I never could figure out what to say."

"Do you think she could handle it?"

"I don't know."

"If you think you have a problem, why did you get engaged?"

Tom was silent.

"Tell me how it happened, Tom."

"I told you we were in the same class. So we started studying together." Tom looked up. "I liked to talk to her. It's really hard to talk to most people, but we could go on for hours about anything. I just enjoyed knowing her. But then she started doing things like taking my hand, holding my arm against her while we walked somewhere. I hated it." Tom swallowed. "But what could I do? I couldn't say, 'Please get your hand off me.' Once I just said we should break things off. Then every time I went into the institute, she was there. She didn't understand. It was like slapping her face every time I passed her and ignored her. So I stopped going to institute. But then my college bishop called me in. After that I went back. I saw her and we talked; we started doing our homework together again. She thought it meant something. Instead of being easy like before, it seemed like she expected something."

"It's called wanting to get married."

Tom didn't smile. "Later our institute teacher called me in. 'You know Carolyn loves you,' he told me. Then he started talking about all the missionaries who come home and wait for the perfect girl. They get too fussy and then they're thirty and not married. He thought I didn't want to marry her because of her looks." Tom hesitated. "It started me wondering. Maybe I was confused. Maybe if we went ahead and got married, things would work out, so I proposed."

"Do you think she's pretty?"

Tom looked at the floor. "I guess so," he said. "But I feel only friendship for her. When she tries to get close, I feel uncomfortable."

"It begins with friendship." The president frowned.

"I know that, but don't you see?" A bead of sweat ran down Tom's face. "I enjoyed her as a friend and I like her as well as anyone I've met, but I can't marry her."

"Just because you're not sure you like girls?" The president gripped the side of his desk then sat back down. "Tom, you're like a son to me, and I don't want to see you hurt. If she's the fine girl you seem to think she is, love could grow."

"Sexual love?" Tom asked. "Do you believe that would grow?" He slumped back in his chair. "I don't anymore."

"If all you've done is what you've told me, then—"

"Then it would be great." Tom stared at the wall.

"Something happened since your mission?"

Tom spoke slowly. "You remember how I was working for Dad right after my release?"

"Yes."

"Well, maybe three months after I came home I got this letter from an elder who had been in my mission. He said he was living in Salt Lake and couldn't we get together and talk about old times. It surprised me. I hardly knew him. Later I figured out why he wanted to talk to me. By 'old times' he meant my experience with my junior companion."

The president shifted his recommend book.

"Anyway, I'd go up to Salt Lake every week for doors or lumber or something. Well, the next time, I decided what the heck, I'd stop in. At the very least we'd talk a little French and then I'd head back."

Tom watched the president as he talked. "His place was just northeast of Temple Square, near a park, in an old, two-story house made into apartments. When he answered the door, his shirt wasn't buttoned and I could tell he didn't have his garments on. Three other guys were sitting on chairs inside. They smiled and said hello, but he didn't invite me in to meet them. He just said we should get something to eat. We went to a restaurant, and all the time he talked about the job he'd had teaching swimming in Los Angeles and what was wrong with the Church.

"He'd forgotten his wallet, so I paid for the food. Then he thought we should go to this place he knew for some music and dancing. It had been quite awhile since I'd just gone out and had fun, so I went. The place was west of the temple, across from the train station. It was pretty crowded though. Some girls were dancing, but mostly it was guys dancing with guys." Tom stopped and waited.

The president looked at his hands, then he looked up at Tom. "You stayed?" he said finally.

"Yes. I stopped in the doorway but Rick—that was his name—he pulled me on inside." Tom was talking quickly now. "I wanted to get out of there at first, but I was curious, I guess. Rick, well, he moved around, talking and having a good time."

"How long did you stay?" The president's voice wavered.

"A couple of hours. Rick would touch my hand and then he'd lay his arm on my back. It seemed all right in that place for him to do that." Tom spread his hands. "It felt as if a burden had been lifted. As if I was finally able to figure something out. I could talk openly about my confusion without feeling stupid or guilty or wrong, and he related. It was like being in France and then suddenly you see an American, someone who speaks the same language. Rick knew what I was feeling before I felt it. That was more important to me than agreeing with him morally."

Tom could see President Williams trying to control his frown. Something burned in Tom's stomach.

"I went to see him every week for a while when I went in for Dad. Then I started getting uneasy about the whole deal. He was always trying to get me to come and stay with them. Rick said they needed another roommate to help with expenses. I felt bad for them but I left anyway." Tom stopped.

"Why did you leave?"

"One day we went over to the community center to play tennis; when we were finished, one of the guys got hold of my garments while I was showering and started waving them like a flag." Tom felt disgust flood him. "I grabbed my things and left. I realized that I couldn't mix with people like that."

"You've never told any of this to Carolyn?"

"Not to anyone."

"Think again about how she'd take it if you told her."

"It won't work, President." Tom slid forward on his seat. "Oh, I think she'd forgive me. Or she might think she could reform me. Maybe she could, but I can't handle the thought of pressure that way. One time this girl came to Rick's apartment. She said that she knew she could change me if I'd just give her the chance."

President Williams rubbed a hand down across his face. He held his fist closed on the top of his desk.

"Carolyn just wouldn't get it," said Tom. "It was hard for me not to go back to Salt Lake. I had to keep away from other places too. I'd see men and I'd want to talk to them because I knew why they were there. I'd look at them and they'd look at me. Can you imagine what life would be like for her, married to me?"

"Have you ever gone for professional help?"

"In Denver. I was making a lot of money and I saw all kinds of counselors. Two years. Some told me it was because Mom and Dad had only one child. Some said my mother was too dominant in our house. Then there were those who said that it was perfectly natural." Tom felt sweat dripping down his back. The president had put one hand to his forehead and was leaning forward, elbow down against his desk.

"I knew I could never be happy that way, but then I'd walk to the bus station or through the park and watch the people there. I didn't do anything though. I just talked and felt lonely. One doctor gave me electrical shocks while I looked at pictures. Another gave me drugs to make me vomit when I got excited."

The president cleared his throat again. "We have some professionals in the Church who have developed certain methods based on the gospel."

Tom started to say something, then he stopped and said quietly, "I don't think they'd do any good." He thought. "Do you?" he asked.

The president was silent. "Ah, sometimes they help," he said, looking down at his hands. "They aren't always successful."

"I don't think it's a matter of being cured. I've been this way as long as I can remember. If I was to be cured now it would be something like a lobotomy. I wouldn't be me anymore." Tom realized he was talking too loudly and he softened his voice. "I think what I need to do is to learn to accept who I am and to live with it. I can learn to control it so that I don't bother anyone."

"Do you think you can hold your breath for the rest of your life?"

Tom waited until he could talk calmly. "That sounds like what Rick said: 'You're going to sit in church and sublimate? No one there can understand. If they ever get a hint of who you are, they'll shut you out.'"

The president cleared his throat. Then he reached over and closed his recommend book.

"I thought I had a chance with Carolyn, until just being friends wasn't enough for her." Tom sat back and started again, trying to keep his voice level. "I've tried to break it off, but I couldn't pass her without seeing pain in her face. What can I tell her? How do I describe myself to her? I like her. I've never talked with anyone like her. But I still look twice when I see some men walking on the street." Tom felt his body tighten again.

"Have you made any contacts since you came back?"

"No! And I never will."

"You've given up on just going through with the marriage?"

"I can't. When I was seeing Rick, we went to a sauna. It was a cover for men who wanted to get together. Rick went there to work out and make contacts. I was approached a couple of times. Once when we were leaving, two or three blocks from the place, we saw this guy getting out of his car. He was in the sauna every week, really friendly. When he was about twenty yards from his car, he saw us. I raised my hand to him, but he ducked his head and hurried past us. Then he went scurrying down the street looking both ways to see if anyone saw me wave at him."

President Williams let his breath out.

"Then we passed his car. It was a station wagon with a briefcase in the front seat. There was a lady's hair brush and a baby bottle next to it. On the back bumper was a Happiness-Is Family-Home-Evening sticker. Rick laughed. 'There's somebody who has his cake and eats it too,' he said." Tom sat looking at his hands. "I could never live like that. I couldn't be that kind of a hypocrite. I've been taught not to be promiscuous. I've always believed in that."

The president nodded; they were quiet. Tom took out his temple recommend and pushed it across the desk to President Williams, who folded it. Tom sat looking at the floor. Then he rose and walked to the door, stopping with his hand on the doorknob.

"What will you tell her?" The president moved wearily to the window, his back to Tom. Tom could see that his shoulders were sloped even more than when Tom had come in. He felt angry.

"Just that we can't get married. We haven't sent any announcements yet, so we'll only have to tell our families."

"It's going to be hard on her."

"I know." Tom wiped his hand across his eyes.

"She'll want to know why. You can't break it off without giving her any reason at all." The president slumped into his chair.

Tom's throat and chest were tight; he felt a buzzing in his head.

The president started to say something.

"Can't you see it scares me," Tom said. "How can I be wrong my whole life? You know sometimes when I'm out at my parents' place and I get up in the morning, I forget and it feels great. I haven't read anything or heard anything that says I'd have a good chance of changing by getting married. Isn't that right?"

The president nodded. "Probably," he said.

"I've thought about it and I don't want to do that to her. After what I've told you, could you want me to get married?"

The president didn't move.

"I think of being with her...after we're married. I don't believe I could ever love her physically." Tom's cheeks were wet. "But I can't deny myself any kind of sexuality, can I?"

The president's face was white. Tom, looking at him, knew that he saw the depth of Tom's fear. The president was blinking his eyes quickly.

"You can't give up," the president whispered.

"What am I going to do? You said a minute ago I was like your son. So I am your son. A homosexual. Your son. When I touched Rick, I felt good about it. Sexually good. When Carolyn touches me that way, it feels wrong."

Tom sat down, his hands clenched. He felt his neck tighten again. Tears ran down his face. "I feel like an insect pinned to a card. I can't move. I've prayed and prayed and I feel, 'You're going to be all right.' And that's good, but it doesn't tell me what to do."

The president looked straight at Tom.

"What *am* I supposed to do?" said Tom. "I want someone to tell me."

The president didn't take his eyes from Tom.

"I can't do it."

The president waited. Tom walked to the window and leaned his face against the cool glass. Neither spoke.

"It's better with it out," Tom said finally. "I waited too long to talk to someone." His shoulders started shaking. He looked back at the president, saw him blinking quickly, his face twisting.

"What are you going to do?" President Williams asked.

Tom walked to the door. "I'll tell her. I'll just tell her all of it."

"What then?"

Tom shook his head. "I don't know. Maybe I'll be back." He started to open the door.

"Tom," President Williams said.

Tom looked back.

"Remember, you're still my son."

Excerpt from *14*

John Cameron

Note: The names "Aaron" and "Ron" refer to the same character at two different stages of his life.

MARLA: Aaron!

AARON: Marla! (He laughs to torment her.)

MARLA: You're giving me a complex.

(Members of the chorus enter and sit around Marla. They become a class. Ron is revealed teaching them. Judy abruptly appears on another part of the stage.)

JUDY: Please. This story could have a real impact on a lot of people.

RON: No. (Music out) (Judy is gone. The lights shift and the class comes to life.)

DONALD: My Abnormal Psych professor said puberty is as close to crazy as you get without being completely nuts.

RON: Do you think that's true?

STUDENTS: (Overlapping) Yeah. Yes. Definitely. I was a complete freak.

RON: Is that what makes Holden Caulfield so interesting? Is that why we connect to him—shared fear—experience?

DENISE: I don't think he's that interesting.

RON: Why, Denise?

DENISE: He doesn't think about anything but sex.

RON: Is that bad, or just typical?

LESLIE: I don't think it's too much about sex. When you're that age everything is sex.

DONALD: It still is.

RON (Warning): Donald.

DENISE: I think it makes him kind of two dimensional. He puts everything together in such a sick way—just to suit his needs.

LESLIE: We all do that. We're all biased. Everybody sees the world the way they want to see it.

RON: I'm afraid I have to agree with Leslie. I don't think Salinger is inventing anything new here. Holden is just doing what we all do and that's why so many people relate to this writing even though the situations may be extreme. We all want to fit in. We all want to be reflected in the world around us. And we can do some pretty desperate things to make that happen. Holden's not such a bad guy. Read chapter 15 in your textbooks for Thursday.

DONALD: When are the papers due?

RON: Papers are due on the 23rd and I'm not accepting any lates. (Pause) Did you all hear that? (The students voice less than an enthusiastic acknowledgement.) Good. I'm glad you're excited. It's why I love you.

DONALD: How many pages? (David appears on the fringe of the class.)

RON: For the umpteenth time, Donald, no page limit. (Donald is not pleased.) Just write well. Write enough to say exactly what you need to say.

DONALD: I hate that.

RON: I was counting on it. Go away. (They move like all students leaving a classroom. Some of them stop to talk or observe. Others leave the stage. Ron also begins to leave. He is approached by David.)

DAVID: How was class?

RON: College has become a remedial extension of high school, David. I'm just filling the time that surrounds Spring Break.

DAVID: You want to get a beer tonight?

RON: I can't. I'm grading.

DAVID: You're angry.

RON: Why would you say that?

DAVID: Truly?

RON: Hand to God.

DAVID: But you won't get a beer.

RON: I really can't.

DAVID: I offended you the other day, didn't I?

RON: That's ridiculous.

DAVID: I admire you very much, Ron. I'd like to be your friend—not a diversion. (Ron is caught completely off his guard.)

RON: I'd be a liar if I said I didn't find that tempting. But I'm not good at friend, David. I'm good at funny, flip, and rude. I appreciate the offer, but you should know it's a risky one.

DAVID: I'm willing to take the risk.

RON: Consider yourself warned.

DAVID: Noted. (Changing the subject) I've got some news.

RON: Ooooh, goody. Dish.

DAVID: We have to do a tenure review.

RON: Don't say it.

DAVID: That's right.

RON: You fucker.

DAVID: You're overdue. I got a sternly worded memo from the Dean's office. It should've been done last year. Why didn't you say anything?

RON: Why in God's name would I say anything? Don't buy grief, it's free. Our dear retired chair was too busy calculating his pension so I kept my head low. Can't I get a pass?

DAVID: It needs to be done by the end of November.

RON: Who's on my committee?

DAVID: Oh you're gonna love this—Rose and Jonathan.

RON: This is the act of a friend? Jonathan hates the air I breathe.
(Judy suddenly appears on another part of the stage.)

JUDY: Mr. Sorenson? (Ron ignores her.)

DAVID: I swear I tried, Ron. Everyone else is up to their neck. They all turned me down. What do you care? He can't touch you. And Rose loves you.

JUDY: Mr. Sorenson?

DAVID: You need to go over your student evaluations and get them to Rose.

RON: Okay.

DAVID: By Friday?

RON: Go away.

DAVID: We'll talk.

JUDY: Ron?

RON (To Judy): No! (Music cue)

(Judy immediately disappears. Aaron is revealed. He begins to sing. Ron listens. He remembers and a smile crosses his face.)

AARON:
Oh Say, What is Truth?
Oh say, what is truth? 'Tis the brightest prize

To which mortals or Gods can aspire.
Go search in the depths where it glittering lies,
Or ascend in pursuit to the loftiest skies:
'Tis an aim for the noblest desire.

(Judy again appears.)

JUDY: Why won't you help me? How can you not be angry about what they did to you?

RON: Let me be just as clear as I possibly can. I'm not interested. I'm not involved with the Church any more. I have no axes to grind. My involvement in the experiment was my choice and I don't hold them responsible. If you want to revenge yourself on the Mormons, you'll have to find someone else to help you.

(Aaron speaks to the audience.)

AARON: (At curtain rise the stage is empty. One by one fourteen men enter the stage and take position facing the audience. When the last is in place Jack walks through them and addresses the audience.):
Top of Form 1
I bear you my testimony that God lives—that we are literally the sons and daughters of our Heavenly Father.

JUDY: Please, Ron. Some major publications are interested in this.

AARON: The seed of divinity rests in all of us.

RON: Who?

JUDY: The Rolling Stone, The Voice, The Advocate.

AARON: And our Heavenly Father has given us the means to return to his presence and live with him forever through the fullness of the everlasting gospel.

RON: I'm sorry. I can't.

JUDY: Why doesn't it piss you off that they want to act like it never happened?

RON: Who is they?

AARON: As it was revealed to the Prophet Joseph Smith and the restored church—

JUDY: The University. The Church.

AARON: The Church of Jesus Christ of Latter-day Saints—the only true church.

RON: That's not true.

JUDY: I have an email from the President of BYU. He claims they can't verify electric shock therapy was ever used on campus.

RON: You're lying. (Judy hands him a piece of paper. He reads it.)

AARON: And I bear you my testimony of these things. I know them to be true as surely as I stand before you this day. In the name of Jesus Christ.

JUDY: Ron?

AARON: Amen.

RON: This is not possible. Is this real?

JUDY: I promise you.

RON: But it's a lie.

JUDY: You don't think they can lie?

RON: No. I didn't. I mean… I may have disagreements with the church, but I always believed them to be honorable. How can he say this? I sat in that room. You can't erase us. You can't remove fourteen lives from the records.

JUDY: They already did. And they will continue to if no one ever says anything. Will you talk to me? (Silence. Ron turns and looks at Aaron. After a moment his decision is made.)

RON: I was there.

JUDY: Will you talk to me?

RON: Yes.

(The moment Ron agrees to the interview lights shift and begin to brighten. They're accompanied by a high pitched electronic tone. Judy and the chorus disappear. Ron and Aaron are caught in mid-gesture. The light and sound both increase in intensity until they are close to unbearable and then suddenly stop. There is a rift in the tissue of time. Aaron and Ron are left alone. Aaron can suddenly see Ron.)

AARON: Oh my gosh! (Laughing) Where did you come from? (Ron is completely disoriented by Aaron's recognition.)

RON: I'm sorry. I'm not...

AARON: Were you there just a minute ago?

RON: No. I... I don't think so. (Struggling for understanding.)

AARON: No?

RON: I didn't mean to scare you.

AARON: No, well, no. I'm sure you didn't. (Exiting)

RON: No, please. Don't go.

AARON: Excuse me?

RON: Stay. Please.

AARON: I... uh... I'm supposed to... (shifting into missionary mode) Are you visiting today?

RON: I... I'm... Yes.

AARON: First time?

RON: No.

AARON: Are you a member of the church?

RON: Yes. No. No.

AARON: Would you like to know more? If you give me your name and address...

RON: (overlapping) No, I...

AARON:... I can arrange for someone to visit your home and answer your questions.

RON: I'd rather talk to you.

AARON: Me?

RON: Can I talk to you?

AARON: I... do I know you?

RON: Yes. Maybe.

AARON: I know you? Where have we...?

RON: (Unable to help himself) You're so young.

AARON: What?

RON: How old are you?

AARON: I'm twenty-four.

RON: Twenty-four.

AARON: Would you like to give me your address?

RON: You're a kid.

AARON (Uncomfortable): Yes. I guess I am. Okay. Well, I hope you'll come visit us again. (He again starts to exit.)

RON: Don't go, Aaron.

AARON: You know my name.

RON: Aaron.

AARON: What do you want?

RON: I don't know—something—to talk to you—look at you.

AARON: Are you trying to be funny?...

RON (overlapping): No. I'm just a little confused and...

AARON:... because I don't know how you know me, but I don't know you and I've...
(Aaron begins to move away and Ron blocks his path desperate to hold him there.)

RON (fast): You're name is Aaron Sorenson. You were born in Rhode Island and raised in Iowa. (Aaron stops and looks directly at Ron. Much of the dialogue overlaps.) Your father works in a mill and your mother sells real estate. You don't like your mother very much. You think she's crazy.

AARON: Wait a minute.

RON: You have an older brother you idolized growing up who has since revealed himself to be a total idiot and you worry you might be like him.

AARON: How do you...?

RON: Don't worry, he's adopted.

AARON: What?

RON: You want to be a singer, but you're afraid your voice isn't good enough so you're majoring in English and you don't know why. You're a good Mormon boy. You've never tasted alcohol, never smoked a cigarette, never even had a cup of coffee. You were a missionary in Central America for two years and loved it so much you didn't want to come home. And you're dating a girl named Marla who waited for you the entire two years. She's the best friend you've ever had and maybe ever will have. You've asked her to marry you.

AARON: No, I haven't.

RON: You will. You're thinking about it. You go to church every Sunday— not always enthusiastically—but you're faithful, and you pray, and you cry sometimes when you're alone because you think you're not worthy, and you hope that God will tell you who you are, or what you are. Sometimes you miss Heavenly Father so much you wish you were dead.

AARON: You're scaring me.

RON: You're scaring me.

AARON: What did I do?

RON: It's what you might do—what you're thinking of doing.

AARON: I can't help you. (He starts to leave.)

RON: But you can I think! There're all kinds of life, Aaron. This isn't the only one. You actually do have a choice. (Aaron runs from the stage.) Oh come on you little coward. An opportunity like this may never come again. You're not as good looking as you think you are. (Music Cue)

(Four male members of the chorus appear—a doo wop quartet. They sing as he exits.)

CHORUS:
Then say, what is truth?
Tis the last and the first,
For the limits of time it steps o'er.
Tho' the heavens depart and the earth's fountains burst,
Truth, the sum of existence, will weather the worst,
Eternal, unchanged, evermore.

(Aaron and Marla are revealed sitting at a table in a restaurant. There are dirty plates on the table and Aaron picks at his dessert, preoccupied. Marla watches him.)

MARLA: What's the matter?

AARON: Nothing.

MARLA: Liar.

AARON: Am not.

MARLA: You're mad about last night, aren't you?

AARON: No I'm not. Maybe.

MARLA: So you're gonna punish me now?

AARON: Yes. No.

MARLA: Well then what is it?

AARON: Nothing, I'm fine.

MARLA: You're not fine. You're playing with your food.

AARON: No I'm not. Yes I am. So what? Maybe I'm not hungry.

MARLA: You're always hungry, Aaron.

AARON: Is that a shot?

MARLA: What's wrong?

AARON: Something happened.

MARLA: What?

AARON: Something weird.

MARLA: And…

AARON: I don't want to talk about it.

MARLA: What?

AARON: I don't wanna talk about it.

MARLA: That's it?

AARON: Yeah. I don't wanna talk about it.

MARLA: Okay, fine.

AARON: What?

MARLA: No, fine. I don't wanna talk about it.

AARON: Fine.

MARLA: Fine. (Marla gathers up all the silverware on the table and begins to throw it across the room.) Fine. (Aaron runs to retrieve it.)

AARON: Marla.

MARLA: Fine.

AARON: Stop it.

MARLA: Fine. (She's done. He gathers what's left, apologizing to the other diners. He returns with the cutlery.)

AARON: You're gonna get us thrown out of here.

MARLA: Don't shut me out!

AARON: Okay, don't start throwing the china.

MARLA: Are you gonna talk to me?

AARON: Yes.

MARLA (Silence, and then…): TALK.

AARON: Okay, (beat) what did you think of my solo today?

MARLA: I liked it.

AARON: Do you think I have a good voice?

MARLA: Yeah.

AARON: No, really. How good?

MARLA: Good. What do you want me to say?

AARON: Could I be a professional singer?

MARLA: I don't know.

AARON: If I made records—would you buy my records?

MARLA: Yes, Aaron, I would buy your records.

AARON: Now you're patronizing me.

MARLA: I swear you make me crazy. You're determined to be in a bad mood, aren't you?

AARON: I just want to know if you think I have a good voice. Tell me the truth.

MARLA: You're not Robert Goulet, okay? You're kind of nasal, but you have a good voice.

AARON: Oh that's perfect.

MARLA: Now you're mad.

AARON: Yes. No. I'm just confused.

MARLA: About what?

AARON: Oh man, I don't know. Everything I guess.

MARLA: Are you confused about us?

AARON: No! Why are you asking that?

MARLA: Because I love you, Aaron—More than I think you really know. I can't even remember not loving you. And if you don't love me back I'm not sure what I'll do.

AARON: I love you.

MARLA: How do you know?

AARON: I don't even understand that question. Why would you say that?

MARLA: Because I'm not sure I believe you.

AARON: How can you say that? I would never ask you a question like that.

MARLA: I know you think you do. I just don't know if you do.

AARON: How am I supposed to respond?

MARLA: I'm going. (MARLA gets up to exit.)

AARON: What do you want from me, Marla?

MARLA: I have to study for my Microbiology test.

AARON: You always have to study.

MARLA: I'm in college. I study. That's what most people do in college.

AARON: I want to talk.

MARLA: I don't.

AARON: Why? (She returns to the table.)

MARLA: Cause you scare the crap out of me.

AARON: I hate when you cuss.

MARLA: Crap is not cussing, you dope. Crap. Crap. Crap. Crap. Crap. Crap. Crap. There. I'm going to hell.

AARON: Why do I scare you?

MARLA: Cause sometimes I look at your face and it's like I've never seen it before. I think you only let me see so much—what you want me to see.

AARON: I'm just really, really shallow. This is all the depth I have.

MARLA: Good-bye.

AARON: I'm kidding. I love you.

MARLA: Prove it, Aaron. (She is gone. AARON rises. RON is there.)

RON: I'm still here. (JUDY appears.)

AARON: Leave me alone!

RON: I can't. (To Judy.) I don't know if I can do this.

JUDY: I don't use your name.

AARON: Stay away from me! (AARON runs away. RON calls after him.)

RON: You don't have to be so freaked out. (After a moment, to Judy.) I don't care if you use my name. I'm just not sure if I can go through it all again.

JUDY: I understand that.

RON: No you don't. This is a crusade for you.

JUDY: What is it for you?

RON: Dirty laundry.

JUDY: I don't believe that.

RON: What do you want to know?

JUDY: I want to know what it was like to be on that campus then.

RON: The same I imagine. I can't believe it's changed much. Vietnam was over. Nixon was in trouble. But it was still completely sheltered, completely safe, completely conservative.

JUDY: What about the purge?

RON: What purge?

JUDY: When you were there.

RON: What?

JUDY: The purge of anyone they thought was homosexual. You must have known about it.

RON: No.

JUDY: They couldn't have kept that quiet.

RON: Nothing.

JUDY: My God, they were doing everything they could to catch queers. Campus security used decoys to entrap students in bathrooms. The straight kids could even get class credit for it. They patrolled the parking lots of all the gay bars in Salt Lake City for cars with BYU parking stickers. Salt Lake was fifty miles outside of their jurisdiction so they must have been pretty desperate to get the homos.

RON: I never heard this.

JUDY: Men were outed to their families, expelled—they even withheld their transcripts so they couldn't finish their education at another school. I mean it sounds like the Nazis. It makes me sick to think about it.

RON: I never saw any of that.

JUDY: How is that possible?

RON: I'm telling you I never saw it. The two students you're writing about—what happened to them?

JUDY: One was thrown out because he was seen holding hands with a man. The other was accused of homosexual activity by his roommates and was told he could come back to school when he was no longer gay.

RON: That seems like a good story. Why are you interested in something that happened thirty years ago?

JUDY: Because nothing has changed, Mr. Sorenson. It's 2000 and what happened to those two kids is no different from what happened to you.

RON: It's completely different. Nothing happened to me. I wasn't expelled. You really don't understand.

JUDY: Of course I don't—at least not from your perspective. But there are other perspectives and other understandings and you don't own all of them just because you went through it. Maybe this is bigger and more important than you. Are you willing to consider that for a minute? Look, I'm not out to get you. I just want to help change things.

RON: Ask your questions.

JUDY: How did you get involved in the experiment?

RON: I wanted it. I was queer and I didn't want to be. I wanted to be cured.

JUDY: Was that because of the pressure?

RON: I wasn't pressured. I thought I was sick, that's all. I thought there was something seriously wrong with me—something evil—and I wanted it removed.

JUDY: You weren't sexually active then?

RON: No.

JUDY: Not at all?

RON: I honored my covenants to the Church.

JUDY: So you were pretty closeted.

RON: I didn't have a closet. Being gay wasn't an option. It was a sin—an abomination. How old are you?

JUDY: Twenty-nine.

RON: You're too young to know. It was so different then. Pride and gay were never spoken in the same sentence at BYU then. People didn't even say the word out loud—homosexual. It was whispered so it wouldn't pollute the air. I was taught that the only sin greater than homosexuality was murder, and that's what I believed. How can you be expected to be proud of something that brings you so much shame? People who willingly practiced homosexuality were insane or willfully evil. No Mormon would ever admit they were gay then unless they were looking to get excommunicated.

The Seduction of H. Lyman Winger

Michael Fillerup

There were times, especially lately, when he wondered if he were doing any real good—any human good—other than keeping the Mt. Taylor 2nd Ward safely afloat and on course.

Maybe it was the weather. Monsoon season in the mountains—that late-summer jungle smell and heat. Something. Take this morning for instance. He had arrived forty minutes early for a bishopric meeting he himself had earlier cancelled. Now he had two hours to kill before putting on his bishop's face for sacrament meeting. The All-American greeter.

Time to kill? Lyman ran his fingers through his slicked back hair, more gray than brown now, more silver than gray, and sighed wearily. Nine years and still no hint of release. President Jensen had made that clear at his last stake interview: "Bishop Winger, you're an inspiration to all of us!"

Inspiration? Lyman glanced at the glossy calendar photograph of President Spencer W. Kimball staring down at him with a reprimanding half-frown, half-smile. "The September pinup," Lyman used to quip to his counselors, in an earlier time, when levity was his refuge and relief.

Two hours. He tried scanning the ward list for inactives—*less* actives: political correctness had even infiltrated the House of Israel—to target for President Jensen's new COME UNTO CHRIST campaign. Adams…Agle…Aiken…In years past he would have prayerfully searched the list until a name jumped out at him and then followed up with an immediate and impromptu housecall. After the initial surprise (shock sometimes, offense less often), more often than not the ailing member would break down and emit a tearful confession, not of sins committed but of loneliness, depression, despair. "I was sitting here, waiting, praying for something…How did you know, Bishop?"

The Spirit. The Holy Ghost. A lucky hunch. Fate.

Afterwards Lyman had always felt a near mystical lightening of his burdens, like at the end of a long, arduous hike when you finally drop your backpack and feel buoyant, airborne.

But those moments were rare now. He blamed himself more than anyone or anything. Bishopric burnout. He had grown weary in the work. The stapled sheets of paper felt like lead in his hands.

He considered writing Jenny a letter, but just the thought of putting pen to paper, or print to screen, exhausted him. Instead, he opened the Book of Mormon on his burnished oak desk and searched for random inspiration: "And by very small means the Lord doth confound the wise and bringeth about the salvation of many souls..." But the words were empty, dead. He felt nothing.

He rose slowly from the padded swivel chair, cranked open the window of smoked glass, and greedily inhaled the scent of imminent rain: fresh, clean, evergreen. A shaft of sunlight broke through the gray cloud mass like a conduit from heaven. Like a spotlight. A vision. He thrust his hands outside, palms up, gathering gold dust.

Across the asphalt fire lane, on the ground floor of the new apartment complex with the fashionable but impractical Spanish-tile roof, he noticed a young woman stretching out in front of the sliding glass door. Tall and trim, she was wearing a skin-tight Spandex suit, aquablue, that showed off in frank detail her athletic contours. Legs locked, she bent forward slowly, her buttocks swelling like a pair of perfect blue melons. As her blond ponytail dropped to the floor, her face appeared upside down in the triangular frame of her legs, like a cabaret dancer, and she smiled at him—and winked?

Lyman ducked away from the window. Had she really seen him? Traded eyes? If so, what on earth could she be thinking? Caught with his eye in the keyhole? The bishop no less! His sagging jowls flushed with embarrassment and shame.

There was a loud knock, followed by two soft ones. "Bishop Winger?" A male voice. A young baritone. "Bishop, I'm sorry to bother you. I know I don't even have an appointment, but..."

His name was Curtis Walker. Lyman would remember at that first interview a slender, narrow-shouldered young man with the dark, high-blown hair and pointed beard of a Shakespearean actor. A handsome face gone hollow. Sitting in the stiff-backed office chair, head bowed, lean legs extended, he looked thoroughly defeated. A tiny gold ring was pinned in his left ear. (Stylish: a sign of the times. Several high school boys in town wore earrings and even noserings now, although Lyman had warned his young priests that no one with face jewelry would administer the sacrament—not in his ward!) His baggy shirt drooped to mid-thigh, like a tunic. Midnight black, with shooting stars and crescent moons, it looked more befitting Merlin the Magician. The plunging neckline revealed an abundance of chest hair and a glossy purple scar that curved around the base of his throat like a pukka shell necklace.

Mumbling morosely, he told a sordid tale of big dreams and great expectations run amuck in the fleshpots of L.A.—sex and drugs and money dripping through his fingers. "Like water," he said, choking on his words. His lean, pianist's fingers, the nails chewed to the cuticles, trembled as he spoke. He balled them into fists and began pounding, or rather tapping, softly but persistently, his thighs, as if he were too drained of life and energy to club himself any harder. He wept, begging for forgiveness. "I'm sorry, Bishop. I'm so sorry."

They talked about repentance, a plan to get back on track. Fasting, prayer, scripture study. No, he wasn't ready to partake of the sacrament yet—that would take some time. They scheduled another interview, two nights later. Lyman knew he had to stay on top of this one. Sister Killearn with her chronic corns and recalcitrant teenagers could wait. ("But they don't *like* the scriptures, Bishop! They say they don't like them at all! What am I doing wrong?")

Curtis struggled awkwardly to his feet, like a cripple trying to walk, wincing as if he were in great pain. Lyman hustled around his desk of neatly stacked papers and embraced the young transgressor, noting the bony protrusions of his shoulder blades and the smell of garlic on his breath.

Tonight she was sitting in her beanbag chair in front of the TV intermittently licking an ice cream cone while folding laundry. Her knees were drawn up to her chest, her nightgown taut over her knees, like a little girl at a slumber party. She looked so perfect and unblemished from afar, like a senior portrait in which any pimples or moles are cunningly airbrushed away. She reminded him of Jenny—tall, limber, blond. The potted plants, the beanbag chair, the cinder block bookshelves. Student furniture, student stuff.

But when she held up a pair of frilly pink panties and gave them a crisp shake, Lyman looked back into his office and glanced guiltily at President Kimball's photograph.

He who looketh upon a woman to lust after her has committed adultery in his heart...

I'm looking, not lusting. Admiring. Paternally.

Paternally?

A knock. One hard, two soft.

Curtis.

They had been meeting three times a week. Progress checks. He was still praying vigorously, fasting weekly, poring through the scriptures. He was eating better as well. His cheeks looked fleshier, tinged with a healthy blush. He still wore the pointed beard, the gold earring, the magician's smock, but—give him time. Rome wasn't built in a day. Besides, Lyman liked Curtis. The young man intrigued him. Each interview he uncovered more pieces to the puzzle. He had served a mission in Ecuador, assistant to the mission president. He was an Eagle Scout. Born and raised in Kanab, Utah, where his father served on the high council and his mother taught Gospel Essentials. Why had he come to Mt. Taylor? A fresh start, new faces. No job yet, but he was still looking. Ambitions?

Curtis stroked his dagger beard thoughtfully, like a chess champion contemplating his next move. "I think I'd like to teach."

Lyman raised his brow approvingly, although somewhat surprised. "Teach what?"

"Children," he replied. Sarcastically? It was hard to tell. He was like that, or becoming more like that. Less gushing, more cryptic. Every so often something would slip out. His smile was like a piece of white thread you twist and twist until it suddenly spasms.

Lyman gave him the benefit of the doubt. "I meant what subject?"

He answered deadpan: "Tolerance."

Lyman tossed his gray suit coat on the dresser, set a steaming mug of cocoa on the night table, and plunked down on the king bed with an everlasting sigh. He loosened the stranglehold of his necktie, then his belt, reminding himself to be more faithful to the gods of Nutrisystem. Outside the wind howled as the ponderosa pines swayed like brooding dancers. Mourning women. The house seemed so quiet by contrast, so empty. Jenny gone, Nikki at her stake meeting. It must have gone overtime again. That, or she and Kathy Simpson were solving some imminent world crisis. He felt an overwhelming loneliness challenged only by fatigue.

He switched on his answering machine and waited for the inevitable. The reviews were mixed.

"I think he showed a lot of courage, Bishop. I just hope we can help."

"How could you let that young man desecrate the House of the Lord like that! Good heavens!"

"As Bishop, it's your responsibility to control the spiritual climate of sacrament meeting. Today you failed us…"

"Ex that jerk before someone *really* gets hurt!"

Lyman leaned back against the headboard, closed his eyes, and groaned: "Oh Father, what am I going to do? What would *you* do?"

Sipping the hot cocoa as if it were a slow-acting anesthetic, he recalled in agonizing detail that morning's fast and testimony meeting: Curtis marching boldly towards the stand at five minutes past noon, seconds after Lyman had risen to the podium to close the meeting; the awkward moment's hesitation as Lyman glanced conspicuously at the clock, deferring to Curtis with a cordial smile that cautioned, silently: Okay, but keep it short, please…

He had started out fine, proclaiming in a humble voice barely above a whisper that the Book of Mormon was true, God lives, Joseph Smith was a prophet. In the front pew Sister Marks had nodded her blue-haired head approvingly, along with Brother Marks and the rest of the Old Guard.

"Bishop Winger is a true servant of God," Curtis had stated. "He's a great man. A champion of the underdog."

There had been a noticeable pause during which Lyman, presiding on the stand, had scrutinized more carefully Curtis's backside. Instead of Merlin's gown, he was wearing a white Musketeer shirt with balloon sleeves and black toreador pants that hugged his tight, round buttocks like leotards. Lyman had reminded himself not to judge a book by its cover. It's what's inside that counts. The heart, not the clothes, make the man.

But as these thoughts had flashed through Lyman's mind, Curtis cleared his throat and raised his eyes to the ceiling, like a martyr burning at the stake. Like

Joan of Arc or Abinadi. "I know God loves us," he had said. "I know God loves all his children, no exceptions. The Samaritans of Christ's time were considered the lowest of the low, the scum of the Earth. Yet Christ not only loved them, he sought them out. He spoke of the Good Samaritan. Likewise the lepers."

Curtis had looked down, up, heavenward. "Brothers and Sisters, the AIDS virus is our leprosy, and AIDS victims are the lepers of our time."

Sister Marks had looked angrily ill, as if Curtis had just scratched her BMW with pruning shears. Burly Steve Burgess, on deck to offer the benediction, had blocked a cough with his fist.

Curtis had swallowed hard, his Adam's apple moving up and down like a golf ball trapped in his throat. "God loves these modern-day lepers and Samaritans. Yes, they're a little different. But they need your love and fellowship too. Brothers and Sisters, I need your love and fellowship, and I say this as a gay Mormon man, a modern-day Samaritan."

For the next half-minute the silence was so intense Lyman had thought he could hear snowflakes tapping on the rooftop. His congregation was stunned. Under any other circumstances, it might have seemed comical, cartoonish, with eyeballs springing from their sockets and jaws dropping to the floor.

One of the Lewis twins, bug-eyed among the other deacons, had broken the silence: "He's a faggot?"

The Old Guard had eyed Lyman like a conspiring Sanhedrin. *Do* something! *Say* something! Don't just sit there! You're the bishop!

Lyman had motioned to Steve Burgess to proceed to the microphone, but the muscle-bound mechanic was paralyzed in the soft theater chair. Lyman had risen, thanking all those who had shared their testimonies, and had closed the meeting himself, without a hymn.

Lyman heard a jolt, followed by the metallic reverberation of the automatic garage door opening. Nikki! He cracked open his scriptures and waited eagerly as her busy little body sashayed through the door, like a Wagnerian soprano in miniature. "I'm home!" she announced grandly.

Lyman looked up nonchalantly and smiled. "How'd it go?"

"Great!"

"That's nice," he said, returning to 2 Nephi. All these years and he still couldn't let her inside. "Any news?"

"Not really."

A bad sign. Usually she came home brimming with gossip. Silence meant she was protecting him.

"So what did you think about our little fast and testimony meeting?"

She smiled sympathetically. "Well, I'll tell you what Cindy Burgess said she'd do if one of her boys got up in sacrament meeting and said he was gay. She said she'd throw him out on his ear!"

Lyman looked outside where two pine trees leaned into one another like disconsolate lovers.

"And what would you do, if one of our kids…"

Nikki started to laugh but her smile twisted into a frown that he couldn't quite decipher. Turning her back to him, she reached behind her neck and began unzipping her floral Sunday dress. "You know, whenever I see a good-looking guy like Curtis who—well, who's the way he is—I can't help thinking, 'If he just met the right woman…' Now isn't that stupid?"

It was cold out. A galaxy of frozen stars sparkled on the smoked glass window, but he cracked it anyway, surprised to find a stranger sitting at her dinette table, a woman about her age, shorter, bustier, but athletic like her hostess. She was darker too, an Indian maybe, with a thick black braid trailing down her spine. She was wearing purple pajama-like sweats, and they were laughing over cups of something—coffee, tea? Lyman cranked the window shut, uncertain why the unexpected presence of this outsider so greatly saddened him.

"I hope that doesn't change things. Bishop?"

Lyman tried to control whatever it was he could feel happening to his face. "No," he replied, the word pushing past his lips like a breech birth. "Why would that change anything?" But mentally he tried to retract his embrace their first meeting in his office. Of course it mattered! Of course it changed things! It changed everything! He wanted to read Curtis the riot act: homosexuality was a sin. A sexual sin. Second only to murder. Like fornication. Like adultery. Worse. Much. It was unnatural. Terrible.

But pardonable? Lyman looked at the uncompromising eyes of Harold B. Lee, the November pinup.

He who is without sin, let him cast the first…

He who looketh upon a woman to lust after her…

And he who panteth after a man…?

He heard it everywhere—in the foyer, in the church parking lot, in Gospel Doctrine class.

"We're all born with the light of Christ. From birth we know right from wrong, and that kind of thing's just flat out wrong! Evil! Why do you think there's AIDS? It's the Lord's punishment against those people."

"They say that if the mother isn't modest and the son sees her naked when he's young, he'll become sexually aroused but he'll feel guilty because it's his mother. They say that's what causes homosexuals."

"We're all created in God's image. God wouldn't put a girl inside a boy or a boy inside a girl!"

Born or conditioned? Nature or nurture? The sins of the mothers! The fathers! Lyman longed for an earlier, simpler era when black and white were rigidly defined. Nowadays the lines were perpetually obscured. Hybriding tares and wheats. Crossbreeding sheep with goats.

The whole world was going to Hell in a handbag! In the big cities down south high schools were installing metal detectors to keep guns out of the classroom. Grade school kids were peddling crack cocaine on the playground. He had witnessed the horror stories on the nightly news. Long hair? Earrings? Do you indulge in Coca Cola or other caffeine drinks? Get real, folks! Sometimes even he blushed during his youth interviews.

Mt. Taylor was different. The lead story on the local news wasn't some gruesome murder or driveby shooting but the winterfest or the annual book fair at Windhover School, which was precisely why he and Nikki had fled their southern California homeland twenty years ago, an ironic reversal of Curtis's bad fortunes. To Lyman, Mt. Taylor often seemed a storybook land the darker, meaner other-world was trying to infiltrate via newsprint and TV. Some said it was inevitable, but it didn't have to be. Not here. Let the rest of the world go to pot, but not their little village in the pines. They could put their foot down—feet!—feet down! Like two years ago when a radical group tried to sneak New Age hokum into the elementary school curriculum. President Jensen had mobilized all three wards as well as several other Christian sects in town to counter the movement. Lyman had done his part; Nikki too. Testifying at school board meetings, circulating petitions, writing letters to the editor. "Brethren," President Jensen had admonished, "we must arm the Saints, especially our youth, to do spiritual battle with the adversary."

But it had always been like that. Growing up in the only Mormon family in his neighborhood, Lyman had sensed it at an early age, in every arcane ritual in and out of their home, whether Family Home Evening on Monday night or Mutual on Tuesday or Saturdays picking pears at the stake welfare farm. And every Sunday morning when Mr. Levy trudged across his driveway in his bathrobe to retrieve the morning paper, stopping, squinting, rubbing his booze-blasted eyes as if trying to erase this bizarre suburban mirage, a primly dressed tribe of nine squeezing into an old Plymouth station wagon. Like a ludicrous college prank. Like a scene from *Candid Camera*. Different. Crazy. Peculiar.

It was an attitude. Us versus Them. Mormons had the whole truth, the others didn't. God gave Mormons commandments, standards, the fullness, the higher law, and it was their duty to preserve them. If they failed, nations would dwindle in unbelief, the Constitution would hang by a thread, the moon would turn to blood, Alpha would devour Omega. Occasionally this was stated dogmatically from the pulpit by a local priesthood zealot, but for the most part it was unpronounced. Assumed knowledge. They were sacred keepers of the gate. Preservers of the word. Stewards of the kingdom. God's chosen.

Dear Bishop Winger,
    We appreciate any help you can give our son. God bless you.
        Martin and Susan Walker

Scanning the congregation from the podium, Lyman at first was relieved by the absence of Curtis Walker. Earlier he had cautioned him over the phone: "If you bear your testimony today, I hope you don't say anything that will force me to ask you to sit down. I think that would be embarrassing for both of us."

Silence. Lyman had counted the seconds: one two three four. "Are you telling me you're going to censor my testimony?"

"No, I'm just saying..."

"Yes?"

"I'm just saying what I said: don't embarrass yourself."

"Or you?"

"Me, you, the ward...the Lord."

But when the opening hymn commenced ("As I have loved you, love one another; this new commandment...") and still no sign of Curtis, Lyman was skewered by his own hypocrisy. How many times had he told his congregation church was a school for sinners, not a country club for saints? Maybe Curtis was right. Maybe they really were the modern day lepers. Christ said love the sinner, not the sin. He went amidst the liars, thieves, harlots; he shared the spotlight on Calvary with a murderer and a thief. "This day you will join me in Paradise."

Later, when the Hixon boy offered him the sacrament tray, Lyman pinched a tiny crust of the broken white bread and wiped it on his tongue, but it turned to mud in his mouth.

As snowflakes splattered on his windshield, Lyman thought of Jenny's last letter home. "BREED 'EM YOUNG UNIVERSITY," she had scrawled for the return address. Then: "The Winter Demons have come early, dumping more white graveyards."

Jenny and her melodramatics! She was lonely, depressed, but too proud to admit it. Her roommates had been keeping her up until 3:00 a.m. every morning talking about boy problems, engagement problems, how many missionaries they had on their string. "Stupid nonsense," she had scribbled furiously. So now she hid out in the downstairs lounge playing Rachmaninoff while watching the snow. Each white flake was an angel coming down, a free-falling suicide. "I guess they just couldn't stand it up there anymore. Or maybe they were kicked out for free-thinking, do you think? Nope. Sorry. I repent. That word. Not allowed here. They're just snowflakes. Or maybe the bad guys won after all and God's being cremated? Or how about the ashen remains of the Spirit prisoners? Residue from the fires of Hell? Maybe they're torching all the free-thinkers."

Jenny. She had always been a loner. Even the year she ran on the track team, between races, while the other girls were flirting with the boys or giggling in their little groups, she would be off by herself reading Kafka and Ibsen.

She had never showed much interest in boys, a relief to Lyman and Nikki during her high school years. "A late bloomer," Nikki had said. "When she leaves for college that'll change."

So far it hadn't. "Give her time. She's shy, that's all. It'll just take the right kind of guy to bring her out of her shell. Look at you!" Nikki still viewed herself as Lyman's social savior.

He worried, though. What if...Suppose...? He didn't say this to Nikki but wondered if she shared his fear. What if what? What if she was? What if she wasn't? So what if she was or wasn't? That shouldn't matter. Shouldn't was the key. What? One of ours? Of course not! It's always the weirdo down the street.

Weirdo?

He kept thinking of incidents where he had failed her. Their other children, Derek and Stefanie, had marched uprightly to the church-sanctioned drummer. Missions, temple marriages, children, elders quorum president, Primary president.

Jenny was a different number—had been from day one. The other young women had snubbed her for being vocal and rocking the ark. He recalled Sister Sampson's lesson on "Individual Worth." Mid-way Jenny's hand had shot up: "How does that make us all special, if *everyone* is a child of God? By definition, everyone can't be unique." Moans, groans, eye-rolling and head-shaking. There she goes again! The bishop's kid!

They had damned her for thinking and so, to a degree, had he.

Braking at the intersection, Lyman switched off his wipers and watched the snowflakes crash softly on his windshield. The rapid accumulation of flakes created an impressionistic picture in white lace. It was an underground hostel, an ice cave, where Curtis and the other misfits of the world huddled in secluded corners, quietly holding hands, while Jenny pounded the keys of a baby grand piano.

"I noticed on the Ward Talent Survey you marked acting and directing. And you said you attended acting school in L.A."

Lyman gripped the plastic receiver and closed his eyes, reconsidering. He took a long, deep breath. "Curtis, I'd like you to direct the ward road show."

Lyman waited through the anticipated silence.

"You'd be working with the youth mostly. The actual production isn't until April, but I need a commitment now so the kids—"

"Have you prayed about this, Bishop?"

"Of course," Lyman said, but this was another half-lie.

"Do you think they really want me—I mean, after...you know?"

"I don't care if they want you. *I* want you—the *Lord* wants you."

"Thank you, Bishop. I won't let you down. I promise."

No scriptural references forbidding homosexual acts? And just where did he get *that* little piece of folklore?

Lyman ran his finger down the *Topical Guide to the Scriptures*, shaking his head: LEV 18:22 Thou shalt not lie with mankind...it is an abomination; DEUT 23:17 there shall be no sodomite of the sons of Israel; ISAIAH 3:9 (2 NEP 13:9) declare their sin as Sodom; ROM 1:27 men burned in their lust one towards another; 1 COR 6:9 nor abusers of themselves with mankind; 1 TIM 1:10 them that defile themselves with mankind; JUDE 1:7 as Sodom and Gomorrah going after strange flesh; GEN 13:13, 18, 20 men of Sodom were wicked and sinners before the Lord exceedingly...

His conversations had been getting more bizarre, leaning more and more dangerously over the edge. Women were the niggers of the church. Why couldn't they hold the priesthood? Joseph Smith ordained Emma and Eliza R. Snow—that was a fact. He also carried talismans and crystals. He blessed a handkerchief and gave it to Wilford Woodruff—"Put this on the heads of the afflicted and they'll be healed!" Back then miracles and visions were encouraged, not snuffed out. Not like now. If it's not in the *General Handbook*, it's evil, wicked, Satan speaking.

"I mean, you realize Joseph Smith was a manic depressive?"

"A *what*?"

"It's typical of men of religious genius."

"Religious gen—"

He was a kook, a nut, an encyclopedia of heresies. He was gay for pity's sake! Yet Lyman listened to him, mesmerized. Arriving for a nine o'clock appointment, he wouldn't close up his office until after midnight. He had learned to schedule Curtis early and block out the entire evening. One moment Curtis would speak with a stubborn defiance bordering on arrogance, his hands fluttering like spastic birds: "You and your inspired programs! Look what they've done for me! I really tried to put my shoulder to the wheel. Can I help how I was born? Am I a victim of my Maker? God's little accident? If so, there are lots of little accidents running around. Lots. Lesbians, mostly. And returned missionaries—like me. You may think I'm your first but don't kid yourself. You've got others. Plenty. I know for a fact."

A moment later he would be slouching in the office chair, his El Greco face drooping, the penitent prodigal: "Thanks for listening, Bishop. You're a true friend. I know you're in a difficult position. You want to do the right thing, but you also feel an obligation to uphold church tradition. It's a head-heart, justice-mercy tug-of-war, but you'll win. You're a great bishop—one of the few I've known who cares more about people than making money."

Lyman was touched, moved—flattered? He stiffened, cautioning himself. Flattery. The devil's hammer and sickle. But the instant the seed of doubt was planted, Curtis countered as if he had read Lyman's mind: "And I'm not just saying that to butter you up. I don't play that game, although you probably think I do."

During their interviews Lyman often sensed a powerful spirit burning inside his little office. He too had questioned the superstructure of the church and its obsession with prolific mandates and large and spacious buildings. Lately there seemed to be more and more church and less and less religion. He found himself, on certain issues, agreeing with Curtis.

"You're right. We don't teach, we indoctrinate. We smother these kids with programs. My daughter Jenny..."

But following such conversations, driving home, Lyman always felt guilty of betrayal, like chicken Peter denying the Christ.

Still, Lyman wanted to ask him questions. When did he first realize…Was it a sudden revelation or a gradual unfolding? Is it like you kiss a girl and nothing happens, you kiss a boy and it does? He didn't ask. He was afraid to, although he freely admitted that he couldn't think about the act—a man and a man. It was too repulsive.

Oh? And what was so un-repulsive, so superior, about a woman and a man? Coupled. Locked. Or two women?

A man and a woman—that's how God decreed it. It was natural.

Natural? What if you have a natural attraction to the same sex? Isn't *that* natural—for you? Who's to say what's natural?

Look at the animal world. A male deer mates with a female. That's natural. A buck trying to mate with another buck would be unnatural. An aberration. An anomaly.

Then why did God create me this way? Unnaturally?

Why did he create alcoholics? Lepers? Cripples? Schizoids? We all have our crosses to bear.

A cross? To bear?

They went around and around. Lyman was trying to be open-minded, understanding—he really was. He was trying to understand *him*.

"Doesn't God love all his children?"

"Of course he does. He loves us but not everything we do. Just as I love my children but not everything they do."

"Jesus Christ is a woman. A man, yes, but a woman too. All of God's children are conceived female. One little chromosome changes us. It makes you male, female, Down Syndrome. We're all women in embryo. It's only a matter of time, Bishop. Only a matter of time."

Early Sunday morning he cracked the smoked glass window and found the ponytailed blonde sitting at the dinette table in pajama-sweats eating a bowl of cereal or something. Her swarthy friend, also in baggy sweats, swept into view and set a carton of milk on the table. She slid her bottom onto the blonde's lap, laced her arm around her neck, and gave her a long, tender kiss on the lips. They executed the maneuver as smoothly as two skilled lovers. Or a seasoned married couple who move together as one.

Lyman looked away—sickened, he assured himself. It was gross, disgusting. Yet he edged back towards the window and watched until the blonde helped the brunette up off the floor and led her gently, by the hand, out of view.

Lyman stared at the legal pad covered with mindless scribble: ovals, X's, spirals, and, conspicuously, in the lower left corner, a big circle with a carefully darkened dot slightly off-center—like a target, he thought. Or a woman's breast. No, a target, he corrected. Get your mind out of the gutter. You're the bishop.

He gazed around his office for reminders: the framed calligraphy on the far wall, compliments of Sister Newton: "Wherefore, be faithful, stand in the office which I have appointed unto you; succor the weak, lift up the hands which hang down, and strengthen the feeble knees. D&C 81:5."

It was Monday, Family Night, when good bishops, good Latter-day Saints, ought to be home communing with their wives and children. But he felt so alone in this, utterly alone. He knew it was largely his fault. The past few months he had gradually distanced himself from his two counselors, canceling bishopric meetings or speeding through the agenda. He had no confidants—not Nikki, not President Jensen...He couldn't fathom taking his petition to the stake president, the iron rodder who snacked on bitter herbs.

Worse still, his prayers had left him confounded. Grand visions fired by passionate conviction and resolve one moment clouded into mists of darkness the next. What was happening to his mind, his soul, the world? Wasn't anything just plain yes or no, true or false anymore?

Hunting was true. Absolute. You went out, you shot a deer. You killed it, skinned and ate it. That simple.

And if you didn't eat it? Killed it for sport only?

He no longer trusted his judgment or his bishop's gift of discernment. Would the spirit abide in a tainted vessel? Physician, heal thyself!

He stared at the window and saw nothing but fog and ice frothing on the smoked glass, his eyes, his life. Diverting his eyes, he tried to think of sunnier times, family days and nights. Returning home from business trips, his children swarming him like locusts, searching his pockets for candy and souvenirs, finding nothing, frowning like sad clowns: "Dad?" And just when it appeared as if tragedy had struck—ta da! A handful of Mars Bars would magically materialize in his hand, and his three precious little ones would jump up and down, clapping, shouting, "Daddy! Daddy! Daddy!"

Rising slowly from his swivel chair, he exited his office, and wandered down the empty hallway into the foyer where he encountered the glass trophy case for the Mt. Taylor 2nd Ward. The lack of championship trophies and overabundance of sportsmanship and participation certificates seemed a sad metaphor for his ministry.

Pressing closer, Lyman studied his reflection on the glass, but the face staring back seemed foreign to him. The jowls were soft and pouchy, the eyes tired and diluted, with little saddlebags drooping underneath. The delta of wrinkles fanning out from the corners of his eyes had deepened and widened, curving mournfully downward, like rows of sad, crooked mouths. The age spots on his cheeks had burgeoned and darkened, like splashes of mud. His hairline had retreated another quarter of an inch. The peninsula of salt and peppered hair that occupied the top of his skull was fast becoming an island surrounded by a moat of glossy pink flesh.

He placed his fingers on his lower left cheekbone and pulled slowly downward. The flesh grew flat and taut but the lines remained, like pencil marks. Like the irrefutable rings in the cross section of a tree trunk. By nature he was not vain, had never given his physical appearance much time, thought, or concern. But all of these, in concert, reminded him of one irrefutable fact: he was growing old.

He returned to his office and looked at the smoked glass. He wanted in the very worst way to break his private pledge. If he could crack it just a hair—one little peek into paradise might melt his winter malaise. He glared at the December photograph of President Joseph F. Smith, a sage-like face with wire-rim glasses and a long, stringy Confucian beard.

It's not what you think. It's not *why* you think.

He listened for Curtis's saving knock. The rescue.

Silence.

"I know this is hard for a lot of you. It's been hard for me. But I think—I mean I really believe this is what we have to do. We each have to ask ourselves: if this were my child, how would I want him to be treated by his fellow brothers and sisters in Christ?"

Steve Burgess, the elders quorum president, stared at his black binder while Nate Simpson, Lyman's first counselor, stroked his crabapple chin. The other members of the Ward Correlation Council, squeezed shoulder to shoulder in Lyman's office which suddenly seemed no bigger than a rabbit hutch, dropped their eyes on the pale blue carpeting.

Sister Frazier, the Relief Society president, was the first to look up. "I agree with you, Bishop."

Lyman removed the lid from the little green candy jar on his desk and offered it to Brother Zartman, the executive secretary with the pink-patched face. He dipped his scab-crusted paw into the jar and removed a handful of Reese's Pieces. Lyman motioned for him to pass the jar around.

All month Lyman had been mentally rehearsing for the debate.

"Do you believe Jesus Christ atoned for the sins of the world?"

"Do you believe God loves all his spirit children?"

"Do you consider yourself a follower of Christ?"

And all month he had listened to the voices of his pioneer forebears howling through the night. Every time he had looked at the grim ancestral photographs on his bedroom wall, his great-great-grandfather's gray beard would catch fire as he raised what remained of the arm he had forfeited to frostbite at Winter Quarters, shaking his stump angrily: I didn't sacrifice *this for that!*

Of course, Curtis hadn't made things any easier. The ward members weren't ostracizing him half as much as he was ostracizing himself. Why couldn't he just come to church and participate like everyone else? No, he had to dress like Merlin the damn magician and preach his oddball doctrine—the philosophies of Curtis! He had to make a spectacle of himself. Everything was a statement, a crusade.

"Does this mean the rumor's true? Brother Walker'll be directing the road show?"

Lyman eyed Ken Sawyer, the sunbleached Young Men's president, keenly. "Is that a problem?"

"Well, no—it shouldn't be I guess. I mean—well, it shouldn't. But maybe for some of the youth…"

"You let me handle the youth."

"I think we need to do anything we can for him," Sister Frazier said.

Nate Simpson removed his bifocals and wiped them with a Kleenex. "Well, yeah, I suppose we ought to help—like if a bank robber were shot down trying to escape, you wouldn't just stand there and watch him bleed to death."

Bank robber? Lyman tugged at his collar. A drop of sweat escaped from his armpit and crawled down his rib cage. He smiled at Sister Frazier. "Is it hot in here, or is that just me?"

Brother Burgess passed him the candy jar: "Bishop?"

Nikki curled up behind him, running her foot up and down his hairy calf, pressing her milk cow breasts against his back, cooing in his ear. Nothing happened. He tried to give himself a little help, but it was hopeless. He closed his eyes and shook his head. No. Stop. It wasn't working. She was big, bawdy, gross—*they* were. Bossy tubs of fat that sloshed, sagged, wobbled.

He closed his eyes and tried to summon up passionate nights from his past but instead saw Curtis perched on their oak headboard like a grinning Cupid miming their would-be moans and groans and oohs and ohhhs as they stroked and thrust and humped and grunted, whispering in his ear throughout: Normal? Godly? Superior? The only true and ordained way? Righteous? Once the erotic heat takes over, we're all fools, Bishop! The greatest of human comedies.

"Brother Walker, have you engaged in any homosexual activity?" Lyman tilted back in his swivel chair, distancing himself.

"Ninety percent of all males have engaged in some form of homosexual activity—if they're being honest."

"I'm not asking about 90 percent. I'm asking about you. As your bishop." He inserted a qualifier. "Since your confession."

Curtis bowed his head and stared at his cupped hands with the same forlorn look of abandonment Jenny had worn that hot, muggy day in Provo when Lyman had waved goodbye to her at the Heritage Halls dormitory.

"Curtis, I don't want to lose you," he said, quickly correcting himself. "*We* don't."

This time he had an appointment: Wednesday, 7:00 p.m. Every other time he had tried to catch Curtis at his eastside apartment the blinds had been drawn and the lights out. Once he had heard soft rock playing inside. He had pressed the doorbell, knocked loudly, called his name.

No answer.

Tonight the windows were darkened, but the porch light was on and an envelope was taped to the door with neat block letters in red ink:

Dear Bishop Winger,
    I'm going back to Tinsel Town! For good this time. I met with Pres. Jensen Thurs. night. There's no hope—none. (Not in this life.) Thanks for your friendship. You are one of the very few.
Love, Curtis

P.S. See you in Paradise.

    The quarterly youth fireside was at Sister Johnson's house. "Everything You Always Wanted to Know about Church Standards but Were Afraid to Ask." After the opening song and prayer Lyman, the guest speaker, randomly drew three-by-five cards from a Tupperware bowl and read the anonymously scribbled questions: "Why can't we date until we're sixteen?" "Is it true only Mormons can go to the Celestial Kingdom?" Although painfully predictable, he responded to each with an appropriate blend of gravity and humor.

    However, the last card he drew didn't contain the question he posed: "Here's an interesting one. 'What is the church's stand on homosexuals?'"

    The Mohawk heads of the Lewis twins catapulted to attention. "You mean queers?" Larry grunted. Terry pinched his nose: "Fairies?"

    Titters, giggles, a fake fart in back. This was going to be even harder than he had anticipated. "No," Lyman corrected calmly. "Homosexuals." He waited for the next wave of giggles to pass, then tried to explain the difference between having a same-sex preference and committing homosexual acts. The former, maybe you can't help; maybe you were born that way or maybe it was conditioned, or maybe it's a combination. Anyway, that's irrelevant. We all have weaknesses, right? For some people it's alcohol, for others it's a bad temper. Whatever. But we can control our actions. It's not a sin unless we act—

    J.D. Walters's beefy arm went up. "Didn't Christ say to think it is to do it in your heart?"

    Lyman was prepared for this one. "Yes, that's true. And I suppose if we were all perfect, sinful thoughts would never even cross our minds. But for most of us— you may be the lone exception—"

    Chuckles. Elbows. Nods.

    "You may be the exception, J.D., but I think if we were judged by our thoughts, the rest of us would earn a one-way ticket to the Eternal Hothouse, if you know what I mean."

    More chuckles. Elbows.

    "So to get back to your comment, yes, we're accountable for our thoughts, but I think we're judged mainly by our actions. It's being able to control the urge, resist the temptation…"

Gangly David Christensen in the gray turtleneck sweater pushed his Ben Franklin glasses up on the bridge of his nose and asked, hopefully it seemed, "But can a gay person go to the temple?"

David? Lyman felt a little sick inside. His legs grew wobbly and the family portrait above Sister Johnson's fireplace clouded over. He momentarily gripped the velour sofa to steady himself. Poor David who had always been so solemn and compliant during his annual bishop's interview; who prayed morning, noon, and night, read the scriptures fervently, fanatically. Plagued, it seemed, by an obsessive conviction to be good. Solemn to the point of sadness. A loner like Jenny, except he lacked her intellectual acumen for self-defense. Lyman wanted to reach out and embrace him, to apologize—but for what? David's condition? Or his own ignorance? Or was the problem too comprehensive, too complex? God's law, or his handiwork? How do you apologize for God? Can you?

"Good question, Dave. Likewise, can they hold the priesthood?"

Heads were shaking; sour mouths set firm. David waited.

"Let's go back to the previous question. Is it a sin to prefer the same sex?"

"Depends on how good it is," wisecracked Larry Lewis.

"All right, let me re-phrase that: is it a sin to have a same-sex preference? I like guys but not girls? Instead of girls?" Unanimous nods. The McCarty girl tilted her auburn head and twisted an eye; her valley girl gape. "Hunh?"

Patience, Lyman reminded himself. Patience.

"Have I committed a sin?" he asked gently.

J.D. Walters piped up. "You bet! Burn, Bishop, burn!"

"What sin, J.D.?"

"Well..." His freckled face contorted, like a parody of the proverbial dumb jock. "Because you like...guys?"

Okay, here was the knockout punch. Do or die time. "J.D., suppose you look at a girl and think, 'Wow! I'd sure like to sleep with her!' Have you ever done that?"

J.D.'s face burned beet red. "So if you never have sex...?"

Lyman smiled. They were getting it. Progress, slowly but surely. It would take another generation of wandering in the wilderness before the old traditions died out for good, but these young people—hope! Here was hope!

Lyman winked at Sister Johnson, gawking beside the potted fern in front of the plate-glass window. They'd have to hire a crane to lift her chin off the floor when this was over.

"Okay," Lyman said, "let's suppose you're a single man and you hold the priesthood. Is it okay to have sex?"

Silence. Dead dumb silence. They had turned into a forest of tree stumps. Heidi McCarty's mouth had opened wide enough to swallow a basketball. He would lose them if he didn't make his point quickly. "Of course you can't! You can only have sex if you're married, right? So what does a single person do?"

J.D., sensing Lyman's impatience, spoke hesitantly. "They don't have sex?"

"Yes! Exactly! They live a chaste life. Same deal with a homosexual."

There were vigorous nods, smiles, even a little back patting. Let's end it here, Lyman thought, on a high note. He threw in the modern day leper analogy, offered the benediction, and the young people attacked the Safeway fruit punch and Oreo cookies spiritedly.

Slipping into the bucket seat of his Pontiac Sunbird, Lyman looked up through the sun-roof at the stars and smiled. He'd done well—*we* had, he corrected, chatting aloud to God. I really think the light clicked on. And David—I've got to talk to David. Please help me help David...

Turning onto Aspen Drive, Lyman looked up at the residual moon, a silver crescent at the top of a blacked-out sphere: the mouth of tragedy. He wanted to spin the lunar wheel and reverse it, making top bottom and bottom top. Like the old Primary song: "If you chance to meet a frown, do not let it stay; Quickly turn it upside down, and smile that frown away." An answer? To whose question?

As his headlights swept across the tarnished black shell of an old Subaru wagon, a big metal beetle rotting at the end of the cul-de-sac, he felt his soaring spirit plummet from its heavenly height like a skydiver with a bum parachute. It was not the junky vehicle that brought him down but the personage standing beside it. In a white tunic, beige slacks, and white deck shoes, he was standing with arms folded in the yellow cone of the streetlight like a celestial messenger waiting to be beamed home.

Lyman pulled into his driveway but didn't press the remote to raise the roll-top door. It occurred to him that Curtis had never been inside his home—no reason in particular; they had always met at the church. But Lyman didn't want him in his home tonight, or on his property, for that matter. In light of tonight's meeting, Curtis's sudden appearance seemed an anticlimactic intrusion.

A what? No, that didn't make any sense. What was it then?

Lyman slid out of his bucket seat to intercept Curtis, who was sauntering across the pavement, his skinny, bearded, all-white image reminiscent of John Lennon on the cover of the *Abbey Road* album.

"Hello, Curtis!" Lyman tried to sound cheerful and upbeat although in truth his bowels had twisted like a garden hose with a bad kink.

"How did it go tonight?" Curtis asked. The streetlight picked the gold ring out of his ear. "The fireside?"

"Good," Lyman said. "Very good."

"That's what I heard." He flashed his know-it-all smile.

Heard? Lyman hadn't left the Johnson home five minutes ago. How could Curtis have heard? Did he have spies? Did his pierced ears stretch to China? Was he—ah, hell, of course. He was Joseph Smith, remember? Maybe he'd been God, too, in a prior life.

"It went fine," he repeated.

Curtis smiled again, but differently this time. The smart aleck smirk had given way to a tentative tremor. His wiry arm circled Lyman's bearish shoulders. "That took a lot of guts," he said. "Thanks." Curtis hugged him tightly, like a lover, like a friend.

Lyman was stunned. The stars overhead had all fallen and were swirling madly around his head like mosquitoes or runaway atoms. As he staggered towards his front door, the hidden sensors around the driveway reacted to his body heat, showering him with light and momentarily blinding him.

"That's a start!" Curtis hollered.

Lyman's hand froze on the brass doorknob. A what?

"A foot in the door," Curtis said. "One small step for a man, a giant leap for mankind."

Lyman looked back and saw Curtis nodding as if they were old allies. War vets. A light flashed on in the house across the street, like a big square eye opening. Lyman tried to smile back, but something—a hand, a claw, something fiercely tangible—gripped him by the shoulders. "No, it isn't," he muttered, fishing for his house key. Turning, hollering, "No, the hell it isn't!"

Curtis called back coolly. "Otherwise it's not fair."

"What?" Lyman bellowed. "What's not fair? You're accepted. Full fellowship. Full brotherhood—if you play by the same rules."

"Not with my spouse."

"Your *what?*"

"My lover's coming up from L.A. I'm not going to give him up again. President Jensen's going to tell me to. Maybe even you will. But I won't. I can't. You wouldn't give up your wife, would you?"

Lyman cupped his hands over his ears. No. He wasn't hearing this, seeing this. He couldn't bear to look at Curtis, his pixie smile and pointed beard. He closed his eyes and in his mind two naked men materialized, one hairy, the other smooth, intertwined like two big alabaster snakes. He shook his head, trying to blur the image.

"No!" he roared. He was angry now. Past patience, past long-suffering, past gentleness, kindness, persuasion. He was hyperventilating. He could hardly talk. Brother Hancock was right, Sister Marks was right—all of them, 100 percent correct. Give them an inch and they'll take a yard. Give them a pew and they'll take the whole tabernacle.

"What does a single LDS man or woman do? They can't just go out and—and copulate at will. They contain it. They sublimate. No, it's not easy. Sure it's hard—darn hard. But it can be and must be controlled. If you want to be a member in good standing. If you want to bear the priesthood. If you want the blessings of the temple."

Curtis shook his head sadly. He looked disappointed, hurt. "You're comparing apples and oranges, Bishop."

Lyman charged, headdown, fists clenched, reminiscent of his high school football days. Curtis stood his ground, unflinching, and Lyman pulled up short of plowing into him. They were nose to nose, Lyman inhaling Curtis's garlicky breath. "How? How is it different? How are you an apple, me an orange? You people don't want equality, you want preference! Asterisks! Special house rules."

"You've got a choice, we don't. You choose to be single."

"How do you know? Suppose I'm born a eunuch—where's my choice?"

"I'm part of God's creation. This is my sexuality, not my cross to bear."

"Okay—all right. Suppose someone likes doing it with three-year-olds or with horses or sheep or elephants. Does that make it okay?"

Curtis's expression remained neutral. A mug shot.

Lyman taunted him. "Hey, God made me that way! Can I help it? Where do you draw the line, Curtis? Where?"

"What right have you got to draw it?"

"I don't but God does."

"How do you know that's where he drew it?"

"By revelation! By the voice of God! And if you don't accept that—what's the point of being in the church? If you only accept what you think you feel you want to believe—whatever's easiest—"

"Don't you see? If so called revelation can change—blacks receiving the priesthood for instance—then God's commandments can change. They're relative to a particular time and place. It's only a matter of time, Bishop."

"A matter of—" Lyman was tired of arguing, defending, accusing, debating. He was tired. "No!" he hollered, waving off Curtis, waving off the world. "No!" all of the way back to his porch where he stopped and gazed into the little hemisphere of glass on the door. His reflection stared back at him like Jacob Marley's ghost, and he studied it as if for the first time, far more creased and pouchy and oppressed than he had remembered, like the worm-eaten portrait of Dorian Gray. "No," he groaned. "No no no no."

The Term Paper Artist

David Leavitt

I.

I was in trouble. An English poet (now dead) had sued me over a novel I had written because it was based in part on an episode from his life. Worse, my publishers in the United States and England had capitulated to this poet, pulling the novel out of bookstores and pulping several thousand copies.

Why should I have been surprised? My publishers were once Salman Rushdie's publishers too.

I didn't live in Los Angeles then. Instead I was on an extended visit to my father. After his retirement a few years ago, he moved down from the Bay Area to Glendale because his wife, Jean, teaches at a university not far from there. They own a newish house, rambling and ceremonial, rather like a lecture hall. This house, which originally belonged to a movie producer, includes a "media room," the electronic controls of which are so complex that even after five years, neither one has figured them out; a lighting system more various and subtle than that of most Broadway theatres; a burglar alarm they can never quite explain to Guadalupe, the cleaning lady, who seems always to be tripping it accidentally. The trouble may be that the house was built in the mid-eighties, when technology was already amazing but not yet simple. And because technology, like money, is measured by our needs—had she lived in our age, George Eliot might have said that—most of this gadgetry, by the turn of the decade, was obsolete. These days machines, like clothes, seem to lose their value merely with the passing of seasons.

In any event, it was to my father, and his complicated house, that I had come that fall. I had come because I couldn't write in my own house, and also because I was dating an actor: an actor who, as it happened, had gotten a part in a movie almost as soon as I'd arrived, then flown off to spend six weeks in the Andes. And as I was inclined neither to visit him in the Andes, nor to return to New York, where I had fallen into bad habits, I settled down into the life of my father's guest room, which is a pleasant, lethargic one except in one detail: because New York wakes up three hours earlier than California, when I got out of bed in the mornings, it was invariably to find faxes of a not very pleasant nature lying outside the door to my room. And this particular morning—the morning of the day I would meet Eric—the fax that lay outside the door to my room was particularly unpleasant. My American publisher, it told me, had decided to suspend publication of the paperback edition of my novel; in spite of the revisions I had made over the summer, in spite of the book already having been announced in the catalogue, "counsel" had decreed it still too dangerous to print.

There was a bad smell in the room, mossy and rotten, as if the fax itself gave off noxious vapors.

I mentioned nothing to my father except the smell. As a rule, I was trying to learn to take blows better, or at least to take them without letting them distort the natural progress of my days. So as usual I had my morning coffee at the local Starbucks. Then I drove around for a while, listening to Dr. Delia, the radio shrink. Then I tried out the computerized massage chair on display at the Sharper Image in the Beverly Center, and then I stopped in at Book Soup on Sunset to thumb through the latest issues of *The New Yorker*, *The New York Review of Books*, and *The New York Times Book Review*, as well as whatever books happened to have landed that morning on the "new arrivals" table. You see, it was terribly important to me in those days to stay abreast of what my *confrères* in the writing trade were up to. Competitiveness, not to mention a terror of losing the stature I had gained in my early youth, played a much more singular role in my life than I have heretofore admitted. Indeed, I suspect it plays a more singular role in most writers' lives than they are willing to admit. And the level of success makes no difference. The young poet cringing to learn that his enemy has been awarded the Guggenheim for which he has been turned down is merely a miniature version of the hugely famous novelist cringing to learn that her university colleague has won the Nobel Prize for which she has shamelessly campaigned: we are speaking, here, of the emotions of vacancy, which scale neither enhances nor mitigates; for panic and emptiness (the words are Forster's) always feel like panic and emptiness, no matter the degree.

After Book Soup, I ate lunch alone at the Mandarette Café on Beverly, then drove over to the UCLA library to research the new novel I was working on, which concerned the aftermath of the Cleveland Street Affair. This was a scandal that took place in London in the years immediately preceding the Oscar Wilde trials. Essentially, in 1889 Her Majesty's police had stumbled upon a homosexual brothel at 19 Cleveland Street, the clients of which included Lord Arthur Somerset, a major in the Royal Horse Guards and equerry to the prince of Wales, whose stables he supervised. Telegraph boys—one of whom had the astounding name of Charles E. Thickbroom—provided the "entertainment" at this brothel, as well as most of the evidence against Lord Somerset.

My idea was to merge his story with that of his brother, Lord *Henry* Somerset, who had fled England for Florence ten years earlier after his wife had caught him *in flagrante delicto* with a boy called Henry Smith. (Lady Somerset would later become a famous temperance advocate.) History has tended to confuse, even to fuse, the brothers, and I was following history's lead.

So there I sat, in a carrel in the stacks of the UCLA library, with an open legal pad and a pile of books in front of me, doing, if truth be told, very little. Partially this was because by nature I am not a researcher. I grow impatient with facts. And yet I cannot deny the more pressing reason for my indolence: it was fear. An aureole of worried expectancy seemed to surround the prospect of this next novel. I thought I could hear it in the voice of my agent, my editor, even my father. Would I ever be allowed to forget what had happened with *While England Sleeps*? I wondered. Or would the scandal that had attached itself to the novel's publication—to quote a helpful journalist—"taint my aura" forever? I couldn't yet say.

Thus my UCLA afternoon, like all my UCLA afternoons, proceeded. Instead of studying the "blackmailer's charter," which in England criminalized "acts of gross indecency between adult men in public or private," I got a Diet Coke from a vending machine. Instead of reading up on the Italian Penal Code of 1889, by virtue of which Italy became such a mecca for homosexual émigrés, I martyred myself to *Publishers Weekly*. Instead of investigating Florence's amazingly casual attitude toward sodomy, I investigated whether anyone sexy was loitering in the photocopy area. Finally around three, having devoted at best a paltry hour to the skimming of history books and the jotting down of notes, I left. Impending traffic on the 210 was my excuse. And yet somehow I managed, as always, to find time for a visit to the Circus of Books on Santa Monica Boulevard, where I wasted just enough minutes browsing at the porn magazines to ensure getting stuck in the same rush hour traffic I'd departed the library early to avoid. It was six-thirty by the time I pulled into my father's driveway.

Feeling rather cross, I got out of the car and went inside. Three people I didn't know were drinking iced tea in the living room. They looked at me. I looked at them. "Hello," we all said, and then Jean and my father—one bearing a platter of raw vegetables, the other a bowl of mushroom pâté—emerged through the swinging door from the kitchen. "Oh, hi, David!" Jean called cheerfully, and introduced me.

The three people, all of whom stood, turned out to be Cynthia Steinberg, a sociology professor at Rutgers and a colleague from Jean's graduate school days; her husband, Jack; and their son Eric. Eric, I quickly learned, was an economics major at UCLA who hoped to attend Stanford Business School; and as my father has taught for several decades at that august institution, this little drinks party had been arranged so that Eric could ask questions, get advice, and perhaps (this is my conjecture; it was never stated) ingratiate my father into writing him a letter of recommendation.

Now, it has actually become quite a common occurrence for old friends of my father's and Jean's to bring their children over for academic advice. And probably because I was so used to the well-heeled, eager-eyed boys and girls I tended to encounter, all of them hell-bent on making an executive impression, Eric surprised me. For one thing, he had large, placid blue eyes with which, as I accepted Jean's proffered glass of tea, he stared at me: a stare that had no caution in it. Eric wasn't exactly handsome; his nose obtruded, and he had thick, stupid lips—the best for kissing. Still, imperfect features can fit together with a mysterious harmony that is altogether more alluring than beauty. And it was this somewhat cobbled-together aspect of his appearance that attracted me: his long legs in khaki pants, which he could not keep still; his brown loafers, above the scuffed edges of which, when he slung one leg over the other, a tanned and hairy ankle was exposed; his too-short tie and brown jacket; and the hair that fell into his eyes: yes, I am back at his eyes; I always end up back at his eyes. For what took me off guard, as I sat across from him (Jean was talking about GMATs), was their frankness. They were like the eyes of children who are too young to have learned that it is not nice to peer. And Eric did peer; at me, at my father, at the garden through the plate-glass windows. His mother asked all his questions for him. He only nodded occasionally, or muttered a monosyllable.

It took me ten minutes before I realized how stoned he was.

Eventually talk of business schools dried up. "So are you living in L.A. now, David?" Eric's father asked.

"Just visiting," I said.

"David lives in New York," my father said brightly. "He's out here working on his new book."

"Oh, you're a writer?" This was Eric speaking—the first question he'd asked since I'd arrived.

"When I'm able to work," I said, "I call myself a writer."

"David's done very well for himself," Mrs. Steinberg informed Eric. "You know I wasn't going to say anything—I figure you must hear it all the time—but I really loved *Family Dancing*."

"Thanks. Actually, I don't hear it all the time."

"What do you write?" Eric asked.

"Novels, short stories," I said, and braced myself for the question that would inevitably follow: *What kind of novels? What kind of short stories?* But Eric only smiled. His teeth were very large.

"And you make a living at it?"

"Usually."

"What did you major in?"

"English."

"Great. Where'd you go to school?"

"Yale."

"Cool. My teacher—I'm taking this English lit class? My teacher went to Yale. Her name's Mary Yearwood. She's probably about your age."

"I don't know her."

"She's an expert on Henry James. Did you go to grad school?"

"No. I pretty much started publishing out of college."

"I'd really like to read some of your books. Maybe you could tell me the titles."

"Well, we'd better be going," Mrs. Steinberg said, rising very suddenly from the sofa. "We've kept you folks long enough."

"No, no." My father did not sound very convincing, however, and soon the Steinbergs were moving toward the door, where farewells were exchanged. Meanwhile I hurried into the kitchen and wrote the titles of my books on a memo pad advertising Librax.

"Thanks," Eric said, as I handed him the list. "I'll definitely pick one up." And he held out his hand.

We shook. His handshake was—everything about Eric was—long, loose, generous.

They left.

"A nice kid," my father said.

"Very nice," Jean agreed. "Still, Cynthia's worried. Apparently he's a whiz with computers—but not exactly verbal."

"C's in English won't get him into Stanford," my father said. (We had all strolled into the kitchen.)

"What does English matter if you want to go to business school?" I asked.

"It didn't used to. But then there were always too many technicians, and so what we're looking for now are all-around students with a good background in the humanities. You, for instance, my boy"—he put a hand on my shoulder—"would probably have had an easier time getting into Stanford than Eric Steinberg will."

"But I didn't want to."

"I still wish you'd applied. You could have been the first student in the school's history to get a simultaneous MFA and MBA—"

"Yes, I know, Dad."

Jean went up to her study while my father took some yellow beets from the freezer and put them in a microwavable dish.

"By the way, do you still have that stink in your room?" he asked.

"Yes," I said. "It's the strangest thing. I started noticing it after the tremor."

"Tremor! What tremor?" He walked over to the intercom. "Jean, did you feel a tremor?" he shouted.

"No, I didn't!" she shouted back. For some reason they always yelled at each other through the intercom, as if they didn't quite trust it to carry their voices.

After that I changed my routine. Instead of wasting my mornings on the road, I went directly from Starbucks to the library, and stayed there until lunch.

I wish I could say I got a little more work done over the course of those days than I might have otherwise, but I didn't. Instead I spent most of my time looking up various literary acquaintances in the periodicals index to see how much more work they had published in the previous year than I had; or chasing down those bad reviews of *While England Sleeps* that my publisher had had the good sense not to forward to me (the worst of these, in *The Partisan Review*, was by one Pearl K. Bell, whose son had been my classmate); or reading and rereading the terrible press I'd gotten during the lawsuit. Also, I looked every day to see if anyone (Eric?) might have checked out any of my books. (No one had; I took the occasion to autograph them.) After which I'd lunch, drive around, and end up more often than not (no, I am lying; every day) at the Circus of Books.

Coming home one evening, I walked through my father's door only to hear Jean shouting through the intercom that I had a phone call.

"It's Eric," Eric said when I picked up. Not "Eric Steinberg," just "Eric"—as if he took it for granted that I'd remember him.

"Eric, how're you doing?"

"All right, yourself?"

"Great."

"Cool."

There was a silence. Naturally I presumed that since Eric had called me, he would also shoulder the responsibility for keeping the conversation going. He didn't.

It soon became apparent that if I didn't say something, no one would.

"So what are you up to?"

"Oh, you know, the usual. Studying. Partying." Another silence. "So I bought one of your books."

"Really. Which one?"

"*The Secret Language of the Cranes.*"

"Oh, right."

"Yeah."

Long pause.

"And did you like it?"

"Yeah, I thought it was pretty cool. I mean, to write all that! It takes me an hour to write a sentence."

"It's just a matter of practice," I said. "Like sports. Are you an athlete?"

"Not really."

"I was just asking because you looked to be in pretty good shape."

"I swim three times a week."

"At UCLA?"

"Uh-huh."

"Is there a good pool?"

"Pretty good. Olympic size."

More silence.

"Well, I appreciate your calling, Eric," I said. "And buying the book. Most people who say they're going to never bother."

"That's okay. I don't read much generally, but I thought your book was pretty interesting. I mean, it showed me a lot of things I didn't know, not being gay myself."

"I'm glad to hear you say that," I said in one breath, "because sometimes I think gay writers only write for a gay audience, which is a mistake. The point is, human experience is universal, and there's no reason why straight people can't get as much out of a gay novel as gay people get out of a straight novel, don't you think?" (I grimaced: I sounded as if I were giving an interview.)

"Yeah" was Eric's reply.

A fifth, nearly unbearable silence.

"Well, it's been great talking to you, Eric."

"My pleasure."

"Okay, so long."

"Later."

And he hung up with amazing swiftness.

The next morning I was at the library when it opened.

I stayed all day. Did you know that Lord Henry Somerset's father, the Duke of Beaufort, invented the game of badminton, which was named for his estate? Well, he did. Also, Osbert Sitwell once wrote a poem about Lord Henry, in which he lampooned the notorious expatriate as "Lord Richard Vermont," whom "some nebulous but familiar scandal / Had lightly blown…over the Channel,/ Which he never crossed again."

Thus at the age of twenty-seven
A promising career was over,
And the thirty or forty years that had elapsed
Had been spent in killing time
—or so Lord Richard thought,
Though in reality, *killing time*
Is only the name for another of the multifarious ways
By which Time kills us.

When I got home that evening, there was a message in my room that Eric had called.

"Hey," I said, calling him back, calmer now, as well as more curious.

"Hey," Eric said.

Apparently it was not his conversational style to phone for any particular reason.

"So what's up?"

"Not much, man. Just kicking back."

"Sounds good. You live in a dorm?"

"No, I'm off campus."

"Oh, cool." (Lying down, I shoved a pillow behind my head, as I imagined Eric had.) "And do you live alone?"

"I share a house with two other guys, but I've got my own room." He yawned.

"And are your roommates home?"

"Nope. They're at the library."

"Studying?"

"You got it."

"And don't you have studying to do?"

"Yeah, but I bagged it around seven. Actually, I was feeling kind of bored, so I started reading another one of your books."

"Oh really? Which one?" (How I longed to ask what he was wearing!)

"*Family Dancing.* And you know what's weird? It really reminds me of my family—especially the one called 'Danny in Transit.' I'm from New Jersey," he added.

"Wow," I said. *Family Dancing* was the last thing I wanted to talk about. "So what do you do with your spare time, Eric? Besides swim three days a week."

"You've got a good memory, Dave."

"Thanks. It goes with the territory."

"Like that story of yours! So let's see, what do I do with my spare time." (I heard him thinking.) "You mean besides jack off?"

"Well—"

Eric laughed. "Let's see. Well, I like to party sometimes—"

"I'm sorry to interrupt, but I have to ask—when you say party, do you mean literally party, or get high?"

"Can be both, can be both."

"You were stoned at my father's house the other day, weren't you?"

"Shit! How'd you know?"

"I could just tell."

"Do you get high?"

"Sometimes."

"Man, I am so into pot! Ever since I was thirteen. Listen, do you want to come over and get stoned?"

I sat up. "Sure," I said.

"Cool."

Long pause.

"Wait—you mean tonight?"

"Yeah, why not?"

"No problem, tonight's fine. I just don't want to keep you from your studying."

"I told you, I bagged it."

"Okay. Where do you live?"

"Santa Monica. Have you got a pencil?"

I wrote down the directions.

Through the intercom, I told Jean I was going out to a movie with my friend Gary, after which I got into the car and headed for the freeway. The rush hour traffic had eased, which meant it took me only half an hour to arrive at the address Eric had given me, a dilapidated clapboard house. In the dark I couldn't make out the color.

From the salty flavor of the air, I could tell that the sea wasn't far off.

Dogs barked as I got out of my father's car and opened the peeling picket gate, over which unpruned hydrangea bushes crowded. The planks of the verandah creaked as I stepped across them. In the windows, a pale orange light quavered.

I knocked. Somewhere in the distance Tracy Chapman was singing "Fast Car."

"Hey, sexy," Eric said, pulling open the screen door.

I blinked. He was wearing sweatpants and a Rutgers Crew T-shirt.

"Glad you could make it." He held the door open.

"My pleasure," I said.

I stepped inside. The living room, with its orange carpet and beaten-up, homely furniture, reminded me of my own student days, when I'd shopped at the Salvation Army, or dragged armchairs in from the street.

"Nice place," I said.

"It's home," Eric said. "I mean, it's not like your dad's house. Now *that's* what I call a house. Say, you want a beer?"

"Sure." I wasn't about to tell him I hated beer.

He brought two Coronas from the kitchen, one of which he handed me.

"*L'chaim*," he toasted.

"Cheers," I said.

Then Eric leapt up the staircase, and since he gave no indication whether or not I was supposed to follow him, I followed him. He took the stairs three at a time.

At the top, four doors opened off a narrow corridor. Only one was ajar.

"Step into my office," he paid, passing through. "And close the door behind you."

I did. The room was shadowy. An architect's lamp with a long, folding arm illuminated a double mattress on the floor, the blue sheets clumped at the bottom. Against the far wall, under a window, stood a desk piled with textbooks. Clean white socks were heaped on a chair, beneath which lounged a pair of crumpled jockey shorts.

In the space where a side table might have been, a copy of *Family Dancing* lay splayed over the Vintage edition of *A Room with a View*.

"Have a seat," Eric said. Then he threw himself onto the mattress, where, cross-legged, he busied himself with a plastic bag of pot and some rolling papers.

"You can move all that," he added, indicating the chair.

Gingerly I put the socks onto the desk, nudged the shorts with my left foot, and sat down.

Unspeaking, with fastidious concentration, Eric rolled the joint. Much about his room, from the guitar to the recharging laptop to the blue-lit CD player (the source of Tracy Chapman's voice), seemed to me typical UCLA. And yet there were incongruous touches. For one thing, the posters did not depict acid rock musicians or figures from the world of sports. Instead Eric had thumbtacked the Sistine Chapel ceiling onto his ceiling. Over his bed hung the *Last Judgment*. Caspar David Friedrich's *Wanderer in a Sea of Mist* stared into the back of the door.

"Have you spent much time in Europe?" I hazarded.

"Yeah, last summer. I went to Italy, France, Amsterdam."

"You must have liked Amsterdam."

"I basically don't remember Amsterdam."

I laughed. "And Italy?"

"Man! Rome was amazing! Rome really blew me away!" Licking the joint, he sealed it, then picked up a lighter from the floor.

"The last time I went to Florence I tried to find the hotel where Forster stayed," I said. "I only mention it because I see you're reading *A Room with a View*."

Eric lit the joint. "Come on down here," he said, slapping the other side of the bed like someone's behind.

"I'd better take off my shoes."

"Yeah, Dave, I'd have to agree that would be a good idea."

He was mocking me, but agreeably, and, flushing, I did what I was told. Down among the sheets the world smelled both fruity and smoky.

Eric toked, passed me the joint. Lying back, he stretched his arms over his head.

"*Two weeks in a Virginia jail*," Tracy Chapman sang, "*for my lover, for my lover*." And on the next line, Eric joined in: "*Twenty-thousand-dollar bail, for my lover, for my lover...*"

"You've got a nice voice," I said when he'd finished the song.

"Thanks."

"Me, I'm tone-deaf. I get it from my dad."

"Your dad seems like a decent guy."

"He is. I liked your parents too. Have they left yet, by the way?"

"Finally." He breathed out bitter fumes. "I mean, my parents, they're nice and all, but after a few days—you know what I mean?"

"Sure."

Propping myself on one elbow, I looked at him. His eyes were getting red. In silence, I watched the way his swollen lips seemed to narrow around the joint, like some strange species of fish; the way his stomach distended and relaxed, distended and relaxed; the meshing of his lashes, when he closed his eyes.

"This is good pot," I said after a while.

Eric had his feet crossed at the ankles. From beneath his T-shirt's hem, the drawstring of his sweatpants peeked out like a little noose.

I forget what we talked about next. Maybe Michelangelo. Conversation blurred and became inchoate, and only sharpened again when Eric looked at me, and said, "So do you want to give me a blow job?"

I opened my eyes as wide as my stoned state permitted. "A blow job?"

"Yeah. Like in your book. You know, when Eliot's sitting at his desk and Philip sucks him off."

"Oh, you remember that scene."

"Yeah."

"And what makes you think I'd want to give you a blow job?"

"Well, the way I see it, you're gay and I'm sexy. So why not?"

"But you have to want it, too. Do you?"

"Sure."

"How much? A lot?"

"Enough."

"Are you hard now?"

"Yeah, I guess."

"You guess?"

I reached over and grabbed his crotch. "Yeah, I guess so too."

"Well, go ahead." Eric crossed his arms behind his head.

Untying the little noose of the drawstring, I pulled back his sweatpants and underwear. Like his handshake, his cock was long and silky. It rested upon a pile of lustrous black pubic hair rather like a sausage on top of a plate of black beans: I apologize for this odd culinary metaphor, but it was what entered my mind at the time. And Eric was laughing.

"What's so funny?"

"Nothing, it's just that…you're really gay, aren't you?"

"Is that a surprise?"

"No, no. I'm just…I mean, you're really into my dick, aren't you? This is so wild!"

"What's wild about it?"

"Because it's like, here you are, really into my dick, whereas probably if you saw, you know, a vagina or something, you'd be sort of disgusted, or not interested. But if you showed me your dick, I'd be like, I could care less."

"You want me to show you my dick?"

"Not really."

"You want me to give you a really great blow job, Eric?"

"Actually, I had something else in mind."

All at once he leapt off the mattress. I sat up. Putting his cock away, he started rummaging through the mess on his desk.

"Here it is," he said after a minute, and threw a copy of *Daisy Miller* at me.

"*Daisy Miller*?"

"Have you read it?"

"Of course."

"I have to do this paper on it. It's due next Tuesday." He read aloud from a photocopy on the desk: "'Compare and contrast Lucy's and Daisy's responses to Italy in Forster's *A Room with a View* and James's *Daisy Miller*.' This is for Professor Yearwood," he added.

"Uh-huh."

"And I've really got to ace this paper because I got a C on the midterm. It wasn't that I didn't do the reading. I'm not one of those guys who just reads the Cliffs Notes or anything. The problem was the essay questions. What can I tell you, Dave? I've got great ideas, but I can't write to save my ass."

He lay down on the mattress again and started flipping through *Daisy Miller*. "So last year my friend bought a paper from this company, Intellectual Properties Inc. They sell papers for $79.95, and they've got, like, thousands on file. And my friend bought one and got caught. He ended up being expelled." Eric rubbed his nose. "I can't risk that. Still, I need to ace the paper. That's where you come in."

"Where I come in?"

"Exactly. You can write my paper for me. And if I get a good grade, you can give me a blow job." He winked.

"Wait a minute," I said.

Eric reached for, and switched on, his laptop. "Actually I've already started taking notes. Maybe you can use them."

"Hold on! Stop."

He stopped.

"You don't honestly think I'm going to write your paper for you, do you?"

"Why not?"

"Well, I mean, Eric, I'm a famous writer. I have a novel under contract with Viking Penguin. You know, Viking Penguin, that gigantic publisher, the same one that published *Daisy Miller*? And they're paying me a lot of money—*a lot* of money—to write this novel. On top of which what you're proposing—it's unethical. It goes against everything I believe in."

"Yeah, if I were asking you to make up the ideas! But I'm not. You can use my ideas. I'm just asking you to put the sentences together." He stubbed out the joint. "Shit, you're a really great writer, Dave. I'll bet you never got less than an A on a paper in your life, did you? Did you?"

"No."

"Exactly." He brushed an eyelash off my cheek. "So the way I see it is this. I've got something you want. You've got something I need. We make a deal. I mean, your dad teaches at Stanford Business School. Hasn't he taught you anything? Now here are my notes."

He thrust the laptop at me. Words congealed on the gray screen.

I read.

"Well?" Eric said after a few minutes.

"First of all, you're wrong about Daisy. She's not nearly so knowing as you make out."

"How so?"

"It's the whole point. She's actually very innocent, maybe the most innocent character in the story."

"Yeah, according to Winterbourne. I don't buy it. I've known girls like that, they only act innocent when the shit hits the fan. Otherwise—"

"But that's a very narrow definition of innocence. Innocence can also mean unawareness that what other people think matters."

"I see your point."

"Oh, and I like what you say about George being part of the Italian landscape. That's very astute."

"Really? See, I was thinking about that scene with the violets—how he's, like, one with the violets."

"Which book did you enjoy more?"

"*A Room with a View*, definitely."

"Me too. I don't—what I should say is, I'll always admire James. But I'll never love him. He's too—I don't know. Fussy. Also, he never gets under Italy's skin, which is odd, because Forster does, and he spent so much less time there."

"The paper's supposed to be ten to fifteen pages," Eric said. "I need it Tuesday a.m."

"I haven't said yes."

"Are you saying no?"

"I'm saying I have to think about it."

"Well, think fast, because Professor Yearwood deducts half a grade for every day a paper's overdue. She's a ballbreaker."

"And what'll you do if I do say no?"

"You won't say no, Dave. I know you won't because I'm your friend, and you're not the kind of guy who lets down a friend in need."

It seemed natural, at this point, to get up off the bed and head downstairs, where Eric put a paternal arm around my shoulder. "Dave," he said. "Dave, Dave, Dave, Dave, Dave, Dave, Dave, Dave."

"By the way," I said, "you do realize that both Forster and James were gay."

"No shit. Still, it makes sense. The way they seem to understand the girls' point of view and all." He opened the creaking screen door. "So when do I hear from you?"

"Tomorrow." I stepped out onto the verandah.

"It'll have to be tomorrow," Eric said, "because if you don't write this paper for me, I've got to figure out some alternative plan. And if you do—" Pulling down his sweatpants, he flashed his cock, which was hard again—if it had ever gotten soft.

"How old are you, by the way?"

"Twenty last month. Why?"

"Just wondering."

He reached out a hand, but instead I shook his cock. "Whoa, no way!" Eric said, laughing as he backed off. "For that you have to wait till Tuesday."

"Only kidding," I said.

"Later," Eric said, closing the door, after which I headed back out into the salty night.

"Society garlic," Jean said the next morning.

"What?"

"That smell in your bedroom. It was the flowers. They're called society garlic because they're pretty but they stink. And Guadalupe picked them and put them in your bedroom. You remember she took that ikebana course?" Jean sighed loudly. "Anyway, we're airing the room out now."

"Guadalupe didn't realize it at the time," my father said. "She just thought they were normal flowers."

Jean poured some cold tea into a mug and put it in the microwave. In the wake of last night's adventures, I'd completely forgotten about the odor in my bedroom, which had apparently troubled my father to a considerable degree. "Yesterday while you were at the library I must have spent an hour and a half going through your room," he said. "Top to bottom, and I still couldn't figure out where the smell was coming from. Toward the end I was worried something had crawled into the wall and died."

"What movie did you see last night?" Jean asked.

"Oh, we didn't end up going to a movie. We just had coffee."

"Gary's a nice fellow."

"I forgot to tell you," my father said. "That other friend of yours phoned last night. Andy, is that his name? And he says he's in the Andes." He laughed.

"I know. He's making a movie."

"He left a number. I'm not sure what the time difference is, but I can check."

"Don't worry. I can't call him back now anyway. I've got to get to the library."

"You certainly seem to be working hard these days," Jean said. Then she took her cup of tea up to her study. My father started the *Times* crossword puzzle. "Younger son of a Spanish monarch," he read aloud. "Seven letters."

"*Infante*," I said. Needless to say, it worried me to imagine him searching my room top to bottom: had he discovered the stash of pornography in the dresser drawer?

After that I left for the library. You will notice that in my account of these weeks I have not made a single reference to the act of writing, even though it is the ostensible source of my income and reputation. Well, the sad truth was, for close to a year, my entire literary output had consisted of one book review and two pages of a short story (abandoned). Research was my excuse, yet I wasn't really interested in my research either, and so when I got to the library that morning I bypassed the 1890s altogether, opting instead for a battered copy of Furbank's biography of Forster. According to Furbank, Forster met James only once, when he was in his late twenties. The master, "rather fat but fine, and effectively bald," confused him with G. E. Moore, while "the beautiful Mrs. Von Glehn" served tea. Yet even as Forster felt "all that the ordinary healthy man feels in the presence of a lord," James moved him less than the young laborer he encountered on the way home from Lamb House, smoking and leaning against a wall. Of this laborer, he wrote in a poem,

No youthful flesh weighs down your youth.
You are eternal, infinite,
You are the unknown, and the truth.
And he also wrote,
For those within the room, high talk,
Subtle experience—for me

That spark, that darkness, on the walk.

Poor Forster! I thought. He'd never had an easy time of it; had passed his most virile years staring at handsome youths from a needful distance while his mother dragged him in the opposite direction. Rooms "where culture unto culture knelt" beckoned him, but something else beckoned him as well, and the call of that something—"that spark, that darkness, on the walk"—he hadn't been able to answer until late in his life. No, I decided, he wouldn't have warmed much to James, that conscientious objector in the wars of sexuality, exempted from battle by virtue of his "obscure hurt." (How coy, how typically Jamesian, that phrase!) Whereas Forster, dear Forster, was in his own way the frankest of men. Midway through his life, in a New Year's assessment, he wrote, "The anus is clotted with hairs, and there is a great loss of sexual power—it was very violent 1920-22." He gathered signatures in support of Radclyff Hall when *The Well of Loneliness* was banned, while James distanced himself from Oscar Wilde during his trials, fearful lest the association should taint. And this seems natural: fear, in the Jamesian universe, seems natural. Whereas Forster would have betrayed his country before he betrayed his friend.

I closed the Furbank. I was trying to remember the last time a boy had inspired me to write a poem. Ages, I realized; a decade. And now, out of the blue, here was Eric, neither beautiful nor wise, physically indifferent to me, yet capable of a crude, affectionate sincerity that cut straight through reason to strum the very fibers of my poetry-making aeolian heart. *Oh, Eric!* I wanted to sing. *Last night I was happy. I'd forgotten what it was like to be happy. Because for years, it has just been anxiety and antidotes to anxiety, numbing consolations that look like happiness but exist only to bandage, to assuage; whereas happiness is never merely a bandage; happiness is newborn every time, impulsive and fledgling every time. Happiness, yes! As if a shoot, newly uncurled, were moving in growth toward the light of your pale eyes!*

I got up from where I was sitting. I walked to the nearest pay phone and called him.

"Hello?" he said groggily.

"Did I wake you?"

"No problem." A loud yawn. "What time is it anyway? Shit, eleven." A sound of nose-blowing. "So what's the word, Dave?"

"I've decided to do it."

"Great."

"You need the paper Tuesday, right? Well, what say I come by your place Monday night?"

"Not here. My roommate's sister's visiting."

"Okay. Then how about we meet somewhere else?"

"As long as it's off campus."

I suggested the Ivy, a gay coffee bar in West Hollywood that Eric had never heard of, and he agreed.

"Till Monday, then."

"Later."

He hung up.

I went back to my carrel. I gathered up all the 1890s research books I'd kept on hold and dumped them in the return bin. (They fell to the bottom with a gratifying thunk.) Then I went into the literature stacks and pulled out some appealingly threadbare editions of *A Room with a View* and *Daisy Miller*, which I spent the afternoon rereading. Believe me or not as you choose: only four times did I get up: once for a candy bar, once for lunch, twice to go to the bathroom. And what a surprise! These books, which I hadn't looked at for years, steadied and deepened the happiness Eric had flamed in me. It had been too long, I realized, since I'd read a novel that wasn't by one of my contemporaries, a novel that smelled old. Now, sitting in that library near a window through which the fall sun occasionally winked, a naïve pleasure in reading reawoke in me. I smiled when Miss Bartlett was unequal to the bath. I smiled when the Reverend Beebe threw off his clothes and dived into the sacred lake. And when Randolph Miller said, "You bet," and the knowing Winterbourne "reflected on that depth of Italian subtlety, so strangely opposed to Anglo-Saxon simplicity, which enables people to show a smoother surface in proportion as they're more acutely displeased." That was good. That was James at his best. *Oh, literature, literature!*—I was singing again—*it was toward your pantheon that fifteen years ago, for the first time, I inclined my reading eyes: not the world of lawsuits and paperback floors, the buzz and the boom and the bomb; no, it was this joy I craved, potent as the fruity perfume of a twenty-year-old boy's unwashed sheets.*

That afternoon—again, you can believe me or not, as you choose—I read until dinnertime.

"Dad, are you using your computer?" I asked when I got home.

"Not tonight."

"Mind if I do?"

From his crossword puzzle he looked up at me, a bit surprised if truth be told, for it had been many weeks since I'd made such a request.

"Help yourself," he said. "There should be paper in the printer."

"Thanks." And going into his study, I switched on the machine, so that within a few seconds that all too familiar simulacrum of the blank page was confronting me.

Very swiftly—blankness can be frightening—I typed:

"That Spark, That Darkness on the Walk":

Responses to Italy in *Daisy Miller* and *A Room with a View*

by Eric Steinberg

After which I leaned back and looked admiringly at my title.

Good, I thought, now to begin writing. And did.

I dressed up for my meeting with Eric at the Ivy that Monday. First I got a haircut; then I bathed and shaved; then I put on a new beige vest I'd bought at

Banana Republic, a white Calvin Klein shirt, and fresh jeans. And at the risk of sounding immodest, I must say that the effect worked: I looked good, waiting for him in that little oasis of homosexual civility with my cappuccino and my copy of *Where Angels Fear to Tread*. Except that it hardly mattered. Eric arrived late, and only stayed five minutes. His eyes were glazed, his hair unwashed, his green down vest gave off a muddy smell, as if it had been left out in the rain.

"Man, I feel like shit" was his greeting as he sat down.

"What's the matter?"

"I haven't slept in three nights. I've got this huge econ project due Wednesday. Airline deregulation."

"You want some coffee?"

"I have had so much coffee in the last twenty-four hours!" He rubbed his eyes.

We were silent for a few seconds. Waiting, I'd been curious to know what he'd make of the Ivy, the clientele of whom consisted pretty exclusively of West Hollywood homos. Now I saw that he wasn't awake enough to notice.

"So do you have it?" he asked presently.

"Yeah, I have it." Reaching into my briefcase, I handed him the paper. "Seventeen pages, footnoted and typed in perfect accordance with MLA style rules."

Eric thumbed through the sheets. "Great," he said, scanning. "Yeah, this is just the sort of shit Professor Yearwood'll eat up."

Stuffing the paper into his backpack, he stood.

"Well, thanks, Dave. Gotta run."

"Already?"

"Like I said, I've got this econ project due."

"But I thought..."

My voice trailed off into silence.

"Oh, that," Eric said, smiling. "*After* I get my grade. I mean, what if she gives me a D?" He winked. "Oh, and *after* I'm done with fucking airline deregulation. Well, later."

He was gone.

Rather despondently, I finished my cappuccino.

Well, you've learned your lesson, a voice inside me said. Ripped off again. And not only that, you can never tell anyone. It would be too embarrassing.

I know, I know.

Alas, it was not the first time this voice had given me such a lecture.

I drove home. My father and Jean were out. Locking myself in the guest room, I took off my Banana Republic vest, my Calvin Klein shirt, my no longer fresh jeans. Then I got into bed and called the phone sex line, a particularly desperate form of consolation, to which I had not resorted for several weeks. And as is usual in that eyeless world (Andy calls it "Gaza"), various men were putting each other through panting, frenetic paces on which I couldn't concentrate; no, I couldn't concentrate on "the bunkhouse" by which one caller was obsessed, or the massage scenario another seemed intent on reenacting. Finally, feeling heartbroken and a little peevish, I hung up on Jim from Silverlake in the middle of his orgasm, after which I lay in bed with the lights on, staring at the vase from which the society garlic had been emptied; the phone, smug on its perch, coy as a cat, not ringing; of course it wasn't ringing. For Eric had his paper, and so there was no reason he would call me tonight or tomorrow night or ever. Nor would I chase him down. Like Mary Haines in *The Women*, I had my pride. He'd get his A. And probably it was better that way, since after all, the terms of the arrangement were that he would let me suck him off once, and if I sucked him off once, I'd probably want to suck him off twice; and then I'd want him to do it to me, which he wouldn't. Falling in love with straight boys—it's the tiredest of homosexual clichés; in addition to which Los Angeles circa 1994 was a far cry from Florence circa 1894, from that quaint Italian world to which Lord Henry Somerset had decamped after his divorce, that world in which almost any boy that caught your eye could be had, joyously, for a few *lire*, and without fear of blackmail or arrest. And though they would eventually marry and father children, those boys, at least they had that quaint old Italian openness to pleasure. I'd thought Eric had it too. But now I saw that more likely, he viewed his body as something to be transacted. He knew what a paper was worth—and he knew what *he* was worth; what his freshness and frankness were worth, when compared with some limp piece of faggot cock from the Circus of Books; some tired-out, overworked piece of dick; the bitter flavor of latex. (Do I cause offense? I won't apologize; it was what I felt.)

And in the morning, I did not go to the library at all. Made not even the slightest pretense of behaving like a writer. Instead I spent the whole day wandering the city. (The low business in which I got myself involved need not be catalogued here.)

Likewise the next day. And the next.

Then Eric called me.

At first, glancing at the Librax pad, I didn't quite believe it. I thought perhaps it was another Eric—except that I recognized his number.

"Dave, my man!" he said when I phoned him back. "You have got the Midas touch!"

"What?"

"An A, man! A fucking A! And an A- on my econ project!" I heard him inhale.

"That's great, Eric. Congratulations."

"Thanks. So now that you've done your part, I'm ready to do mine."

"Oh?"

"What, you're surprised?"

"Well—"

"Dave, I'm disappointed in you! I mean, do you really think I'm the kind of guy who'd let you write his paper and then just, you know, blow you off?"

"No, of course not—"

"On the contrary. You're the one who's going to do the blowing. You just tell me when, man."

I blushed. "Well, tonight would be okay."

"Both roommates away for the weekend. Plus I've got some great pot. I bought it to celebrate."

"Fantastic. So—I'll come over."

"Cool. See you in a few." He hung up.

Feeling a little shaky, I took a shower and changed my clothes. By now the beige vest from Banana Republic had gotten stretched out, and the Calvin Klein shirt had a ketchup stain on it. Still, I put them on.

"Hey, Dave," he said at his door half an hour later. And patted me on the shoulder. Eric was drinking a Corona; had put *Sergeant Pepper's Lonely Hearts Club Band* on the stereo.

"Hey, Eric. You're certainly looking good." By which I meant he looked awake. He'd washed his hair, put on fresh clothes. On top of which he smelled soapy and young in that way that no cologne can replicate.

"I feel good," Eric said. "Last night I slept fourteen hours. Before that, I hadn't slept in a week." He motioned me upstairs. "And you? What have you been up to? Hard at work on another bestseller?"

"Oh, in a manner of speaking."

We went into his room, where he shuffled through the pile of papers on his desk. "Here it is," he said after a few seconds. "I thought you'd want to see this." And he handed me my paper.

On the back, in a very refined script, Mary Yearwood had written the following:

Eric: I must confess that as I finish reading your paper, I find myself at something of a loss for words. It is really first-rate writing. Your analysis of both texts is graceful and subtle, in addition to which—and this is probably what impresses me most—you incorporate biographical and historical evidence into your argument in a manner that enriches the reader's understanding of the novels (in my view *Daisy Miller* must be looked upon as a novel) without ever seeming to intrude on their integrity as works of art. Also, your handling of the (homo)sexual underpinnings in both the James and Forster *oeuvres* is extremely deft, never polemical. And that extraordinary early poem of Forster's! Wherever did you find it? I applaud your research skills as well as your sensitivity to literary nuance.

Looking back at your midterm, I have trouble believing the same student wrote this paper. Never in my career have I seen such a growth spurt. Clearly the tension of the exam room strangles your creativity (as it did mine). Therefore I have decided to exempt you from the final. The paper, thought out quietly in privacy, is the form for you, and so I shall assess your future performance purely on that basis.

Last but not least, if you're not averse, I'd like to nominate this paper for several departmental prizes. And if you have a chance, why don't you stop by my office hours next week? Have you thought of graduate school? I'd like to discuss the possibility with you.

> Grade: A

I put the paper down.

"So?" Eric said.

"I guess she liked it," I said.

"Liked it! She went apeshit." Kicking off his shoes, he sat down on the bed and started working on a joint. "You know, when I first read that part about the midterm, I choked. I thought, Shit, she'll say it's too good, someone else must have done it. But she didn't. She bought it!"

"I tried hard to make it sound, you know, like something a very smart college junior might write. I mean, as opposed to something Elizabeth Hardwick or Susan Sontag might write."

"And now I don't even have to take the final!" He laughed almost brutally. "*Stan-ford Biz School, here I come!* You really slung it, Dave."

"Well," I said.

My pulse quickened.

Very casually he put down the joint, unbuttoned and took off his shirt. Then his T-shirt.

He lay back. What a friend of mine called a "crab ladder" of hairs crawled from his belt up over his navel to disappear between small, brown nipples.

He lit the joint, took a puff.

"Dave Leavitt, come on down," he said. "You're the next contestant on the new *Price is Right*."

He started taking off his socks.

"Let me do that for you," I said.

And did. I licked his feet.

Above me, I heard him exhale. Reaching up, I felt his warm stomach rise and fall.

"Eric," I said.

"What?"

"I want to ask you something. I know it wasn't part of the bargain. Even so—"

"You can't fuck me," he said.

"No, not that. What I'd like to do—I'd like to kiss you."

"Kiss me!" He laughed. "Okay, sure. As your bonus for getting me out of the final."

I pulled myself up to shadow his face with my own; licked the acrid flavor of the pot from his tongue; sucked his soft, thick lips.

"You're a good kisser," I said after a few minutes.

"So they tell me."

"Who, girls?"

"Yeah."

"And how do I kiss, compared to girls?"

"Not bad, I guess."

"Afterwards, you'll have to tell me if I do something else better than girls do."

"To tell the truth, I'm kind of curious to find out myself," Eric said.

Then for about half an hour, though he made other noises, he didn't speak a word.

II.

Things started looking up. My editor moved from Viking Penguin to Houghton Mifflin, which decided to bring out the paperback of *While England Sleeps*, as well as my new novel. "So it's a done deal," my agent said on the phone. "Oh, and by the way, I'm putting down a March of ninety-six delivery. Is that feasible?"

"Sure," I said. "Why not? I'm working harder than I have in years." Which was true. The quarter was drawing to a close, and I had two term papers to finish: "Mirror Imagery in Virginia Woolf" for Mary Yearwood, plus "Changing Attitudes toward Sex and Sexuality in 1890s England" for European History. Also, the day before I'd come home from the library only to get a message that someone named Hunter had called. Needless to say, I'm not of the generation that knows many people named Hunter. Still, I called back. Hunter told me he was a sophomore, a buddy of one of Eric's roommates. Could I meet him for lunch at the Fatburger on Santa Monica? he wanted to know. He had a business proposition to discuss.

Of course I went. Hunter turned out to be one of those muscular blond California boys who drive Jeeps and really do call every male person they know except maybe their fathers "dude."

"I'm a friend of Eric's," he began.

"Oh?"

He nodded. "And we were partying the other night, and I was telling him I was up shit creek with my World War II history paper, so he goes, 'Why don't you call up this dude I know, Dave Leavitt?'"

"He did."

"That's right. He said, well, that you could help me out. I mean, how am I supposed to finish this history paper, *and* my comp sci project, *and* my poli sci project, in addition to which I've got this huge econ final? Huge." Hunter took an enormous bite out of his Fatburger. "You understand my problem, dude?"

"Sure," I said. "As long as you understand my arrangement with Eric."

"I'm listening."

"I mean, did he explain to you how he, well, pays me?"

"Yeah."

"And are you willing to pay the same way?"

He crossed his arms. "Why not? I'm open-minded."

Mimicking his gesture, I sat back and looked him over. He didn't seem to mind. He had dark skin, longish blond hair brushed back over his ears, abundant blond chest hair, tufts of which poked upward from the collar of his shirt. An unintelligent handsomeness, unlike Eric's. Nor did he provoke in me anything like the ample sense of affection Eric had sparked from the first moment we'd met. Still, there is something to be said for the gutter lusts, and so far as these were concerned, Hunter possessed the necessary attributes—muscles, vulgarity, big hands—in abundance.

"So what's the assignment?" I asked.

"That's the trouble. I've got to find my own topic."

"History of the Second World War, right?" I thought. "Well, something that's always interested me is the story of the troops of black American soldiers who built Bailey bridges in Florence after the armistice."

"Bailey what?"

"Temporary bridges to replace the ones that were bombed."

"Cool. Professor Graham's black. He'll like that."

"Almost nothing's been written about those soldiers. Still, I could do some research—"

"It supposed to be a research paper," Hunter added helpfully.

"When's it due?"

"That's the bitch. The twenty-first."

"The twenty-first!"

"I know, but what can I do? I only found out about you yesterday."

"I'm not sure I can manage a research paper by the twenty-first."

"Dude, please!"

He smiled, his mouth some orthodontist's pride.

I don't know what came over me, then: a lustful malevolence, you might call it, that made me want to see just how far I could go with this stupid, sexy, immoral boy.

"All right," I said. "There's just one condition. With this time constraint, the terms are going to have to be—how shall I put it?—more exacting than usual."

Hunter put his elbows on the table. "What did you have in mind?" he asked.

"Okay, how does this sound? Just to be fair, if you get a C or lower on the paper, you don't have to do anything. If you get a B, it's the same as with Eric: I give you a blow job. But if you get an A—"

"You can't fuck me," Hunter said.

Why did these boys all assume I wanted to fuck them?

"That wasn't what I was going to propose," I said. "What I was going to propose was…the opposite."

"That I fuck you?"

I nodded.

"Sure," Hunter said swiftly. "No problem."

"Have you ever fucked another guy?"

"No, but I have, you know, fucked a girl…back there."

"You have."

"Uh-huh."

"And did you like it?"

"Well…" He grinned. "I mean, it felt good and all, but afterwards—it *is* kind of gross to think about. You know what I'm saying?"

I coughed. "Well, I guess it's a done deal, Hunter."

"Great."

We shook.

"Oh, and Hunter," I added (what possessed me?), "just one more thing. There is the matter of the security deposit."

"Security deposit?"

"Didn't Eric tell you?"

"No."

"Well, naturally I require a security deposit. On my work. I'm sure you understand that."

"Sure, but what…kind of security deposit?"

I gestured for him to lean closer.

"Do you wear boxers or briefs?" I whispered.

"Depends. Today briefs."

"Good. All right, here's what I want you to do. I want you to go into the bathroom, into the toilet stall, and take off your pants and underwear. Then I want you to jack off into your underwear. You know, use them to wipe up. Then I want you to put them in your coat pocket. You can give them to me when we get outside."

"But—"

"You don't have to worry, there are locks on the stalls."

"But Eric didn't—"

"Or we could forget the whole thing…"

He grimaced. Suddenly an expression of genuine disgust clouded his handsome face, so forcefully that for a moment I feared he might knock over the table, scream obscenities, hit or kill me.

Then the expression changed. He stood up.

"Back in a flash," he said, and strode into the bathroom.

Exactly five minutes later—I checked my watch—the bathroom door swung open.

"Ready?"

"Ready."

We headed out into the parking lot.

"Here you go, dude." Surreptitiously Hunter handed me a wad of white cotton.

My fingers brushed sliminess as I stuffed it into my pocket.

"And are you always that quick?"

"Only when I need to be."

He climbed into his Jeep and switched the radio on loud.

"So I'll have the paper for you the afternoon of the twentieth," I shouted over the noise.

"Sounds like a winner."

"Oh, and incidentally, Hunter, if you don't mind, maybe you could do it in the back of your Jeep."

"Do what?"

"If you get an A."

"Oh, man!" Hunter laughed. "Shit, you have really got a filthy mind. I like it." Then he nearly slammed the door on my fingers.

Simple as that, I became an industry.

Days passed more quickly. I got up early in the mornings, sometimes as early as my father, who was usually weeding in the garden by six. Then I went to the library. Did you know that at the end of World War Two, after the Germans bombed the bridge of Santa Trinità in Florence, all four statues of the seasons which graced its corners were recovered from the river? Everything except spring's head. Posters went up, in which a photograph of the head appeared under the words, "Have You Seen This Woman? $3000.00 reward." Rumor had it that a black American soldier had kidnapped the head. Only no one ever turned up to claim the ransom.

Not until 1961—the year I was born—was the head finally found, buried in mud at the bottom of the Arno.

Actually, I'd known this anecdote well before I started researching Hunter's paper. I'd even seen a reproduction of the poster itself when I'd gone to Florence a year earlier with Andy: heading into the Palazzo Medici-Riccardi one morning to look at Benozzo Gozzoli's frescoes of the *Procession of the Magi*, we'd stumbled on a photo exhibit commemorating the bombings that had nearly destroyed the city's medieval center. And there, amid the rubble-strewn piazzas and the women cheering the American liberators and the children in bread lines, the poster had hung, boldly American in its idioms, like the Wanted posters I used to study anxiously while my mother waited in line at the post office. Around it, in photographs, young black enlisted men—one of whom had been suspected of the theft—built Bailey bridges. If they felt the sting of injustice that must have been their daily lot in the military, their faces didn't show it. Instead, expressionless as ants, they heaved steel beams, and gradually restitched the severed city.

As I recall, Andy didn't take much notice of the soldiers. Good homosexual that he is, he was in a hurry to get over to the Accademia and see the David. And I should have been more interested in the David too; after all, he is my favorite sculpture, as well as the erotic ideal in pursuit of which Henry Somerset and his brethren had poured into Italy all those decades ago. And yet it was those soldiers—not the David—whose faces bloomed in my mind as we trudged up Via Ricasoli; to which I should add that I was in the middle of being sued then; in Italy, as it were, in flight from trouble; invention was almost painful to me. So why, at that particular moment, should a novel have started telling itself in my head? A novel I knew I could never write (and all the better)? A novel in which a young black soldier comes to Florence; from a distance, as he hammers planks, an Italian boy watches him, every morning, every afternoon...

The thing I need to emphasize is this: I never wanted to write that novel. I wanted just to muse on it as a possibility; listen to the story unfurling; drift with it, the way as a boy I used to keep up a running soap opera in my head. Every day I'd walk in circles around the pool outside our house in Stanford, bouncing a red rubber ball and spinning out in my mind elaborate and unending variations: pure plot. Sometimes I'd look up and see my mother watching me from the kitchen window. And when my ball got a hole in it, my father was always ready with his little packet of patches to seal it up.

A curious thing about my father: when, many years later, he moved down south, he gave away without compunction most of the sentimental objects of my childhood. Stuffed animals, Corgi cars, books. Yet he kept that ball. He still talks about it. "David's ball," he says, which I must have bounced a thousand miles in circles around that pool, in those days when invention was the simplest sort of pleasure or folly.

I think that was what I was trying to recapture: all the gratitude of authorship, with none of the responsibility implicit in signing one's name.

And how hard I worked! Mornings in the library, afternoons at my father's computer. For Eric's history project, I was able to cannibalize a good deal of the research I'd already done for the Somerset novel—that novel which, like the Bailey bridge novel, I was now certain I would never write. An essay I'd done in college on *Between the Acts* formed the basis for "Mirror Imagery in Virginia Woolf." And Hunter: well, thanks to that unwritten, even unwhispered bit of story, he ended up getting the best paper of all three.

And why was that? This is the thing of which, I suspect, I'm going to have the hardest time convincing you. After all, a bond of genuine affection united Eric and me: it made sense that I should want to do well by him. Toward Hunter, my feelings could best be described as an admixture of contempt and lust. Nor did he like me any better than I liked him. Contempt and lust: how is it possible that from such a devalued marriage as this, art could have been conceived? Yet it was. Indeed, as I look back, I recognize that there was something startlingly clear, even serene, about my partnership with Hunter, which no yearnings for domesticity defiled. Eric, on the other hand, I was always calling up and asking if he wanted to have lunch. He'd meet me when he had the time, which was rarely, since lately he'd gotten busy with his juggling lessons.

Yes, juggling lessons.

Sometimes I'd go over to his house and lie on his bed, stoned, while above his head he hurled three red pins, or three sticks, or three white balls. Only the occasional "shit" or "fuck" interrupted his quiet, huffing focus. A ball bounced toward the window, or the pins clattered. Then he picked up the pins and started fresh, as the dense odor of his sweat claimed the room.

He said he was hoping to get good enough to juggle on weekends for extra cash. He said he was working up to fire.

And need I mention that those evenings never evolved into the erotic? Of course one hoped. Yet Eric was scrupulous, and—more to the point—not that interested. Sex with me, to his view, was a reward for a job well done.

With Hunter, by contrast, sex was payment for services rendered. I hope I've made the distinction clearly.

And of course he got his A. I learned only from Eric, who'd gotten A's too and called me up before Christmas break to whoop about it. "Hasn't Hunter told you?" he asked when I inquired, and when I said no, went silent. Then I tried to phone Hunter, but he was never at home. This didn't surprise me, betrayal being the usual result when one starts making gentleman's agreements with people who are not gentlemen.

Anyway, what more should I have expected from a boy who buys a term paper, then tries to pass it off as his own?

In the end I had to track him down at the UCLA pool. Dripping chlorine, the golden hair on his chest made my mouth water. I wanted to drink him.

"Hey, I've been meaning to call you," he said as he toweled himself.

"I've been trying to call you too. You're never home."

"Sorry about that, dude. I've been busy. By the way, my professor really loved that paper! I appreciate it."

"No problem."

He dried under his arms.

"So anyway, the reason I'm here, Hunter, is that I'd like to know when you intend to fulfill your half of the bargain."

"Softer, your voice carries!"

"What, you don't want any of your friends to know I wrote your paper for you?"

"Softer!" He pushed me into a corner. "Look," he said, his whisper agitated, "it'll have to be after I'm back from break. Right now I'm too busy."

"No, it'll have to be before you leave for break. Didn't your mother teach you it's never a good idea to put things off?" I patted him on the arm. "Tell you what, why don't you come over to my dad's place tomorrow around noon? He's away for the weekend. We can put the Jeep in the garage."

"The Jeep!"

"You did get an A, Hunter."

"But I—"

"What, you thought I was just going to write that paper for nothing? Uh-uh. You be there at noon."

I gave him my address, after which he limped off toward the showers.

He was not a bad kid, really. It was just part of his affably corrupt nature to try to get away with things. Of such stuff as this are captains of industry made.

Probably the aspect of this story that puzzles me most, as I look back, is how word of my "availability" circulated so quickly through the halls and dormitories of UCLA those next months. I don't mean that it became common knowledge among the student body that David Leavitt, novelist, was available to write term papers for good-looking male undergraduates; no articles appeared in *The Daily Brain*, or graffiti (so far as I am aware) on bathroom walls. Still, in a controlled way, news got out, and as the spring quarter opened, no less than five boys called me up with papers to be written. And how had they gotten my number in the first place? I tried to imagine the conversations that had taken place: "Shit, Eric, I don't know how I'm supposed to finish this paper on 'Ode to a Grecian Urn' by Friday." "Why don't you call up Dave Leavitt? He'll do it for you if you let him give you a blow job." "A blow job, huh? Sounds great. What's his number?"

Or perhaps the suggestion was never so direct. Perhaps it was made in a more discreet language, or a more vulgar one. The latter, I suspect. In fact I'm sure that at some point all the boys, even Eric, made rude, humiliating remarks about me, called me "faggot" or "cocksucker," then qualified those (to them) insults by adding that I was "still a basically decent guy." Or some such proviso.

Business got so good, I started turning down offers, either because I was overworked, or because the boy in question, when I met him, simply didn't appeal to me physically, in which case I would apologize and say that I couldn't spare the time. (I hated this part of the job, but what could I do? Profit was my motive, not charity. I never gave anything for which I didn't get something back.

You'd think I *had* gone to business school.)

All told, I wrote papers for seven boys—seven boys toward most of whom I felt something partway between the affection that ennobled my friendship with Eric and the contempt that characterized my dealings with Hunter. The topics ranged from "The Image of the Wanderer in English Romantic Poetry" to "The Fall of the Paris Commune" to "Child Abandonment in Medieval Italy" to "Flight in Toni Morrison's *Song of Solomon*" to "Bronzino and the Traditions of Italian Renaissance Portraiture."

Of these boys, and papers, the only other one I need to tell you about is Ben.

Ben got in touch with me around midterm of the spring quarter. "Mr. Leavitt?" he said on the phone. "My name's Ben Hollingsworth. I got your number from Tony Younger."

"Oh?"

"Yes. He told me to call you. He said you might…that we could—"

"Relax. There's no need to be nervous."

"Thanks. I'm really…I don't know where to start."

"Why don't we meet?" I offered, my voice as honeyed and professional as any prostitute's. "It's always easier to talk in person."

"Where?"

I suggested the Ivy, only Ben didn't want to meet at the Ivy—or any other public place, for that matter. Instead he asked if he could pick me up on the third floor of the Beverly Center parking lot, near the elevators. Then we could discuss things in his car.

I said that was fine by me.

We rendezvoused at ten-thirty the next morning. It was unusually chilly out. Ben drove a metallic blue Honda, the passenger door to which was dented. "Mr. Leavitt?" he asked as he threw it open.

"In the flesh."

I climbed in. Altogether, with his carefully combed black hair and short-sleeve button-down shirt (pen in breast pocket), he reminded me of those Mormon missionary boys you sometimes run into in the European capitals, with badges on their lapels that say "Elder Anderson" or "Elder Carpenter." And as it turned out, the association was prophetic. Ben *was* a Mormon, as I soon learned, albeit from Fremont, California, not Utah. No doubt in earlier years he'd done the very same European "service," handing out pamphlets to confused homosexual tourists who'd thought he might be cruising them.

"I really appreciate your taking the time to see me, Mr. Leavitt," he began as I put on my seat belt.

"Call me David."

"I'd feel more comfortable calling you Mr. Leavitt."

"Okay, whatever. And what should I call you?"

"Ben."

"Ben. Fine. Anyway, it's no problem."

We headed out of the parking lot. "I just want to make one thing clear," he said. "I want you to know that I've never cheated on anything in my life. Not a test, not a paper. And I've never stolen anything either. I don't drink, I've never used drugs. I'm a clean liver, Mr. Leavitt. I've had the same girlfriend since I was fifteen. And now here I am driving with you, and we're about to enter into an unholy alliance— at least I hope we are, because if we don't, my GPA will go below 3.5 and I need higher than that to get into a good law school. I'm so desperate that I'm willing to do things I'll be ashamed of for the rest of my life. You, I don't know if you're ashamed. It's none of my business."

We turned left onto San Vicente. "Probably not," I said.

"No. And it must sound terrible to you, what I'm suggesting. Still, the way I see it, there's no alternative because one day I'm going to have a family to support, and I've got to be ready. Most of these other guys, they've got rich parents to fall back on. I don't. And since I'm also not black or in a wheelchair or anything, it's that much more difficult. Do you hear what I'm saying? I don't really have any choice in the matter."

"You always have a choice, Ben."

Opening the window, he puffed out a visible sigh. Something in his square, scrubbed, slightly acned face, I must admit, excited me. His cock, I imagined, would taste like Dial soap. And yet even as Ben's aura of clean living excited me, his shame shamed me. After all, none of the other boys for whom I'd written papers had ever expressed the slightest scruple about passing off my work as their own; if anything, it was the sex part, the prostitutional part, that made them flinch. Which, when you came to think about it, was astounding: as if the brutal exigencies of the marketplace had ingested whole, in each of them, all shopworn, kindergarten notions of right and wrong.

In Ben, on the other hand, those same kindergarten notions seemed to exert just enough pressure to make him worry, though not quite enough to make him change his mind.

"So what's the class?" I asked.

"Victorian History."

"And the assignment?"

"Are you saying you'll do it?"

"You'll have to tell me what the assignment is first."

"Jack the Ripper," Ben said.

"Really? How funny. I was just reading about him."

"You were?"

"Yes. Apparently a lot of people thought he was Prince Eddy, Queen Victoria's grandson and the heir to the throne. Since then that's pretty much been disproven, though."

"Wow," Ben said. "That might be an interesting angle to take...if you're interested. Are you interested? I hope you are, because if you're not I'll have to figure out something else, and buying a term paper with cash is something I just can't afford right now."

"Ben, slow down for a second. I have to say, this whole situation worries me. Are you sure you know what you're getting yourself into?"

"Do you mean do I understand what I'll have to do in exchange? Of course! Tony told me, I'll have to let you—you know—perform oral sex on me. And no, I can't pretend I'm comfortable with it. But I'm willing. Like I said, I have this girlfriend, Jessica. I've never cheated on her, either."

We stopped at a red light, where Ben opened his wallet. From between fragile sheets of plastic, a freckled girl with red hair smiled out at us.

"Very pretty," I said.

"She will be the mother of my children," Ben said reverently.

Then he put the picture away, as if continued exposure to my gaze might blight it.

The light changed.

"Of course, if you say no because I'm not so good-looking as Tony, well, there's nothing I can do about that. Still, I do have rather a large penis. I understand homosexuals like large penises. Is that true?"

"Sometimes." Laughing, I patted his knee. "Look, you know what I think? I think *you* should write your paper. And I'll read it over for you, how does that sound? Free of charge, as it were. And if you do get a C in history, well, so what? It won't matter in the long run. And meanwhile you won't have cheated on Jessica, or compromised your ethics."

"But I'm fully prepared to compromise my ethics." Ben's voice grew panicked. "Also the security deposit. Tony told me about that too, and I've already taken care of it. Look."

Reaching across my lap, he opened the glove compartment. A bleachy odor of semen wafted from the opening.

Pulling out a pair of rumpled boxer shorts, Ben tossed them into my lap.

"When did you do this?" I asked, caressing slick cotton.

"Just now. Just before I picked you up." He grinned. "So what do you say, Mr. Leavitt? Will you do it?"

"All right." My mouth was dry.

"That's great. That's terrific."

He turned onto Saturn Street.

I wiped my fingertips on my jeans.

As I'd told Ben, I already knew a little about Jack the Ripper. This was because Prince Eddy, whose candidature for the post "Ripperologists" were forever bandying about, stood also at the center of the Cleveland Street scandal. Indeed, several historians believed that Lord Somerset had fled England primarily to take the heat off Eddy (also a regular client at the brothel) as a favor to his old friend and protector the prince of Wales.

It would have been interesting, I thought, to write a paper linking Prince Eddy's homosexuality with the hatred of the female body that seemed to have been such a motivating element in the Ripper crimes. Unfortunately, fairly hard proof existed that Eddy had been off shooting in Scotland on the date of two of the murders, and since Ben's assignment was to make a strong case for one suspect or another, I decided I'd better look elsewhere. M. J. Druitt, a doctor whose body was found floating in the Thames about seven weeks after the last murder, was certainly the candidate toward whom most of the evidence pointed. Yet for this reason, it seemed likely that many of Ben's classmates would argue for Druitt.

Who else then? Among the names that came up most frequently were those of Frank Miles, with whom Oscar Wilde had once shared a house; Virginia Woolf's cousin James Stephen, who had been Eddy's tutor; the painter Walter Sickert; and Queen Victoria's private physician, Sir William Gull. Indeed, a large percentage of the suspects seemed to have been physicians, which is no surprise: to disembowel a woman's body as precisely as the Ripper did that of Mary Kelly, you would have to possess a detailed knowledge of human anatomy. And if Donald Rumbelow is correct in proposing that the Ripper's weapon was a postmortem knife "with a thumbgrip on the blade which is specifically designed for 'ripping' upwards," the evidence that he was a medical man appears even stronger.

So: the Ripper as doctor, or anti-doctor. As far as this "angle" went, the argument that intrigued me the most came from someone called Leonard Matters, who in 1929 had published a book claiming that the Ripper was in fact a "Dr. Stanley." His brilliant young son having died of a venereal infection after traveling to Paris with a prostitute named Mary Kelly, this good doctor (according to Matters's theory) had gone mad and started scouring the alleys of Whitechapel, bent on revenging himself not only against Mary Kelly, but prostitutes in general.

A second possibility was to talk about class. This struck me as an interesting if somewhat experimental approach because regardless of who actually committed the crimes, the Victorian imagination—of which gossip is the strongest echo—associated Jack almost obsessively with Buckingham Palace. If he was not a member of the royal family, then he was someone close to the royal family, some mad failure of stately blood who would periodically troll the streets of East London in search of whores to murder and eviscerate. And couldn't that be looked upon as an allegory for the exploitation of the working classes by the upper classes through history? A Marxist argument proposed itself. After all, as victims Jack chose exclusively prostitutes of an extremely degraded type: older women, alcoholic, with too many children and no qualms about lifting their petticoats in a squalid alley to pay for a drink. To write about the Ripper as a personification of the bourgeoisie's contempt for the workers would certainly provide a provocative twist on the assignment. Or perhaps such a twist would be *too* provocative, especially coming from a boy like Ben.

A third possibility was to talk about xenophobia: for if the Ripper suspects could be categorized, then the last rough category (after doctors and aristocrats) was immigrants.

And as I mulled over each of these angles, the one thing I could not get out of my mind was a police photograph I'd seen of the corpse of Mary Kelly, the last of Jack's victims and the only one to be killed in her room. Her body had been found on the bed, quite literally split down the middle. The nose had been cut off, the liver sliced out and placed between the feet. The kidneys, breasts, and the flesh from the thighs had been dumped on the bedside table, and the hand inserted into the stomach.

Even in my own epoch of serial killers and snuff films, of Charles Manson and Jeffrey Dahmer, I'd never seen anything quite like that.

Three days passed in research. Each morning I'd wake vowing to conclude the afternoon with a decision, and each afternoon I'd go home having failed. Then only a week remained before Ben's paper was due, and I hadn't even started writing. It felt as if something had seized up in me, the way the screen of a computer will sometimes freeze into immobility. Nor did it help when Ben stopped by my carrel one afternoon to give me a book I'd already read and returned. "It's called *The Identity of Jack the Ripper*," he said. "And according to this guy, at first they thought the Ripper was a Polish barber who went by the name of George Chapman, but then they found out that he had a double, a *Russian* barber, and that this double—"

"Also sometimes used the name Chapman. I know."

"Oh, you've already read it? Well, never mind, then. I just thought in case you hadn't—"

"Thanks."

"Say, you want a Seven-Up or something?"

I said why not.

We repaired to the vending machines, then taking our drinks outside, sat on a bench in the library courtyard. It was a warm spring day, better than most only in that the air was unusually clear. A breeze even seemed to carry the scent of mountains.

For a time the only noise in that courtyard, aside from the buzz of yellow jackets, was the pop of our drink cans opening. Then Ben said, "Strange, all this."

"What?"

"Just…our sitting together."

"Why?"

"I'm not sure quite how to explain. You see, in the church—did I tell you I'm a Mormon?"

"No."

"Well, in the church we have this very clear-cut conception of sin. And so I always assumed that if I ever committed a really big sin, like we're doing now…I don't know, that there'd be a clap of thunder and God would strike me dead or something. Instead of which we're sitting here in this courtyard and the sun's shining. The grass is green."

"But what's the sin?"

"You know. Cheating."

"Is cheating really a sin?"

"Of course. It's part of lying."

"Well," I said, "then maybe the fact that the sun's shining and the grass is green means God doesn't really care that much. Or maybe God doesn't exist."

Ben's face convulsed in horror.

"Just a possibility," I added.

Ben leaned back in disillusion. "So you're an atheist," he said. "I suppose I should have expected it. I suppose I should have guessed that most homosexuals would be atheists."

"Oh, some homosexuals are very religious. In fact, it wouldn't surprise me to find out one or two were actually Mormons."

"Ex-Mormons."

"A lot more than two of those. But to get back to what you were saying, I wouldn't call myself an atheist. Instead I'd say I'm a skeptical lapsed Jew, distrustful of dogma."

"Tony's Jewish too. Last night he was telling me about his circumcision—"

"His *bris*."

"—and how in Israel they use the foreskins to make fertility drugs." He shook his head in wonder.

"Are you circumcised, Ben?"

"No, actually." Blushing, he checked his watch.

We got up and walked toward the library. "Well, back to the salt mines," Ben said at the main doors. "By the way, I hope you realize I'm working my butt off too. I really bit off more than I could chew this quarter."

"Oh, I'll bet you can chew more than you think."

"Probably. Still, I wanted to make sure you knew. I mean, I wouldn't want you thinking that the whole time you were sweating out this paper, I was playing pinball or something." He wiped his nose. "By the way, have you decided who did it yet?"

"Not yet. The problem is, everyone has a different theory about the Ripper, and every theory has a hole in it." Which was true. Indeed, looked at collectively, the theories ramified so far afield that the actual murders began to seem beside the point. For if you believed them all, then the Ripper was Prince Eddy *and* Walter Sickert. The Ripper was Frank Miles *and* M. J. Druitt *and* Sir William Gull. The Ripper was an *agent provocateur* sent by the Russian secret police to undermine the reputation of their London brethren. The Ripper was a Jewish *shochet*, or ritual slaughterer, suffering from a religious mania. The Ripper was a high-level conspiracy to squelch a secret marriage between Prince Eddy and a poor Catholic girl. The Ripper was Jill the Ripper, an abortionist betrayed by a guilt-ridden client and sent to prison, and therefore bent on avenging herself on her own sex.

Not to mention the black magician and the clique of Freemasons and (how could I forget him?) Virginia Woolf's cousin (and possibly Prince Eddy's lover), the handsome, demented James Stephen.

But which one? Or all of them?

Saying goodbye to Ben, I returned to my carrel. As it happened I'd left the photograph of Mary Kelly's corpse lying open on the desk. And how curious! As I sat down, that "butcher's shambles" no longer made me nauseated. Perhaps one really can get used to anything.

And upon this degraded body of the late nineteenth century, I thought, *some real demon swooped, ransacking its cavities like a thief in search of hidden jewels, and finding instead only a panic, an emptiness, a vacancy.*

But what demon? Who?

I looked up.

Modernism and espionage, Diaspora and homosexuality, religious mania and anti-Semitism and most vividly—to me most vividly—desire and disease, gruesomely coupled.

"Fantastic," I said. For all at once—sometimes inspiration really is all at once—I saw who Ben's Ripper had to be.

The Ripper was the spirit of the twentieth century itself.

I worked fast those next days, faster than I'd ever worked on anything else. Looking back, I see that the pleasure I experienced as I wrote that paper lay in its contemplation as a completed object, like the Bailey bridge novel I was sure I would never begin. Or a Bailey bridge, for that matter. Bank to bank I built, and as

I did a destination, a connection, neared. It was the same end I'd hoped to reach in my Somerset book: a sort of poeticization of that moment when the soul of my own century, the soul of vacancy itself, devoured the last faithful remnants of an age that had believed, almost without question, in presences.

After that, from the unholy loins of Jack the Ripper, whole traditions of alienation had been spilled, of which I was merely one exemplary homunculus. Eric was another. Eric with his cheerful, well-intentioned immorality. And Hunter. Even Ben. We were the nightmare Mary Kelly had dreamed the night she was murdered.

I finished, to my own surprise, three days early. That same afternoon my agent called. "Congratulate me," I said. "I've just done the best work of my life."

"Congratulations," Andrew said. "Now when do I get to see pages?" To which request I responded, rather unconvincingly, "Soon."

How could I have explained to him that the only thing that made it possible for me to write those pages was the knowledge that they would never bear my name?

I called Ben. He sounded happy and surprised at my news, and as before we arranged to meet on the third floor of the Beverly Center parking lot.

He was waiting in his car when I pulled up. "Nice to see you, Mr. Leavitt," he said.

"Nice to see you too, Ben." I climbed in. "Beautiful day, isn't it?"

"Mm." He was staring expectantly at my briefcase.

"Oh, the paper," I said, taking it out and handing it to him.

"Great," Ben said. "Let's go up to the roof and I'll read it."

"Read it?"

"What, you think I'm going to turn in a paper I haven't read?" He shook his head in wonderment, then inserting the key in the ignition, drove us up into sunlight. To be honest, I was a little surprised: after all, none of the other boys for whom I'd written had ever felt the need to verify the quality of my work. (Then again none of the other boys had been remotely scrupulous in the second sense of the word, either.) Still, I couldn't deny Ben the right to look over something that was going to be turned in under his name; in addition to which the prospect of seeing his astounded face as he reached the end of my last paragraph did rather thrill me; even in such a situation as this, I still had my writer's vanity. So I sat there, my ripper's eyes fixed on the contoured immensity in his polyester slacks, and only balked when he took a pen from his shirt pocket and crossed out a line.

"What are you doing?"

"I just think this sentence about Druitt is a bit redundant. Look."

I looked. It was redundant.

"But you can't turn in a paper all marked up like that!"

"What, you thought I was going to turn in this copy? Are you kidding? No way! I'll type it over tonight on my own computer."

He returned to his reading. Periodically he jotted a note in the margin, or drew a line through a word or phrase. All of which made me so nervous, he might have been Michiko Kakutani sitting in the next seat, reviewing one of my novels while I watched.

Finally Ben put the paper down.

"Well?" I said.

"Well…" He scratched his head with his pen. "It's very interesting, Mr. Leavitt. Very…imaginative. The only thing is, I'm not sure it answers the assignment."

"How so?"

"The assignment was to make a case for someone or other being Jack the Ripper. And basically, what you're saying is that it doesn't matter. That any of them, or all of them, could have been Jack the Ripper."

"Exactly."

"But that's not what Professor Robinson asked for."

I spread my hands patiently on my lap. "I understand what's worrying you, Ben. Still, try to think about it this way. You have a murder mystery, right? A whodunit. Only there's no clear evidence that any one person did it. So the B student thinks, I'll just make a case for the most likely suspect and be done with it. But the A student thinks, More is going on here than meets the eye. The A student thinks, I've got to use this as an opportunity to investigate a larger issue."

"I can see all that. Still, this stuff about twentieth-century modernism—I have to be honest with you, Mr. Leavitt, to me it sounds a little pretentious."

"Pretentious!"

"I mean, very intelligent and all. Only the spirit of twentieth-century modernism—that can't hold a knife. That can't strangle someone. And so I'm afraid Professor Robinson will think it's—I don't know—off-the-wall."

Clearly Ben had the limited vision of the B student.

"Well, I'm sorry you're disappointed," I said.

"Oh, I'm not disappointed exactly! It just wasn't what I expected."

"Fine. Then I'll go home this afternoon and rewrite it. You just have to tell me who you think actually did do it—"

"Mr. Leavitt—"

"Was it M. J. Druitt, or James Stephen, or Dr. Pedechenko? Or how about Jill? It could have been Jill."

Ben was silent.

Then: "Mr. Leavitt, you can't blame me for being worried. A lot rests on this paper for me. You, you've got nothing to lose."

Was that true?

"And *you* don't risk expulsion if you get caught."

"Well, naturally, and that's exactly why I'm offering to rewrite it." (My anger had dissipated.) "After all, Ben, you're the customer, and the customer's—"

"Do you have to make it sound so…commercial?"

"Isn't it?"

"I'm not sure," Ben said. "I never have been."

Once again he took out his pen. From the bottom of his breast pocket, I noticed, a tear-shaped blue ink stain seeped downward. "You must have put your pen away without the cap," I said.

"Did I? I guess. I do it all the time."

"Me too."

With my forefinger, I stroked the stain. Ben's breathing quickened.

"Look," he said, "about the paper. You don't have to rewrite it. I mean, if I didn't appreciate it, it probably says more about me than about you, right?"

"Not necessarily—"

"And anyway, I didn't come to you to get a B paper, I came to you to get an A paper. And if I don't recognize an A paper when I see one, all that points up are my limitations."

"Maybe." I moved my finger downward, to brush the cleft of his chest. "Or maybe it only points up the fact that I have a wider experience of these things. Remember, I've never gotten anything less than an A on a paper in my life—for myself or anyone else."

"Mr. Leavitt, please don't touch me like that. Someone might see us."

"I'm sorry." I took my hand away.

"Thank you," Ben said, clearing his throat. "And now I guess I owe you something, don't I?"

"Oh, don't worry about that. For that let's just wait until you get your grade. Then we can—"

"No, I'd rather get it over with, if you don't mind. Not have it hanging over my head." He played with his collar. "Obviously we can't do it here. Where can we do it?"

"My dad's place," I said swiftly. "He and his wife are in Singapore."

Without a word, Ben switched on the ignition and drove me back to my car. "Follow me," I said, and he did, down Santa Monica to Cahuenga and Barham, then onto the 134, the flat, trafficked maze of the Inland Empire.

Around one-thirty we pulled into my father's garage. "Come on in," I said, switching off the burglar alarm. "Make yourself at home. You want to take a swim in the pool first?"

"I didn't bring a suit."

"You don't need one. No one will see you but me."

"Actually," Ben said, "I'd rather just—you know—get down to business, if that's all right with you."

"Fine," I said. "It's this way." And we headed together down the long corridor into my bedroom.

"This is nice."

"Thanks. It's not really mine. Just the guest room. But I try to put in some personal touches when I'm here. That little painting, for instance. My friend Arnold Mesches did it."

"What is it, a turkey?"

"A portrait of a turkey."

"That's funny."

I took off my shoes. "By the way, would you rather I leave the lights on or off?"

"Off."

"All cats are gray in the dark, right? All right, then, why don't you just...take your clothes off and lie down on the bed. And I'll be back in a minute."

"Okay."

Like a discreet masseur, I stepped into the bathroom, where I brushed my teeth and got out some condoms. Then I walked back in. Ben was sitting naked on the edge of the bed, shivering a little.

"Are you cold?" I asked.

He shook his head.

"Wow," I said, sitting down next to him. "Lucky I've got extra-large condoms."

He wrapped his arms around his chest. "Mr. Leavitt, you embarrass me when you say things like that."

"Look, Ben," I said, trying to sound paternal, "I've been thinking about it, and if you don't want to—"

"No, it's okay."

"But it's also okay if you don't want to. I mean, you can still have the paper. Don't tell Tony, though." I winked.

"What's his like?" Ben's voice was surprisingly urgent.

"Tony's? Oh. Fine. Smaller than yours, of course."

"Straight or curved?"

"Straight."

"The other night he was telling me that in his fraternity, they take the pledges and shave their balls."

"Yeah?"

"If they pass out from too much drinking."

Something occurred to me. "You're not in a fraternity, are you, Ben?"

"No."

I brushed my fingers against his scrotum.

"Your balls are pretty hairy. I could shave them for you, if you wanted." I hesitated. "You know, we could pretend you were the pledge."

Ben started shaking.

"Or that I was Tony—"

"Shut up."

And pulling my face toward his, he thrust his tongue down my throat.

Don't think he wanted me. He didn't. Yes, he stayed that night, allowed me to initiate him into even the most specialized modes of intimacy—and initiated me into one or two as well. Yet as we sat down across from each other at breakfast the next morning, I could tell from his eyes that it wasn't me he was thinking about. Maybe Jessica, or God. Probably Tony. Not me.

He left shortly thereafter, having first extracted from me a promise never to tell anyone what had happened between us—a promise I naturally kept. And as I watched his car disappear onto California Boulevard, I couldn't guess whether he'd ever do it again, or do it only once again, or change his life and do it a thousand times. I knew only that during our night together, the marrow of identity had been touched. Whether it had been altered, however, I couldn't say.

A lull ensued. Spring break took most UCLA boys to a beach. With my father and Jean still in the Orient, I resorted to old habits: an hour each morning at the library, followed by Book Soup and lunch at the Mandarette Café. Then Andy was back in town for a few days between shoots; and my friend Matt Wolf from London. I got busy.

Something like my old life claimed me.

Naturally I was curious to find out, when spring break ended, what grade Ben had gotten on his paper; also, whether he'd bother to call and tell me what grade he'd gotten on his paper.

When finally I heard news of the matter, however (this was early April), it wasn't from Ben but from Eric.

Eric and I hadn't been in touch much lately. My suspicion was that he had a new girlfriend, the sort of thing he would never have discussed with me. So I was surprised and happy when he called me up one Sunday morning at seven and ordered me to meet him for breakfast at Ships on La Cienega.

He was waiting in a corner booth when I got there. A placid, sleepy smile on his face, he held the menu with fingers marked by little burns. "Juggling fire?" I asked.

"I got fifty bucks on Venice Beach last Sunday," Eric said.

"Congratulations." And I sat down. His skin was porphyry-colored from the sun.

"I must say, I never expected to hear from you at seven in the morning," I said. "You're not usually such an early riser."

"Depends on the season. Anyway, I had some news to tell you."

"Tell me."

"I just thought you should know, apparently some guy you wrote for—Ben something—got caught last week."

"Caught?"

"Tony Younger called me. Banana waffles for two," he added to the waitress, "and another cup of coffee. Anyway, yes. Apparently what happened was that when this guy Ben got back from spring break he found a message waiting from his history professor, the gist of which was to get over to her office hours pronto. So he went, and she basically told him that after reading his paper, and comparing it with his other papers, she'd come to the conclusion that it wasn't his own work. Too sophisticated or something. Then she gave him a choice. Either he could admit he hadn't written the paper, in which case he'd get a C and the incident would be dropped, or he could protest, in which case he'd get an F and the whole thing brought before the honor board."

"Damn. What did he choose?"

"That's the clincher. Apparently this Ben, this idiot, not only confessed he hadn't written the paper, he practically got down on his knees and started begging the professor's forgiveness. Tony's roommate was outside the office, he heard the whole thing." Eric shook his head in disgust. "After that he went straight to his room, packed up his things, and left. And since then—this was three days ago—no one, not even Tony, who's one of his best friends, has heard a word from him."

"Eric," I said, "I have to ask. Did he mention me?"

"Always thinking about others, aren't you, Dave? But no, he didn't."

"As if it matters. As if it makes it any less my fault."

"Hey, take it easy." The waffles arrived. "You're too quick to blame yourself," Eric went on, pouring syrup. "I mean, it's not as if this Ben guy didn't know the risks. He came to *you*. Don't forget that. And he could have fought it. Me, I would have said"—his voice went high—"'Miss Yearwood, Miss Yearwood, how can you think I'd *do* something like that!' And cried or something. Whereas he just gave in. You can't break down like that! The way I see it, they're testing you twenty-four hours a day. They want to see if you can sweat it out. If Ben couldn't take the pressure, it's not your problem. Still, I'd say it's probably better if you kept a low profile around campus for a while." He patted my hand. "Me, I'm lucky. I've finished my humanities requirements. And if I win a prize for that paper, it'll go a long way toward Stanford Biz School, provided I get a high enough score on my GMATs. Did I tell you I have GMATs coming up?"

He hadn't—a lapse he now corrected in lavish detail—after which we said goodbye in the parking lot, Eric cheerful as he drove off into his happy future, me wretched as I contemplated the ruin of Ben's academic career, a ruin for which, no matter what Eric might say to assuage my guilt, I understood myself to be at least in part responsible. For suddenly it didn't matter that I hadn't gotten caught; it didn't matter that no one knew what I had done except the boys themselves, none of whom would ever squeal on me. Because I had written my paper, and not Ben's, he had suffered. Blame could not be averted. The best I could do was try to bear it with valor.

I got into my father's car. For some reason I was remembering a moment years before, in elementary school, when a girl called Michele Fox had put before me an ethical dilemma familiar to most American schoolchildren at that time: if a museum were burning down, she'd said, and you could save either the old lady or the priceless art treasure, which would you choose? Well, I'd answered, it depends. Who is the old lady? What is the art treasure? To which she responded—wisely, I'm sure—"You're missing the point, David Leavitt." No doubt I was missing the point—her point—since Michele had few doubts in life. (She grew up to be a 911 operator.) As for me, I tortured that little conundrum for years, substituting for the generic old lady first my aunt Ida, then Eudora Welty; for the priceless treasure first the Mona Lisa, then Picasso's *Guernica*. Each time my answer was different. Sometimes I opted for life, sometimes for art. And how surprising! From this capriciousness a philosophy formed itself in me, according to which only particularities—not generalities—counted. For principles are rarely human things, and when museums burn—when any buildings burn—the truth is, most people save themselves.

What I'm trying to say here is, I made no effort to get in touch with, or help, Ben. Instead, that afternoon, I booked a flight to New York, where by the end of the week I was once again installed in that real life from which the episode of the term papers now turns out to have been merely a long and peculiar divagation.

III.

I ran into Ben about a year later. This was in the Uffizi Gallery, in Florence, where I'd gone to research (I am actually now writing it) my Bailey bridge novel. I was looking at Bronzino's portrait of Eleonora di Toledo, and Ben was looking at Bronzino's portrait of the baby Giovanni, fat-cheeked and clutching his little sparrow, and then, quite suddenly, we were looking at each other.

"Ben?" I said, not sure at first that it was he.

"Mr. Leavitt!" To my relief, he smiled.

We walked upstairs, where in the little coffee bar on the roof, I bought him a cappuccino. Ben looked better than he had when we'd first known each other. For one thing, his hair was both longer and messier, which suited him; also, he'd foregone his old Mormon uniform in favor of denim, down, hiking boots: ordinary clothes, boy clothes, in which his body, somehow ampler-seeming, rested with visible ease. Nor did he appear in the least surprised to be sitting with me there. "Actually," he said, "since I've been in Florence I've bumped into six people I knew from school. It might as well be Westwood Village." He took a sip from his cappuccino. "I never knew coffee could be so good before I came to Italy."

"How long have you been here?"

"In Florence, three days. In Italy, two weeks. I'm with my friend. No—I guess I should say my lover." He leaned closer. "Keith and I talk about this all the time. Lover's stupid, and friend's too euphemistic, and partner sounds like a business arrangement. So Keith says, 'Just say you're with Keith.' But then people say, 'Who's Keith?' And I'm back to square one."

"Well, you don't have to worry with me," I said, smiling. "Anyway, how did you meet Keith?"

"It was after I quit school, while I was living with my parents in Fremont. The thing was, I just kept having this yen to go into San Francisco. The usual story. So one night I was driving up and down Castro Street, and finally I worked up the courage to stop in at a bar. The next thing I knew someone was buying me a beer."

"And that was Keith?"

"Oh no. Keith came later." Ben's cheeks reddened. "He likes to tell people we met at a party, but the truth is we met on the street. He cruised me, we went back to his apartment and fucked. The rest is history." Ben drained his coffee cup. "And what about you, Mr. Leavitt? What have you been up to this year? Still living with your father?"

"No, I'm back in New York."

"Oh, great. And who are you writing term papers for there? NYU boys? Columbia boys?"

"Actually, I'm working on a novel."

"Better, I guess." His tone was somehow reproachful and affectionate all at once.

We were quiet for a moment. Then I said, "Ben, about that paper—"

"So you heard what happened."

"Yes. And I'm sorry. Probably you were right, probably it was pretentious. Or at least, not the right thing for you. I always tried to make my papers sound like they came from the people they were supposed to be coming from. I guess in your case, though, I got carried away. Infatuated, almost. The thing was, I fell in love with an idea."

"You're a writer. Writers are supposed to fall in love with ideas."

"Exactly. And that's why I should have been more careful. After all, if I'd done the paper the way you'd asked me to—"

"If you'd done the paper the way I asked you to, I'd be graduating from UCLA and on my way to law school and engaged to Jessica. Or graduating from UCLA and on my way to law school and a queer with a whatever you want to call him. Instead of which I'm drinking coffee with you on the roof of the Uffizi." He leaned back. "I'm not saying you didn't screw things up for me. I'm just saying the jury's still out on whether it was all for the best or not. And of course I'd be a hypocrite if I pretended it was only for the paper. It was never only for the paper."

"So what are your plans?"

"Well, for now I'm studying social work at San Francisco State. My goal is to go for my master's, then work with PWAs."

"That's great."

"Oh, and also—this may surprise you—I've been trying my hand at fiction writing."

"Really."

"Well, I figured, why not? See, since I moved in with Keith, I've been reading every gay novel I can get my hands on. I even read two of yours. I liked *The Lost Language of Cranes* all right. I didn't much like *Equal Affections*."

"I probably should have written it as a memoir. I still might."

"Interesting. As for me, I was thinking our little adventure might make a terrific story."

"That's a good idea," I said. "Writers often disguise their lives as fiction. The thing they almost never do is disguise fiction as their lives."

There wasn't really any way to answer this remark, and so for a few more moments we were both silent. Then Ben said, "And how about you, Mr. Leavitt? Do you feel comfortable with what you did?"

I spooned up the last remnants of my cappuccino foam. "Well, I'll never look at is as the proudest moment of my life, if that's what you're asking. Still, I'm not ashamed. I mean, is it wrong for the ghostwriter to say yes to the First Lady because she can't write? Was it wrong for Marni Nixon to dub Natalie Wood's voice in *West Side Story* because she couldn't sing?"

"You tell me. Was it?"

But I couldn't answer.

We got up shortly after that. It was nearing one, when Ben and Keith had a date to meet outside Café Rivoire. From the spot where Savonarola had burned the vanities, I watched them kiss each other on the cheek, two handsome, nicely dressed young men. Then, arms linked, they strolled together down Via Calzaiuoli.

And how did I feel? Ashamed, yes. Also happy. For the one thing I hadn't explained to Ben—the one thing I could never explain to Ben—was that those papers, taken together, constituted the best work I'd done in my life. And perhaps this was precisely *because* they were written to exchange for pleasure, as opposed to those tokens with which one can merely purchase pleasure. Thus the earliest troubadours sang, so that damsels might throw down ropes from virginal balconies.

Still, I couldn't have said any of this to Ben, because if I'd said any of this to Ben—if I'd told him it was the best work I'd done in my life—he would have thought it a tragedy, not a victory, and that I couldn't have borne.

From Savonarola's circle, I turned toward the Uffizi corridor, opening out like a pair of forceps. Pigeons, masses of them, circled in the sky, sometimes alighting on the heads of the statues: the imitation David, Neptune, Hercules, and Cacus, with their long fingers and outsize genitals. *And toward this nexus, great waves of men once moved,* I thought, *drawn by the David himself, by the dream of freedom itself.* It would have made a wonderful paper....Meanwhile bells rang. Ben and his companion had disappeared. "Time for lunch!" called an old man with bread, and the pigeons flocked and swooped to the earth.

Duets

Eric Samuelsen

SONDRA: Whenever Richard Cory went downtown, we people on the pavement looked at him. He was a gentleman from sole to crown. Clean favored, and imperially slim.

SHERILYNN: I crave beauty.

CANDACE: It was a Sunday like any other Sunday.

SONDRA: And he was always quietly arrayed, and he was always human when he talked, but still, he fluttered pulses when he said "Good morning," and he glittered when he walked.

SHERILYNN: Crave it.

CANDACE: It was cold out. We were all bundled up. Which was dumb because they'd turned the heat up too much like they do all winter long.

SHERILYNN: But my garden: weeds. Crochet, cross-stitch; turned out ugly and weird. I tried to blog: my sister's the only one who reads it.

SONDRA: And he was rich, yes, richer than a king, and admirably schooled in every grace. In fine, we thought that he was everything to make us wish that we were in his place.

CANDACE: I'd gotten Misty Reynolds for the special musical number: playin' piano, "Nephi Seer of Olden Times."

SHERILYNN: And then one Sunday, there she was.

CANDACE: Someone I'd never heard of.

SHERILYNN: And then she sang.

(SONDRA begins to sing.)

SONDRA: "Jesus, the very thought of thee, with sweetness fills my breast. But sweeter far, thy face to see, and in thy presence rest."

(As she sings, SHERILYNN and CANDACE look around, trying to locate the source for the voice.)

CANDACE: Who the livin' heck is that?

SHERILYNN: Sweet....

CANDACE: Most of our sisters, and bless their heart, love 'em to death, but most of 'em have those namby-pamby little girl voices; 'please don't pay attention to me, I'm just a girl.'

SHERILYNN: So sweet.

CANDACE: Boy do I not have patience for that. I'm a woman: hear me roar. Or, you know, sing. (The song finishes. She turns.) My heck, that's a great voice you got there.

SONDRA: Thank you.

CANDACE: Not to be pushy, but I'm Ward Music Chair? Always on the prowl for soloists. And choir members.

SONDRA: I have sung in choirs.

CANDACE: Voice like yours, I bet you have. Anyway, we meet every Sunday after the block, four fifteen.

SONDRA: I can't today. I'm sorry.

CANDACE: Candace Freeman.

SONDRA: Sondra DeRosa.

CANDACE: Nice to meetcha. Well, in future, I sure as heckfire hope you can make it. Not to be too blunt about it, but we need that voice.

SHERILYNN (approaches.): Hey.

CANDACE: Sherilynn Richards.

SHERILYNN: Hi.

CANDACE: Our best alto, easily. Not that our ward choir's anything special. Nine altos, one bass, two tenors. And the sopranos, well, Allison Rodriguez is pretty good, but with six kids, she can't always make it. Though we do provide child care, if that's an issue.

SONDRA: We don't have children yet. Listen, I really do....

CANDACE: If there's one thing I've learned, it's that you just plain can't have a choir without someone to watch the kidlings. What about your husband? Does he sing too?

SONDRA: He does. He's a baritone.

CANDACE: Wow, another guy for the bass section! Bring him along! We'd love to have you both!

SONDRA: We'll see if we can make it. (She exits.)

CANDACE: That voice. You know them?

SHERILYNN: I heard they're in Tammy Martin's old place. (Pause.)

CANDACE: What about you? You comin' to choir?

SHERILYNN: As always.

CANDACE (Light shift. She turns to audience.): And of course, Sondra didn't come to choir that week. Or the week after. Or the week after that.

SHERILYNN: Good ol' Candace never gave up.

CANDACE: Once again, choir's at four fifteen. Love to see you there.

SONDRA: Thank you. I'll try.

SHERILYNN: And then she'd just slip away.

CANDACE: She was a ghost. Flitting in and out. It's not like we're unfriendly; people made overtures.

SHERILYNN: "Hi, I don't believe we've met…"

CANDACE: "So are you guys new? I'm…."

SHERILYNN: Like I said, a ghost. She'd drift in, find a seat near the back. Wait for the closing prayer, and… disappear.

CANDACE: Well, after a couple of months, I quit trying. It's like my husband always says: the Church is a volunteer organization, and choir is a volunteer organization *within* a volunteer organization. Can't force people to show up.

SHERILYNN: That voice, though.

CANDACE: Though like I tell him, there are men who can sing just fine, and choose not to come to choir if there's a football game on instead.

SHERILYNN: So sweet and pure.

CANDACE: I wondered if it was our piddly little choir embarrassed her. We sang in Church twice when I knew Sondra was there, and maybe that turned her off.

SHERILYNN: We sang "How Great Thou Art," and it sounded like a dirge.

CANDACE: And Ali Rodriguez held the high note way longer than she needed to: (Demonstrates, singing.) "How great thou art. How greeeaaaaaaaatttttt thou art." Embarrassing.

SHERILYNN: Choir director then was Cathy Anderson.

CANDACE: Cathy's fine; I recommended her, and she's got some musical sense. But everything so… slllllllooooooooowwwwwwwww.

SHERILYNN: Cathy does prefer a languid tempo.

CANDACE: Even the really rousing hymns, like "Master the Tempest is Raging" or "Shall the Youth of Zion Falter." (Sings.) 'No!' Love that hymn. Even that one. We just plod along.

SHERILYNN: And then, so unexpected. Like four months after we first heard her in Church, she came to choir. And brought her husband with her.

CANDACE: Sondra?

SONDRA: Hi. Is this where we....

CANDACE: Yes! Absolutely!

SHERILYNN: Sondra, so glad you could make it!

SONDRA: Oh, and this is my husband. Mark.

CANDACE: Well, he was just plain gorgeous.

SHERILYNN: There's a poem I remember from school. Richard Cory, I think it was called, and it described this guy as 'clean favored, and imperially slim.' Said: 'he fluttered pulses when he spoke and he glittered when he walked.' That was Mark. Average height, slim and graceful, dark hair he wore a little long. Something about him. A light.

CANDACE: Where had she been keeping that man?

SHERILYNN: Smiling, friendly. Smart. And then we started singing, and without being even a little bit obnoxious about it, he would offer suggestions.

CANDACE: I like choir members who speak up like that. I do it too, when needed.

SHERILYNN: Never disrespectful, never pushy. But, my gosh.

CANDACE: 'Listen,' he said. 'I know it's my first time here. And I know this hymn has such a lovely message, we want the congregation to hear every word. But it is marked at 160. I just think if we picked up the tempo a little, that major minor thing he's doing with the altos will point up the lyric.' I didn't even know what he was saying, but it sure sounded good.

SHERILYNN: And his voice was like hers. Clear and sweet and unpretentious. And never a wrong note.

CANDACE: We actually had three other basses, which never happens, and he kept working with them too, helping them find their parts.

SHERILYNN: Two of the young men came, from one of our Samoan families, the Tinoasusopas. Nice kids, nice voices, but they couldn't read music. He worked with them.

CANDACE: By the end, he was high fiving and fist bumping those kids, and they were laughing, and he was calling 'em, like, 'homies.' Which didn't seem weird coming from him. And then, when they all knew their parts and didn't need him, he switched to tenor and sang that part perfectly too. And when we sang it through the last time, we actually had something our ward choir had never had, ever. A blend.

SHERILYNN: And we performed the next Sunday, and it was amazing.

CANDACE: I mean, it was a high council speaker, and of course whenever the choir sings they say something like 'and thanks to the choir for that beautiful number.' Even when we just finished butchering something like 'Oh how lovely was the morning' like we did that one time.

SHERILYNN: But this time, just, quiet. And the speaker got up, and he was…he didn't say anything for a long time. And when he did speak, he just said 'that was so beautiful. Thank you.'

CANDACE: And after the meeting, everyone was patting Cathy on the back and telling her how great she'd gotten the choir to sing, and we all knew, it wasn't her.

SHERILYNN: Mark and Sondra had transformed us.

CANDACE: And then we didn't see them for another two months.

SHERILYNN: Either of them.

CANDACE: We'd heard things. She'd refused visiting teachers. He'd turned down a calling. I'm not in the loop to actually know, but you do hear things.

SHERILYNN: I'd see her sometimes, in the neighborhood.

CANDACE: I'd see him too. He rode a bike to work. Rode it right past my living room window every morning at 8:41. It's possible I may have occasionally seen to it that I was at that window at that time.

SHERILYNN: They were never unfriendly, or anything. Just… absent.

CANDACE: I knew he was busy; you'd see him coming home from work on that bike, nine, ten o'clock at night.

SHERILYNN: And then one day, in the spring, months after they'd moved in, I saw her at Joann's Fabric. My oldest, Laurie, got asked to prom; and it's so hard to find modest prom dresses for a reasonable price. So I was looking to maybe see if I could sew her one. And there was Sondra.

SONDRA: Hi.

SHERILYNN: Sondra. We've missed you in choir.

SONDRA: We enjoyed it.

SHERILYNN: You're always welcome back.

SONDRA: Thanks. (After a second.) Well....

SHERILYNN: Listen, you don't know where they keep the tulle?

SONDRA: Tulle?

SHERILYNN: Yeah. It's for a....

SONDRA: No, I get it, you've got a daughter.... . I think it's right over there.

SHERILYNN: Thanks.

SONDRA: So, tulle, prom, did I get that right?

SHERILYNN: Yes indeed.

SONDRA: You can't possibly have a daughter old enough for prom.

SHERILYNN: Well, thank you for those kind words! But, yeah. And get this: her sixteenth birthday is two days before prom this year.

SONDRA: Good for her.

SHERILYNN: Of course, you know, they can't just call on the phone to ask someone out. No, no, it's this entire elaborate ritual.

SONDRA: I remember that.

SHERILYNN: I don't. I was in high school in Germany—a lot of these traditions...

SONDRA: Germany, huh? Dad in the military?

SHERILYNN: How'd you guess? Yeah, career Air Force.

SONDRA: Well, I grew up in Idaho, so....

SHERILYNN: So you know. It was cute: The guy, he'd somehow gotten a heart shaped pizza pan, and he baked this pizza, and underneath it, this invitation: 'Laurie, you've stolen my heart. Will you go with me to prom?'

SONDRA: That is cute.

SHERILYNN: Of course, she hardly knows him. And the pizza tasted like dog food, but… .

SONDRA (Laughing.): That's hilarious. What do you think of this? (Holding up a fabric: possibly mimed?)

SHERILYNN: I like the color.

SONDRA: With your daughter's dark hair, right?

SHERILYNN: You've met my daughter?

SONDRA: I've seen her in the neighborhood.

SHERILYNN: Well. You're right, this would be a good color for her.

SONDRA: And maybe with this….

SHERILYNN: Anyway. So of course, she had to answer the same way. Not pizza— she hid her reply in an order of sushi.

SONDRA: I love sushi.

SHERILYNN: Me, not so much. But she'd heard he liked it. It's all about the high school grapevine; she doesn't know the boy, but her best friend knows his best friend, so… .

SONDRA: Do you have a pattern?

SHERILYNN: I do. But I'm not much of a seamstress—I just hope this works.

SONDRA: Yes. (A pause, then with a bit of a rush.) I've actually done a bit of sewing. Um…would you like some help with it?

SHERILYNN (Pause, looks at her, open-mouthed.): I would completely love that.

SONDRA: Okay then.

SHERILYNN: And the next day, she came over, and we spent an afternoon with Laurie, measuring, cutting it out. Laurie was furious with me at first.

CANDACE (As LAURIE.): Mom! You remember eighth grade? You remember? A certain pinafore.

SHERILYNN: You looked cute in that.

CANDACE (As LAURIE.): I looked like a freak! I looked like a polyg!

SHERILYNN: I admit, it was a trifle old-fashioned....

CANDACE (As LAURIE.): You ruined eighth grade! And now you're going to wreck my prom!

SHERILYNN: Honey, we cannot afford a two hundred dollar... .

CANDACE (As LAURIE.): One eighty five!

SHERILYNN:... .expensive dress you're going to wear once in your life.

CANDACE (As LAURIE.): It's the prom! Why can't I... .

SHERILYNN: You're going to like it. It's going to be cute.

CANDACE (As LAURIE.): Arrgghhhhggghhhh!

SHERILYNN: And she stomped out of the room.

SONDRA: Sherilynn. Wait 'til she sees it.

SHERILYNN: So. With seriously minimal cooperation from my daughter, we worked on it together. And it became very clear, very early on, that I was not in Sondra's league.

SONDRA: I think it's ready for a fitting.

SHERILYNN: Sondra, I can't believe this.

SONDRA: I think it turned out.

SHERILYNN: Laurie!

CANDACE (As LAURIE, offstage.): I'm busy.

SHERILYNN: We need you for a fitting.

CANDACE (As LAURIE, offstage.): I'm busy! I'll do it later.

SHERILYNN: We need you now.

CANDACE (As LAURIE, entering.): Why, what's the big deal, I'm chatting on Facebook, why is it so frickin' important....? (She stops.)

SHERILYNN: We need to have a fitting while Sondra's here. And she cannot be expected to wait around for you to... .

CANDACE (As LAURIE.): Okay, whatever. Is that it?

SONDRA: Yes.

CANDACE (As LAURIE.)(Shocked pause. Reverently.): It's gorgeous.

SONDRA: Well. Let's try it on.

CANDACE (As LAURIE.): Yeah. (She takes the dress, and exits.)

SONDRA: We'll have to wait 'til we see it on her, of course.

SHERILYNN: Sondra. You're a magician.

SONDRA: Oh, I can do a few things.

SHERILYNN: But as she packed up her sewing machine, I could tell she was pleased.

SONDRA: So, choir, again? This Sunday.

SHERILYNN: We'd love to have you.

SONDRA: We'll try and make it.

SHERILYNN: And prom was... magical. All the things you hope it will be for your daughter. Her date even looked...less geeky than most boys look at seventeen. And I looked at her, with her wrist corsage and her hair and makeup perfect, and I thought, this is my gift to my daughter. And Sondra's gift to us both.

CANDACE: And suddenly, Mark and Sondra were choir regulars. Cathy Anderson didn't know what hit her. Summer became fall, and still, they came, to Church and to choir. And Mark, suddenly he was indispensable. They put him in the Elder's Quorum Presidency. They called her to Primary. Every Sunday, they'd sing, and choir attendance... I mean, when you sing as good as we were singing, it makes people want to join in.

SHERILYNN: Sondra and Mark sat near the front in Sunday School, and every Sunday he'd speak up and everything he said was smart and thoughtful and, you know, spiritual.

CANDACE: Fall led to Thanksgiving, and we started working on Christmas music. The biggest choir event of the year—the annual Christmas program.

SHERILYNN: It's always my favorite Sacrament meeting, just lots of music and reading from the Gospel of Luke.

CANDACE: At Christmas, the stake does this choirfest thing, where all the ward choirs sing two carols each, a very nice event, and absolutely competitive even though it's not supposed to be. And most of the choirs in the stake had been like ours had been—too few men, dull hymns sung in very safe arrangements. We've never won. Not that there's a prize. So: this year. We sang this 'Oh Come All Ye Faithful' Mark had found, where the piano part was Pachelbel's canon? Killed it! And then we sang this arrangement of 'Come Oh Come Emmanuel' that blew everyone away. We were easily the best. Everyone in the stake said so.

SONDRA (Sings.): Oh come oh come Emmanuel, and ransom captive Israel, that mourns in lonely exile here, until the Son of God appear. Rejoice! Rejoice! Emmanuel shall come to thee, Israel.

SHERILYNN: Christmas is joyful, it's supposed to be a celebration of Jesus' birth. But what Sondra and Mark seemed to understand was that Christmas is also melancholy. Jesus is born, and that's glorious. But he brings us salvation through suffering; he's being born so that he can die. This baby, in a manger, is going to die for us, for our sins. For the times we snap at our kids, for the times we fight with our husbands. For the kids dying in Darfur and Somalia. And Mark and Sondra, their voices were perfect, like Jesus is perfect. But beneath the sweetness, there was also tremendous sadness. Maybe because they couldn't have kids. Maybe because of something else. I don't know—it's not my business to know. But when I hugged her, after our performance, I could see a tear starting in the corner of her eye. And I knew I was close to crying too.

CANDACE: Most choirs take a couple of weeks off after Christmas. Not us. Cathy Anderson knew we were on a roll, and I recommended that we sing 'Ring Out Wild Bells' for New Year's. With Mark and Sondra leading the way, we nailed that one too.

SHERILYNN: And Laurie got asked to the Valentine's Day dance at school, and Sondra helped with her dress for that, too.

CANDACE: I had this plan. I talked to the bishop, and he approved it. The thing is, we hardly ever do anything special for Easter. My Mom was Catholic, and she told me what a big deal they make of it, and we should too—it's just as important a day for us too, we Mormons.

SHERILYNN: And she started coming over, mornings. Once a week maybe. Just to chat.

CANDACE: Honestly, it's like the Easter bunny is more important than Jesus's resurrection. What's with that?

SHERILYNN: Not, like, heavy conversations. Kids, our childhoods, and what books we liked and had we seen that movie.

CANDACE: I mean, seriously, what *is* it with that? I never actually thought about it before, but… rabbits don't lay eggs. They're mammals. I think.

SHERILYNN: The most serious we got was when she admitted she and Mark sometimes saw R-rated movies, and I confessed I did sometimes too.

CANDACE: I mean: rabbits? And eggs?

SHERILYNN: And we both liked fantasy novels; I turned her on to Mercedes Lackey, she got me going on Terry Pratchett.

CANDACE: Ducks lay eggs; why isn't it the Easter duck?

SHERILYNN: I got to looking forward to my time with her. Chatting.

CANDACE: And why do we paint 'em all those colors? This is making my head hurt. (She retreats.)

SHERILYNN: So, tea? You drink tea?

SONDRA: Herbal tea. I looked it up, it's not against the word of wisdom.

SHERILYNN: I guess. (sips.) It's really good.

SONDRA: I love it. (Short friendly pause.)

SHERILYNN: You know, I've been meaning to ask you for a long time....

SONDRA: What?

SHERILYNN: Your name.

SONDRA: Oh.

SHERILYNN: I mean, not Sandra. Sondra. Is there a story there?

SONDRA: It's embarrassing.

SHERILYNN: So there *is* a story!

SONDRA: It was my Dad. He named me after... .

SHERILYNN: What?

SONDRA: Clint Eastwood's girlfriend.

SHERILYNN: Clint Eastwood's girlfriend?

SONDRA: Sondra Locke. She was in a bunch of his movies. *The Outlaw Josey Wales. Every Which Way But Loose.*

SHERILYNN: Haven't seen 'em.

SONDRA: Oh, I have. That's my namesake up there; I've seen every movie.

SHERILYNN: She was...gorgeous?

SONDRA: Not really. Sort of a washed-out blonde. Pretty, I guess, in sort of an abused-girl way. Plus....

SHERILYNN: What.

SONDRA: Well. She basically took her top off every movie.

SHERILYNN: Seriously!

SONDRA: Yeah. Pretty much every film. I think maybe that's what my Dad liked about her.

SHERILYNN: Okay, that's creepy.

SONDRA: You never met my Dad. (Awkward silence.) So, I had some issues. If it weren't for Mark, I probably still would.

SHERILYNN: I can imagine. (She takes SONDRA's hand, squeezes. After a moment.) How was she?

SONDRA: Hey, she had more goin' on up there than I ever will. (And after a shocked silence, they burst out laughing together.)

CANDACE (With a disgusted look at them both.): Anyway. Easter. I wanted: a musical Easter. No bunnies, or ducks. Just music.

SHERILYNN: There's so much beautiful Easter music.

CANDACE: Our choir was good enough to handle 'Our Savior Thou Who Wearest A Crown.' It's Bach, but we can do Bach now, with Mark and Sondra. And I found a great duet arrangement for Sherilynn and Allison to sing of 'That Easter Morn.' But then I got this brilliant notion. A duet, with Sondra and Mark, singing 'Morning Has Broken.'

SONDRA: She wanted us to sing Cat Stevens.

CANDACE: But Cat Stevens didn't write it. It's a hymn—he just recorded it. And it's so beautiful.

SHERILYNN: She got the bishop to approve it.

CANDACE: I knew there might be people in the ward who wouldn't like it. There'd be people who'd even say 'he's not even Cat Stevens anymore, he's Yussuf bin Imaterrorist or whatever. But it would be Mark singing it. It would be Mark, with that presence and style and that beautiful voice.

SONDRA: I didn't think it was a good idea. But Mark wants us to.

SHERILYNN: See… (catches herself.) Sorry. My husband, Ben, got laid off. And… .we were getting help from the Church; Ben hated that. Eligible for food stamps, which Ben hated even worse.

SONDRA: I was over almost every day.

SHERILYNN: You go to Church and you sing in the choir, and you have friends—it does all help.

SONDRA: My Dad was the same way.

SHERILYNN: The whole thing, the stress, the anxiety. It changed Ben. Pulled him inside himself. Pulled him away from me. (Brightly.) So: 'Morning Has Broken'?

SONDRA: It is pretty. Candace is right about that. It's very pretty. I just....

SHERILYNN: So... .

SONDRA: It's about fresh starts. Starting all over. A new world. And.... sorry, I can't really tell you more than that.

CANDACE (Singing.): 'Morning has broken, like the first morning. Blackbird has spoken, like the first bird. Praise for the singing. Praise for the morning. Praise for them springing, fresh from the word.'

SONDRA: Those lyrics.

SHERILYNN: I love the lyrics. That's what I like about the song, is the lyrics.

SONDRA: Me too.

SHERILYNN: So you like it, and you don't like it.

SONDRA: I know I probably sound crazy.

SHERILYNN: No more than usual.

SONDRA (Laughs.): You....

SHERILYNN: So what's the matter?

SONDRA: Fresh starts. I'm not sure how much longer Mark and I... have.

SHERILYNN: What? (Knock on door, doorbell, some similar device.)

CANDACE: I come bearing gifts! (Hands SONDRA music.) I really like this arrangement.

SONDRA: Thanks.

CANDACE: And Sherilynn. Listen, Allison's pulled out—a much-too convenient attack of laryngitis, if you ask me. So....

SHERILYNN (Warily.): What?

CANDACE: I was wondering if you'd like to duet with me.

SHERILYNN: Candace! No.

CANDACE: Why not? You switch to soprano, and I pick up your alto part and it'll be fine.

SHERILYNN: Soprano!

CANDACE: You'll do great.

SHERILYNN: I felt uncomfortable enough supporting Allison!

CANDACE: Let's just run through it. Sondra, be a doll and play for us, would you?

SHERILYNN: Candace, seriously. I can't do this.

CANDACE: Nonsense, you have a beautiful voice. Stop hiding your light under a barrel. Or whatever the scripture says.

SONDRA: I don't even play all that well.

CANDACE: It's in D, you'll be fine. And a one and a two....

SHERILYNN: And so we practiced. And suddenly, Sunday went from a day I was sort of looking forward to to a day I was dreading.

SONDRA: And we didn't really finish our conversation. Saturday night, day before Easter, she stopped by. Terrified.

SHERILYNN: Terrified.

SONDRA: She's so self-conscious about her voice. Which she shouldn't be, she has a lovely voice. But she couldn't hear that.

SHERILYNN: Sondra, honestly. Can't you sing it for me?

SONDRA: Candace has pretty much made up her mind.

SHERILYNN: But this is basically a solo.

SONDRA: It's a duet. You support each other.

SHERILYNN: I've got the lead, though.

SONDRA: Just the melody. But that's what's wonderful about music. Two voices complementing each other.

SHERILYNN: One of them quavering with fear.

SONDRA: I know.

SHERILYNN: I'm going to crack on that A.

SONDRA: You never have when we've practiced it.

SHERILYNN: But in front of... .

SONDRA: Sherilynn. You can't think that way. You can't think 'I'm in front of all those people, singing a solo, and I'm not that good.'

SHERILYNN: That's exactly what I'm thinking.

SONDRA (Lightly.): Well, cut it out. (They laugh briefly together.) Is Ben going to be there?

SHERILYNN: Doubt it.

SONDRA: I'm sorry.

SHERILYNN: It's okay. Chance for him to pick up a shift, so....

SONDRA: Yeah.

SHERILYNN: How's 'Morning Has Broken'?

SONDRA: Mark sounds great.

SHERILYNN: And you do too, of course.

SONDRA: He always sounds great.

SHERILYNN: You and Mark. Is he.... ill?

SONDRA: Define ill.

SHERILYNN: What's going on?

SONDRA: It can keep. Let's get through tomorrow.

SHERILYNN: But if he's....

SONDRA: It's not what you think. Monday. I'll tell you everything.

CANDACE: Well, our musical Easter could not have gone better. The bishop had always been supportive, but our Stake President came too, and was nothing but compliments. The choir sounded great, as always. And Sherilynn came through on our duet with hardly a problem. She just started to crack a little on the high note— that A always gave her fits in practice—but she pushed through, and everyone said afterwards our blend was perfect. The one disappointment was surprising. It's not that Mark and Sondra sang badly, exactly—they're too talented to ever sing badly. But, I don't know what it was. They just didn't sound quite...together. It sounded like two good soloists. Not really much like a duet.

SHERILYNN: It's hard, when you know something, some things, and you can't really...put the pieces together. Sondra came late to Church on Easter morning. At first I thought they wouldn't come at all, but they did, finally, appear. Not looking at each other, sitting together, but... apart.

SONDRA: I made it through. I gutted it out.

SHERILYNN: The thing is, our house is just two houses down and....

SONDRA: We came up together, we stood together, the piano started. It was just mechanics, breath support. Shaping vowels and consonants.

SHERILYNN: I saw Mark come home late Saturday night. It was probably one, two in the morning. He parked in their driveway—didn't use the garage door opener. Like he didn't want to make that extra bit of noise.

SONDRA: And then came the choir number, and we stood again, sang again. I couldn't stay for the rest of the meetings. Couldn't handle it.

SHERILYNN: And I came home from church, fed the kids, washed the dishes. Waited for Ben. And then, around eight or nine, I couldn't wait any more. I put Laurie in charge. I'd bought a package of Chips Ahoy cookies, and I put 'em on a plate, and took 'em with me. Like cookies were a legitimate excuse for a visit. And went over.

SONDRA: And Sherilynn came over. And Mark opened the door for her. And excused himself, and went back into his study, where he'd been since we got home from Church. And he shut the door. (Pause.)

SHERILYNN: I brought cookies.

SONDRA: Yeah. Thanks.

SHERILYNN: Chips Ahoy.

SONDRA: I thought so.

SHERILYNN: I wasn't sure.... I thought maybe cookies.... I feel so stupid.

SONDRA: You sang beautifully today.

SHERILYNN: So did you.

SONDRA: No.

SHERILYNN: You did.

SONDRA: No.

SHERILYNN: You really did. (Pause.)

SONDRA: And then we just sat there. Forever. Like we knew where the conversation needed to go but had no idea how to get it there.

SHERILYNN: And that's when I blurt. Just blurt things out. (To Sondra.) I saw Mark. Last night.

SONDRA: Did you?

SHERILYNN: He parked in the driveway.

SONDRA: He didn't want to wake me.

SHERILYNN: I thought maybe....

SONDRA: But I was still up. So....

SHERILYNN: Look, this is none of my business, but....

SONDRA: You want to know if Mark is seeing someone. And how you can help if he is.

SHERILYNN: Yes.

SONDRA: How are you and Ben doing these days?

SHERILYNN: We're fine. You know that; it's been tough for us.

SONDRA: But Ben still loves you.

SHERILYNN: Of course he does.

SONDRA: And you love him?

SHERILYNN: Of course.

SONDRA: I don't know how to even say this. I'm talking around it and talking around it and I still can't bring myself....

SHERILYNN: You think there may be another woman.

SONDRA: Oh no. Not at all.

SHERILYNN: Oh!

SONDRA: No, really. That's the least of my worries, believe me.

SHERILYNN: So....

SONDRA: And I love him dearly. He's kind, and he's thoughtful, and he's so wonderfully talented. From the first time I met him, I worshipped the ground he walked on. I still do.

SHERILYNN: I don't understand.

SONDRA: Sherilynn, I'm not afraid my husband is seeing another woman. I'm afraid—in fact, I know—he's seeing another man.

SHERILYNN: Shock. Like a fist. Try to breathe. Try to breathe.

SONDRA: He told me last night. It's not the first time. They haven't... done anything. But he's met someone, and they are deeply, deeply in love.

SHERILYNN: Oh, Sondra.

SONDRA: I've told people this before. Twice, good friends, like you have become. They say the right things each time. Then they stop calling.

SHERILYNN: I would never do that.

SONDRA: I hope not.

SHERILYNN: I won't.

SONDRA: Okay.

SHERILYNN: But.... how long... ?

SONDRA: He told me when we were dating. He said he was fighting it, that it was this dark evil part of him and he was desperately trying to overcome it. Like a... an addiction.

SHERILYNN: That's what it is, too! Evil, an addiction!

SONDRA (Sadly.): No. It's not. It's just who he is. Part of who he is.

SHERILYNN: I don't understand.

SONDRA: I loved him, completely. I knew, absolutely knew, that I could help him change. I knew that with my help, he could become...whole. And pure. And mine. And God's.

SHERILYNN: But what? He's given up?

SONDRA: No, Sherilynn, it's not... look, I know you and Ben are going through a rough patch right now. But you still... he still desires you, right? He still...

SHERILYNN: Yes.

SONDRA: When Mark kisses me.... well, he doesn't much, anymore, but when he kisses me, everything about it's wrong. It's like when you're in a play, and you have to kiss someone, but you're thinking the whole time about standing so you're in the light, and your costume itches and what's your next line. And you want it to look good, but it means... .you know.

SHERILYNN: Nothing.

SONDRA: It's ripping him apart. He loves me, I know he does, as much as he's able. But he doesn't want me. It's disgusting to him, creepy and weird. And every time, he's forcing himself to... .

SHERILYNN: And he meets other men.

SONDRA: Yeah. And he falls for them. And then, he can't stand himself, he hates himself, he withdraws. Won't go to church, won't pray. Punishing himself. And then we sing together. And for a second, just for those few moments when we're singing... it's all we have. It's the only way we can ever be together.

CANDACE: The sirens woke us.

SHERILYNN: But today....

SONDRA: He was with him last night. He got home, I screamed at him, I lost it completely.

CANDACE: One in the morning, coming down our street.

SONDRA: Completely out of control.

SHERILYNN: Oh, Sondra. (Hugs her, they're both crying.)

CANDACE: I thought maybe, it could be one of the older couples in the ward.

SONDRA: I was so wrong. I was so... . selfish.

CANDACE: But then I saw Sondra, sitting on her porch in her nighty, hugging her knees, rocking.

SHERILYNN: So on we worked and waited for the light,

SONDRA: Because this was it, this was the man he wanted to be with for the rest of his life. It was all he could think of.

SHERILYNN: And went without the meat and cursed the bread,

CANDACE: Utterly bereft. (Gunshot sound effect. SONDRA screams distantly.)

SHERILYNN: And Richard Cory, one calm summer night, Went home and put a bullet in his head.

SONDRA: My fault. Mine.

SHERILYNN: Clean favored, and imperially slim.

SONDRA: I sinned. I sinned against love. I sinned against the man I loved most in the entire world.

CANDACE: Sherilynn was standing on the lawn, looking up at her. And I thought, hug her. She's your friend, she's in trouble, she's in pain. Hug her!

SHERILYNN: It doesn't make sense. It doesn't make sense.

SONDRA: I thought. I would give anything to sing with that man. For the rest of my life. Anything. Anything.

FINAL BLACKOUT

Hunters and Gatherers

Bernard Cooper

Rick had been searching for the Pillings' address for over twenty minutes, and the hungrier he became, the harder it was to concentrate on the dimly lit street signs, the six-digit numbers stenciled on curbs. Westgate Village was a planned community an hour away from the downtown loft where Rick lived, its street names a variation on the same bucolic phrase Valley Vista Circle, Village Road, Valley View Court. Each one-story ranch house looked nearly the same except for the color of its garage door, and Rick, who'd skipped lunch, began to wonder if the entire suburb was a hunger-induced hallucination. Jerry Pilling, giddy as a kid at the prospect of throwing a party, had given Rick hasty directions over the phone so many weeks ago that Rick now had a hard time deciphering his own scrawl. He pulled over to the curb, squinted at what he'd written on a scrap of paper, and tried to retrace his turns. All the while, digestive juices sluiced through his stomach and a dull ache came and went.

Rick was about to give up and head for a phone booth when a Mustang crept past, the driver peering this way and that, on the prowl for an address. Jerry had described the party as a chance for his wife, Meg, to meet a group of his gay friends, and after much wrangling she'd finally agreed, but only on the condition that she could invite her hairdresser, the one "avowed" homosexual she knew. Rick had a hunch that the man driving the Mustang was Mrs. Pilling's hairdresser—the skin of his face was shiny and taut, his silver hair moussed—and decided to follow him. "Avowed" had about it a quaint, anachronistic ring, and Rick pictured a dandy in an ascot, hand raised as he swore some sort of oath. Sure enough, the Mustang pulled up to the right address within minutes. A house with double doors and deep eaves, it sat at the end of a cul-de-sac. "Pilling" was chiseled on a wooden sign, the front lawn glowing greenly in the dusk.

Rick had met Jerry Pilling on a midnight flight from New York to Los Angeles. Returning home from his one-man show at a SoHo gallery, Rick was solvent and optimistic for the first time in a year. Seatmates in the back of the plane, the two of them struck up a conversation, or rather, Rick listened across the dark heartlands of America as tiny bottles of Smirnoff's accumulated on Jerry's tray table. "Meg and I are Mormons," Jerry told him, shaking the last drops of alcohol into his plastic tumbler, "so we aren't allowed to drink. But I bend the rules depending on the altitude." He touched Rick's arm and his breath, as pungent as jet fuel, sterilized the air between them. "I'm terrified of flying." This was the first of Jerry's confessions; soon they came with escalating candor, the consonants softened by booze. "Do you know any Mormons?" asked Jerry. "Personally, I mean."

"Only impersonally." Rick laughed.

"Well, take it from me, not all of us are polygamists who bathe in our holy undergarments. There's lots of ways to be a Mormon; at least, that's the way *I* see it."

"There's a Mormon guy at my gym," ventured Rick, "who wears the garments under his workout clothes, even in summer."

"Or proselytize on our bicycles."

"I'm sorry?"

"Not all of us proselytize on our bicycles."

Rick pictured Jerry wobbling on a Schwinn.

"Listen," said Jerry, giving Rick a let's-lay-our-cards-on-the-table look. "Are you by any chance... I don't mean to be presumptuous, so forgive me if I'm wrong, but you haven't said anything about a wife, and I was wondering if you're..."

"Gay?"

"I knew it!" blurted Jerry slapping his armrest. "I have a sick sense—sixth sense—about these things. I am, too!"

To Rick's way of thinking, Jerry was unduly excited by this coincidence, as if he'd discovered they had the same mother. Still, he found something intriguing about the portly, candid stranger beside him. He eyed Jerry's wedding ring and, with no prompting whatsoever, Jerry launched into the story of his marriage. "I only recently told Meg that I fooled around with men in college. Groping a house brother, that sort of thing." This piqued Rick's interest and he had to steer Jerry back to the subject when, trying to recall the name of his fraternity, he was sidetracked into a muddled pronunciation of Greek letters. "The point," continued Jerry, "is that I wanted to write off my college flings as trial and error, youthful confusion. But after six children and twenty years of marriage, I couldn't ignore my thing for guys. College men especially. Studious types. Blond. With glasses." Jerry sighed. "The more I tried to pray it away, the stronger it got."

The plane hit a patch of turbulence over Kansas. Snug in his seat and buffered by vodka, Jerry didn't seem to notice. Passengers shifted beneath their blankets. A baby bawled in the forward cabin. "We counseled with the church elders, Meg and me, and they thought that male companionship—strictly platonic, of course— would help me 'scratch the itch,' as they put it. So we decided to stay married and faithful, and I'm going to make some homosexual friends." Jerry brightened. "We'll have to have you over for dinner."

"The church *wants* you to have gay friends?"

"Hey," said Jerry, shifting in his seat. "They didn't say homosexual or not. But 'male companionship' is open to interpretation, don't you think?" He stirred his drink with an index finger, then sucked his finger and took a swig. "According to the church, if me and Meg get divorced, old Jerry here wanders around heaven for time immemorial, a soul without a family."

It was delicate: Rick didn't want to challenge Jerry's religious beliefs, but he found this punishment cruel and unusual, not to mention superstitious. "Do you really believe that's what would happen?"

"The idea scares me whether I believe in it or not. An outcast even after I'm dead. Lifelong bonds coming to nothing. Estranged from my very own kids." He chewed an ice cube and shivered. "I joined Affirmation, a group of gay Mormons, and they say the church is run by humans, and humans don't know everything there is to know about the Creator's plan; only one judgment matters in the end, and at least He'll know what made me tick and how I tried to do what's right. But Rick," said Jerry, leaning close, "here's where I part company with the folks at Affirmation: they're skeptical about a man staying married."

"You mean about a gay man staying married?"

"Isn't that what I said? Anyway, living in a family makes me happy. My kids are turning into people I like. You should see the little ones swamp me when I walk through the door. Chalk it up to my having been an only child, but even when they're fighting and crying, the chaos is kind of cozy, you know?"

"What about your wife?"

"I'd tried to tell her when we were dating, but she'd shush me and say the past didn't matter. It probably didn't occur to her I was messing with men. She wanted a husband and I wanted to be normal; in that respect we were meant for each other. And here I am." Jerry looked around, then whispered, "I'm the only man Meg has ever slept with. And let me tell you, I've never pretended. I've always loved her and I always will. In the bedroom, too. Love must count for something, right?"

"It should," said Rick. He wished that Eric, the man he had lived with, was still alive and waiting at home. "If it were up to me," he told Jerry, "love would stop trains and change the weather."

The seat belt signs were turned off and a low electronic bell rang throughout the cabin. "Sorry if I talked your ear off," said Jerry. "I ought to keep my big mouth shut. But keeping quiet wears me out a lot more than talking." His head lolled toward the oval window. Rick leaned forward and gazed out, too. Beads of condensation gathered on the glass. Dawn-tinted fields and rooftops and roads were visible through thinning clouds.

The double doors swung open and there stood Mrs. Pilling, her tight auburn curls a miracle of modern cosmetology. She glanced back and forth between Rick and her hairdresser, smiling nervously. "Did you and Oscar come together?" she asked. Perhaps she assumed that Rick and Oscar had crossed paths in the small province of their "lifestyle." Rick felt a pang of sympathy for Meg; *she's trying to hold up the walls*, he thought, *just like the rest of us*. Dressed in slinky blue culottes, eyelids dusted with matching shadow, Meg appeared every inch the camera-ready hostess; the only thing missing, lamented Rick, was a platter of canapés. He felt certain her stylish outfit was meant to show her husband's unconventional friends that she was a woman with flair, not the stodgy, narrow-minded matron they might have expected.

"It's serendipity," Oscar told her, handing over a pungent bouquet. "We met tonight on this very doorstep."

Jerry Pilling darted out the door. "Gentlemen," he bellowed, "welcome to the hinterlands!" His hail voice and vise-like handshake were far more manly than Rick remembered. Dressed in loose black linen, Oscar rippled as Jerry pumped his hand. "Meg's raved about you," he told Oscar. "Says you're the only man who can give her hair volume."

"Noblesse oblige," said Oscar. He turned toward Mrs. Pilling. "Meg, dear, you'd better get that nosegay into some water."

Rick and Oscar followed the Pillings into a spacious living room, as ornate, thought Rick, as a rococo salon. Overstuffed sofas and chairs were covered in plaids and herringbones and stripes. One wall was an archive of framed family photographs. Jerry and Meg pointed to the pictures and boasted about their kids in unison—a long, overlapping roll call—and it sounded to Rick as if they'd given birth to a happy hive, several more than the half-dozen children Jerry'd mentioned on the plane. Snapshots in which the whole family posed together had the voluminous look of class pictures. Rick imagined the Pillings' grocery cart loaded to the brim with potato chip bags, Cheerios boxes as big as luggage, six-packs of soda, gallons of milk. While the Pillings, as verbose as docents, led him along the wall, Rick searched every tabletop for a bowl of peanuts or a wedge of cheese, finding instead an endless array of ceramic animals, dried flowers, and colorful blown-glass clowns. The clowns looked as though they were molded out of hard candy, and Rick could almost taste their antic faces.

"Where *is* your brood?" asked Oscar.

"Simon's at debating. Mandy's at ballet. The rest of the kids have already eaten. They're in their rooms doing who knows what." Jerry nodded toward a hallway that burrowed deep into one wing of the house. Light seeped from beneath its row of doors.

"I'll check on the kids," said Meg.

"How 'bout I show you the grounds," said Jerry, slapping them both on the back.

The yard was a vast expanse of concrete, a kidney-shaped swimming pool in the center. Lit from within, the pool threw woozy refractions onto the surrounding cinder-block walls. Pool toys bobbed atop the water like flotsam from a shipwreck. An inflatable shark, bleached by the sun, floated belly-up. Jerry bent down at the edge of the pool and fiddled with the water filter, which made a shrill sucking noise; from behind, it looked as if he were trying to drink the pool through a straw. Blood sugar plummeting, Rick wondered if it would be impolite to ask for a Coke, or whether he should wait until something was offered. He scolded himself for being a recluse; if he got out of the studio more often, he might know how to behave in these situations.

The sliding glass doors rumbled open and Meg ushered the remaining guests into the warm night. Mitchell Coply was Jerry's dentist. A man in his early forties, he had the slim, diminutive build of a schoolboy. A lock of hair sprang onto his forehead no matter how often he brushed it away. His puckish appearance was contradicted by tired, melancholy eyes behind his gold-rimmed glasses. During the round of introductions, Mitchell was soft-spoken and shy about eye contact, the kind of man incapable of concealing his sadness. Jan Kirby was an agent who worked with Jerry at a real estate office that specialized in new housing developments throughout the San Fernando Valley. Tall and broad-shouldered, Jan wore a pin-striped pants suit and running shoes. After meeting the other guests, she stood perilously close to the edge of the pool and faced the deep end, hands on her hips. Lit from below by the pool light, she looked to Rick like a deity about to part, or walk across, the water. "After dessert," she said in her husky voice, "let's go skinny-dipping." It took everyone a second to realize she was joking. Mrs. Pilling wagged a finger at Jan—naughty, naughty—and gave a fair imitation of laughter.

By the time the guests reassembled indoors to see the Pillings' remodeled kitchen, Rick was actively praying for snack food. The thought of salty pretzels possessed him, though he'd have happily settled for Triscuits, Cheese Nips, anything with weight and flavor. Meg Pilling ran her manicured hand across the width of a new refrigerator, like one of those models who stroke appliances on game shows. The built-in icemaker suddenly dumped a few chiming ice cubes into a tumbler. Mitchell nodded thoughtfully. Oscar applauded and said, "Brava!" Jan asked if the refrigerator could heel or play dead. Only after the demonstration did Rick notice the absence of cooking odors. The windows of the double ovens were dark, the granite countertops barren. Copper pots hung above the electric range in descending size, mere decoration. Rick tried to fight his hang-dog expression; hadn't Jerry said there'd be dinner?

"Folks," announced Jerry, after corralling everyone into the living room. "Have a seat. The wife and I have a little surprise." The four guests squeezed among an avalanche of tasseled pillows, sinking side by side into the couch. "Honey," Jerry said to Meg, "you've got the floor."

Meg Pilling walked to the center of the room. She taught at Westgate Elementary, which explained her exemplary posture and the lilting, patient cadence of her voice. Rick had no trouble envisioning a troupe of mesmerized second-graders following her every order. He wondered if she was about to ask them to make their dinner out of paste and construction paper.

Meg cleared her throat and gazed into the upturned faces of her guests. "Jerry and I wanted to do something fun and unusual, so we've planned a really outlandish night." She grinned and shot a look at her husband. Jerry beamed back. "I bet you're all just itching to know what it is." As if on cue, everyone mumbled and shifted about. "Well...," she said, milking the suspense, "we're going to give you each five dollars and let you go to the store on your own—there are several excellent supermarkets in the area—so you can buy something to fix for a potluck!"

No one stirred or spoke. Rick wasn't sure he'd heard her correctly.

"We have all the cooking utensils you'll need," said Meg. "And that brand-new kitchen is just sitting there, waiting! The only rules are that you don't go over your five-dollar limit, and that you're back here within half an hour."

"Do we have to actually cook what we buy?" asked Mitchell. The idea of culinary effort seemed to depress him. "Can't we buy something frozen or from the deli section?"

Meg's smile wavered. Through the crack in her composure, Rick thought he glimpsed a hint of misery. "Now that wouldn't be very creative, would it?" She looked at her husband as if to say, *You've got to prod some people into the party spirit.*

"I get it," rasped Jan. "Hunters and gatherers!"

"How primitive," said Oscar.

"I used to love scavenger hunts," said Mitchell. "Of course, those were the days when a kid could knock on a stranger's door without being molested or kidnapped." He pushed his glasses up the bridge of his nose.

"Well," said Meg, reviving her smile, "you're safe in Westgate."

"She's absolutely right," said Jerry. "If you're not back in half an hour, we'll file a report with the Bureau of Missing Persons." He removed a wallet from his back pocket and dealt out five-dollar bills. Peering up from a sitting position, reaching for what amounted to his allowance, Rick had to admit that, fiscally speaking, Jerry fit the paternal role, confident and ceremonious as he handled money.

"Largess!" exclaimed Oscar. He took his five and winked at Rick.

"I ironed them," said Meg, to explain the crisp, unblemished bills. "Are there any more questions?"

Rick was going to ask the Pillings to give him explicit directions back to the house so he wouldn't get lost again, but he was nearly moved to tears by the thought that he could not only buy food for the potluck, but also something to eat right away, even before he got to the cash register. He was first to rise to his feet, a move which, considering the plush upholstery, took some leverage. The others straggled after him, sharing baffled glances. Meg and Jerry each grabbed a knob of the double doors and swung them open. "I wish I had a starting gun," said Jerry.

Mitchell paused in the doorway and asked, "Aren't you coming, too?"

From the way the Pillings looked at each other, it was clear this possibility hadn't crossed their minds. "We'll keep the home fires burning," said Jerry.

"Your best bet is to head back to the freeway exit," said Meg. "Toward the commercial district. You can't miss it." She watched her guests scatter across the front lawn, trudging toward their cars.

"Just look for signs of life," yelled Jerry.

Once inside his car, Rick noticed Jan in a Mercedes parked across the street, her face lit by the glow of a cigarette lighter, cheeks imploding as she took the first drag. Parked behind her, Mitchell furrowed his brow and squinted at a road map, disappearing within its folds. Oscar barreled by in his Mustang, shrugging at Rick and honking his horn. Jerry and Meg stood beside each other in the wide bright doorway of their sprawling home. They waved at Rick as he revved his engine, one fluttering arm per spouse.

—

Anyone who saw the Pillings in their doorway that night would probably take their happiness and compatibility for granted. Rick wondered what, if anything, Jan and Oscar and Mitchell knew about the couple's compromised marriage. He wouldn't have been surprised to learn that Meg and Jerry had let their secrets slip; it's easy, thought Rick, to confide in someone you see at work, or to someone who runs his fingers through your hair, or probes your open mouth.

As he pulled away from the curb, he couldn't help but marvel at the Pillings' elaborate domesticity: offspring, swimming pool, blown-glass clowns. While touring their home, he had sensed that Meg and Jerry meant to impress each other more than their visitors: *See what we have. See what we've done. Our life together is no illusion, no mistake.*

Since Oscar seemed to know where he was going, Rick tried to catch up with the Mustang's taillights, but they shot away like comets near a street named Valley Court. Checking his rearview mirror for Mitchell and Jan, he saw nothing but the empty road behind him. Once again, Rick found himself navigating the maze of Westgate, its lawns trimmed, its houses all alike. He aimed his car toward a concentration of hazy light, a distant promise of people and commerce.

It had been so long since Rick had cooked a meal, he was worried he'd forgotten how. Working in his studio till dinnertime, light-headed from paint fumes, he'd usually stand before the open refrigerator and nibble at scraps of food, or jump into his car and head for Casa Carnitas, the local taco stand. Dinners had been different when Eric was alive. The two of them sometimes dedicated entire nights to the alchemy of cooking; the raw becoming tender, the cold becoming hot. Chopping and stirring and sautéing not only took time but seemed to prolong it, the minutes enriched with their arguments and gossip. When their studio grew warm and fragrant with sauces and roasts, Rick found himself believing that Eric might never succumb to the virus. Not if he could be tempted by food. Not if he gained weight.

"I wouldn't be so worried if I could put on a few pounds," Eric told him one night, peering down at himself as if over the edge of a cliff. The weaker Eric's appetite, the more time he and Rick spent planning and preparing meals. They began to visit farmers' markets, carnicerias, bakeries. At a restaurant supply store near Chinatown, they bought a garlic press, a set of wire whisks, and what they decided was their most frivolous purchase to date: a lemon zester. Although he often couldn't finish a meal, Eric insisted that cooking gave him pleasure, distracted him from the neuropathy that numbed his lips and hands and feet. They had sex less often now that Eric was home all day, groggy from medication, and Rick suspected that their libido, rerouted, had given birth to lavish repasts.

In the early evenings, Rick cleaned his brushes, climbed the stairs to the sleeping loft, and crawled into bed beside Eric. The mattress lay on the floor, surrounded by issues of *Art in America*, bottles of AZT, and crumpled clothes. Rick would reach beneath Eric's sweatshirt and rub his back while they watched cooking shows on television, both of them soothed by the warmth and give of skin. On Channel 13, Madeleine Dupery might fricassee a game hen or make a sumptuous ratatouille, rolling her R's with such panache, they began to doubt she was really French. Then there was Our Man Masami, a chef who dismembered vegetables with a glinting cleaver and laughed a high, delirious laugh as he tossed them into a hissing wok. Rick and Eric took notes while they watched, salivating. They cheered and grumbled like football fans, shouting comments like "Needs something crunchy!" or "Too much cumin!"

Over time, however, it was Rick who grew padded with fat, his trousers tight around the waist, while Eric, whittled by the blade of AIDS, could barely bring himself to eat.

Alarmed by Eric's weight loss, Dr. Santos started him on a regimen of Oxandrin tablets, steroid injections, and cans of a rich nutritional drink. His weight finally stabilized, but his already pale skin continued to grow translucent. Rick began to notice thin blue veins beneath Eric's temples, wrists, and groin, a glimpse into the tributaries, the secret depths of his lover's flesh. Still, Rick held on to the hope that he was only imagining Eric's fragility, making it into something more ominous than it really was. Until one Sunday at the farmers' market.

They were walking back to their car, both of them carrying bags of fresh food. Eric had been in good spirits that morning, eager for an outing. Enormous clouds raced overhead, wind strafing the city streets. Taking a shortcut, they turned down an alley, and a sudden gust funneled toward them. Eric's jacket blew open, the red lining as bright as blood, and he toppled backward, landing on his side, apples and onions spilling from the bags. Sprawled on the asphalt, Eric couldn't move his arm, and Rick knelt down to cradle his head. "Is this happening?" Eric asked. An eerie calm tempered his voice, as if he'd observed, from far away, the fall of some frail, unlucky stranger.

In the emergency room, while Eric was being X-rayed, Rick told the attending physician that Eric must have tripped on a crack in the asphalt and lost his footing. But later, sitting alone in the waiting room, he couldn't stop repeating to himself, *A gust of wind knocked Eric over.*

AZT, it turned out, had made his bones brittle, and so Dr. Santos discontinued Eric's antiretrovirals until his fractured arm had time to heal. This led to complications that worsened Eric's weight loss. The most dire was an inability to absorb nutrients. Now and then he managed sips of broth, cubes of Jell-O, diluted juice, but nothing he ate or drank sustained him. Eric was eventually admitted to the hospital and tethered to an IV. Rick offered to smuggle into the hospital the heavy, soporific dishes Eric had loved as a child: biscuits with gravy, chicken-fried steak. But the foods he'd once loved revolted him now, and Rick's offer made him feel like a finicky child. "Honey," he told Rick, "it's better if you don't try to feed me." For days Rick sat by the bed while Eric faded in and out of sleep, his meals growing cold. Nurses swept through the room and changed the IV bag dripping into Eric's arm, a clear solution that bypassed the tongue.

Despite daily infusions and the few bites of food he forced himself to eat, Eric was dying of starvation. "AIDS-related-wasting," Dr. Santos told Rick in the corridor, "remains one of our most difficult battles." The doctor spoke in a solicitous whisper, but Rick heard surrendering through the ward, drowning out authority and hope. "Do you understand," asked Dr. Santos, "how wasting works?" Rick knew very well how wasting worked: lips papery, cheeks hollow, eyes puzzled, Eric retreated into the stillness and solitude of his body. No wish or prayer or entreaty could restore him. "What more," he asked the doctor, "do I need to know?"

The Westgate Safeway, glaring and imperious, loomed above dozens of smaller shops. Rick pulled into the lot. On the drive here, he'd had to remind himself that a year had passed since Eric's death. Except for teaching two graduate seminars at a local art school, Rick spent most of that year working on paintings of slender, disconnected bones glowing against a black background. Now that the paintings were being shown in New York, Rick had accepted Jerry's invitation as part of a plan to end his isolation and revive his flagging social life. More than once after leaving the Pillings' house, Rick considered finding the freeway and simply driving back home, five dollars richer, but anything sounded better than returning to an empty studio. Besides, he liked the other guests, and he was curious to see how Jerry fared in his double life. Rick had never met anyone like Meg and Jerry, which accounted for the evening's strain, and also its sense of adventure. *It's only one night*, he told himself, parking the car.

The second he stepped through the supermarket's automatic doors, Rick heard a tune he recognized but couldn't identify, its perky, repetitive rhythms urging him down the aisles. Wandering past shelves stocked with eye-catching cans and packages, Rick became one big, indiscriminate craving. Everything looked appetizing. In the pet food section, basted dog bones seemed like the perfect complement to a sharp Stilton or a salmon pâté. In Household Cleaning Products, pastel kitchen sponges looked as edible as petits-fours. The linoleum throughout the store was creamy white and speckled like spumoni. "Your eyes are bigger than your stomach," he remembered his mother saying when he'd heaped his plate with more than he could eat. Once, he'd learned about the world by putting its pretty objects in his mouth—the dusty taste of a wooden block, a bitter waxy bite of

Crayola—and tonight he'd reclaimed, without even trying, this long-lost infant wisdom.

When he rounded the corner, he caught a glimpse of Jan, in her pinstriped suit, striding toward Gourmet Foods. With his head turned, Rick almost ran into a man who was handing out samples of Inferno Chili. Standing behind a folding table, he wore a white apron and stirred a pot that was heated from beneath by Sterno. Peering inside the pot, Rick saw kidney beans, chunks of tomato, and bits of ruddy onion. The concoction bubbled like lava, small eruptions burping from its surface. "Try some?" asked the man. He held out a plastic spoon, a dollop of chili steaming at its tip, the smell robust and peppery.

Before Rick even began to chew, chili lit the wick of his tongue, his taste buds scorched by exhilarating flame. His eyes watered, his nose ran. Perspiration beaded on his skin. He wrenched the spoon out of his mouth and grabbed a can of the stuff, as if reading the ingredients might explain the unearthly surge of heat. "A taste of hell in every bite!" exclaimed the devil on the label, grinning maliciously. Rick opened his mouth, half expecting to exhale fire and torch the store. The man in the apron handed him a tiny paper cup filled with Gatorade. "Only thing that cuts the burn," he said. "That cayenne's got a kick." When he smiled, wrinkles radiated from his brown eyes. His black mustache was waxed at the ends, his jaw shaped like a horseshoe. Rick wanted to thank him, but his throat had closed, leaving him speechless. "Here's one for the road," said the man, offering Rick another shot. At first, Rick wasn't sure if his gallant, folksy manners were real, or his languorous twang authentic. He studied the man through tearing eyes. His nametag read "Earl." Dazed in the aftermath of chili, cool air wafting from the dairy case, Rick couldn't stop staring.

Ordinarily, Rick wasn't attracted to dark-haired men, or to men with mustaches, especially waxed. Any guy who reminded him of potbellied stoves and tooled-leather belts had always struck him as so remote from his own tastes and sympathies as to be practically extraterrestrial. In the past year, though, every man had seemed alien to Rick because he didn't look or smell like Eric. He'd dated two men since Eric's death, but neither involvement lasted long. In the middle of an intimate dinner, he found himself staring across the table at masticating teeth, tufts of hair on the knuckles of a hand, and though he was glad his companions were mammals, these features were vividly physical without being the least erotic. The one time he did have sex, it was to prove to himself that he could excite someone besides Eric. While flailing naked, he'd inventory the way he and his new partner made love: *Now he's plunging his tongue into my mouth, now I'm licking the inside of his thigh.* He might as well have brought a clipboard to bed. After sex was over, Rick knew he'd been a lousy lover, mired in the past, hopelessly distracted, as spontaneous as a metronome. And now, at the Westgate Safeway of all places, while Muzak tinkled in the glaring air, Rick's desire awoke from hibernation. Earl returned Rick's gaze—there was no mistaking—with the same flirtatious curiosity. "What brings you to the Safeway?" asked Earl as he slowly stirred the Inferno.

Coated with dust, its brown enamel faded by the sun, Earl's ancient station wagon looked like a boulder that had rolled into the parking lot. Rick carried the folding table and cooking equipment while Earl gripped a cardboard box filled with cans of Inferno. Now that Earl had taken off his apron, Rick could better see the outline of his body and the motion of his ropy limbs. Earl propped the boxes on the roof of the car and fished in his jeans pocket for keys. The Golden State Freeway roared in the distance. "By the way," said Earl, "you can keep your five bucks; there's no finer way to promote a product than feeding it directly to the people."

"It isn't my money," Rick reminded him. "And besides, Inferno will be the bargain of the party." They lifted the tailgate, loaded the car. As they slid inside and slammed their doors, the station wagon creaked on its springs. "Just throw that crap in the back," said Earl. "I wasn't expecting company." Rick reached down and chucked cans of Sterno, a box of plastic spoons, and a stack of paper cups into the backseat. Crumpled McDonalds's bags and a few empty soft-drink bottles littered the floor. Rick told Earl that the station wagon reminded him of his studio when he was too steeped in work to think about cleaning, to give order to anything but art; the disarray was industrious. "I guess I can see that," said Earl, nodding at the compliment and idling the engine. "It's in me to give a thing my all. Before selling Inferno, I did a stint at a pitiful little radio station in Buford. My spot was called *The Classical Half-Hour*, but it was more like a fancy fifteen minutes. I'll tell you, though, this gig's as solitary as being a DJ. During long hauls, I've been known to interrogate myself just to have a conversation." Earl laughed and shook his head. "The things you'll confess, alone on the road." He twisted a knob on the dashboard and a tape deck sputtered to life. "Johann Sebastian Bach," said Earl upping the volume. "Best antidote I know to a day of Muzak." He threw the station wagon into reverse.

"Do you know your way around Westgate?" asked Rick.

"All I know these days are supermarkets. Everyplace in between is just gas stations and motels. Don't you know where we're headed?"

The directions were locked in Rick's car back at the lot and, after convincing Earl to keep him company, he wasn't about to suggest they turn around. Rick peered through the bird droppings and insect remains that splattered the windshield, doing his best to guess the way back to Meg and Jerry's. He couldn't help but interpret the windshield as a good omen: Earl had traveled numberless gritty miles to meet him, and even if they only spent one night together, the unlikelihood of their having met, combined with the tape deck's welling arpeggios, made their impromptu date seem predestined. "It's funny," said Earl, "to have a passenger." As Rick leaned toward the dash and squinted at street signs, he told Earl about his conversation with Jerry on the plane. All the while, he could sense Earl staring. Lack of subtlety was one of Earl's most appealing traits, and Rick had to use every ounce of restraint and concentration to keep his mind on the road. But when Earl rested his hand on Rick's thigh, Rick dove headfirst into the driver's seat, yanked Earl's shirt from his jeans, and licked his stomach, the flesh warm, taut, and salty. Earl gasped and arched his back, allowing Rick to lift his shirt higher. Rick pulled his head back far enough to see Earl's stomach in the emerald light of the dashboard. Wind from the open windows ruffled Rick's hair and blew into his shirt; the velocity of the car, the rumble of the engine, the bumps in the road felt metabolic. "That," he said, peering up from Earl's lap, "is one beautiful bellybutton." Rick couldn't help but notice that the things he said and did that night were unlike him, or at least unlike the recluse he'd become, and his audacity, like a file baked in a cake, freed him from the cell of himself. He circled and probed Earl's navel with his tongue.

"Yikes," heaved Earl. "You *are* an artist!" He steered the car to the side of the road with one hand and gripped a hank of Rick's hair with the other, pressing him against his stomach. The station wagon grazed the curb and lurched to a stop, its cargo rolling and clattering in the back.

Earl's mouth was wet and generous, his hard jaw covered with stubble. When he moaned, his bony chest rattled with pleasure, an erection tenting his jeans. The more they kissed, the more Rick realized how alone he'd been, and the more alone he realized he'd been, the greedier his kisses became. The restless pressure of Earl's hands had the power to cause and alleviate need. Finally, the two of them pulled apart long enough to catch their breath and make a plan: an appearance at the potluck, back to the Safeway for condoms and Rick's car, then on to Earl's motel.

After ringing the doorbell, the two of them waited on the front stoop, cooking equipment in tow. As Rick reached out to squeeze Earl's shoulder, he remembered reaching beneath Eric's sweatshirt and rubbing the supple muscles of his back. The memory, blunt and unbidden, lingered in his hands.

When no one answered the door, they sneaked inside the house as quietly as thieves. In the living room, Earl's eyes widened. "Beats the rooms at Best Western." The guests had gathered in the dining room, where sliding glass doors opened onto the backyard and the luminous pool. Even from a distance Rick could hear the strain of people trying to keep the ball of small talk aloft. A surprised hush greeted Rick as he walked into the room with a stranger. Everyone eyed them quizzically. Rick apologized for being late and introduced Earl all around, counting on the possibility that the Pillings were too bent on being "outlandish," and too constrained by good manners, to object to an uninvited guest. "I sure appreciate the invitation," Earl said to Meg. There had been no invitation of course, but Earl's gratitude disarmed Mrs. Pilling. "We're glad to have you," she said uncertainly.

Meg had set the table in anticipation of a buffet. The white tablecloth matched the napkins fanned atop it. Empty china bowls and plates shone beneath the chandelier. Rick had to admit that Earl, a stewpot dangling from his arm, made a scruffy addition to the pristine room and the well-dressed guests. Earl was a wild card, a complete stranger who was capable, Rick realized with both alarm and excitement, of almost anything. As a result of their feverish making out, Earl's hair was mussed, his mustache frayed. Rick didn't dare imagine what *he* looked like, though he suspected a hickey was imprinted on his neck. Propped against Rick's chest was a cardboard box. He set it on the table and explained that, for a mere five dollars, Earl was going to treat them to an up-and-coming American meal.

"Up-and-coming, indeed," repeated Oscar, who could skew any phrase toward innuendo.

Rick shot Oscar a warning glance.

Earl cleared his throat, straightened up, and mustered all the salesmanship he had left. "This is just about the most savory pot of chili you'll ever taste," he said in his polished disc-jockey modulations. "Inferno's aiming for a three-year growth plan with a product-recognition goal along the lines of, say, your Dinty Moore or Del Monte." He lit a fire beneath the pot and began stacking cans of Inferno into a pyramid, display-style. "We've got quite a few backers in Dallas, the kind of ranchers who're all wallet and no cows."

Mitchell smiled for the first time that night and Rick was sure he found Earl attractive. Jerry saw Mitchell smiling at Earl, and his body tensed. It occurred to Rick that Jerry might harbor a secret crush; didn't Mitchell possess the collegiate look, glasses and all, that had made the airborne Jerry rhapsodic? Noticing the devil on the cans, Meg folded her arms and turned to share a look of consternation with her husband. When Meg saw Jerry staring at his dentist, the same hunch that occurred to Rick seemed to cross her mind. Her arms slipped loose and fell to her sides.

This was the aspect of parties that Rick found most wondrous and suffocating: one suddenly became entangled in the invisible lines of lust or envy or resentment that stretched between the guests. Suddenly, Rick was walloped by an idea: a diagram of the party would be his next painting! He saw, against a backdrop of muddy color, filaments of glowing emotion.

Once Earl had completed his pitch, the others took turns presenting their purchases. Jan dredged from a Safeway bag, one by one, a can of baby corncobs, a tin of Norwegian sardines, and a glass jar crammed with tiny white cocktail onions that, even beneath the glittering light of the chandelier, looked haplessly subterranean. She placed the offerings on the table. Everyone eyed the foreign labels. "It's gor-may," she enunciated. "I once had a girlfriend who lived for pickled foods." Meg blushed, as if "pickled foods" were a euphemism. Jerry began to struggle with the jar of onions, huffing and gritting his teeth until Jan grabbed it from his hand and twisted off the lid with a flick of her wrist. "You loosened it for me," she told him, and Rick imagined that she'd had to say that, or something equally reassuring, to many men in order to downplay her prowess and spare them embarrassment. She dumped the onions into a bowl.

Mitchell contributed three boxes of Lunchables, a packaged assortment of lunch meats, crackers, and processed cheese spreads that could be served in various combinations. He ripped open the boxes and, hunched in an occupational posture, prepared a plate of meticulous hors d'oeuvres.

Oscar proffered a one-pound box of marzipan from Heidi's Kandy Kitchen, a concession he'd found tucked away in a strip mall. Everyone oohed at the replicas of ripe fruit, the box exuding a sweet almond odor. Meg said, "They're precious," and gingerly nibbled a miniature orange. What happened next was something that Rick, who considered himself visually sophisticated, if not downright jaded, had never conceived of, let alone seen. Meg let loose a warble of horror and her right eyelid began to widen and contract, the eyeball adrift in its socket. Her otherwise mild and maternal presence gave way to a kind of lascivious rapture, and if Meg hadn't been mortified into silence, Rick would have expected her to purr with delight, lick her own shoulder, or nip at the air. The instant Jerry became aware of what was happening, he pulled out a chair, into which Meg plummeted. With one hand she applied pressure to her tremulous brow, and with the other held her eyelid closed by the lashes. While she was trying without success to control her eye, her jaw went lax and revealed a mash of marzipan. When Meg realized she was flashing food at the stunned guests, she shut her mouth with such force, her teeth snapped together like the clasp of a purse.

"Oh, my God!" yelped Mitchell. "I read about it in dental school but I've never seen it happen firsthand!"

"What is it?" barked Jan. She stood erect and ready, as though prepared to pin Mrs. Pilling to the floor if the spasms worsened.

Meg waved her hand as if to say, *Don't look at me, please.*

Everyone crowded closer.

The body is such a mystery, thought Rick; *you forget that your eyes are apertures. That your skin is a huge and vulnerable organ, that your muscles have a will of their own.*

Mitchell bent over Meg. "Is it Marcus Gunn reflex?" he asked.

Meg nodded.

"You've heard of it?" marveled Jerry. "I'm very impressed." He dashed through the swinging door and retrieved a glass of water from the kitchen. While Meg took a couple of grateful gulps, Jerry rested his hands on her shoulders, his wedding band catching the light. "Hasn't happened in years has it, darling?"

Meg poked and kneaded her own cheek as if putting the finishing touches on a clay bust. "I think it's stopped," she said. The guests gazed at Mrs. Pilling and waited to see if the twitching returned. A warm breeze blew through the screen doors. A swing set clanked in the backyard. Crickets throbbed on the lawns of Westgate. At last, Mitchell pronounced the episode over and there came a collective murmur of relief.

"Marcus Gunn reflex is rare," explained Mitchell. "It's caused when the chewing muscles and salivary glands are connected to the muscles that control the eyes. Anything can set it off: certain food, emotional stress, even novocaine injected into the wrong spot."

"It's painless," said Meg, "but unpredictable and terribly embarrassing."

"And congenital," added Jerry. "Her mother first noticed it when she was nursing Meg in the hospital. 'It made my baby look like a little sucking glutton,' she used to tell me. 'So blissful at the teat.'"

Meg twisted around and glared at Jerry. "Thank you," she said. She took a deep breath and hoisted herself out of the chair. "Will you excuse me?" Meg fled into the kitchen. Jerry hurried after her. No sooner had the swinging door stilled than there arose the angry clank of pots and furious blast of tap water. Rick realized with a wince that the Pillings weren't familiar with the acoustics of their new kitchen—all that decoy noise did little to mask their voices. "I'm embarrassed enough as it is, Jerry, without you regaling your friends with stories about my breast-feeding. They don't have to know everything about me."

"What do you mean, 'embarrassed enough as it is'?"

"I can't look at those people without thinking about what they do with each other in bed."

Oscar sighed a facetious sigh. "One look at me and people think of sex."

"They don't do anything with each other," said Jerry. "They didn't even know each other until tonight."

Jan peeled the lid from the tin of sardines. A regiment of fish stared back, darkly iridescent. "What are these marinated in anyway?" she asked. "Motor oil?"

Earl surveyed the buffet. "This," he said, "is one cockamamie potluck." He hummed under his breath and dished chili into bowls.

"'Luck' is the operative word in 'potluck,'" mused Oscar. "On the groaning board before you, what looks like mere food is actually manifestation of chance." He waved a hand over the table. "Things come together in ways you'd never expect."

"And fall apart in ways you'd never expect," added Mitchell.

"Then don't think about what they do in bed, Meg."

"I can't be around them and *not* think about it. That's the problem with homosexuals."

"But the party was your idea as much as mine."

"No, Jerry. It was *your* idea. I agreed to this party because, after consulting with the elders, I was ready to do whatever it took to live up to our vows, to keep you happy and faithful. But you know what I found out tonight, Jerry? I found out I'm old-fashioned. And I'm tired of being polite. Men lying with men, women with women: it's a sin, period. And you condone it." Silverware clanked like scrap metal. "I saw you looking at that Mitchell."

Mitchell took a bite of chili and his eyes began to water. "Even if I were attracted to Jerry," he said, "I'd never date a patient. Especially not heterosexual. It's hard enough to find someone compatible; why would I want to make the odds impossible by going after a straight man? Besides, abscesses and gum recession don't exactly fan the flames of lust." He sniffed, removed a handkerchief from his back pocket, and blew his nose. "This is delicious," he said to Earl.

"Jerry was cruising the pants off you," said Oscar. "The man could use a few lessons in the art of the clandestine glance. Especially if he plans to stay married." He surveyed the table. "Meg is a lovely woman when she's not besieged by queers."

"Besieged?" said Rick. "I seem to recall being invited."

"In Texas," said Earl, "the married ones go to another town when they want to fool around. They'll do everything with another man but kiss him on the lips, and they think that makes them…"

"Pure as the driven snow," said Oscar. "It's amazing, all the intimate things you can do with another human being and still remain a virgin."

"Don't tell me you weren't ogling him," said Meg. "I have eyes."

"That's an understatement," said Oscar.

Jan fished a baby corncob from a bowl. "Hold on, you guys. I don't blame her for being upset. It's another case of the wife getting the short end of the stick. I'm awfully fond of Jerry, but at the office, he's one of the boys when he's with gay men and one of the men when he's with straight women." She poked the cob—a pale, extraneous finger—into the air for emphasis. "Jerry wants it both ways, which would be harmless, I guess, unless you were married to him and had a horde of kids to take care of. None of us would want to be in Meg's position."

"Of course not," said Rick. "But the way Jerry explained it…"

Meg hissed, "You twist things around till they suit you."

"I'm trying to do what's best for—"

"—me and the kids? Spare me the piety, Jerry."

"For all of us, I was going to say. So I think a man is handsome; what's that have to do with how I feel about you?"

"Nothing," said Meg. "And it hurts."

"I know what Jerry's going through," said Mitchell. "My ex-wife is still furious because I told her I was gay. And because I didn't tell her sooner."

"In other words," said Oscar, "she's mad at you for failing at the marriage *and* trying to make it work."

A glass broke in the kitchen. "Look what you made me do," shrilled Meg.

Mitchell gazed into his plate. "Do you think we should leave?"

"Not me," said Rick. "I don't care if they start throwing knives. I've waited all night to eat and I'm not going anywhere until I'm full." He loaded his bowl, took Earl by the hand, and walked outside. At the pool's edge, Rick and Earl yanked off their shoes and socks. They dangled their legs in the tepid water and shared the bowl of finger food. "Sure would be nice to stay in one place for a while," Earl lamented. "Tomorrow I've got a gig at a Market Basket in Placerville." Rick might have felt a pang of sadness about Earl's leaving, but the temperate air, the plentiful stars, and the pool as bright and fathomless as daylight fortified him against despair. *Compared to losing Eric,* he thought, *all my future losses are bound to be bearable.* The second he thought this, he knew it wasn't true. "I wish I lived here," said Earl. "This would be a good place to stay put." His words were so plaintive, so burdened with yearning, that Rick laughed when Earl added, "But then I'd probably be in the kitchen scrapping with my wife."

Oscar and Mitchell and Jan walked toward the pool, a talkative trio. Each of them held a china plate filled with incongruous food. Rick recognized in their speech and gestures small flourishes of good will—a stray touch, a teasing retort—that a stranger might mistake for flirtation. When Jan delivered the punch line of a joke—"And the priest says, 'Young lady, when you get to heaven, St. Finger is going to wag his peter at you'"—laughter replaced the silence of the night. Somehow a party had sprouted in the Pillings' backyard like a dandelion through a crack in the sidewalk. Rick leaned against Earl, swinging his legs until waves slapped at the sides of the pool, rafts and life buoys drifting on the choppy turquoise currents.

The sound of churning water drew two of the Pillings' children from their rooms. They materialized from behind the swing set at the far end of the house. The youngest, a barefoot girl in an oversize T-shirt—Rick guessed her to be about ten—sauntered toward the strangers. She plunked herself down by the water and tried to garner, without seeming to, as much attention as possible. When the inflatable shark drifted toward her, she flung out a leg and kicked it in the snout. The shark wheezed and sailed away. "I'm Yvonne," she announced.

"That's not her real name," said the boy from the opposite side of the pool, hands thrust in his pockets. Rick had no trouble imagining him as a grown man who inhabited the periphery of parties, lobbing skeptical remarks into the crowd, eyes animated by the same watchfulness that shown in them tonight.

"I'm the governess," said the girl.

"She's my little sister," corrected the boy. "She likes to act bratty and pretend she's things she's not."

The girl went on, undaunted. "Are you friends of Mr. and Mrs. Pilling?"

The guests paused, considering her question.

"Excuse us," came the voices of Meg and Jerry from inside the dining room. Everyone turned to face them. Jerry stared forlornly into the backyard, as if he were outside the house looking in. "I'm afraid it's late," he said, pointing to his watch. Meg said, "We hate to be party poopers." Their voices, as if strained through the wire mesh of the screen doors, were timid and thin.

Rick and Earl shook water from their feet and, while lacing their shoes, glanced at each other with such overt erotic promise, Oscar clicked his tongue.

Jan and Mitchell hurried their conversation, determined to fit in a few remarks before parting. "I bet your ex-wife will be more forgiving when she finds another husband," said Jan. "If I knew more heterosexual men, I'd set her up on a blind date." Mitchell agreed that things would be easier once she was coupled, but behind the gold-rimmed glasses, his eyes conveyed their native doubt.

The little girl and her brother bolted across the concrete, flung open the screen doors, and ran into the dining room. Yvonne nearly collided with her father, embracing his leg, and Rick wondered what it would be like to be grabbed by your brash and affectionate child just when love seemed most farfetched. The boy gravitated toward his mother but remained aloof. Ever the considerate hostess, Meg flicked on the outdoor light, a magnet drawing moths whose frantic shadows churned against the house.

"Shall we take our leave?" asked Oscar. And the visitors headed inside.

Rick received a postcard from Arizona that depicted a jackelope, the imaginary offspring of an antelope and a jackrabbit. A postcard from Florida showed a freight train's flatcar loaded with an orange the size of a house. Earl sent the most surreal cards he could find, either because he favored them or because he thought they'd appeal to the artist in Rick. They arrived every few weeks, a reminder that the world's oddities were inexhaustible.

Eventually, however, the cards stopped coming, as Rick knew they would. Earl never asked for a reply or included a return address. Besides, Rick was at work on a new painting and, apart from a nagging set of technical and aesthetic preoccupations, he had little to talk about. He'd come to think of his encounter with Earl as a thing completed, an improvised composition that one more brushstroke would ruin.

And then, just as Rick was about to relegate his evening in Westgate to the past, a letter arrived from Meg and Jerry. It was one of those Xeroxed family newsletters sent out at Christmas. Listed in alphabetical order were the academic and athletic victories of the Pillings' six children. Rick noted with amusement that there was no mention of a girl named Yvonne. Apart from parental hyperbole, the highlights of Meg and Jerry's year were reserved for the last two sentences: "We visited the Big Island of Hawaii in September, where we glimpsed the fury of a live volcano. Upon our return, Jerry assumed a position on the church's high council."

Rick turned the letter over, searching for a salutation scrawled in the margins, or for some note that would say what had become of Jerry and whether his equivocations persisted. But the margins were empty and even the signatures were photocopied. Rick slid the Pillings' letter into the rolltop desk he'd inherited from Eric, and swiveled around to face his latest painting. The cavernous studio contained a commotion of paintbrushes, dropcloths, and coffee cans encrusted with acrylics. Beyond the windows, sunlight burned through passing clouds, then slid over streets and billboards and buildings. The fluid, moody light animated his painting. Its imagery was based on his recollection of Saturday morning cartoons in which trails of enticing odor wafted from hot pies or freshly baked bread; then as now, he loved how they rippled through a room to caress a face, burrow into nostrils, and beckon the hungry with curling fingers. Follow. Taste. Be sated. Rick leaned forward. Thanks to hours spent feathering wet paint with a small brush, tendrils of scent reached across the canvas. One moment they seemed to float closer. The next they seemed to recede.

Strong Like Water

Robert Hodgson Van Wagoner

The same week Karmine discovers her husband is having an affair with a man, she takes her mother to a doctor, who finds a tiny patch of cancer on the tip of the old woman's nose. Abby, Karmine's seventy-five-year-old mother, cannot be convinced she has not contracted the malignancy from her late neighbor, a young woman stricken with lymphoma, who regularly, at the conclusion of Abby's visits, kissed the old woman on the nose. Abby's little spot is a garden variety cancer, the result of too many years' unprotected exposure to the sun, years and years of wear; its removal requires but a small operation and the maintenance of a periodic check-up. All the same, Abby is sure she's caught lymphoma from kissing. She is convinced she will shortly die.

"You're not going to die," Karmine says. "There's nothing fatal about a tiny spot on the end of your nose." It is snowing hard—icy flakes click softly against the windshield. It is the sound, Karmine imagines, of parakeet feet, unnumbered parakeet feet, walking on glass. She turns the wipers to the highest speed. The blades rush back and forth, and though Karmine doesn't entirely realize what is happening, the vigorous back and forth, this motion of winding a watch, has begun to stiffen her neck.

"Lymphoma," Abby insists. She examines her nose in the visor mirror, but doesn't touch the cancer. "I should have never let her kiss me."

Karmine is Abby's youngest child, and for all practical purposes, Abby's only child. Harlan, Karmine's older brother, lives in Detroit, an automotive engineer. He calls Abby weekly and visits as he can, usually on major holidays. It causes a guilty moment, this resentment Karmine feels for her brother, his distance and freedom from Abby's unreasonable aging. Karmine resents Harlan for his careless assumptions, and for his useless and insufficient gratitude. She resents him most, however, for the same reason she resents her father, who is dead—she resents them both for leaving her alone and terrified Abby will die.

"You're not listening," Karmine says. "There are no lymph nodes on the end of your nose. And even if there were, you don't catch cancer like some virus."

Abby pushes the visor to the ceiling and as an after thought—though they are almost home—checks that she's locked her door. "This is the beginning of the end," she says calmly. "You remember this conversation. This is the beginning of the end. I give myself three months."

In Abby's driveway, Karmine turns off the car. The windshield wipers stop, and she is immediately grateful for the stillness. "The beginning of the end," as far as Karmine is concerned, has long passed. The end had begun five years earlier when Karmine's father, a man ten years older than Abby, died of heart failure. On the day of her father's funeral, Karmine hadn't given her despondent mother three months, much less five years. Now she is distressed, put off, by Abby's arbitrary death predictions. She is put off by the arbitrariness of death. For five years Abby has deteriorated—lost much of her sight, some of her balance, a little of her memory—but she has not died. Abby slips away much like a child grows, in increments beyond perception, with only memory and the passage of time for measurement. The more frail Abby seems, the more frightened Karmine becomes. Strange, it strikes Karmine, that now, when Abby can no longer offer the comfort and reassurance of the mother, that she, Karmine, is most terrified of losing her. Perhaps it is because they need each other again, as in the child's early life. For very different reasons they need, though they can no longer truly help one another. Karmine sometimes wonders if it would have been easier (for her, for Harlan, for Abby) had Abby, in fact, died as predicted, shortly after her husband's death.

"I hope Peter doesn't take this too hard," Abby says. Peter is Karmine's husband. "I was hoping he'd come along today. He'd have been very upset by the lymphoma. I don't think Peter is going to take this well."

Karmine gets out and comes around to help Abby. Abby adores Peter, and Peter adores Abby. They have adored each other for twenty-six years, since before Karmine adored Peter. Peter's adoration of Abby was one of Karmine's first reasons for loving Peter. In the twenty-five years of Karmine and Peter's marriage, Peter has made no distinction in time and concern and service between Abby and his own mother. So much adoration, in light of all Karmine must keep to herself, must keep from her mother, only complicates the needing—needing Peter, needing Abby.

"Peter had a meeting after school," Karmine says. She takes Abby's elbow, pulls her gently from the car, bracing herself against a slip. It is still snowing, and Karmine intuits the uncertain footing. Her muscles, without permission, flinch and tighten, a phenomenon she remembers from years of carrying infants across Utah winters.

"A meeting," Abby scoffs. She knows few meetings keep Peter away. "I hope it wasn't a *church* meeting."

"Not church," Karmine assures. "A meeting with the administration to plan this year's tour. He would have canceled had it been anything else."

Abby grunts but seems satisfied with Karmine's explanation. Near the back door the old woman stops and looks at her yard. January and already a hard winter. Drifts from Peter's shoveling stand as tall as Abby, taller in places. He has shoveled off her carport roof, beaten the snow from her bushes. The temporary stain of Ice Melt stretches like blue carpet from the carport where Abby's car awaits Peter or one of the older grandchildren, Harlan when he is in town—the few people who drive the aging vehicle now and then for the sake of maintenance.

"It's going to snow for a long time," Abby says, shuffling toward the door. "I can feel it. I wish you Mormons would stop praying for snow."

"We stopped that a long time ago," Karmine says. "We're praying for snow-blowers now."

Because of Peter, Karmine and Abby can say these things to each other. Karmine's conversion to Peter's faith, the fact that she abandoned her parents' faith, works because Abby loves Peter. It works because Karmine and her parents, always suspicious of Mormons, loved Peter more than they suspected Mormonism. To his credit, Peter never once asked Karmine to convert. He married her suspecting full-well she never would. Peter, himself, suspects Mormonism, has been openly skeptical at times, which is why, perhaps, he has never been promoted beyond choir director in the lay clergy. On the other hand, the remarkable results he pulls from one hopeless congregational choir after another may be the better answer. Peter is very good at what he does.

Inside Abby's house, Karmine helps her mother remove her winter clothing; she hangs Abby's coat in the closet, removes the old woman's boots and covers her feet with lamb-skin slippers. Positioned haphazardly about the house are a half-dozen walkers, four pronged canes, landmarks of Karmine's determination to keep her mother on her feet. They are rentals, some with wheels, some without, different designs procured in the hope that variety and novelty will tempt Abby to use one. Karmine picks up the nearest walker and places it next to the couch, where her mother sits.

"Diane next door was skin and bones by the time she went," Abby says. She shakes her head sadly, but without the drama Karmine has come to expect from her mother. Abby, convinced she has lymphoma, seems remarkably content to have it. It occurs to Karmine that her mother is more concerned with the fact, the certainty, of the disease than troubled by the consequences of having it.

"You're going to lose some skin off your nose, Mom." Karmine smiles. "There's no bone at the end of your nose, only cartilage. Your nose is already down to skin and cartilage."

Abby glances at her daughter, a look of mild reproach. She points at her nose without touching it. "It's like the entrance to a coal mine," she says. "One little opening for all those miles and layers of tunnels inside."

Karmine imagines her mother as a diagram, something late nineteenth century, with obscure, ominous markings, a cut-away illustrating a network of roughly organized mining tunnels beginning at the tip of Abby's nose, arrows and measurements for the miniature miners burrowing away inside. It is an image Karmine understands; it explains so much. The hollowing, the consumption, a bite at a time, from the inside out. She wonders what such a diagram of herself might reveal, how intricate the tunnels would be, what pieces of what would be missing. And a diagram of Peter? How much of Peter would be gone?

"Well," Karmine sighs. "When the doctor takes off the tip of your nose, I'll have him shine a light down the shaft. If the back of your head glows, we'll run tests for lymphoma."

Abby throws her head back and laughs. Karmine smiles, and after a moment, begins to laugh, too.

"I have to tell you something," Abby finally says. She smoothes the front of her blouse. "For the last week, your father's been spending the nights. He sleeps right where I'm sitting. Here, on the couch."

Karmine blinks rapidly. She resists an impulse to open her mouth wide, as in a yawn, to open the chamber and release a sudden pressure behind her ears. For the past nineteen years, since converting to Mormonism, she has slowly assumed the accouterments of the faith. It is no longer beyond her, as it was before her conversion, to consider the spirit world viable, the distance between mortals and their predecessors small. It was a thing she sometimes hoped for and sometimes dreaded. Yet, even after so many years, she is not certain her hope constitutes actual belief.

She stares at the couch, then at the carpet by the heat vent. Since before her father's death, her mother has slept on the living room floor. Every night for five years, Abby has unrolled the foam-rubber mattress, made her bed with sheets and blankets. Every morning she has removed and folded the bedding, rolled the mattress. What began as a consideration to her ailing husband is now a safeguard against falling out of bed. And, too, it is warmer, she claims, on the floor near the heat vent.

"Every night?"

"Except last Thursday," Abby clarifies. "He didn't come at all last Thursday." She seems mildly perplexed by this.

Karmine starts to shake her head but stops herself.

"When I wake up to use the bathroom he's here, so I put a blanket on him. It's been so cold, you know." Abby pauses, absently petting the cushion beside her. "His hair still has that beautiful black curl."

Abby is pleased with her secret, as pleased to have such a secret as to have her husband again spending the nights. Karmine does not begrudge Abby her pleasure, nor her visions, but she is distressed and angry, nonetheless. She is angry because a sign, if it is a sign, should bring more comfort than distress. Comfort to her, Karmine, as well as to Abby. She is angry, too, because her mother, who has never believed in the supernatural, the preternatural, the spiritual, has without question accepted the whole as real. Karmine has heard of such things before, which distresses her. Whatever the cause, whatever the reality, she suspects that in the world at large people experience similar occurrences quite regularly. And usually (in Karmine's limited experience) to their own demise.

Abby stands, using the walker to leverage herself up. "I'm going to show you something." She abandons the walker and haltingly crosses the room. She passes into the hall and returns a minute later carrying an accordion folder. Before returning to the couch, she drops the folder in Karmine's lap.

"Diane next door went about this thing the wrong way," Abby says. "The way she shriveled away to nothing."

Karmine opens the folder. It is full of papers, pamphlets, envelopes. She pours it all out. "The Hemlock Society," she says.

"My damned eyes," Abby laments. "Given the clientele, you'd think they'd print everything in large print."

Karmine stares at the pile. She can not make herself touch the papers. She is thinking that Peter will soon have to climb on the houses, Abby's and their own, and shovel off the snow. Peter is a large man, very strong and sure on his feet. He is capable of shoveling heavy snow for hours, throwing it, if need be, fifteen or twenty feet without shifting his feet for balance. His physical strength, and the way he smells after hard work, musky but without the stink Karmine has smelled on other men, are qualities she has always loved. Karmine wonders what Abby would say about Peter. She wonders what Peter would say about the Hemlock Society.

"You do not have lymphoma, Mother," Karmine says. *"You simply do not have lymphoma."*

"Fine." Abby smiles. "But browse a little, anyway. Tell me what you think."

Her children grown, no longer demanding so much time, Karmine often walks to the high school to watch Peter rehearse the Wind Ensemble. Summer through fall, marching band season, she takes an active role, sewing uniforms for the flag team, filling large water coolers for those long pre-game rehearsals. Peter respects her opinion; he asks for her criticisms and suggestions. And over time, Karmine has assumed ownership, staked a claim in his artistry. Standing high on the bleachers to better view the formations, sitting in the band room listening to Peter work the counterpoint between the trombones and French horns, Karmine has sometimes lost herself in the precariousness of Peter's work. All those awkward children struggling too hard to be indispensable, yet fearing, as they squeeze those oft-times paltry notes to life, that the opposite is true. And during transitional years, when the performances have not been the best (though even in the bad years the bands are large), Karmine has watched the talented students try to bring the others along, knowing that some people are at their best bridging chasms created by those around them.

It has been a week since she's last attended a rehearsal, and though it is bitter cold outside, she still walks the two blocks to the high school. Peter smiles, appears pleased, when she comes in. Students are opening cases, sucking on reeds, screwing on slides. It is already much too noisy to talk, and Peter is much too busy, so Karmine removes her coat and pulls a chair from Peter's office.

"You're feeling better!" a young flutist calls. Some of the other students wave. Karmine smiles and nods and returns the waves. Apparently, Peter has explained her absence as illness, and perhaps this is, after all, not such a bad explanation. In the middle of the band, their youngest child, Timothy, warms up with the French horns. If he is surprised or pleased or unhappy to see Karmine, he doesn't indicate it. This is Timothy's usual response, and Karmine is not offended. She knows it must be difficult for a fifteen year old boy to have his father for a teacher and his mother for a teacher's aide.

Karmine knows she is taking this step toward routine, the routine that is her routine, because she can determine no other step to take. So far, Peter has not said what he intends to do. What are you going to do? As a question, a sentence, it dangles between them, a road block that no one has yet ventured to challenge. Their three children know nothing.

Karmine is not sure what it means, that her husband is having an affair with a man. She is not sure she understands the specifics of such an affair. She is not sure she understands the generalities either. For her ignorance, she cannot blame Peter. He has tried—and there is something of a tidal wave in his efforts—to convince Karmine to listen, to let him talk.

She watches Peter tune the band. From the podium, he leads his students through a series of simple sounding exercises, etudes derived from the mountains of tricky-sounding exercises he has, over the years, simplified because they did not work. When it comes to training a band, Peter says, the deceptively difficult is almost always more useful than the blatantly difficult. Peter claims this to be one of his most valuable secrets, a secret not because he hides it, but because so many of his colleagues find it difficult to understand. Karmine, sitting in this same chair listening to these same exercises, has watched Peter produce some of the state's finest high school bands.

Karmine has seen the man Peter loves, but she does not know him. He plays keyboard, does freelance work for the ballet, the opera, local theaters and studios. For years, Peter has brought in extra money playing freelance—the ballet, the opera, local theaters, studios. French horn, like Timothy. Peter has a reputation for being consistent and dependable. Peter claims it has been evolving for years, this love affair, though only recently has he allowed it to become physical. Physical?, Karmine wonders. When she thinks of physical, Peter as physical, she sees him throwing snow twenty feet without shifting his stance, she sees him moving quickly for such a large man, and confidently, down the basketball court at the church gymnasium. Only recently has he allowed it to become physical. Karmine does not feel much of anything one way or another for Peter's pianist.

What she does feel is foolish. She feels foolish for having never suspected Peter, and though now, looking back, there may have been much to suspect, she is still uncertain as to which of those things, exactly, she should have suspected. It is not computing well, Peter's claim after a quarter century of marriage that he has, through the years, been desperately lonely in his attraction to some man. Surrounded by his family, in bed with his wife, he has been so hopelessly lonely it is all he can do to hold his secret until morning. And from morning until night. Twenty-five years. Where was she those twenty-five years? This is not Peter's question, but her own. When Peter arrives at this point in his story, Karmine refuses to hear more, but she cannot help but remember odd moments, like finding him in the bathtub, lights out, weeping for no explainable reason—no reason he was willing to explain, anyway. More times than she can separate into a single memory, Karmine has felt surprise, relief, when, after weeks without a single caress, he has suddenly reached for her under the covers.

About this, their love-life, she feels the greatest confusion, for while his touch has been unpredictable (with passing anniversaries, little more than seldom), when he does touch her, he is a wholly unselfish lover. Peter has declared extraordinary gratitude during lovemaking, particularly when Karmine has been needful, giving herself over to selfishness. Not always, but often enough, their lovemaking has been of a quality and sincerity that tempers, almost removes, the uncertainty grown in the gentle but passionless companionship between touches. Yes, she has been uncertain, but her uncertainty has moved along like a narrow highway cutting at night through the wheat fields of some distant state, rolling slightly, taking the pit of her stomach one moment, compressing her the next. Up or down, it hasn't much mattered, because the road has still taken her forward. Until now, the rolling highway has never dropped too quickly nor risen too steeply.

Karmine studies Peter as he tests the trumpet section, player by player, to see if a difficult fanfare has been mastered. He taps his baton against the stand, meting out the beat so the nervous students can concentrate on the manuscript and the fingering. Without harassing, Peter teases the students, and his smile, when he encourages or criticizes, never changes. He is forty-seven, two years older than Karmine, and except at his center, where he has begun slightly to spread, he has managed to remain respectably firm. On the podium, rehearsing and performing, he moves lithely like a dancer, like an athlete.

Karmine, too, has maintained herself. She has given birth to three children but, being small and elastic, has never struggled with weight. All the same, her confusion during Peter's periods of disinterest has often found her looking twice in mirrors. Though Peter insists it isn't so, Karmine knows she has failed her womanhood, that her womanhood has failed her, and in a way, to an extent, beyond anything she might have feared while turning this way and that in the mirror, wondering when Peter will reach for her again.

Peter wants to know what she is going to do. Karmine does not even know what the options are. She is waiting for him to decide what he is going to do. She knows less today than she did a week earlier when, for that instant after his confession, she had understood how some people can kill their mates.

The bell rings and the students begin disassembling their instruments. Wind Ensemble is the final class of the day, and the students move off at different speeds. Some remain seated, rehearsing their parts. Timothy waves, finally, and carries his French horn to his father's office. It has been the same ritual for all of their children, Peter carrying instruments to and from school each day, even on days he does not drive, so the children, without the hassle of dragging the instruments back and forth on their own, will have them at home to practice.

"I'm going to the writing lab," Timothy calls, hurrying from the office. "I'll be a little later than usual."

Karmine smiles and without cause or precedent doubts her son's excuse.

The room is nearly empty before Peter finishes with the questions and answers and excuses that detain him. Karmine attempts her typical concern for the few students who stop to tell her how they've been. Peter gathers his music and puts it in a folder. He steps down from the podium.

"This is a good sign, maybe?" he asks. Karmine can tell by his open, awkward posture that he wants to embrace her but doesn't dare.

"It's not really a sign at all," she says.

Peter nods agreeably. Lately, they are both thin-skinned. It is too easy to draw blood. She doesn't apologize.

"I haven't told you about Mom's visit to the doctor," she says. "That's why I'm here."

"Okay," Peter says. They both know she might have waited until home, but neither points this out. "Do you want to sit?"

"No." Karmine looks at the door.

"Okay," Peter says again.

Karmine pauses; she does not like the sound of spite, particularly in her own voice. "It's nothing serious, really." She feels lame and awkward, doesn't like this beginning but presses on. "Mom has a little skin cancer. Which really isn't the problem—" She shakes her head, disgusted with herself. "She's convinced she has lymphoma."

"Lymphoma?"

"That spot on the end of her nose." Karmine sighs. "She thinks she caught lymphoma from Dianne before she died."

"Dear Momma," Peter says knowingly. He purses his lips and looks at the ceiling.

"She gives herself three months."

"So long?"

"That's not all." Karmine breathes deeply. "Apparently, Dad's been spending the nights. Sleeps on the couch. She covers him in the night with a blanket when she gets up to pee."

"Holy cow!"

Karmine smiles despite herself. She has always liked Peter's self-depreciating use of phrases like "holy cow" and "groovy" and "neato."

"Dad's hair is as black and curly as ever."

"Your dad always had nice hair."

Karmine thinks of the Hemlock Society. She has hidden the accordion folder in the downstairs freezer, behind a case of orange juice. She's mentioned it to no one.

"She's going to be mad as hell if she doesn't die."

Karmine has finally said what she's come to say. Knowing this, Peter watches her for a moment.

"Maybe I should talk to her. Do you think it would help?"

Karmine shrugs. She is determined not to show Peter the gratitude she feels. Though she knew he would make such an offer, she is more relieved than she'd thought possible.

"It might," she says.

Peter begins sleeping in Karmine's sewing room. Karmine calls it her sewing room though she has only recently moved the sewing machine and the table up from the basement. For eighteen years the room has been Marcee's, and it still is, though Karmine's only daughter is away at school, a freshman at Brigham Young University. Marcee lives with her older brother, Jake, and his wife. Jake is a graduate student in music composition and his wife is trying to finish her bachelor's degree. Karmine suspects her daughter-in-law is also trying to get pregnant. Nearly daily, Karmine resists the impulse to call Marcee and beg her to major in prelaw, premed, to resist the Mormon pressure to marry young. Except for the sewing table, the machine and Peter, Marcee's room remains the same. Karmine wonders what they will do the next time Marcee comes home for a weekend. She wonders what they will do when Timothy begins asking questions.

It has been three weeks. When she counts the days, Karmine does not know how time can pass so fiercely, with the blurring velocity of a summer storm, and not blow or wash or dissolve anything away. Peter is still here, and Karmine, and maybe Peter's pianist, though she is not certain. Abby is still around, and her lymphoma, though the tip of her nose is now missing. The Hemlock Society is still frozen, gathering frost behind the case of orange juice in the downstairs freezer. Abby's daily question remains the same, and Karmine's answer:

"I'm still reading," she lies, assuring Abby she is sifting through the pamphlets, the newsletters, the legal action forms. "And by the way," she sometimes adds, "how's Dad?" She can't resist the irony—that at about the same time her father returns from the dead to sleep with her mother, her own husband retreats, moves to their daughter's room.

And so, after three weeks, it is the *nothing* that torments Karmine most. Peter is kind and gentle and patient, the things he has always been. He defers and defers with courage and stamina and humility. For her more than for himself, he has moved from their bedroom. He is trying to do his part, whatever that is, but has, at present, so little to work with. Karmine resists helping him, but still longs for a something more than this nothing, a longing she also dreads, knowing that most desires are answered one way or the other, sometimes too absolutely, in the mere passage of time.

"There are two middle-eastern women sitting in my car," Abby tells Karmine. It is late afternoon, clear and cold. The sun is preparing to set. Karmine shifts the phone to her other ear.

"Middle-eastern? Like from Saudi Arabia?"

"How should I know?" Abby shrieks. "They're wearing those veils over their faces. How do you expect me to know which of those countries they're from?"

Without thinking, Karmine turns off the stove. The oven is on, too, a casserole inside, but Karmine has not for any conscious reason turned the surface element off and does not think to do the same with the oven. Instead, she wedges the phone between her ear and shoulder and places her hands, palms flat, on the warm oven door. She leans forward, siphoning heat into her hands and thighs.

"Well, Mom...," she says.

"Don't 'Well, Mom' me," Abby snaps. "They've been sitting there all day. I want to know what they're doing. What if they steal my car?"

"Do they look like they're trying to steal your car?" Karmine, who cares nothing for Abby's car, has begun to feel frantic. Peter appears in the doorway; he's been reading in another room. Still pressed against the stove, Karmine watches him from the corner of her eye. Without looking directly at him, she grimaces for his benefit. He puts his hands in his pockets and leans against the door frame.

"What would that look like?" Abby asks. Karmine can see her mother bent before the kitchen window, squinting blindly to make out the two veiled women sitting in the old Chrysler.

"Like they're trying to start the car, Mom." Karmine shakes her head. She's neither asking the correct questions nor giving the correct answers. "I don't know, maybe they'd be fiddling under the dashboard."

"They're not fiddling," Abby declares. "They're just sitting there, the same as they've been sitting there all day."

"It's awfully cold to be sitting—"

"I know how cold it is," Abby says. "Any minute they're going to want to come inside and get warm. What am I going to do then?"

Karmine looks at Peter. "I'm coming over."

"Good," Abby said. "And bring Peter. Who knows what these people intend to do."

Karmine lets Peter drive—she has always let Peter drive. They've spent so much time sidestepping, it feels strange to be sitting side by side, sharing the same air.

"Have you said anything to the children?" Peter asks.

"No."

"They'll hate me." Peter does not look at Karmine when he makes this declaration. He steers with both hands, looking straight ahead. Karmine's self-consciousness evaporates. She studies him openly.

"Probably. At first, anyway," she says. And she knows it is true. Peter is not trying to elicit pity, nor is he asking her to keep his secret. His is a pronouncement, part of an ongoing progression toward a circumstantial, consequential awareness. It has been coming to them both in one line snippets.

"The church will excommunicate me." Yes

"Our friends will desert us." Yes.

"We are too old, too damaged to start again." Yes.

Yes.

It is not the first time in these three weeks Karmine has felt sorry for Peter, for what Peter is doing to himself. At times, Karmine has even forgotten what Peter is doing to her. And perhaps this is why she has said nothing to anyone. If she cannot find a way to hold him, she can at least for a time protect him.

"I've stopped seeing him," Peter says.

Karmine chews on her lip and watches the road.

"I'll understand whatever you decide to do," he says. "But I've stopped seeing him. I've stopped seeing him no matter what you decide. I can live without all of that. I didn't know it before, but I do now. There are too many other things I don't want to live without."

Peter looks at Karmine, she can feel it; he takes his eyes from the road until Karmine's silent, forward glare convinces him she will not look back. She wants to know about the "all of that," why a month ago, two months ago (years ago for all she really knows), he couldn't live without it. And she wants to know about the "other things," too, the "many other things" he, at one point, had been willing to risk for "all of that." Peter's decision to stay doesn't surprise Karmine. She has expected it. But she wants to know about the "all of that" and the "many other things," the interchangeability, particularly considering what seems to her a ponderous inequality between the two. Had Peter somehow felt it an even trade, a man in exchange for a wife and three children, a life, so many lives?

Karmine rolls down the window and turns her face into the frigid wind.

At Abby's house, Peter parks at the base of the driveway. Karmine and Peter climb from the car. They pause, doors open, to look up the drive to the carport. At the back of the yard, the car hunkers beside the barn-like workshop, under the pitched overhang. Abby has turned on the carport lights, and unless the Arab women are ducking, the car is empty.

"Must've heard the Marines landing," Peter says. He closes his door and starts up the drive.

"They're probably in the house torturing Mom," Karmine says. She follows Peter.

Abby is waiting at the back door, coat in hand. She's seen them pull in. "That was good thinking," she says. "Blocking the driveway so they can't make off with the car."

Karmine kisses her mother on the cheek and steps into the house. "Peter watches a lot of spy movies," she says. It has been two days since Karmine's last visit. As a rule, she sees her mother three, four times a week; she calls her twice a day. In two days, the house has taken on a sour odor. Abby looks tired and disheveled and frantic.

"You should have called us earlier, Mom." From the kitchen window, Karmine can plainly see no one sitting in Abby's car.

"When did you first see them?" Peter asks. He has joined Karmine at the window.

"Yesterday night," Abby says. "Or maybe yesterday morning. I keep hoping they'll just go away."

"I think they finally have," Karmine says.

Abby hurries slowly to the window. She looks at the car, then casts her daughter a disgusted glance. Karmine smells Abby, the sour, acrid odor of the house, but stronger. "You need a closer look," Abby says. She moves to put on her coat. Peter helps her.

It hasn't snowed for nearly a week. The stratified flow of passing storms has tattered the customary Utah inversion. It is clear and painfully cold—a cloudless February night. Abby shuffles between Karmine and Peter, allowing her children to guide her by the elbows. When they reach the car, Peter produces a key and unlocks the passenger door.

"Look at them," Abby exclaims. She taps angrily on the side window. "Don't they have any respect for other people's property?"

"Mother," Karmine says. She opens the door. She is trying not to plead. "There is no one in the car. There are no middle-eastern women sitting anywhere in this car."

Abby stares at her daughter. She turns and stares at the Arabs. "What are you doing in my car?" she demands. "This is America. Don't you know you can't just sit in other people's cars?"

"Look," Karmine insists. She slides onto the front seat.

"What is she doing?" Abby asks Peter. "Is she crazy?"

"Karmine," Peter says. He offers his hand.

Karmine gets out reluctantly. "You try," she tells him.

"Someone with some sense needs to do something," Abby agrees.

Peter leans over so the Arab women can see his determined face. "I think you need to leave now," he says, sternly. "You've been here long enough."

"Are they leaving?" Karmine asks.

Abby slaps at her daughter's hand.

"Maybe they don't speak English," Peter suggests. He clears his throat and begins to speak in broken Danish. Karmine is horrified and on the verge of hysterical laughter. Peter, who has spoken little Danish since his Mormon mission, begins gesturing wildly, perhaps to compensate for his limited vocabulary. He steps away from the car and points at the street. He wags his finger, scolding. He offers his hand, a pantomime twice enacted, and helps the women from the car. He looks cautiously at Abby.

"Just drag them out of there," she declares.

"Mom," Karmine pleads. Peter puts his hands in his pockets.

"Why did you even bother?" Furious, Abby turns and shuffles back toward the house. Karmine tries to take her elbow, but Abby won't have it. Peter shuts and locks the car, then follows silently, a step or two behind the women.

"They're going to have to pee," Abby predicts. "What am I going to do when they want to use my toilet?"

After the diagnosis, Karmine calls Harlan and tells him their mother's kidneys are failing. Too old for a transplant, too much damage everywhere else. Bad breath, vomiting, hallucinations, edema. Her bones hurt and her lungs are filling with water. Harlan wants to know if he should come yet.

"We probably have a few months," Karmine says. "But come if you want."

Harlan thinks they should start looking for a nursing home. Abby has enough money, and if not, Harlan will cover the rest. Karmine and Peter have sacrificed enough already, he decides. *Sacrifice*, Karmine thinks as she listens to her brother, the engineer, draft their mother's final days. Here is the thing about sacrifice: The investment and the expense make it impossible to pull up and back out. Though there seems nothing left to gain, there is far too much to lose. Karmine does not explain this to Harlan, but she knows she will never put her mother in a nursing home. Abby—and Karmine, too—are confused enough as it is.

"Keep me posted," Harlan says.

Sure, Karmine thinks, I'll send you a memo on Mondays.

Since receiving the diagnosis, there is something of an "I told you so" in Abby's disposition. She cannot be convinced that lymphoma hasn't caused her kidneys to fail. Nor can she be convinced that her hallucinations are not reality. She is rather content to have proof of her dying, and much too content, as far as Karmine is concerned, to be dying. The doctors have given her medication. An obligatory, if meager, attempt at cure to go along with a most sincere effort to secure her comfort. And though Karmine can not deny her mother's failings, she is struck by Abby's lucidity in the midst of so much confusion. She is amazed by her wellness as she falls increasingly ill.

"You're going to have to read faster," Abby tells Karmine. "At the rate we're both going, I'm liable to die before I get a chance to kill myself."

"It's a sin to kill yourself," Karmine says.

Abby laughs and touches her breast. "*This* is a sin."

Karmine agrees. In truth, she has little use for sin—Abby's, Peter's, her own. She knows she is supposed to believe in the hand of God, in the dangers of sin and the blessings of trial. Fate, however, has assumed an increasing appeal. It is satisfying, for example, to nod at fate when considering the circumstances that make it convenient, a relief, even, to spend her nights with Abby, away from Peter. To attribute the same to God only angers her. After so many years of attending church, of giving her time and money and energy to a religious society, she is

surprised at how little her faith draws her now, at how little, frankly, she wants
anything to do with it. Karmine's non-Mormon parent is dying, her husband has
been sleeping with a man, and Karmine can find no contingency plan in the church's
version of God's scheme. That the Mormons will probably throw Peter out does
not concern Karmine. Karmine suspects she would pay little attention even if they
suddenly threw her out too. It startles her that she can so easily accept this failing
after so many years of trying. There is simply neither time nor energy to waste on
that which cannot help her.

    For two weeks, Karmine stays with Abby, taking only short breaks when she
becomes desperate enough to allow Peter or Timothy to take a shift.
    "Maybe we need to hire a nurse's aide," Peter suggests. "Someone to watch
her during the day so you can have a break."
    Karmine has not been sleeping well. She has not been feeling well. She will
not let Peter relieve her for much longer than an hour, two at the most, even on
weekends. She is afraid Abby, whose increasingly vigorous campaign to enlist
Karmine's help in dying, will turn to Peter instead. It is strange to Karmine that
after twenty-five years of marriage she does not know what Peter will do if Abby
asks. Peter's suggestion offers a wisdom and a compromise Karmine thinks she
can accept. There have been moments of anger so compelling she's been forced to
flee, leaving Abby alone, though only for minutes, while she walks, runs, drives
around the block.
    "How would you feel if we hired a nurse to spend some time with you during
the days?" Karmine asks Abby.
    Abby has taken to sitting by the kitchen window, where she can watch the
Arab women. In her favorite chair (Peter and Timothy have moved it at Abby's
request), she sits and watches and waits for them to need her bathroom. Peter has
offered to drive them away, to park the car elsewhere, but Abby has become far
too interested in these exotic women who can sit for weeks without food or water
or toilet.
    "That would depend," Abby says, "on whether I could find a nurse more
willing to help me than you seem to be."
    Karmine is too tired to hide the anger. "You might. Or you might find someone
who thinks you should be locked away in a nursing home for your own protection."
    "You wouldn't do that?" Abby whispers.
    "No," Karmine says. She begins to cry. "I will never put you in a nursing
home."
    "I don't want a nurse," Abby says. She turns back to the window. "I don't want
anyone but you."
    Karmine goes for a walk around the block.

    Peter visits daily, bringing groceries and books, videos. On occasion, Karmine
allows him to touch her.

When Timothy can stay with Abby, Peter takes Karmine places—to dinner, to movies, for long drives. Karmine is worried about Timothy, about his eating and his school work and his emotional well-being. But Peter is reassuring. Though difficult, the past weeks have been good for Peter and Timothy. Lots of time together, lots of learning.

"Sometimes there are good things, too," Peter tells Karmine.

It is becoming easier for Karmine to acknowledge, with favor, Peter's efforts. He is solicitous without presumption. Committed and consistent. He has canceled his freelance work to be more available to Karmine and Timothy and Abby. Less available to anyone else. Peter's face seems older to Karmine, worried and pale, and she is inclined, in her own need, to let him derive whatever comfort he can from the comforts she accepts from him.

"Mom's seeing something new these days," she tells him.

Peter, as usual, is interested.

"Hippies in the back yard having a party," Karmine says. "They've rigged lights to the house. Last night was non-stop drinking and screwing and frolicking in the snow until dawn."

"Cool," Peter says. He is impressed and amused, which, for reasons Karmine can't explain, pleases her.

"That's not all," Karmine continues. "There was music, very loud music. Mom was frantic some neighbor was going to call the cops."

"It's not possible to have a frolic without music," Peter says with concern.

"Henry Mancini," Karmine says. "Judy Garland. Frank Sinatra. Nat King Cole."

"Nasty, that hippie music," Peter agrees.

"This morning, after they gave up and left, she wanted to go out and take a look at the mess. When we get out there, she says, 'Tricky bastards.'"

"Tricky bastards!" Peter whistles. He loves it when Abby curses.

"'What do you mean?' I ask her."

Peter takes Karmine's hand. She does not withdraw it.

"She says, 'No footprints.' 'You're right,' I say. I figure maybe the medication has started working. My mistake. Apparently, before leaving this morning, the last two hippies spread a long rope between them and pulled it across the yard, under the snow. While she was watching, they refluffed the snow."

"Tricky bastards," Peter says with admiration.

Karmine nods. "Now she's in a panic about the electric bill. All those lights."

"Well," Peter says. "Tell her if the bill goes up, we'll pay the difference."

Patiently, Peter is waiting. Karmine knows he will wait, without asking, without pressing, without knowing, forever if necessary. This is the quality in Peter that Karmine, of late, values most, and distrusts most as well, for it is but more of the same patience and silence and determination that has led them through the past twenty-five years. It is a gift, Karmine thinks, to be able to embrace uncertainty, as Peter has. Certainty—Karmine's own certainty in Peter's regret, in his good intentions, her certainty that her mother's death quickly approaches—is difficult enough to embrace.

"You've been wonderful with Mom," Karmine says.

"I love your mother."

"I know." Karmine lifts her chin. "But thank you anyway."

Peter watches Karmine. "Someday, maybe you'll be able forgive me." He seems very sad, suddenly. Karmine sees him soaking in the bathtub, lights out, weeping.

"Forgiveness isn't the problem," Karmine sighs. "I forgave you a long time ago."

When Harlan calls, he talks to Abby first. He doesn't mention a nursing home to his mother, but when Karmine takes the phone, he is agitated. Karmine pictures him on the other end, spitting into the receiver.

"This is out of control," he tells Karmine. "She told me the hippies just hang it out or squat to pee in the snow."

"That's better than it seems, Harlan," Karmine says. "It means they're not asking to come in and use the bathroom."

"Shit!" Harlan says. "Admit it, Karmine, it's time for a nursing home. This is just too much for you guys to handle."

"We're doing fine, Harlan."

Harlan pauses on the other end. "Look," he says. He is trying to be calm. "I think I need to insist, Honey. I know you're doing everything you can, but when it comes right down to it, we have to worry about Mom."

"I know you're worried." Karmine looks at her mother. The kitchen light is off. Abby sits before the window; she watches the hippies drink and dance and screw in her snow. Peter sits beside Abby, watching with equal intensity. "Mother is dying, Harlan. I can think of a hell of a lot of ways to make the dying more difficult. I haven't come up with too many ways to make it easier."

"All right," Harlan sighs. "Maybe I can get away the end of next week. This isn't something we can really decide over the phone, anyway."

"It'll be nice to see you," Karmine says.

She lights the candle in the potpourri dish while Harlan restates his position one last time before saying good-bye. Without returning the phone to its cradle, she leans on the counter, over the fragrance. The small ceramic pot is barely warm, but she can already smell the cinnamon. The potpourri is a gift from Peter. Karmine admires the design and the efficiency, that a single candle under a miniature pot can spare at least one of the senses the by-products of dying flesh. Karmine watches the flame in the tiny stove, the patterns it plays on the surrounding tile. Harlan, she thinks, would be offended most of all by Abby's odor.

Karmine joins Abby and Peter by the window. It has begun to snow. Large flakes fall evenly through the glow of the carport light.

"Harlan says he may come the end of next week."

Abby points. "The clothes they don't wear. It's amazing those crazy people don't get sick."

"Maybe they're part of that one club," Karmine says. "Those folks, you know, who cut away the ice in frozen lakes and go swimming."

"I can think of better things to do," Abby grunts, trying to pull herself from the chair. "Like sleeping. It's past my bedtime."

Together, Karmine and Peter put Abby to bed. Karmine unrolls the foam-rubber mattress and makes the bed beside the heat vent. Abby still insists on the living room floor, though the getting down and the getting up have become too much. On the couch, Karmine spreads a sheet and places a folded blanket across the arm rest. A symptom of her failed kidneys, Abby seldom needs to use the bathroom, but she will wake up, nonetheless, to check on the hippies and to cover her sleeping husband with a blanket.

"Would you like me to turn up the thermostat?" Karmine asks. She covers her mother with a quilt. Abby's eyes are already closed. She doesn't hear Karmine's offer.

Karmine waves Peter from the room then lingers for a moment, watching her mother breathe. This watching, it seems a remarkable need, an instinct. Countless parents standing every night over sleeping children, watching them breathe. Countless children standing every night over sleeping parents, watching them breathe. Sometimes, standing over her own sleeping children, Karmine has whispered secrets, voiced the impossible for the simple necessity of giving the words to someone who matters. It is her diary, of sorts, secreted deep inside her children's brains. Unconsciously, her children know things about their mother, and Karmine is satisfied to believe that her secrets have forever changed her children, and their children, even if but slightly.

"Oh, Momma," Karmine whispers. "I think I know what to do."

In the hallway, Peter is waiting. Karmine allows him to touch her. He touches Karmine's hair first, and then her face. When he kisses Karmine, she moves closer. Peter is weeping, but Karmine takes his hand anyway and leads him to the bedroom.

It is her childhood bedroom and Abby, in Karmine's absence, has covered the walls with photographs of Karmine and Harlan, Karmine's family, Harlan's. Karmine kisses Peter and begins to remove his clothes. Peter does not help, but makes himself available, like a young child being undressed for a bath. There is a sequence, and Karmine moves deliberately.

When Karmine, too, is finally undressed, she lies back and closes her eyes. With her eyes closed, she can concentrate on Peter's movements. They are small and refined and accurate. She listens to Peter above her, sobbing silently. She runs her fingers down his ribs, to the swell of his hips. Karmine loves Peter, and she is sorry for him. But for once she has the benefit of prescience. She knows for all his efforts and all her own that this particular desperation is inevitable.

"You're going to be fine, Peter" she says. "You're going to be much better than you think."

Peter laughs apologetically, more sob than laugh. He puts his head down, chin to chest, and his hair brushes Karmine's forehead. He moves on, the steady, familiar motion of their twenty-five years together. The motion, Karmine thinks, of water, the Strong One, with the power to wash away earth, extinguish fires, ignore wind. Strong like water, but weak like water, too, flowing always undirected down the paths of least resistance.

Afterwards, Karmine caresses Peter, waiting. She holds him until he climbs from the bed.

"I'm sorry," he says. He gathers his clothing from the floor. "I've got to get hold of myself." Rubbing his face, he stands half stooped, a weight-laden man, then bends the remaining distance and kisses Karmine. "I'll come early tomorrow and shovel. I think it's going to be a bad storm." He leaves quickly, still crying. Karmine hears him pull the back door closed behind him.

Alone, finally, Karmine listens to the popping and the settling of an old house under the accumulations of a rough winter. The furnace ignites, and Karmine hears this too, a rumbling, comforting sound that warms even before the air flees the vents. As a child she would stand barefoot on the floor vents, the air burning the arches of her feet, filling her nightgown with warmth. It was always a temptation, when the heat clicked off, to turn up the thermostat and ignite the furnace again.

Getting up, she takes a blanket from the bed and wraps herself in it. The vents have stopped blowing, so she pauses in the hall to turn up the thermostat. She waits for the furnace to rumble, then switches on the kitchen light. From the refrigerator, she takes the milk, fills a glass, returns both the carton and the glass to the refrigerator. It is an unnecessary preparation just as well left until later, but Karmine prefers, at last, to have it all waiting. She's been thinking about this for some time. Without telling Abby, she has learned which medications will most immediately, most efficiently, do the job. She gathers the bottles, removes the lids, dumps the pills in a salad bowl, the blues with the reds with the greens with the yellows. Changing her mind, she pours the pills into a candy dish. Abby has a sense of humor; she will like eating pills from a candy dish.

Abby's sleep will be short, Karmine knows, so she turns off the light and sits in the chair by the window. Waiting, she watches the snow fall on Abby's play. She listens, can almost hear the music. She cannot help but imagine how strange all those hippies frolicking naked in the snow must seem to the two Arab women.

Partying with St. Roch

Johnny Townsend

I could see that Dennis had a drinking problem. It wasn't as bad as Glenn's had been, of course. I'd dated Glenn for almost a year before he died of cirrhosis, holed up in his apartment with empty beer cans around his bed. He'd frequently point to my flat stomach after we had sex and say, "You may have a six-pack, but *I've* got a whole keg," and then he would pat his extended abdomen. I'd thought it was just a beer belly, but some of that enlargement was due to his damaged liver. After that experience, I vowed I'd never date another drinker.

Then I met Dennis at the Unitarian church in Uptown New Orleans on Nashville. We were both excommunicated Mormons, and we hit it off singing about a God who loved all people equally. We dated for five months and then moved in together, about one month before Dennis's T-cells dropped to 50 and he was diagnosed with full-blown AIDS.

It was late 1989, and we were looking forward to New Year's, hoping for a repeat of the Gay Nineties, at least in name, working together for gay rights with several organizations, not the least of which was ACT UP, carrying signs and shouting slogans in front of City Hall as we demanded more access to medicines. Shortly after we moved in together on St. Roch, just off of Chartres in the Marigny, Dennis developed an addiction to Coke.

That's Coke with a capital C.

He began having me purchase every three-liter bottle of the off brand the local Schwegmann's grocery stocked when I went to do our weekly shopping. I'd pile twelve of the monstrous bottles into my cart and plod my way to the checkout. Every single week, people would smile and say, "You having a party?"

"Nothing but fun at my house," I'd reply, smiling back.

"Kirk, you only bought eight bottles today," Dennis complained to me this afternoon. "I'll never make it through the week."

"I'll stop at the store again tomorrow."

"I need this. I get so little pleasure out of life."

"I'll stop at the store again tomorrow."

The sodas were not diet. I was afraid that at any moment, Dennis would have diabetes to add to his problems, but something about the HIV or his particular metabolism seemed to defy the sugar overload. He remained thin as a rail despite a full daily allotment of calories just from the cola alone. His other favorite treat was chocolate, which was a debatable violation of the Word of Wisdom. And perhaps because the caffeine kept him from fully hydrating despite the vast amounts of liquid he consumed, he also drank a great deal of black tea.

"Do you think I'm a hedonist, Kirk?" Dennis asked. "Do you think I should be obeying all the commandments now that I'm about to die?"

"Shut up and fuck me," I said, forcing a smile.

I was still negative, and Dennis always used a condom when we had sex. The irony was that he was basically a top. He'd only bottomed maybe three or four times ever, but he'd done it just once without a condom, and now he was paying the price. Every day, priests and pastors across the country were still proclaiming that AIDS was God's punishment for our abominable sins, thereby infecting everyone with their hatred. It was impossible not to wonder if they were right. Every evening as I kissed the man I loved goodnight, I would look into his face and wonder if God really despised us this much. One of the last things I heard my stake president say after he told me I was excommunicated was, "Choosing this carefree, frivolous lifestyle to avoid the responsibility of family is wrong. If Heavenly Father still loves you, He'll give you AIDS to help you repent. It's so much kinder than letting you live in your sins for a lifetime, thinking you're not sinning. I'll pray that God gives you AIDS, for your own good." He smiled and held out his hand warmly, as if he'd just said something comforting.

My hand stayed by my side, and his finally dropped as well, a look of confusion on his face. I turned and walked out of his office, and I never went to an LDS church again. Mormonism had always been my rock before, "the one and only true church." Four years passed, in fact, before I ever entered any other church at all. A friend invited me to a meeting at the MCC in the Bywater, in an ancient red brick building along the levee. I didn't like the congregation, so a few months later, I tried a Dignity meeting with some gay Catholics. I didn't care for that, either. I attended a Reform synagogue Uptown on St. Charles and liked that well enough, but I was afraid to stop praying "in the name of Jesus Christ," although I wasn't sure I even believed in Jesus Christ anymore. I realized I was being superstitious, not religious. I attended a Methodist meeting on North Rampart in the Quarter and then an Episcopalian service Uptown and a Hare Krishna meeting on Esplanade. At last I stumbled upon the Unitarian meeting. I had been just about to give up my quest as pointless when I listened to a blonde woman with dreadlocks give a sermon on the importance of protecting the environment, and I decided to come back a second time. I'd been attending ever since. It was refreshing to hear from the pulpit that I could still be a good person even if I was also a sexual one. I looked at Dennis now and felt a stirring in my groin.

"Really?" said Dennis, looking doubtful, almost mournful. "You're still attracted to me?"

"I want you, mister."

I grabbed my crotch, and Dennis's eyes lit up. He hurried over to the dresser and pulled out the two nametags I'd had made. He slipped one on his shirt pocket that said, "Elder Top—The Church of Jesus Christ of Latter-gay Saints" and handed mine for me to put on my pocket, "Elder Bottom" and with the same fake Church name. Dennis leaned forward to kiss me, rubbing against me and smiling as our two missionary nametags clicked against each other. Then, despite the costume, he took off his shirt and knelt in front of me, unzipping my pants as I rubbed his head, trying not to be distracted by the large black Kaposi's lesions on his shoulders and back. He didn't fuck me as I'd suggested but just sucked me off. I watched as his head moved back and forth, wanting to memorize every sexual encounter with him, so that I could replay them after he was gone. With a final thrust, I came, and then Dennis smiled and stood up.

"Your turn?" I asked, pointing to his zipper.

He shook his head. "All I want is more Coke. I know it's a pain, but can you go to another store?"

I nodded and went to grab my cart again. We didn't have a car, and the Schwegmann's on Claiborne was the only store truly within walking distance, about nine blocks from the apartment. The next closest was a grocery on Franklin. I walked the five blocks to the bus stop, waited for almost twenty minutes, and then boarded the 57. A few minutes later, I was at the store.

There were no three-liter bottles here of the off brand that Dennis preferred, but there were several two-liter bottles of regular Coke. I'd tried making this substitution for Dennis before with negative results. He wanted what he wanted, and nothing else would do. It could be annoying, but how could I deny him what few indulgences he had left in life?

If what the Church taught were true, there'd be no Coke in heaven. I'd never even dared try a sip until I went to my first gay bar.

I wondered if it were true that the Church owned lots of stock in Coca-Cola.

I pushed my cart along the pavement until I arrived at the bus stop. What could I try next? There was a Rouse's up closer to the lake. Since I was already taking the bus, I supposed it didn't matter how many blocks I had to go once I was sitting down. The bus jerked to a halt in front of me fifteen minutes later, and I dragged my cart on board. I was the only white person in the vehicle. Whites in general were afraid to ride the buses in New Orleans, afraid they'd be murdered by all those "low-class" blacks who filled the seats. While I did get a few cold stares once in a while, obviously most other passengers ignored me completely. Once, I'd run into my Sunday School teacher Theautrey on the Elysian Fields bus and said hi and shaken his hand. At the Unitarian church the next Sunday, he admitted he'd felt two conflicting emotions: one, surprise that a white person would acknowledge him in public, and two, embarrassment in front of other blacks that *he* was friends with a white person himself.

As a Mormon, I'd learned about how blacks had been cursed with a dark skin for their lack of dedication to God in the Pre-existence. While I'd grown up watching *Diff'rent Strokes* and *The Jeffersons* and didn't feel I harbored much prejudice, whenever I saw a news report of another black murderer or listened to the uneducated speech of blacks around me, I'd doubt just a little my belief that all people were equal. Maybe it wasn't oppression and lack of opportunity that hurt this community. What if they really were inferior spirits? Even while listening to Theautrey teach a class on Sundays and feeling impressed with his knowledge, I'd doubt. Maybe he had some white blood, I'd think. Maybe that was why he was so smart.

I'd hate myself for thinking these things and then get mad at the Mormons all over again for filling my head with such nonsense. Gays weren't bad. Blacks weren't inferior. What kind of religion went around spreading such a plague of hateful teachings in the first place?

Then I'd wonder again if I was going to hell.

I climbed out of the bus across the street from Rouse's and headed for the store. I went straight for the soda aisle, ready to be finished with this interminable chore and get back home to relax. I worked all week at the public library under a tyrannical manager and then came home to a sick partner. Saturday was my day to have fun, and I had to take my fun when I could get it. I tried to make these outings an escape from the confines of my apartment, but all I really wanted to do was listen to Roxette while putting together a thousand-piece jigsaw puzzle of Notre Dame or the Taj Mahal.

No three-liter bottles.

Why did Dennis have to drink so much? Was it his way of thumbing his nose at God?

I looked over the soda section a second time to make sure I wasn't missing anything. There was a section for three-liter bottles, all right, but there weren't any stocked. Was there an epidemic of cola addiction out there?

"Excuse me," I said, stopping a young black man with a nametag. "Could you check in back to see if you have any more of the three-liter bottles?"

The man looked at me, looked at the empty shelf, looked at me again with his lip curled ever so slightly, and headed off without a word. I waited fifteen minutes and then decided to try one last store, a new one that had opened next to the projects near Canal. This would be the last stop on my pilgrimage, regardless of the outcome.

I arrived thirty-five minutes later and pushed my cart quickly to the soda aisle. There was a lone three-liter bottle. An elderly woman looked as if she was contemplating it. I debated whether or not to snatch the bottle before she had a chance to reach for it, but I bit my lip and waited till she slowly moved on down the aisle. I put the bottle in my cart, added one more item from a few aisles away, and headed for the checkout.

Dennis was not going to be pleased.

Was I a bad partner for giving up before I'd accomplished what Dennis asked of me? The man was dying, after all. He'd be gone in only a few months.

Couldn't I sacrifice just a little more for him? Perhaps this proved that fleeting gay relationships were a poor substitute for "true" eternal marriage. It was what I felt every Sunday, too, that my new religion was only a lackluster replacement for the real thing, no matter how much I told myself I preferred these services to the Sacrament and Priesthood meetings of before.

Could one be inoculated against the infection of self-doubt?

I dragged my cart off the steps of the bus twenty minutes later and pushed the metal cage ahead of me slowly, careful going over the cracked and uneven sidewalks of the Marigny. I passed the funeral home and the home of a gay hairdresser who was Clyde Barrow's cousin and then passed the home of a cute guy who routinely invited me to come in whenever he saw me walk by. I always politely refused, of course. He wasn't out today. I walked past the Lion's Inn gay bed and breakfast and finally made it to St. Roch.

The patron saint of the plague.

I unlocked the door underneath the balcony and headed up the stairs. "Kirk! I was afraid something had happened to you!"

"I could only find one more bottle."

Dennis stared at the bottle in disappointment and then managed a smile. "Maybe there will be more later in the week. I just want you to spend the rest of the day with me. We have so little time left together. Tell me more of your mission stories from Germany. You know I like that."

Dennis sat down on the sofa eagerly, and I poured him a glass of cola. Then I opened my other purchase, my first bottle of red wine, and poured myself a drink, too. I brought both glasses over to the coffee table and set them down. Dennis picked up his and looked at mine for a long moment without saying anything. Then I picked up mine and took a sip. Not bad.

"Tell me again about that time you decked your zone leader," said Dennis, leaning back and smiling.

"Well, naturally, it was an accident," I began. I sat back on the sofa, too, and Dennis swung his legs up so that his feet were resting in my lap. I sipped my wine with one hand and rubbed his feet with the other. I looked over at the man I loved, and wondered how I was going to fit the whole of eternity into the next few months. "It all started the day my zone leader told me in front of everyone that I didn't measure up to his expectations…"

I continued with my story, distracted by a new lesion on Dennis's leg. I began embellishing, just to add some variety, and Dennis grinned as I went on.

These are the good old days, I realized as I talked. One day soon, I'd look back and miss these times. I tried to memorize every detail of the room, the torn vinyl sofa we'd bought at Goodwill and had a friend deliver, the coffee table I'd carried two blocks from a garage sale, a mediocre piece of art Dennis had painted. When I finished my story, Dennis asked for another, this one about the middle-aged German man who'd fucked me one day when I'd broken the mission rules and took a long walk on my own.

We both smiled as I began telling the story. When I finished, I poured Dennis another glass of cola, and I sipped more of my wine. Then I had Dennis tell me one of his own favorite mission stories, back when he thought it was a healthy thing to spread the teachings of the Church. We smiled and laughed and drank, happy for a few brief moments on the torn, aging sofa.

In the back of my mind, I wondered where I'd packed my Book of Mormon, and if maybe I should read for a while after Dennis fell asleep.

Strange Bedfellows

Ken Shakin

After the dance spirits were high. Which was fine. Let the boys have some fun. Long as it stops at midnight the men would let them carry on. Needless to say, the boys wanted to keep on dancing. But a promise is a promise. He told them they could let themselves go, have all the raucous play young men can muster, as long as at the stroke of midnight they all went home to bed.

As they made their way home, Brother Smith can hear laughter all around. He shares a chuckle with Brother Jones. They agree, it was nice to see the boys getting on, dancing together and enjoying each other's company. It was a good idea to turn the schoolhouse into a dance hall for the night to celebrate young Smith's coming trip to Colorado as well as Brother Jones' arrival. Both men enjoyed watching the young men dance and sing and horseplay. Their manly chuckle is like an inside joke. They can remember the fun they had when they were that age. Tonight they'll rekindle some of that nostalgia when they lie in bed and talk. Last time Brother Jones visited they didn't get to sleep til daylight. The bond between these two men is so intimate that though they see each other rarely these days, when they do they pick up right where they left off, filling each other in on everything that's happened in each other's absence. Brother Jones of course is full of exciting news from Salt Lake City with all the latest from the Latter-Day Saints headquarters. Brother Smith has such admiration, respect and maybe a bit of envy thrown in for this friend whose importance in the Mormon Church takes him on these travels. Part of the reason he organized the dance was to show off his own local power as the most important man of this small Utah town. At home he showed off his family, something Brother Jones has neglected to have. He's been advising him for years to finally get married. If I can have two wives, you can at least have one. Brother Jones was always a man of special character. His keen intellect needs constant stimulation. The routine of family life would wear on him. Brother Smith continues to advise him towards marriage not because he thinks it would be good for him. Rather because it would help his standing in the church, which is something important. A Mormon man should be married.

At the house the women and girls are all asleep. The men and boys stand outside the Smith door to say goodnight and at once the big shuffle starts. Who's sleeping with whom. It starts when young Smith says he wants to sleep with his best friend since he won't be seeing him again until he gets back from Colorado. That leaves his brother, Jonathan, alone in his bed. It gets confusing because some are not saying what they're thinking. Young Smith's best friend and his little brothers were supposed to sleep with one of the old men from Illinois who are passing through since the one will be sleeping with the father of the house as the wives sleep in the other room with the girls. It seems to Brother Smith that the real reason they don't want the old man from Illinois around is because he'd dampen the high spirits of the boys and with young Smith added, the higher spirits. At the dance young Smith's best friend was overheard whispering jokes about how he didn't look forward to spending the night next that smelly old fart. It was uncalled for, but understandable. He obviously wanted to spend the night with young Smith before the trip. Those two are like brothers. And it's clear that the old man is a bit unkempt. But this shuffle sets off a round of shuffling that complicates it further as some of the other young men want to join in by removing the young boys from the bedroom and sticking them with the young boys from their own houses. The other fathers are busy agreeing on that when Brother Smith cuts the confusion with a firm decision. Young Smith can sleep with his best friend if the old man from Illinois doesn't mind sleeping with Jonathan. The old man agrees and that settles it, with only the young men and boys to figure the rest out. There's always complications with sleeping arrangements. Brother Smith looks forward to eventually adding another room to the house. With six girls and the baby stuffed in one tiny room the house is breaking at the seams, the wives continuously bickering about who will sleep with the girls and who will share his bed. The good thing about having a visitor is that it put that female bickering to rest, for the time being.

He looks forward to a peaceful night with Brother Jones, a night of important conversation and brotherly affection. The rest of the bedfellows will have to make do. Jonathan might not like the idea of sharing his bed with the old man from Illinois, but at least he's keeping quiet about it. He's such a quiet boy. He was the only one who didn't seem to be having fun at the dance. He went home early. Maybe this is just what he needs. The old man might give him some confidence. The boy lacks confidence, forever in the shadow of his brother. Young Smith is such a handsome and energetic boy, it's difficult to be his younger brother. Lately the two Smith boys have not been getting on, one of the reasons why this trip to Colorado was a good idea. Brother Smith feels a bit selfish in wanting Brother Jones exclusively in his own bed for the week. He'd even thought about suggesting Brother Jones sleep with Jonathan a night or two. But now it's all worked out. Everyone gets to sleep with their dearest. And who knows, the old man from Illinois might be able to impart some wisdom on the boy as only a man of years can. Maybe a bond will form. Which is something the boy clearly needs. The prophet Joseph Smith took boys into his bed frequently. As Brother Jones once quoted, the prophet strongly recommended for men and young men to sleep together "locked in the arms of love, to sleep and wake in each other's embrace and renew their conversation."

Inside the humble wood house a calm takes over from the party mood. The two men go to their bed and the old man to join the boy in his. Brother Smith wastes no time in asking Brother Jones his impressions of the evening. He blushes when he's given compliments for his beautiful family and upstanding small community. It's a fine life he's made for himself. Brother Smith wants more than anything to hear about the world outside, about all the rich experience his friend has in his wandering missionary life. But the subject of his own small world, his family, brings up mundane troubles for which he could use his learned friend's advice. What words can he offer to help him deal with the constant bickering between the two women? Brother Jones tells him to find the love inside to give more to each. Babies will keep them busy and out of each other's hair. And what should he be doing about Jonathan? The boy is sullen. As a father it pains him to see one of his sons cowering in the heroic shadow of the other. Brother Jones reminds him that as boys grow into men they become themselves and no one can say who that person will be. Brother Jones himself had been a shy boy. Until the men of the church, one in particular, took him under his wing, he'd thought himself incapable of doing anything of substance. What Jonathan needs is the love and support of the older wiser men around him.

The man around him tonight is older and wiser. The old man from Illinois holds the skinny boy in his arms as they try to fall asleep. Hard to imagine two stranger bedfellows than these. He tried to talk to the boy. They spoke as he got in under the covers but the boy seemed afraid to say what's on his mind, silently staring at the door. The old man remembers what it was like to be a boy of that age. Much as he might dream of his youth he's glad to be long through with that most awkward stage of life. Now as a father and grandfather of some two dozen children his greatest pleasure in life is in watching youth at play. To see the joy in their innocent faces is a joy in itself. He would have liked to spend the night with those other boys, to hear about the simple things that concern them. This Jonathan is different. He's within himself. He needs a David to give him confidence. All evening, watching the young men dance with each other, seeing the Jonathans and Davids pairing off, the old man had such fond memories awaken in him that he felt moved to tears. The passion is in those bonds we make. With our friends. With our family. If he has any regrets in his full life they center on his youngest grandchild. He hasn't seen the boy in years. He can only picture him now as either a young man or a dead man and fears the latter is more probable. The boy came to no good after his father died, the old man's youngest son. That's when bad became worse. That whore mother of his gave him charcoal to draw sinful pictures instead of teaching him scriptures. She was too busy drinking and fornicating. Rumor had it that the boy had been picked up as a vagrant and put in a home. He doesn't even want to find out. It breaks his heart to think about that beautiful child escaping his reach and falling into an abyss of evil. The guilt will follow him to the grave. He tried to help. If only he'd given the boy the love he thirsted for. Instead he beat him and left him dry. He can hear the men in the next room speaking affectionately with each other in low solemn tones of admiration. He can hear one of the women tending to a crying baby in the girl's room next door and the sound of the woman's sweet coo makes him feel even more tender towards the boy in front of him. He cradles him tighter. He wants him to know that he's loved by God and men, that he has nothing to fear from that love. He closes his eyes and whispers to him, kissing the back of his head. Jonathan, Jonathan. It'll be alright.

Jonathan is wide awake. Staring at the door next to the bed. The old man's quiet attention is stirring his heart. He feels like gulping down the lump in his throat. He would love to bask in the love of this man, to be his Jonathan. He would love to be his own brother's Jonathan. To be Jonathan for all the men and boys he's ever admired. More than anything else his soul aches for that. But he can't. He knows that he can't. It won't be alright. His eyes are wide open but all he can see is what he feels and it won't go away. It's there denying him what he most desires. It grows as the man behind him tightens his grip.

Gay Messiah

Excerpt from All of Me (Can You Take All of Me?)

Dirk Vanden

Headed back to Sacramento, I stopped the van on that graveled turn-out, near those dilapidated mail-boxes, and read the computer printout Joshua had given me, just as we were leaving:

GAY MESSIAH, PART ONE:
ICDLITE—1969

On Christmas Eve, 1969, John and I went to Dave's Baths in San Francisco, and both of us took tabs of 'windowpane' LSD, just before we left our car parked on an empty side-street in the financial district, and walked the block or so to the steam-baths, tucked away on two floors of a warehouse. The wet reflective streets were deserted. A nearby church was broadcasting recorded bells playing Christmas Carols, and we almost fell down laughing when they started pealing a very scratchy "Oh, Come, All Ye Faithful!"

We both responded "I'm cumming! I'm cumming!"

As we went through the front doors, Eartha Kitt was singing *"Santa Baby!"* setting the mood for a much different sort of Christmas celebration.

There were festive scallops of silver and purple tinsel, down each side of all the hallways—with a sprig of mistletoe tacked, with a little lavender bow, above each and every doorway.

I was beginning to feel a sense of displacement. It was like stepping into an episode of *The Twilight Zone*. In the background, The Rolling Stones were singing *"Two Thousand Light Years From Home."*

As I started toward my room, striding down the hall toward me was one of the most beautiful men I had ever seen! He was blond with blue eyes, with a short, trimmed auburn beard. His long, shining hair curled up at his shoulders. He was dressed as the attendants at Dave's always dressed: in tight bell-bottom denims and a T-shirt displaying a perfect body. He seemed to glow.

His T-shirt was one I had never seen before and it shocked me at first—which it was surely meant to do: On the front was a copy of that famous painting of Jesus-in-drag with his arms outstretched, and two disciples clinging to his robes, with a cartoon bubble above his head saying *"Cum unto me!"* Under the painting, in crude letters, it read "JESUS WAS A FAG!"

On the back it had that other famous painting that hurt to look at, 'The Crown of Thorns,' depicting Jesus suffering excruciating agony, dying. Below that, the crude lettering read, "THAT'S WHY THEY CRUCIFIED HIM."

He said "Merry Christmas!" and kissed me briefly, on the lips, on his way to do something for somebody. When he kissed me, brief as it was, I felt a sudden infusion of brilliant energy. It started my engine! I felt young and supremely self-confident.

To this day I will not swear that he was a real attendant at Dave's or an angel, or an acid-induced hallucination. But I can remember him vividly, even now. When I turned to look back at him, just to make sure I had seen what I'd seen, he was gone.

But I was feeling much better. Kissing him had been like an injection of energy. My body was starting to feel really good. It felt like I was starting to glow!

There were only a few others wandering around in the halls or watching an old Christmas movie on TV in the lounge, where an eight-foot cedar tree was gaudily decorated and colorfully twinkling with bubble-lights. The dimly-lit steam room was empty, so I climbed to the top shelf and moved back into my favorite spot, the darkest, hottest corner of the room. My body felt as though it were shifting gears—from low, to second, to third, and then sliding into overdrive. I felt delicious!

It seemed like my mind was unfolding, like an enormous flower blossoming.

Walter Carlos, who went on to become Wendy Carlos, played Bach's "Jesu, Joy of Man's Desiring," on a Moog Synthesizer, far out in space! And a gigantic mollusk crawled across the hot steamy black tiles and slowly engulfed me.

The steam-room vanished; the earth vanished! I became aware of myself as a tingling, sparkling sphere of light, suspended in space, in a vast, empty darkness. At first I felt appallingly alone, but then, other tiny, sparkling lights appeared in the darkness—dim and widely separated at first, but then more and more appeared until there seemed to be millions of us. We were all moving to the tempo of the music—dancing in space—but it soon became obvious that we would all converge at the same point, where now I could see a brilliant white light, burning and pulsating—far brighter than the lights that were zooming toward it—welcoming us! The sphere of light grew brighter and hotter as I flew closer, until it finally filled the entire range of my vision, and then I went crashing into it—and *came!*

The Universe exploded! Bach exploded—and became fireworks in space!

Then, dimly, a bearded face, surrounded with long blond hair that sparkled like a halo in the steam, rose up from my crotch and kissed me wetly. "Merry Christmas," he whispered, then vanished into the mist.

When I finally regained enough strength to move, I went to the showers and turned one on full blast! It felt fantastic—like a deliciously-refreshing cup of cold spring water on a hot summer night. The splashing, bubbling water seemed to be drawing something out of my body and I watched in awe as writhing, slithering, little creepy-crawley cartoon-monsters came oozing out of my body to go, wildly protesting, screeching and screaming, swirling down the drain. They were my "Sins!" I recognized them!

When the shower was finished, I felt refreshed, renewed, amazingly clean! In a word, I felt "reborn!"

Just then, on the background music tape, Barbra Streisand was singing, "On a Clear Day," and I had the most overwhelming impression that God was speaking with Barbra's voice and that She was talking to me, directly, telling me to look around. So I did. I turned and looked into a room which seemed to be behind a large window behind the wash basins, where a long-haired, bearded naked man stood looking back at me.

There was no doubt in my mind who it was; I recognized him instantly, easily! It was someone I had once adored, but had abandoned, many years ago because it seemed he had abandoned me! I had seen that face, that beard and long hair, in a thousand religious illustrations: It was Jesus! The Come-Unto-Me Jesus—Jesus knocking on your door—Jesus and the little lamb—even the glow-in-the-dark plaster Jesus who stood guard in my grandmother's bedroom.

But then, the door opened and the "window" wavered, and I realized I was looking at my own reflection in a mirror.

Jesus grinned and winked at me, and God sang, "*See who you are!*"

The conclusion was obvious: I was Jesus!

The idea should have terrified me, but instead, something in my brain went *click-click-click* and I thought "Oh! All right. Of course! Why didn't I see it before?" Suddenly it all made perfect sense!

Gentle Jesus, meek and mild!

Then, through the open doorway, another long-haired, bearded, naked man came in. Obviously he, too, was Jesus! He smiled beatifically and nodded—a little almost-Oriental bow—and went into the showers. As I stepped out into the theatrically-lit, purple-carpeted, tinsel-draped corridor, a dozen other naked and near-naked Jesuses—black ones, brown ones, tan-and-pink ones—were moving to the music like some kind of bizarre avant-garde ballet! In the background music, singers were pretending to be musical instruments, making a dance-tune out of "Oh, Come, All Ye Faithful!" I joined the parade and went up to my room with a happiness welling up inside me, ready to explode.

There was something divinely ironic about learning all this on Christmas Eve, in the House of *David*. Homosexuality was the "Key of David!" Half of our Gay institutions were named after the King of the Jews who said of Jonathan, when he died: "*Greatly beloved were you to me; your love to me was wonderful, passing the love of women.*" The other half were named "Lambda." We were the "Lambs who had gone astray!" The "first fruits of the Lamb of God!" Revelations flowed through my head like a river! We were the "last" who would soon be "first!" We were those "redeemed from the earth, who sang, as it were, *a new song*!" We were the "Eunuchs" who had made ourselves eunuchs for the Kingdom of Heaven's sake. We were the seeds the Sower had sown, long, long ago, finally blossoming! In us were all the prophecies fulfilled! Jesus had returned, not as one man, but as millions of lovers of men.

Look out, world, here come the meek!

I had the impression that I was the last one to discover the incredible Messianic-Riddle. "*Whosoever solveth the Puzzle winneth the Prize!*" Today was like a very special "Surprise Party" just for me! It seemed that everyone else had been waiting for me to solve the final mystery, and then the celebration would begin! It was going to be the biggest party the world had ever known!

And then we were going to merge!

I decided my time had come. For some reason, I had been "chosen"—God knew why, even if I didn't. I opened the door of my cubicle—ready to reveal to the world the answer to the riddle—the end of the divine mystery—and proclaim the return of *The Son of Man*—by the millions—and was almost engulfed by an enormous roiling, gurgling, anger. Pure fury! Something beyond terror was out there, in all those other little cubicles, just waiting to gobble me up and silence me forever.

I slammed the door and locked it, then frantically—my heart pounding madly, my hands shaking almost uncontrollably—I found the little pink tranquilizer I'd brought along, just in case something like this happened. John called them his "bummer-stoppers." I swallowed it dry and sat huddled in the corner of my bunk, clutching the covers around me, like a little kid alone in the dark, until I fell asleep.

John wakened me by banging on my door, wanting to go somewhere for breakfast! Acid always made him hungry for greasy fried bacon and eggs with hash browns and buttery toast.

CODA

That event is why I came to write my books—why I did everything I did after that. That one event in my life totally changed my life. Or, rather, it illuminated my life. It told me why I was who I was. Somehow, improbably, I was a Jesus-clone. That would slowly start to make more and more sense as the years went by. I had unknowingly accepted and incorporated a kind-of secret code—a computer-program—hidden in the Biblical stories of Jesus. As a child, in Sunday School, I had sung "I'll be a sunbeam for Jesus!" Unlike all the other kids, I had meant it. I had "*believed*" it. That made it my operating system. The others went on to make babies, like good Mormons. I went on to be a Sunbeam. If you open a sunbeam, it turns into a rainbow! My "vision" changed my attitude toward myself—toward all Gay people. I allowed myself to stop feeling guilty and sorry for myself for being Queer. I stopped condemning others for being weak and imperfect. Instead of a perversion, it became a Divine Commandment—and I finally started to enjoy it!

It's okay to forgive yourself for loving men. Jesus told you to!

Forgiving yourself is like spiritual masturbation!

I finally understood that I was who I am because of what I'd been taught to believe. My brain had been programmed, like a computer, to be "Like Jesus." "Gentle Jesus, meek and mild." "Love each other." "Judge not." I wasn't the bad guy everyone, including myself, wanted to believe. I was actually one of the good guys. Only nobody knew it yet.

The next day I decided that, somehow, I had been selected by some higher power—*God* or *Fate* or *Karma*—to tell the Gay world—or maybe the whole world—the story I've just told here—but after I'd come down, back to earth, had gone home and slept for twenty hours into Boxing Day, I discovered that my "task" was not going to be easy to accomplish.

John actually laughed at me and called it "religious bullshit." That, of course, started the end of my relationship with John. He was Jewish and had no idea what I was talking about: "Christian bullshit."

If I had the courage, or stupidity, to tell my wonderful story to various friends, they all acted as though they had forgotten appointments, or had just remembered crucial errands they had to run—or dogs to walk, or places to go—and they would then keep forgetting to call for months on end. When we met in the bars they would tell me how busy they'd been.

It was like being Queer and being rejected, all over again, *déjà vu* on a higher level!

It took awhile, but I finally realized that I sounded like one of those crazy, wild-haired, bearded Acid-freaks, out on the street corners, babbling about *The End of The World!* I was talking about Jesus, and nobody wanted to hear about Jesus. They had left all that religious bullshit behind when they stopped going to whatever brand of church they had grown up in. As far as my friends were concerned, Jesus was a phony-baloney boogie-man invented by the new kind of Medicine-Men—Religious Priests—to scare the ignorant savages into behaving themselves—and paying their tithing—or the various equivalents. *Faith in Jesus paid the salaries of psalm-saying hypocrites and child-molesters.* My Gay friends had all out-grown their religions and wanted nothing to do with my "new one"— which is what it sounded like to them.

I finally decided that it didn't really matter what I did, or didn't do, if my "vision" were true, it would happen without my announcing it. If it were not true, then it would be less embarrassing just to shut up about it. If it were true, then that also meant that, two thousand years ago, some guy named Jesus actually knew what he was doing—"sowing the seed"—and that—if that were true—then "harvest time" was nigh....

That was forty years ago, and, as far as I know, I haven't been harvested yet. (Or maybe I have and just don't know it!)

But had I not known that my *Jesus-trip* was the result of LSD, I might have totally believed it, and tried to start a new religion, with Dave's Baths as my designated Holy Place, incorporating "my vision" like Joseph Smith, and Paul of Tarsus—and who knows how many other Prophets and Seers and Revelators? Epileptic Grand Mal Seizures and LSD, several different kinds of mushrooms and peyote, "Shewbread" and "Soma," all open the same doors, give you variations of the same visions.

I understand the impulse to try to "jump-start a dead horse" (Dobbin Dubinski). But that impulse is mitigated by the knowledge that Grand Mal seizures and Amanita Muscaria mushrooms and Lysergic Acid only show you what is in your own head—so it remains completely possible that the entire experience was totally a product of my own, vivid imagination.

But, to me, to this day, it still seems to be the most real and valid experience of my life.

It was "My Vision." That's who I think I am—and that's who I think you are.

Love & Kisses! Gabriel Horny/Joshua Adamson

PS: I am truly a "fisher of men."
I catch them and eat them~
and throw them back again!
LOL! JA/GH

The Dream

Levi S. Peterson

Niles awoke from a strange dream to find that his snoring had once again driven his wife from their bed. On his way to the bathroom, he peered into the darkened living room and, as he expected, saw her form upon the sofa. Returning to bed, he retrieved what he could of the dream, fully expecting to ponder it with amusement while drifting off for another hour or two of sleep.

Niles and Thora were younger in the dream, perhaps in their fifties. They were at an academic conference in a hotel and had a room many stories up, but he, an early riser, had gone down to the lobby to work on his paper, and then, breakfast time having come, he had returned to their room and found her conversing in the corridor with a couple of other women. He opened his mouth to utter a cheery "Good morning," but was arrested mid-word by the collective gasp of all three of the women as they turned to look at him. He looked down at himself and saw that over his suit he had pulled a female garment, a sleeveless party dress of flamboyant orange silk. The skirt flared with stiff petticoats, something like a ballerina's tutu. With a surge of anger, he stripped off the dress and threw it to the floor with a vindictive strength. That was the point at which he had awakened, greatly relieved to know he had been merely dreaming.

Unfortunately, his review of these details failed either to amuse him or to lull him into a pleasant early morning drowse. Instead, it forced unwelcome questions upon him. Did the donning of a dress in a dream signify that the identity of a woman lurked in his subconscious? Was he emotionally the female that, before his birth, his mother had hoped he would prove to be? He rallied almost instantaneously from these absurd, nonsensical questions, the answer to which was an abrupt No! He had been born a male, had always felt himself to be a male, had always wanted to be a male. Irritably, he got up, put on his robe, and, having fetched in the morning newspaper, went to the study to read it.

The paper said that an aspiring assistant professor who had been denied tenure had filed suit against the university, claiming that the formality of his attire—he habitually wore classic-fit chinos, a navy blazer, and a tie—had been the single negative point adduced by his departmental tenure and promotion committee, which was composed of professors who—according to the suit—prided themselves on an informality approaching slovenliness. Wishing for more facts, Niles read the brief article a second time. But even as he tried to fix his thoughts on the ins and outs of academic selection, his mind returned to the puzzling dream. He could easily see its immediate source: an episode in a recent movie featuring a den of male transvestites, immaculately made up in female attire. The dress he had found on himself in the dream was resplendent, richly decorated and satiny, like those in the movie. What wasn't so easy to see was why putting on a dress in a dream should prove worrisome to a seventy-six year old man. Time had been—a very long time ago, in high school—that he had donned a dress and high heels for a skit at an assembly or, while wandering through the state fair, had seen college students in dresses and wigs on an open stage, and had thought of it all as mere tomfoolery.

He heard his wife close the bathroom door and remembered that she had early duty at the welfare center where she served as a volunteer. He went to the kitchen and began to prepare breakfast. He planned to tell Thora about the dream, knowing that its sheer implausibility would amuse her. But the more he thought about it, the more it seemed a needless indiscretion to mention it, as if in some vague manner it wasn't so implausible after all. Better to let sleeping dogs lie, as it were.

While he poured milk onto his cereal, she came into the kitchen, fastening a brooch to her blouse. He glanced at her appreciatively, aware that even in her seventies she was beautiful. She was of medium height, five feet six or so, a height—as she often observed dryly—universally considered desirable for women who wished to bolster the confidence of the men they were attached to. She had an angular chin, lips that curved into a perpetual smile, and a mound of curly hair tinted to an auburn luster. As for Niles, he was tallish—six feet two, or at least he had been before he began to grow old and shrink; his face was long, bland, and clean-shaven, as became the countenance of an obedient Mormon in the twenty-first century. However, the large, round spectacles, which he had put on while reading the newspaper, gave him—as he esteemed—something of an owlish appearance.

"Any big plans for the day?" Thora asked as she seated herself.

He looked out the window, unsure. There were sunbreaks in the clouds. It seemed like he ought to do something worthwhile. "Maybe I'll start on a paper," he said.

He pondered that idea for a moment, then said, "Maybe I'll go to the library and roll up my sleeves and dig into those westerns." He was referring to a large collection of popular cowboy novels in the university library which he himself had gathered years ago.

"I thought you had lost interest in those," she said.

"True," he said. "I did lose interest in them."

"Though you've written some very nice papers about other books," she said.

"Thank you," he said with a nod. "The thing about these cowboy novels is that they are all about the same imaginary cowboy. Every one of them! And he is a pretty anemic cowboy at that."

After they finished eating, they rinsed their dishes and put them in the dishwasher. At the door he paused and said, "But maybe I should give those westerns another try. I have been thinking lately that an old man could do worse than honor the intentions of the young man he used to be."

"Well, then," she said, nodding, "maybe that's what you ought to do."

She was the first to leave the house, pausing at the door to say simply, "Goodbye," and to hear him reply, "Drive carefully." He would have paid no attention to this perfunctory departure had he not felt an extraordinary impulse to give her a hug, or perhaps a parting kiss, either of them a gesture so rarely exchanged between them that he couldn't remember when they had last done so. They had never been demonstrative people. They had grown up in undemonstrative families where affection had been expressed between adults and older children through kindness and consideration, but not through touching of any sort—a reticence which, as might be expected, their own children had inherited. The exception to the reserve between Niles and Thora had been, of course, while engaging in sexual intercourse. Unfortunately, as old age grew upon them, his embarrassment over an increasing inability to achieve a climax had deprived them of even that intimacy.

A half hour later he left the house and walked to the bus stop. At the intersection of Moormeade and Grover, he realized with some surprise that he could remember the day when he had first understood that cross-dressing was more than mere tomfoolery. It was soon after he had begun his mission. He and his companion had shared a train compartment with what he at first took to be three women. However, with mounting astonishment, he inferred from their intonations, gestures, and posture that two of the three were men in fashionable female attire. Even now, past seventy, he still responded to the sight of a transvestite with a smothered sense of incredulity.

After a brief wait at the stop, he caught a university-bound bus. The vehicle was crowded, and he found himself obliged either to cram himself into a half-seat next to an obese man or to stand gripping a pole. He chose the latter. This bus, like all others, smelled of sweat, oil, tobacco, and various undefined essences of an unpleasant sort. Its stark green metal walls were mercifully interrupted by wide windows. Above them on either side stretched a row of relentless placards advertizing, among other things, a bank, two grocery stores, a subscription to the *New York Times*, an Internet service provider, and a maverick brand of green olives.

For a few minutes he tried to concentrate on the oft-postponed task he had impetuously decided to reconsider that morning, the production of a scholarly article on the image of the American cowboy in the popular fiction of the early twentieth century. But the flashing scene outside the windows—freeway lanes filled with speeding automobiles, roadside buildings, a background of forested hills, and above that a mottled sky—distracted him. Suddenly feeling a need to be honest with himself, he granted the utter irrelevance of any article he was capable of writing. The scenes he presently looked upon, both inside and outside the bus—*his* world, the world of now—were an infinity away from the world that had inspired all those cowboy novels he presumed to study.

He therefore surrendered all too willingly to ruminations on the bizarre dream that had unsettled his early morning. However, as before, he found himself quickly drawn into worry, if not about the implications of the dream, then about worry itself. It seemed odd that a seventy-six year old man would be worrying about his sexual identity. It seemed that, if he were a woman in a man's body or a man who desired carnal knowledge of other men, he would have known about it and dealt with it one way or another long before now. But then he was a worrier by temperament. He had a robust instinct for worry. All his life he had suffered from bad things that never materialized. They were beyond counting.

Soon the bus was crossing the lake on the mile-long floating bridge. He saw a few early sail boats and, only a couple of hundred feet above the blue, shining water, a float plane. After forty years, he was still startled to find himself a part of this scene. Juniper-covered plains, dissected by barbed wire fences and dotted here and there with the derrick of a furiously whirling windmill, were his natural habitat. Which brought him back to the cowboy novels—but only momentarily, for a memory now came to him of the men's restroom in a movie house where a certain fellow with tousled red hair and face marred by acne frequently loitered, waiting— so rumor had it, likely true—to make assignations of the unspeakable sort.

Why had he been so afraid of the red-haired fellow? Would he have been utterly paralyzed had the fellow advanced a proposition? Why did he now suddenly feel worried for having remembered the incident? Strangely, it roused the question every maturing boy faces, *how do I know that I am not one of them, the queers, or, as people called them nowadays, the gays?*—a question he had thought settled to his satisfaction even before he and Thora were married—*no, a man as interested as I am in his fiancée's intimate parts is no gay.* Suddenly, as of this morning with its strange dream of an orange dress, it was as if somehow the question of his sexual orientation had not been settled at all.

He got off the bus at the inner campus stop and crossed the main quad to the library. He entered the east wing and trudged along a corridor. The morning sun shining through high arched windows and the scent of floor wax touched him with nostalgia. The curator of the special collections—an apparently ageless man he knew only as Mr. Seymour—let him directly into the stacks, saying as he formerly had, "It's against policy, but since it's you...."

Niles lingered there for several hours, pulling off the shelf, one after another, hardback novels whose covers were sometimes frayed and invariably faded. They bore titles like *Silver Creek Raiders, Shorby of the Z-Bar Ranch, Bordeen Wins Again, Flashing Guns, Thunder on the Prairie,* and so on. How had Niles got into this business in the first place? In graduate school his favorite professor had lectured on the sociological value of popular literature, which by definition had no pretensions to quality. Figuring out what you could know about westerners from the popular western novel had struck Niles as a charming idea. So once he was settled as an assistant professor on the present campus, he had applied for a small grant from the library committee and, with the assistance of a downtown used book dealer, spent it on close to 1500 novels, which were cheap because nobody else wanted them. Unfortunately, as they began to come in, he realized you couldn't know anything about real westerners from these novels. For the most part, they weren't even written by westerners, and the titles gave a deceptive appearance of variety to what was actually a single, age-old story of heroic action, dressed in slightly different details from book to book. The same character could be found in cheap novels about sailing the high seas, jousting with medieval knights, and fighting Bedouins in the sands of Tunisia.

Toward noon, Niles emerged from the library, determined to grab a bite of lunch at the union cafeteria and return to the task of deciding, once and for all, whether his early dismissal of the novels had been too hasty. For a few moments he stood on the library steps, blinking in the bright sunshine, making no move toward the cafeteria because that troublesome question confronting all teen age boys— *how do I know that I am not one of them*—had returned to his mind just now. But after a few moments more, he relaxed, having suddenly recalled an incident from long ago. After a football game in a town far from home, he and a high school friend had gone to bed in an unheated motel room, taking off their coats, shirts, and pants, and crawling between the sheets dressed only in their briefs. The friend instantly cuddled up to him, as he apparently did at home with his little brother, but Niles jumped—quite literally—out of the bed. The friend said nothing, but the rest of the night each slept on his own side of the bed. Wasn't it sheer untutored instinct that had made him jump? No shred of homosexuality there.

With that, he changed his mind about lunch at the cafeteria. He would go home for the day, though he would keep focused on the possibility—admittedly slim, but still a possibility—that the American readers who had bought the novels composing his collection when they were new understood something about the cowboy that had evaporated from the collective American mind during the succeeding decades. If these novels, cheap as they were, reflected that understanding—and if Niles could discern and articulate it—*that* would make an article worth writing!

However, as he made his way across the quad, he found himself unable to concentrate on this new insight. A new angle to his frantic leap from the motel bed on that cold night had just occurred to him. It might have been acquired behavior, socially conditioned by the derisive banter of boys in the shower room after PE, who directed mock accusations of homosexuality at one another in strident and scornful voices because no one, including the accuser and the accused, believed them. Their banter and their mock accusations—didn't they tutor and educate? The lesson they taught was that boys don't touch, hug, embrace, or fondle one another, or stare at one another's intimate parts in the shower room even if they want to. They must show a studied indifference, a blithe oblivion, as if they were fence posts rather than sentient sexual creatures. So his aversion to being hugged by a high school buddy might not have been sheer untutored instinct at all.

In the middle of the quad, he ran into an acquaintance named Jerry Bovig, a lab assistant from the biology department whom Niles had met fifteen or twenty years ago at a Mormon-sponsored Messiah sing-in. Ironically—as Niles now observed to himself—Jerry was the last person among his acquaintances whom he wanted to meet on this particular day, Jerry being not only Mormon but also gay. Jerry didn't mind talking about being gay. In fact, he gave firesides in private homes on being gay and keeping church standards, which meant that he had dedicated himself to celibacy forever. As for his colleagues in the biology department, they knew he was gay and were okay with that. However, they didn't know he was a Mormon, and he had asked Niles not to tell them.

Jerry was headed for the union cafeteria and asked Niles whether he didn't want to come along for some lunch. Not wishing to seem homophobic—and having the memory of many pleasant conversations with Jerry over the years—he agreed. In the cafeteria, Niles followed Jerry's example and ordered from the Mexican menu, reputed to be the least unpalatable of the cafeteria's offerings, and they carried their trays to a small table in the overflow room.

"How are things in your ward?" Jerry asked while they ate.

"Same as always," said Niles. "Sacrament meetings made unintelligible by the hoots and shrieks of dozens upon dozens of little children. Sunday School lessons read directly from the correlated lesson manual. High Priest quorums divided by the perennial debate over whether Adam-ondi-Ahman is in Missouri or Iraq. At least that's the way it was last time I attended. Actually, I haven't checked in lately."

"I've been ward chorister for a couple of months now," Jerry said. "It's a job I like."

"Well, you're lucky," Niles offered. "However, don't let it be known that you like it or they'll take it away from you and give it to somebody else."

Jerry chuckled. "You seem to have a clouded view of things."

"Yes, I suppose I do." Niles was wondering why, considering how anxious simply remembering that red-haired fellow in the theater restroom had made him, he didn't feel anxious in the actual presence of a known homosexual. But then he realized he *was* beginning to feel anxious, not so much about having lunch with this friendly man, but about what people like Jerry did to the Mormon concept of the pre-existence, which held that God assigned gender to the unborn beings of the spirit world. Men who desired other men and women who desired other women implied some kind of terrible mistake in design on the part the Almighty, an obvious impossibility for any respectable theology. Moreover, a dream on the part of a man about putting on an orange dress was also an obvious affront to any respectable theology. That is, whatever kind of deity a church happened to believe in, by all measures it ought to the kind of deity that wouldn't trouble believers with dreams of that sort. Cross-dressing shouldn't happen in a well-ordered cosmos. Not even in a dream.

After lunch, Niles went back to the special collections room in the library, more or less certain that he wanted to have nothing more to do with his collection of popular westerns. Even if diligent research could demonstrate that early twentieth century America had an understanding of the cowboy that had evaporated from the collective national mind during the succeeding decades and even if that research could go on to demonstrate that the 1500 or so novels housed in the special collections library reflected that now vanished understanding, Niles wasn't the man to undertake it. He was too old. Too weary. Too indifferent.

However, second thoughts quickly beset him. Abandoning an intention held for forty years was no light matter. It had to be pondered, weighed, decided upon only after due process. He asked Mr. Seymour for a chair, which he placed in the aisle where the western novels were shelved, feeling magnanimous and perhaps a bit self-congratulatory about his fidelity to promises from the distant past. But after he had seated himself and fingered through a number of the westerns on the shelves before him, Niles realized all over again how remote they were from the real cowboy, that hired hand on horseback, as Eugene Manlove Rhodes had called him.

Niles had known some of those hired hands on horseback during his boyhood. They were nothing like the walking fashion manikin that passed for a cowboy now, whom you were likely to meet on a city street or in an airport or sports arena. That fashion rack was nothing more than *wimpus americanus* togged out in boots, jeans, pearl-buttoned shirt, and ten-gallon hat. And most assuredly, those real cowboys were nothing like the cowboy heroes in these novels, who weren't togged out in anything except vapid, colorless words. Readers were free to visualize them in any attire they wished. There was a lot of verbiage about nickering horses and wind-whipped waves of grass and spooky-eyed cattle and coyotes wailing in the distant haze. But there was nothing to make a cowboy hero in one western stand out from the heroes in a hundred others. There wasn't anything to make him a western person.

That settled it. Niles was seventy-six and retired and not in line for promotion or tenure and therefore in no need of publications or symposia on his résumé. He zipped his file case, folded the chair, returned it to Mr. Seymour, and shook this faithful factotum's hand, saying he doubted he would ever see him again.

There being no express bus from the campus back across the lake till much later, he took a local that followed a tedious, meandering route. Across the aisle sat a fellow dressed in shabby grey pants, a soiled sports shirt, and running shoes with a hole worn through at the point of each big toe. Incongruously perched atop his head was a brown, flat-crowned western hat. Here, Niles reflected, was a prime example of *wimpus americanus* usurping the signs and symbols of a better breed of man than himself.

Yet, curiously, as he went on to recall, the real cowboys he had known during his boyhood were often dressed as shabbily as this fellow. They wore boots and jeans for work, not for fashion. One of them he could remember, Orville Canover, was a pathetic creature, actually. Niles recalled seeing him one late spring day at his mother's house, where he had been staying. He said he had been let go by his employer after the spring roundup. Moreover, his employer had run out of cash the previous autumn and owed him nine months pay, which was $30 a month with room and board. He had had the room and board, the room being furnished with a bunk with woven rope for springs and the board being rice, beans, and prunes, which he had to cook for himself, of course. At the moment, he was barefooted and mowing a patchy lawn with a push mower. His scuffed, run-over-at-the-heels boots stood neatly placed in the dirt pathway leading to the front door. He wore faded jeans and a soiled white shirt and a ragged vest from an old three-piece suit.

The city bus had got behind a yellow school bus which, with blinking yellow and flashing red lights, was making frequent stops to let off students. These seemed to be little tykes—kindergarteners, apparently—which explained the bevy of mothers that stood waiting at each stop corner. Shortly, the school bus turned up a side street, and the city bus picked up speed. However, Niles scarcely noticed, having begun to think about a problem with his authentic example of American manhood, the real cowboy. Weren't those two fellows in that movie that had swept the nation not so long ago, *Brokeback Mountain*, specimens of the real cowboy, the working cowboy? One was a Montana ranch hand, the other a Texas rodeo rider. They wore scuffed boots, blue jeans, denim jackets, and high-crowned Stetsons. And they were in love with each other. They kissed, they made love in that unspeakable manner, they yearned to be together.

When he got off the bus and walked the final few blocks to home, Niles felt himself drained and dejected. It wasn't precisely a physical fatigue. It was perhaps more a weighty disappointment, and it had something to do with that abominable dream of having put on an orange dress. All day he had been set at hair trigger for thoughts and memories that somehow undermined him. Was he so sure that he had always felt himself to be a male, had always wanted to be a male? Hadn't there been the sweetest, most tender of moments in his mother's lap when he had wrapped his arms around her neck and had assented with all his heart to being her little Nilesina, as she sometimes called him? Nilesina! What a travesty to impose upon an unsuspecting child! Say he had been born a girl. Would she have really called him by a name as revolting as that? At any rate, it had influenced him to endorse heartily Thora's selection of very ordinary names for their children— Steven, Mary, Dorothy, and Lisa. Thora, of course, had never been overly charmed with her own name, which derived from a pioneer ancestor who had died on the plains of Nebraska.

Thora was across the street chatting with a neighbor when he arrived home. He waved at the two women and went inside, where the dining table was set and a pot roast with potatoes, carrots, and onions simmered quietly on the back burner of the kitchen range. He was moved by deep affection. Thora's suppers were always gratifying, always calculated to please him. He had been favored beyond all desert by more than fifty years of her companionship. He recalled the extraordinary impulse he had had that morning to give her a hug, or perhaps a parting kiss, and wished that he had done so. But perhaps it didn't matter. He knew she knew he loved her. Always. Every day.

After supper he helped Thora place the dishes in the dishwasher. Following that, he went into the study to check his e-mail. There was a message from Steven, asking Thora for the name of the de-worming medication they had used on one of their dogs fifteen or twenty years ago. Being online, Niles couldn't resist looking up the word "transvestitism" on *Wikipedia*. Reading about it made him anxious again and also angry, because it seemed a shame, an outright injustice, that a man of his age and dignity should be asked to prove once again that he was qualified to be called a man. It was as if he were taking his prelims all over again, that nightmarish week-long series of examinations by which he had qualified, not for a PhD, but for the mere right to advance to candidacy for a PhD And all because of a single strange dream.

At that point, Thora came into the study and Niles told her about Steven's request for information. Ceding the computer to her, he went into the family room and for an hour worked out on the stationary bicycle in the family room while he watched television. Following that, he showered and put on his pajamas and then sat in something of a stupor on the edge of the bed. Presently, Thora came in and began to undress, talking all the while about an excitable Vietnamese char woman at the welfare center who had mistaken powdered milk for floor detergent. When she glanced at Niles, as she did from time to time, he averted his eyes, not wishing to reveal the depth of lust that an old, impotent man could feel while his wife prepared for bed. He thought again for the thousandth time of getting something to alleviate his condition, but ended for the thousandth time by deciding the side effects were too daunting.

Once abed, he turned this way and that several times, plumping his pillow each time he did it. Thora turned out the light and climbed in on her side. "Did you have a good day?" she asked in a soft voice.

"More or less, yes, I did," he affirmed. "I gave up once and for all on those western novels. The world will have to languish in ignorance about them as far as I am concerned."

"Maybe it's just as well."

"I ran into Jerry Bovig," Niles added. "I had lunch with him. I ordered an enchilada."

"Sounds good," Thora said. "How's Jerry doing?"

"He's about the same as always. He's still doing fireside chats on celibacy for homosexuals."

"Well, that's too bad."

"Too bad?"

"Yes. If they are born that way, if it's their nature, then they ought to be able to marry like anyone else."

Niles plumped his pillow again, feeling all tensed up and in need of another session on the exercise bike. He hadn't realized Thora had become so liberal. Not that it mattered. What mattered was that he needed a way to get rid of his self doubts. Or at least to repress them, to smooth them over and go on behaving as if he didn't have any. Once upon a time, carnal knowledge of this affectionate and willing female—a nightly business when she wasn't having a period—had allowed him to smooth over his self doubts and go on behaving as if he didn't have any.

"Good night," Thora murmured.

"Good night," he replied.

He was wishing there was something more to say. With a racing heart, he suddenly blurted, "You are a good wife."

There was a long silence and then she said a simple, "Thank you."

There was a rustling of the covers and he realized she had pulled herself close to him and, before returning to her side of the bed, had brushed his forehead with her lips.

Their brief exchange was of course an eventuality beyond all expectation, a violation of the undefined reticence that had existed between them for decades. But the perturbations of his day evaporated, his muscles relaxed, and he felt coming over him that sweet soporific lull that precedes slumber.

Nestle's Revenge

Ron Oliver

Valentine's Day, 2000
Her Grace,
The Duchess of Milton
St Gerome's Home for the Aged,
Welpington-on-Green, UK

Lady Milton:

I trust this letter finds you well and in good spirits. I'm sure the days pass pleasantly in Welpington-on-Green although, having never been to England myself, let alone out of the state of California, I can only assume the recent A&E documentary on your life did the place justice. And while the tone of *Lavinia: The Madwoman of Milton* was surely condescending—Indeed, Harry Smith was often so insulting I was surprised you didn't beat him within an inch of his life with your prosthetic arm—it did at the very least present an interesting view of your life. One point in particular caught my attention and, before I introduce myself properly, let me just ask you this:

Do your butterflies still talk?

Please pardon my directness; indeed, I do have to consider the possibility that you've simply tossed this letter into the garbage and continued with your lunch— tapioca pudding and puréed cream corn, if A&E got their facts right. But I'm going to bet you're still with me, good Lady. You see, when I watched your story on the small color television we have here in the common room, something in your eyes just told me you'd believe my story.

And that you'd understand about Nestle.

I'm not exactly sure why Kyle gave his toy terrier a name synonymous with sweet or delicious. It's not as if he wasn't aware of what an unpleasant little beast it was; in fact, as I think back to the night we met, I'm positive he deliberately avoided the topic of pets. But I should have known better; in West Hollywood's hierarchy of required accessories only cell phones outnumber canines, with the rule of thumb being the bigger the muscles, the smaller the dog. And my ex-husband certainly is well-built.

Oh, I see I've slipped a bit and let the cat out of the bag. Or dog, if you'll pardon my little joke. I am indeed, as my Aunt Lillian often said, "a gay." But I suspect a lady of your lineage will barely bat an eyelash at this startling revelation. I believe it was a friend of your mother's, Mrs. Patrick Campbell, who uttered the now famous line, "Does it really matter what these gentle, affectionate people do, so long as they don't do it in the street and startle the horses?"

I would hope you share her sentiments as I finally begin my tale...

My dear friend, Paris DeLamour, noted astrologer and psychic of the transvestite persuasion, had recently signed a deal to appear in her own weekly television program called, aptly, *Paris DeLamour, Noted Astrologer and Psychic.* Granted, it was only on the local cable access station but for Paris, who had dreamt of stardom ever since her unhappy childhood as epileptic Clark Nesbitt of Puce, Nebraska, this was a cause for celebration.

Her previous forays into show business had been miserable failures, given her suffering from a rare condition known as Chronic Short Term Recall Disorder. In spite of possessing a distinctive, almost pleasant singing voice, she was sadly unable to commit to memory any song lyrics beyond the first she had learned as a child; and, while "I Got Rhythm" is a wonderful tune, it did not give her the sort of repertoire upon which one can build a career.

And so we met that night at Revolver, a local lounge catering to gentlemen who prefer the companionship of other gentlemen, for what was supposed to have been just one drink.

The first thing that I saw as I came out of the coma was Kyle's face, staring down at me with that very familiar, disapproving frown. The sickly green tint of the hospital room deepened into focus around him and I could make out a steely-eyed doctor peering at me from her clipboard, then glancing at a nurse. Nobody spoke. The silence in the room was, as they say, deafening and since I, like nature, abhor a vacuum, I felt compelled to rasp a sentence through my parched lips:

"Did I miss last call?"

I was kept in the hospital for two more days of what they referred to as "observation" but as Kyle told me later they simply wanted to make sure I couldn't score another bump of crystal before my body chemistry had the chance to return to what, in my case, passed for normal. Apparently, there had been some concern about brain damage.

I should pause in the narrative here and, with your kind permission, educate you regarding the subject of crystal methamphetamine, or "Tina," as she's known to an army of wide-eyed championship house cleaners. An intriguing combination of stimulant, aphrodisiac, and hallucinogen, Tina is practically currency in the gay bar scene and with my job as a professional event planner in and around Hollywood I had more than a fair share of it greasing my palm nightly. It became, I'm ashamed to say, my favorite sin and, finally, the proverbial straw which broke my husband's back.

Kyle had delivered his ultimatum with a deceptively casual air, catching me off-guard while he filled Nestle's dinner dish with the obscenely expensive designer dog food the tiny beast demanded. Drugs or marriage, it was up to me. We would leave West Hollywood or we would leave each other. As simple, and as complicated, as that.

I looked around our stunning Doheny Avenue condo, at the evidence of our life together, the sleek furniture from Shelter and Diva, the fastidiously framed black-and-white erotic photographs from Weber and Ritts, the Williams-Sonoma chromed espresso maker. I looked at Kyle; even after a long and difficult day at the bank, managing the accounts of cranky gay men—bitter at suddenly facing the fact that after selling off their life insurance policies for the money they needed to "die with dignity," they were now going to actually live—he was still the most beautiful man I had ever met. His brown eyes were fixed on my face, waiting for an answer as, at his feet, that animated tissue-box cozy smugly devoured the doggie equivalent of dinner at the Ivy.

I found myself wondering two things: one, how much would all this stuff fetch us at the Yard Sale surely looming in the future and, two, where on earth were we going to live?

My dear Duchess, should you ever find yourself appearing as a special guest on one of those television game shows where they ask obscure questions in return for vast sums of tax-free money and should one of those obscure questions be "Where is the World's Largest Thermometer located?" you will now be in luck. You see, I happen to have spent almost eight months of my life staring at said thermometer through the window of our rented two-story house.

The answer is Baker, California.

Glorious Baker, Population 2,000. Only a three-hour drive from West Hollywood, but at least twelve light years away from the twenty-first century. However, it was not a town without a certain charm; there was always the Dairy Queen.

Kyle had no problem finding a job; a managerial position at the Bank of America's local outpost had opened up, following a particularly nasty double murder/suicide at a nearby trailer park. My situation was, however, considerably more challenging. You may find this hard to believe, but in a town like Baker there are very few career opportunities for a gay man in his early thirties whose sole skill is planning the perfect dinner party.

I tried the entrepreneurial route, taking out an advertisement in the *Baker Gazette* for an "Event Planner," offering my services to make any gathering "a memory to last a lifetime." The single call I received inquired about my ability to "make them little animals outta balloons." When I assured the prospective client that while I could not at the time, I would be more than happy to learn if the price was right, the sound of the phone being hung up was like an arrow to my heart.

I did not renew my advertisement the following week.

Despondent, bored, and more than a little homesick, I tried all the usual remedies. I went to the local gym—"Stan's Workout Center and Hardware Store"—but, upon asking about their aerobics schedule, was met with a stare so blank I found myself unable to lift even a single weight thereafter. I checked out the local library, figuring to make the most of my exile by reading the classics: *Valley of the Dolls,* possibly, or, in a pinch, the new edition of *Mommy Dearest.*

But the town council, with the urging of a local church group, had passed an ordinance declaring any book with "in excess of four profanities per chapter: unfit for community standards." Needless to say, the only literary works left in the place had the words "Jesus," "God," "the Light" or "Flopsy, Mopsy, and Cottontail" in the titles.

And so, as easily as Kyle seemed to adapt to our new life, even going so far as to plan and design a barbecue pit for the backyard—my very soul spiraled into an abyss of afternoon television talk shows and tearful phone calls to Paris DeLamour in a desperate attempt to stay in touch with the outside world.

But through it all, no matter what, there was always Nestle.

Nestle needed to go for a walk. Nestle need his water dish refilled. Nestle had to be fed. Nestle had to be brushed. Nestle had to be let in, let out, taken to the vet's, picked up from the vet's, walked again, fed again, brushed again: and since Kyle was at work, and since work was *all the way* across town (a five minute drive, mind you), who do you suppose was left on full alert Nestle duty?

Dear Lady Milton, I am not an animal hater. And despite what many have said about me in the media, especially as they have cast long shadows upon the issue of my humanity, let me assure you that what happened to the dog was an accident.

Just an accident.

You see, I was upstairs in the bedroom cleaning out one of my old knapsacks—truth be told, I wasn't just cleaning that knapsack, but it was the last place I had looked in my desperate search to find even a single hit of acid, a grain of coke, *anything* to alleviate the spine-decalcifying tedium of life in Baker. Nestle was at my feet as usual, demanding, in that high pitched *yip! yip! yip!* of his, another walk in the park or perhaps it was fresh water or maybe that I play fetch with him, tossing that ridiculous rubber hamburger Kyle had given him the Christmas before. Whatever it was, I was ignoring it, playing what I had come to know as the "Nestle isn't here anymore" game, the object of which is fairly self-explanatory. And that's when I found it.

A tiny little ziplock baggie. Inside, another little baggie. And inside that...

Enough crystal meth to get me through the summer.

Everything around me seemed to melt away—Ethan Allen bedroom suite, the clapboard house with its single, hopeless hibiscus tree in the backyard, the whole hideous little town—as I considered my options. I could flush the drugs down the toilet and forget I ever found them. I could take a little bit now and then flush the rest down the toilet and forget I ever found them. I could take a little bit now and save the rest for later.

Or, I could keep my promise to Kyle: to try and stay clean, to give our new lives a chance, to really work at being a better, drug-free me.

I looked at the bag in my hand and felt a lump of shame rise in my throat. Had it come to this? Had the move to Baker caused me to slide so far down the moral chute that my wedding vows, to love, honor and cherish Kyle as long as we both should live, meant nothing if there was a possibility of satisfying my baser instincts?

I glanced out the window again, where the World's Largest Thermometer was topping 114, and decided to snort the whole bag.

Now before you shake your head in disapproval, good Lady, rest assured that I didn't bend to my addiction that day. I couldn't. Because it was at that exact moment that someone forfeited our game of "Nestle isn't here anymore" by leaping up like a demented kangaroo rat and grabbing the bag of crystal between his shaggy jaws! Before I could even threaten him with the possibility of a future hanging in a Korean butcher shop window, the demonic mutt was out the door!

I chased him along the upstairs hallway and into the guest bedroom, where he scuttled into the tiny bathroom. Cornered against the toilet, he snarled at me, baring his fangs as I reached down toward him.

"Good Nestle… just give me the crystal, Nestle, and everything will be fine. Just give it to me…"

He tried to make a break for the door, but I caught him by his silver Tiffany dog collar and held tight. The dog squirmed and struggled against my grasp, but I clamped down on his head, forced his jaws open, and reached into his mouth with my fingers.

His tiny, piranha teeth snapped and bit at me as he desperately tried to fight back, but I just held tighter, digging deeper and finally grabbing a corner of the slippery, saliva-drenched plastic. I yanked it out and let the little beast go. With a bark and a yelp, he scrambled away from me, his claws clattering against the tiles as he fairly flew out the bathroom door, leaving me alone with the baggie.

The *empty* baggie.

His teeth had gouged a good sized chunk out of it, and what little of the drug remained inside was now soaked in terrier spit. I looked around the floor hopefully; the tiles were clean and dry, and there was no sign of my crystal anywhere.

In the parlance of the narcotics *cognoscenti*, a "bump" of crystal is usually a single thin line of the powdery drug, about an inch long and less than a sixteenth of an inch wide. One or two "bumps" is more than adequate for, say, a man of six feet in height and 180 pounds in weight to experience the drug's effects. By my conservative estimate, there were about twenty "bumps" in that baggie.

The average toy terrier weighs approximately fifteen pounds.

Suddenly, from out in the hallway, I heard a strange gurgling sound. I moved out of the bathroom and cautiously stepped toward the hall, already dreading the sight I had guessed was about to greet me.

Nestle, shaking, drooling Nestle. Now in the full throes of a massive crystal meth overdose, the dog had backed himself into a corner, eyes glazed wide and teeth bared. And he didn't look terribly pleased about it.

"Nestle... good boy..." I coaxed.

He growled in return, a thick wave of foamy saliva oozing from his jaws. This was going to be a problem. I glanced at my watch; Kyle was due home soon, and I was definitely going to have a hard time explaining why his beloved terrier was performing selections from the road company version of *Cujo* in the upstairs hallway. But maybe, I reasoned, if I could just get the dog out of the house and lock him in the garage for a couple of hours, he'd dry out in time for his walk before bed. I made a move toward him holding my hand out, palm up, like Kyle always did to soothe the monstrous little throw rug.

"Good doggie... how about a nice walk?"

His fur rose on his haunches and he snarled at me again, his ears flattening in attack mode. With no further warning, he lunged at me!

One of the more curious side effects of crystal meth is the user's inability to accurately determine distance or strength. With that in mind, it really should have come as no surprise to me when, instead of hitting me, Nestle launched himself on a remarkably graceful arc about ten feet through the air and sailed cleanly out the second floor window.

The sudden, deathly silence below told me everything I needed to know before I made it down to the backyard.

"Where's Nestle?" was, of course, the first thing out of Kyle's mouth as he came home twenty-five minutes later. I kept my eyes on the pot of boiling angel hair pasta on the stove in front of me, nervously adjusting the apron I had thrown on in a desperate attempt to appear domestic.

Normal. Everything very normal. That was my plan.

"He was out in the backyard a few minutes ago," I replied, which was more or less true.

"I told you not to leave him alone," he retorted, slamming his briefcase on my perfectly set table and knocking an entire basket of breadsticks to the floor.

"It was just a few minutes," I said, perhaps a little too nonchalantly; it was hard to concentrate with the pasta steam billowing up into my face. "What could possibly happen to him in a few minutes?"

"Coyotes don't get paid by the hour!" Kyle shouted as he hurried out the back door. Still trying to figure that one out I followed, with the steaming pot in my hand, and did my best Marjorie Main impression at the doorway.

"Dinner's almost ready," I called after him. But by then he was already halfway across the yard, shouting Nestle's name at the top of his lungs. I turned the burner down to let the pasta simmer and, kneeling to pick up the breadsticks, I felt a shiver of cold water run down my spine as I caught a glimpse of my hands. I wondered if Kyle had noticed them.

For in spite of soaking and scrubbing with water hot enough to turn my knuckles red, there were still traces of black earth under my fingernails.

Dirt from burying that scruffy little ditch rat's body under the hibiscus tree.

Kyle scarcely spoke to me for the rest of the night. We ate in silence, he barely touching his meal, and even the slice of key lime pie on his plate—his favorite dessert—was met with only a suspicious glare.

"What's this for?" he grumbled.

"Dessert," I said. "I thought you'd like it."

"What I'd like to know is what happened to Nestle," he muttered, getting up from the table without taking a single bite of the pie. And so it went, all evening, until he crawled into bed and turned off the light, plunging me and the new issue of *Wallpaper* magazine into darkness.

"All you had to do was watch him," Kyle snorted, as he turned over and burrowed down into his pillow. "That's all you had to do."

I chose not to reply. What was I supposed to say, anyway? That I had watched him? That, in fact, I'd had a ringside seat as his beloved pet flew out the window and landed in a broken pile of triple digit grooming bills and absurdly expensive dog food receipts on the ground below? I rolled over onto my side and closed my eyes, hoping things would look, if not better, at least more tolerable in the morning.

Three hours later I awoke to the knowledge that we were not alone in the house.

I wasn't sure at first what I'd heard. But something had definitely reclaimed me from a deep sleep, my body immediately tense, and my ears tingling in spite of the silence. I looked over at Kyle, still dead to the world, a trail of drool staining his pillow. Not wanting to wake him with a false alarm—no sense adding insult to injury—I quietly eased my naked body from beneath the covers and padded on silent bare feet out of the room.

I stood there at the end of the upstairs hallway for a moment, listening to the house. Nothing. Only the distant hum of traffic rumbling along the freeway back to Los Angeles; back home. I glanced down at my once gym-trained and pool party-tanned body, now a pale gray in the thin moonlight, and patted my stomach. To my horror, it rippled; not the ripples of muscle, mind you but the ripples of cheese and potato chips, and enough Entemann's boxed cakes to cause a stampede at Jenny Craig.

No question, kind Lady Milton—I was losing it. First goes the career; then the body; and finally, you find yourself standing completely nude in the middle of your house, thinking you're hearing things.

That's when I heard the sound. A dry, scraping noise, like a dead tree being dragged off to a woodpile slaughter, followed by the hollow clink of something metal. I looked over the railing, to the floor below, but saw nothing there. The sound came again, a little closer this time. I leaned back into the bedroom where Kyle slept silently, snorelessly, on; whatever it was, the sound certainly wasn't coming from him. I listened again, as the strange scraping noise became louder, the metallic whisper closer.

It seemed to be coming from the stairs.

Barely aware of being naked, I crept cautiously down the hallway. The moon squeezed through a tiny hall window, bathing the empty landing in silver and leaving the rest of the staircase to tumble off into shadows below.

And it was from those shadows that the sound came. Closer.

Closer.

I tried to move, tried to scream, but somehow my feet had sunk into cement and my voice had fled in terror! The hideous rasping, scratching sound continued until it seemed as if the very walls themselves were alive with it! I could only stand there, naked and shivering, as what I knew to be impossible happened in front of my eyes!

A twisted limb stabbed out from the darkness. Matted fur, claws bent at impossible angles, it slapped at the next step, uncontrollably it seemed, and pulled the rest of the hideous vision into the light.

It was Nestle!

The dog's body, shattered by the fall, forced itself to continue up the stairs, one wrenching inch at a time. Clumps of dirt hung like icicles from its mangy fur, bloodied spittle dangling from the slack jaw. Its head lolled limply at the end of its broken neck, the expensive Tiffany collar tapping against the stairs with that horrendous metallic sound. Yet, in spite of its injury, it reached the top of the landing and somehow managed to turn its demon eyes toward me.

They were completely white, as if the horror of the animal's resurrection had bleached them to their very core. But still the beast seemed to stare with those slick ivory orbs, as if accusing me of its murder. The broken jaw began to work with a ghastly rhythm, the grim keening of bone grinding against bone, and I somehow knew that if I listened it would drive me mad. I clamped my hands tightly over my ears and closed my eyes and waited for what I knew was to come...

Rinnnggggg!

The sound of the alarm on the bedside table wrenched me, taut and sweating, from the nightmare. My eyes snapped open, focusing on that damnable—forgive my language, but that's how I'd come to think of it—thermometer in the distance, reading eighty-two degrees already and it wasn't even nine in the morning.

I reached over to Kyle's side of the bed, to wrap myself in his arms long enough to shake off the dream, and found myself face to face with Nestle.

I screamed, a high-pitched wail, and scrambled backwards out of the bed, falling hard to the floor. Kyle rushed out of the bathroom, already in his suit with a toothbrush dangling from his mouth, to find me cowering in the corner.

"The dog," was all I could manage. "The dog!"

Kyle reached down to the bed and picked up a small pile of freshly printed flyers, gathering a few more off the floor where they'd fallen. He held one up for me to see; it was a computer scanned picture of Nestle's face, framed by "Missing Dog" and "Reward Offered" as well as our address and phone number.

"Yeah," he nodded, dropping the pile into my lap. "I made them up this morning. You stick a few up around town while you're getting the groceries today, I'll hand some out at the bank."

I stared down at those beady little eyes, peering out from the nest of its furry face, and felt a wave of nausea pass over me. Kyle didn't notice a thing as he headed back into the bathroom.

"But don't leave until after the landscaper finishes," he said, between spits. "He looks kind of suspicious to me."

"What landscaper?" I asked, still in a daze.

"The one in the backyard."

He came back out of the bathroom, fingers impatiently negotiating a Windsor knot into his tie and I turned so he wouldn't see the blood drain from my face.

"God, what's the matter with you? I told you about this half a dozen times. He's putting in the barbecue today!"

As soon as Kyle left for work, I rushed out to the backyard with a tray of ice cold lemonade and no idea what I was going to do.

The landscaper's muscular form was bent over a wheelbarrow, unloading a pile of bricks and placing them next to his garden tools; shovel, pickaxe, rake. His once-white tank top, dirty with sweat and dust, pulled up with each brick he lifted, revealing a narrow band of his taut tanned waist. His close cropped blond hair glistened with sweat.

"Thought you'd like a drink," I said. He turned and looked at me with crystal blue eyes and suddenly the tray felt just a little heavier. Only twenty if he was a day but let me tell you, Lady Milton, Caravaggio in his wildest absinthian dreams couldn't have painted beauty like the common laborer standing before me.

"Thanks," he mumbled, hiking the loose fitting workpants up over his thin hips. He wiped at his sweating forehead with the back of his hand and I don't mind telling you that simple action caused enough rising and falling of muscles across his upper body to register on a seismograph. I poured him a glass, babbling.

"It's not store bought. It's fresh. I made it myself. From lemons. Well, lemons and water. And sugar. But not too much sugar. That's the thing people always get wrong when they make lemonade. They put in too much sugar, to make it sweeter. But then why do they bother at all? I say, if you want something sweet, then don't have lemonade."

I laughed alone. He just stood there, looking at me, so I handed him the drink. For a brief moment, as he took it, our fingers touched on the sweating glass. I introduced myself and waited for his reply.

"Harold," he mumbled, taking the drink from me quickly. He downed it in a single, long gulp as I stood there silently, watching the muscles in his throat roll like waves. He lowered the glass and noticed me staring. He held the glass out to me. "Not too sweet."

"Right," I nodded, taking the glass back. This time, he was careful not to let his touch graze my hand.

"You live here with the other guy?" he asked.

"Yes."

"Alone?"

"Yes."

"Just the two of you?"

"Just us."

He looked at the house. Looked at me. Nodded.

"Thanks for the drink," he grunted, turning back to pick up his shovel. He started to move toward the far corner of the yard.

Toward the hibiscus tree.

"What are you doing?" I asked, maybe too quickly.

"Gotta move the tree," he said, without breaking his stride.

"Why do you have to move the tree?" I asked, urging a calm layer over my voice.

"Cuz that's where your... that's where he wants the barbecue."

"No!" I blurted, hurrying toward him. "I mean, you can't move that tree. We love that tree there. It's perfect, right there." "He said he wanted the barbecue here. He told me to move the tree over there, I'm gonna move the tree over there." He raised his shovel and, in one quick stab, plunged the blade into the soft earth at the base of the hibiscus.

"Wait!" I shouted. He stopped, and turned slowly to look at me. A droplet of sweat rolled down his left temple and he squinted to keep it out of his eye. "He changed his mind. He told me he decided to put the barbecue over... there!" I pointed vaguely toward the other side of the yard. Harold shook his head with a smirk.

"Look, buddy. I don't want to get involved in some kinda..." His nostrils flared slightly with distaste. "Some kinda family feud, okay? The guy told me what he wanted done just before he drove outta here this morning, and he was pretty specific. You want something different, you talk to him, alright? Me, I'm moving this tree."

He returned to his shoveling and began to dig around the base of the tree. I backed up slightly, toward the brick pile, waiting for him to find the remains of Nestle, and wondering if I could make it to the bus station before he called Kyle. I bumped into something sharp and metallic and looked down to see what it was.

Don't you find, good lady, that sometimes, fate just comes along and hands you an opportunity? And wouldn't you agree that you ignore that opportunity at your own peril?

The landscaper continued digging with strong, deep stokes, sweat now pouring freely down his face.

"You just put this tree in? Ground's pretty soft around here, like somebody was just digging it or something."

I didn't answer. I was too busy aiming.

"Huh?" was all he got out as he turned to look at me, at the pickaxe in my hand, the sharp end making a wide, sweeping arc down toward him.

He reeled backwards before it connected, but couldn't move fast enough to avoid the blow. The point of the axe glanced off his forehead and skidded across his face, cutting a swath of blood and torn flesh on its way to gliding into his open mouth. His grunt of shock ended abruptly as the axe punctured through the back of his skull.

His body convulsed, limbs lurching wildly, as evidence of a last few coherent thoughts flickered across his face. He fell forward, but the pickaxe handle jammed into the soft earth and kept him from hitting the ground, supporting his body on its knees as if in prayer. Blood spilled from his mouth and down the axe handle, splashing the grass below him as he died, and I decided I'd better pour myself a glass of lemonade.

There was work to be done.

Although the television documentary mentioned your many trips to America, it did not say whether or not you had ever visited Joshua Tree National Park. Situated as it is halfway between those twin islands of high culture, Los Angeles and Las Vegas, I wouldn't be surprised if it hadn't made it onto your travel agenda. However, if you do find yourself in the area again in the future, I would highly recommend stopping by; it is a truly beautiful place. Twenty miles of desert terrain punctuated by breathtaking vistas of giant rock formations and incredible views of distant horizons, one could drive for half an hour without seeing even a single human being. Nothing but the stark skeletal "Joshua trees," rather optimistically named by the Mormons because they appear to be praying. They couldn't have been more wrong for, in fact, the poor things are actually wrenching themselves upwards toward the heavens in a misguided attempt to find sustenance in the unforgiving sky. Not unlike the Mormons themselves, one supposes.

Still, it is a spiritual place and one where Harold will, I hope, have found some peace. Granted it was probably a rather rough start, what with his corpse being stripped naked and left out in the open on a rock. But the body is only a vessel they say, and I like to think that Joshua Tree was only a brief stop on his way to a better life.

As a side note, Kyle was quite right about coyotes; they don't waste any time at all. Why, I'd barely reached the truck and they were already starting to appear from behind rocks and cacti, drawn by the smell of the freshly dead landscaper.

What's that expression, "It never rains, it pours"? You know, I don't think I really understood exactly what it meant until that day. For no sooner had I abandoned Harold's truck out behind a seedy little bar on the highway, being careful of course to wipe for fingerprints—those years watching *NYPD Blue* paid off after all—and rode my bike the eleven miles back to Baker that the Mormon boys showed up.

I suppose it makes some kind of cosmic sense, really. I went to the Joshua Tree. The Mormons came to me.

I was in the back yard, preparing to dig up Nestle's remains in order to dispose of them once and for all, when the doorbell rang. I ignored it. It rang again. I ignored it again.

But you've got to hand it to those missionary types; they are persistent.

"Hello?" came a voice from the side of the house. I immediately stopped digging and turned to see the two young men tentatively walking into the backyard. One blond, blue-eyed, and lanky, the other a strapping red-haired lad, they both wore the same taut haircuts, short sleeved white shirts tucked into ill-fitting black slacks and clip on ties. They carried leather-bound Bibles, zipped up as tight as their faces.

"Hello," I replied, non-committedly, casually leaning on my shovel in a way that blocked any view they might have had of the hibiscus tree. As they approached, I noted their clip on name tags, rather incongruously labeled "Elder Howe" and "Elder Niles" since neither of them were an hour past eighteen years old. They were sweating, dank circles under their arms, droplets of perspiration dotting their foreheads and upper lips, but in spite of their discomfort they summoned the grimly determined smiles of used-car salesmen before they spoke.

"Good afternoon, sir," Elder Howe offered, extending a hand to shake. I ignored it, being neither of the mood nor with the time to suffer these religious fools gladly—no matter how handsome they were. "I'm Elder Howe, this is Elder Niles, and we'd like to share something wonderful with you."

I raised a hand to stop his pitch.

"I already have something wonderful, thanks. It's called a life, and it doesn't need whatever you're selling, so why don't you guys just…"

Suddenly, Elder Niles clutched his stomach and doubled over, grunting in pain.

"Eric!" Elder Howe bent to help his friend, but Elder Niles pulled away, and through gritted teeth I could make out one word:

"Bathroom!"

Elder Howe looked up plaintively.

"May he use your… "

"First door on the left," I nodded, and without further ado Elder Niles loped toward the house. Elder Howe gave me a sheepish look.

"He's from Iowa," he said, as if that explained everything. I suppose he read my blank face as a lack of understanding, rather than the lack of interest it was, and continued. "He's not used to the food in California. We went to a place called Burrito Villa and I guess it didn't go down too well."

"Yes," I nodded. "I guess it didn't."

There was a long pause as he looked around the yard. He seemed to be thinking, trying to find something to talk about I supposed, as his friend evacuated his bowels in my once-pristine bathroom.

"You live here alone, sir?"

I was about to respond with something sharp and clever, when I heard the noise behind me. I froze. Elder Howe turned to look at me, waiting for an answer. Had I really heard what I thought I heard?

"Sir?"

There it was again. *Yip! Yip! Yip!* A high-pitched muffled sound. I turned to look at the source. It was coming from the hole behind me. Beneath the hibiscus tree.

I swear to you, good Lady, I knew it was impossible. I knew it couldn't be. But it was. I knew that voice.

It was Nestle.

Yip! Yip! Yip!

I didn't dare to move. Elder Howe looked at me strangely, waiting for me to say something, but I couldn't speak. I just kept staring down into the hole, the dirt, the darkness, dreading what was going to happen next.

"Sir, are you all right?"

Couldn't he hear it?

Yip! Yip! Yip!

It was getting louder now, as the beast must surely have been digging itself up and out of its grave.

"Is there something wrong?"

Of course there was!

Yip! Yip! Yip!

Didn't he hear the barking? Didn't he see the earth was about to move as the hideous thing clawed with its filthy paws, up, up, toward the surface?

Elder Howe stepped up beside me and leaned over the hole, peering down into the darkness. I backed away, letting him take a good look. Any moment now I knew the dead dog's head would lurch up through the dirt and the boy would see it and he would tell the police and they would tell Kyle and then Harold's body would be found in the desert and everything was going wrong so quickly.

"Is there something down there?"

I plunged the shovel into the young missionary's back. The sharp edge of the blade cleanly severed his spinal cord and burst out through his abdomen, taking what looked to me like his liver along with it. He gurgled in shock as he grabbed at his torn stomach, unsuccessfully trying to keep his intestines from spilling out through his fingers. The thick, ropy organs tumbled down into the hole, getting tangled up with the hibiscus roots, and Elder Howe fell to his knees, dropping his bloodstained Bible onto the ground next to him. He turned to look at me, his eyes sparkling with fear and confusion, and for one crystal clear moment I knew how he felt. A wave of pity washed over me.

So I swung the shovel again and cut his head off.

"Feeling better?" I asked Elder Niles as he stepped out of the downstairs bathroom.

"A little," he nodded. He still looked pale and if the stench coming from the tiny room behind him was any indication, he had emptied himself of several weeks' worth of food. "I had one of those burritos you know, the spicy ones."

"Elder Howe told me. This might help," I said, offering him a glass of bubbling liquid. He took it gratefully, raising it to his lips. I gave him my warmest smile. "It works best if you drink it down in one gulp."

He stopped abruptly and looked at the drink with suspicion. The smile on my face froze.

"Is there any caffeine in it?" he asked. "We're not allowed to drink anything with caffeine."

I relaxed. "No. No caffeine." That, at least, was true. To my knowledge, they've never put caffeine in drain cleaner.

He smiled and swallowed the stuff in one gulp.

I was still mopping the blood—and the other—off the floor when the telephone rang. It was Kyle. I could tell he was still angry. After grilling me about the groceries and the flyers and whether or not there had been any sign of Nestle, all of which I lied about with remarkable ease given the circumstance, he told me he was bringing his assistant manager and her husband home within the hour. I was supposed to make dinner. That was it. No "Please clean up the two dead Mormons and then make a nice meal for us, honey, I love you." Nothing. He just expected it to be done.

I hung up the phone and looked around the kitchen. An hour? If we were back home in West Hollywood, I could have called any number of fabulous restaurants and had a gourmet meal delivered in less than thirty minutes. But Baker was strictly KFC territory, and if I dared serve deep-fried anything to Kyle I would never have heard the end of it.

No, I needed to prepare a feast, and it had to be delicious. But I certainly hadn't had time to get to the grocery store, what with the murders and all, and there was simply nothing fresh in the house.

Well... almost nothing.

So what was I supposed to do? I ask you, Lady Milton, what was I supposed to do?

Dinner was a huge success. Everyone, even Kyle, commented on the delicious meat; its delicate seasoning, the way it literally melted in their mouths. When the meal ended, Tanya, the assistant manager, shyly asked if she and her husband could take some of the leftovers home. She had, she admitted, never tasted anything like it in her life. What was my secret?

Of course I told her. No caffeine.

They left shortly after dinner, spouting all the usual lies of reciprocation, and Kyle and I were alone again in the silent house. He made a few feeble stabs at conversation as he helped to clean up the kitchen, but I could tell his heart wasn't in it. I suggested he take a walk around the block, showing Nestle's picture to our erstwhile neighbors; it was very possible, I lied, that the dog was even now enjoying the hospitality of one of the friendly locals. Kyle took the bait, gave me a peck on the cheek, and left.

I stood there in the foyer of the dreadful little house, his kiss drying to become an itch on my face, and wondered what had happened to our wonderful life. My husband was grimly wandering the streets of a hick desert town in search of a dog he'd never find, and I was picking Mormon flesh from between my teeth, trying to remember where I'd put the flashlight.

Was this our destiny? Was this to be our future? Where had it all gone wrong? And where was the flashlight?

Twenty minutes of fumbling through the cluttered garage yielded nothing, not even a decent candle to light the pitch darkness of the backyard. How was I going to unearth the remains of that ghastly dog if I couldn't even see the hibiscus tree? Tears came suddenly to my eyes as I found myself thinking about home. It was nine thirty; Santa Monica Boulevard would just now start coming to life. Wednesday night. Half-price Margaritas at Revolver. Go-go boys at Mickey's. Maybe a floor show at Rage, some comedy troupe or a drag queen.

Drag queen. My dear, dear Paris DeLamour. I missed her quick wit, her clever put downs, the withering stare she could summon at will if one of her less attractive fans became a little too adoring. I could almost smell her perfume, something cheap and French, leftover from her mother's last visit to La Rive Gauche.

"You've only been here a month and already he's making you sleep in the garage?"

I opened my eyes in shock. The smell was real. And so was the voice.

It was Paris DeLamour, right there in Baker!

"Darling," she exclaimed, pulling me into the embrace which had earned her the Nebraska State High School Wrestling Championship two years running. "You didn't tell me you were moving out of the country!"

"What are you doing here?" I sputtered, standing back a moment to take in her ensemble; peasant smock, pigtails, gingham blouse and matching—matching mind you—gingham pumps. Salvador Dali meets Loretta Young in *The Farmer's Daughter*. The overall effect was stunning.

"I had a vision. I felt you needed me. Plus, they cancelled my show. Got any Ketel One?"

I couldn't move.

"Hello?" she said. "Anybody home?"

And then the dam broke. I began to sob uncontrollably, great whacking gulping sobs, the kind where your eyes feel like they're going to pour right out of their sockets. Paris took me into her arms.

"There, there. It's alright, darling. Stoli will do. But there'd better be mix."

I looked up into her kind face, eyes thick with caterpillars of mascara, her day-old beard growth beginning to poke through the heavy pancake makeup. Backlit by the naked bulb suspended from the garage ceiling, her wig seemed to glow like a halo. I knew then she was an angel. A caring, loving messenger sent from

Heaven to make everything all right again. And between crying spasms, I told her the whole story.

The town. The World's Largest Thermometer. The house. The dog.

Harold. The Mormons. Dinner.

Everything.

Moments later we were in the backyard, with me digging beneath the hibiscus tree while Paris held aloft her authentic *Charlie's Angels* Zippo to light my way.

Her reaction should have come as no surprise, really. After a childhood spent clawing her way up through the sewers of Midwestern heterosexuality, surviving the vicious taunts and horrendous physical assaults which surely went along with being an effeminate boy in small-town America, Paris had a healthy disregard for common morality. As she explained it, spilling tears over a few less rednecks and religious fanatics was nothing more than a waste of good salt. What I had to do, she insisted, was get rid of the damn dog and forget the whole thing ever happened.

Good friends, dear Duchess, are those who will help you bury the bodies.

Which made what happened next all the more painful. You see, as I continued shoveling the dirt, making my way deeper and deeper into the hole under the tree, I began to realize there was something wrong. Very wrong.

I had dug six feet down but I still hadn't hit the terrier.

"Are you sure this is where you buried it?" Paris wondered, holding the lighter low enough to cast eerie shadows deep into the hole.

"It was right here, right under the hibiscus," I insisted. "I know it was."

"Maybe you were confused, dear heart. I mean, burying your husband's pet dog is enough to make anyone a trifle *désorienté*!"

"I'm not *désorienté*!" I shouted, loud enough to echo through the backyard. In the distance, a dog barked and a window slammed shut. "It was right here!"

I began to dig like a madman, ravaging at the earth with the shovel. Paris backed up as I flailed, dirt flying in every direction! I felt the muscles on my arms shriek as I slammed the spade again and again into the sun toughened ground.

"It's here! It's right here! Damn it, I know where I put that god-damned dog!"

Suddenly, the flame of the lighter flickered out, plunging us into darkness.

"Paris!" I grunted, still digging. "I need that light!"

But there was no answer from the drag queen. Only the strange, rasping sound of breath forced through taut teeth.

"Paris?" I turned to where she had been standing, and peered into the darkness. "Paris, what are you doing?"

A cloud moved away from the moon, casting the backyard in a cold, silver light.

The first thing I saw was one of the gingham pumps, empty, laying on its side on the grass.

And beside that, convulsing on the ground, the former Clark Nesbitt of Puce, Nebraska, now Miss Paris DeLamour of Glamorville, USA was having an epileptic seizure.

I leapt up out of the hole and knelt beside her, trying to calm her down, or at least make sure she didn't break off one of her expensive acrylic fingernails.

"Shh, shh... you're okay, you're okay..." I said lamely, my hands on her shoulders, holding her firmly against the ground. "Just breathe... breathe..."

Suddenly, her head twisted toward me, her eyes snapping open. Her pupils gleamed with platinum moonlight, boring into me with an unearthly gaze as she parted her glistening coral lips to speak.

And I swear to you, kind Lady, this is what came out of her mouth.

Yip! Yip! Yip!

It was Nestle.

Somehow, don't ask me by what demonic power, that hellish toy terrier had possessed my beloved friend!

"Paris!" I shouted at her. "It's evil! The dog is evil! Fight it! Don't let it win!"

But the animal's control of her was complete, its horrendous spirit in command of her every breath. So violent were her convulsions that her scarlet wig pulled away from her skull, exposing the bleached blonde nest of processed hair beneath.

"Yip! Yip! Yip!" she shrieked, her body writhing in pain and terror. "Yip! Yip! Yip!"

"No, Nestle!" I screamed. "Let her go! Take me!! Take me!"

It was no use. The beast held her in its ghastly thrall, determined to enact God-only-knew what hideous revenge upon me. She clawed at the grass, her muscles contorting, the tendons along her neck straining as if to burst.

Yip! Yip! Yip! Yip! Yip! Yip!

Dear God, I could stand the yelping no more! There was only one solution, only one way to free the poor transvestite from the clutches of the horrid thing!

I closed my eyes and prayed for forgiveness as I wrapped my hands around the soft yielding throat of my dear Paris DeLamour.

I'm sure you can imagine Kyle's reaction when he arrived moments later to find his husband of four years holding the broken neck of a dead drag queen at the edge of a six-foot deep pit in the backyard.

But can you imagine my shock when I saw what Kyle was carrying in his arms?

It was Nestle.

Claws and fur thick with dirt, but otherwise alive and well, staring at me with those beady little terrier eyes.

I could have sworn it was smiling...

I have spent endless nights trying to make some sense of it all.

From what Kyle told the police in his statement, and from the numerous articles on the subject printed in the *Baker Gazette*—this was, after all, the first interesting thing that had happened in the town since they'd built the damn thermometer—I have managed to put together a theory of sorts.

It is my belief that the wretched hound had never died at all. It simply fell into a coma after ingesting all that crystal meth and, when it awoke, dug its way out of the premature grave. Unable to rouse either Kyle or myself from our sleep, it wandered out into the street and found shelter with our next door neighbors, a charming Indian couple with utterly unpronounceable names. Not knowing to whom the dog belonged, and with only the most rudimentary command of the English language, they had set out that evening on a quest of their own. It had only been when they met up with Kyle at another house down the street that the entire situation worked itself out.

Well, not entirely of course. There was still the matter of my murders.

I confessed right away to killing Harold and the Elders Niles and Howe; I saw no point in lying, really, as eventually even the dullards employed as police officers in that town would have connected the rather obvious dots. There was one rather interesting moment when I showed them how I had disposed of the bodies of the Mormon boys; apparently Tanya and her husband were finishing off the last of the leftovers when they were told the truth and it caused quite a fuss at their house.

And while I did admit to strangling Paris DeLamour, I tried to explain that in fact I hadn't really *murdered* her *per se*. It had been a mercy killing, I told them; an exorcism to release her from the unholy grip of that devil dog.

As you can see, by the return address on this letter, your Grace, my sanity was immediately called into question.

There were countless hearings and examinations, during most of which I simply let the lawyers argue amongst themselves.

They tossed around meaningless phrases like "disconnected sociopathy and brain damage due to controlled substance abuse," things like that. But I ask you, who wants to listen to all that legal mumbo jumbo, anyway? I was just happy to be getting out of Baker.

I will admit, however, that I do miss Kyle.

Of course he was exonerated of any involvement in my crimes. And while having a serial killer as an ex-husband should give one a certain "cachet," or at the very least the grounds for a best-selling tell-all book., Kyle has declined all offers—he even turned down Larry King!—and has apparently gone into hiding. With Nestle, I assume.

As for me, well, I'd like to think I have been spending my time here at the Center wisely. I'm taking a few courses in art appreciation and history, with an eye toward becoming a teacher when I'm released at the end of my sentence—if, of course, they still have schools at the turn of the next century.

You'll be happy to know I have been working very hard with my therapist to try to work through the feelings I still have about the dog. About Nestle.

Dr. McDermid, an extraordinarily patient and understanding man, has helped me to see that the toy terrier was just a symbol, a physical manifestation of my intense fear of relationships. And by acting out around those fears, in my case by burying a toy terrier and then ritualistically slaughtering four innocent victims, I was only trying to figure out why I think Paris barked.

Which brings me, finally, to the point of this letter, kind Lady.

Do your butterflies still talk?

And if they do, is it still in the voice of your late husband, the one you slowly poisoned with the arsenic you slipped into his oatmeal during the course of that overseas voyage from the continent to the West Indies two decades ago?

Or have they stopped, letting you sleep at night without the constant reminder of your crime?

You see, there's this spider in my cell. We've become quite close, actually; he's more of a pet now than a nuisance. And I've been thinking that maybe, just maybe, if I can convince Dr. McDermid that I love the spider, he will see that my attitude towards having pets has changed. Then he will know that the therapy is working and perhaps he will make a recommendation allowing me to have a day pass soon.

I would use it to go back to West Hollywood. Just to have one drink, that's all I want. Just one drink as the sun sinks down behind the distant silver castles of Century City. Sitting there in front of Mickey's say, or Rage, licking the salt from the rim of my dollar margarita and watching those handsome young men walk by. That's all I want. If the spider would just stop making so much noise.

He keeps me awake at night, you see. I've tried asking him to be quiet, I need my sleep, but he doesn't seem to listen. So I was thinking that if you found a way to make your butterflies stop, then maybe it would work for my spider, too?

Now, I know you must be a very busy lady, what with your charity work and I'm sure a very full social calendar at the Sanitarium. But if you can find it in your heart to send a reply to me by return mail, my dear Duchess, I would be ever so appreciative. You see, unlike your butterflies, my spider doesn't talk.

He sings "I Got Rhythm." Just like Paris DeLamour did. Exactly like she did. With her voice.

Don't get me wrong. The fact that he sounds like my late, lamented transvestite friend isn't what disturbs me. It's actually rather comforting.

But the spider... like Paris, he only knows the one song. And frankly, it's beginning to drive me crazy.

Please write soon.

Your Servant,

Trevor Bowden
Millwood Center for the Criminally Insane,
Needles, CA

Excerpt from WAIT!
Scene Two of a Full-Length Play

Julie Jensen

CHARACTERS:

WENDY: A gay girl in her 20s. Her father says she's as interesting as wall board.

LU: A gay guy in his 20s. He and Wendy hung out together in high school, because no one else would have them.

VIXEN: A woman in her 20s. A would-be actress. A most amazing person.

SETTING:
An old opera house, which Lu and whomever he can get are trying to restore.

NOTE:
Underscored lines are meant to be addressed directly to the audience.

WENDY: So then one day, I'm at the theatre. Lu scoots in from the dog grooming shop. That's where he works. A job that pisses off my old man. "What is he?" he says. "A beautician for dogs?" To which Lu always answers, "An appreciation of beauty is not limited to the human race."

Well anyway, in he runs. Lu. He's all breathless and tattered. He's got the luncheon arranged, he says. Luncheon with the Dollarnuts. The Dollarnuts!

The Dollarnuts have money. They love the theatre, and they're losing their beans. That is a combination Lu cannot resist.

LU: They simply adore the idea that John Wilkes Booth performed here.

WENDY: But Lu, John Wilkes Booth never performed here.

LU: Of course he did. He played Richard III. Performing the evil king by night, brooding in his hotel room by day. It was here in this town, in this place, that he planned his role on the stage of history.

WENDY: What year was that?

LU: It was 1862, of course.

WENDY: The theatre was built in 1909.

LU: Nonsense. I have playbills to prove it. And so I need a big favor from you.

WENDY: You want me to shovel the pigeon shit out of the lobby. Before the actors show up.

LU: You're a doll. Wish me luck.

WENDY: And he's off like a bee from a tulip. Just then, in comes Vixen. That's her name. Vixen. And my whole life flew. Straight up.

VIXEN: Hello.

WENDY: Hey.

VIXEN: I'm Vixen.

WENDY: Right.

VIXEN: Course my full name is O Vixen My Vixen. *[We hear the first phrase of Beethoven's Fifth.]*

WENDY: You hear that?

VIXEN: I'm named after a poem. "O Captain, My Captain." I forget who wrote it, but I'm named after that. Except instead of O Captain, My Captain, I'm named O Vixen My Vixen. *[First phrase of Beethoven's Fifth again.]*

WENDY: See. There it is again.

VIXEN: And you are?

WENDY: I am. I am. Ahhhh, Wendy. I'm Wendy.

VIXEN: Wendy. I love their milk shakes. Don't you?

WENDY: Yes.

VIXEN: Except, have you ever let one of their milk shakes wait? They turn into plastic foam.

WENDY: I wouldn't know, I eat them right away. *[Pause.]* Vixen, that's a good name.

VIXEN: O Vixen My Vixen. That's my full name. *[We hear the first phrase of Beethoven's Fifth again.]*

WENDY: It happened again.

VIXEN: Is something wrong with you?

WENDY: No, no. I'm fine.

VIXEN: Brain damage or something? My brother has brain damage. He gets this look. Then he receives messages from the silverware.

WENDY: Oh. *[Pause.]* Wall board woman again, just like my dad says. Can't think of a thing to say. So I decide to focus on breathing.

VIXEN: Of course, I changed my name.

WENDY: Yeah.

VIXEN: My old name was....

WENDY: Polly Ann Pucket.

VIXEN: Oh no, you knew me by my other name.

WENDY: You were a cheerleader.

VIXEN: Yes, I was.

WENDY: And part of the Pink Steps.

VIXEN: Yes.

WENDY: And, of course....Miss Walrus.

VIXEN: Yes, I was! And, like, what were you?

WENDY: No one. I was watching you. From afar.

VIXEN: Polly Ann Pucket. That is a very a good name for, like, a cheerleader. But I think O Vixen My Vixen is a better name for, like, the theatre. What do you think?

WENDY: Yes....Yes, I do. I do. Yes. I do. The old man's right, I sound defective. Are you an actress, then?

VIXEN: Yes. Yes, I am an actress. Oh wow, that is the first time I've ever said that out loud to a person. I mean, I go to my parents and I go, "I think I'll go into, like, acting," well, my dad pret-near has a cow. He goes, "You can't be turning into no damn weirdo." I tell him, like, "Dad, they don't have weirdo girls in theatre, only weirdo boys." But, like, he don't believe me. So I'm, like, whatever.

But lately, I have been real serious about it. About acting. I get into these, like, different emotions and think about how to express them on the stage.

So anyway, I'm quite good I think, but I'm not sure. Like, with certain emotions I'm really good, I know that. But I mean there's a lot I haven't done yet. Like a lot of emotions that I haven't expressed onstage yet. That's what it's about, expressing new emotions on stage. It's very deep. Don't you think?

WENDY: Yeah.

VIXEN: Pretty soon I've got to specialize, though. But I just haven't done that yet.

WENDY: Specialize?

VIXEN: Yeah, like queens, maids, whores, whatever. See, I'm gonna probably specialize in whores, because there's a lot of them in a lot of different plays. So if you're, like, a girl, it's a good thing to specialize in, like, whores.

WENDY: Right. I'm looking at her hair. It's orange. I'm looking at her eyes. They're blue. She is a bird of paradise in human form.

VIXEN: I'm early, aren't I?

WENDY: Early?

VIXEN: You know, like, early.

WENDY: Early. Yes. No. It is quite remarkable, I think, time.

VIXEN: I came early so I could work on my audition piece.

WENDY: Audition piece. Right!

VIXEN: I promised myself to do it a hundred times a day.

WENDY: For how many days?

VIXEN: Six months. But I didn't do it. I was overwhelmed, like, by life. And that's more important, I think.

WENDY: Right.

VIXEN: Because life is what the theatre is based on. I mean that is so deep when you think about it, don't you think? Life. Theatre. Theatre. Life. Like wow.

WENDY: I want to tell her I know what she means. And I do know what she means. But I can't. I can't speak in sentences.

VIXEN: So....what's you doing?

WENDY: Just shoveling shit.

VIXEN: You live here, I bet.

WENDY: Yeah.

VIXEN: You live in the same town as this theatre, one of the greatest theatres in the history of all history!

WENDY: Right.

VIXEN: You do not know how truly fortunate you are. For example, I live in Walrus.

WENDY: Right, Walrus.

VIXEN: You see, we do not have a theatre in Walrus. We do not even have a movie theatre in Walrus. We have to go to, like, Chinchilla for everything.

WENDY: Oh yeah. Chinchilla. Suddenly words like...Walrus. And... Chinchilla. Words I've said all my life. They have new meaning now. Wal-rus.

VIXEN: You must know Lu then.

WENDY: Lu. Yes.

VIXEN: I am, like, inspired by Lu. That's what I told my parents. I have to drop everything and follow that man.

WENDY: Follow. Yes.

VIXEN: I have to like commit myself to this work.

WENDY: Commit. Yes.

VIXEN: I have got to be in, like, the same air space with him.

WENDY: Air space. Yes.

VIXEN: You know what he said to me, the first time he met me?

WENDY: Something about dreams.

VIXEN: Yes! How did you know?

WENDY: Just a guess.

VIXEN: He said these words. He said, "Dreams cannot be wasted." That's what he said. I'll never forget it. Because it went straight through my chest like a heart. "Dreams cannot be wasted." Don't tell no one. But it was like the Angel Maroni spoke to me, like he was saying to me, "Cheerleading is wonderful and all, but it is just not enough." And that's when I dedicated myself to, like, the art of acting.
And so how do you know Lu?

WENDY: We grew up together.

VIXEN: No. I cannot believe that. It's like God. Was he ever a baby and who did he date? You can't imagine it.

WENDY: I am posing my face like I understand everything she says. But really I don't.

VIXEN: Did you know that Drew Barrymore was born here, right over there by those ropes. Lu told me all about it.

WENDY: I bet he did.

VIXEN: Yes. Because her mother was in this play, and she was really, really preggers. And then between the acts, she gave birth to Drew, and then she went on and finished the play. I think that's is, like, so inspirational. I would like to give birth on stage, wouldn't you?

WENDY: What is the answer to that question? This Vixen is so thought provoking.

VIXEN: You know, you remind me of someone. I don't know who it is. Do people say that to you a lot?

WENDY: I don't know.

VIXEN: I wonder who it is. Oh, yeah, it's Leo on A-M-C.

WENDY: A-M-C?

VIXEN: "All My Children." You remind me of Leo.

WENDY: Oh. Yeah, right. Leo! You can see how smart she is.

VIXEN: He used to love Laura, but now he doesn't. So when she called him up, he goes, "Do not call me anymore." And she faints. Or else, she's like faking a heart attack.

WENDY: Oh.

VIXEN: But you remind me of him. You do. I'm more like Laura, don't you think?

WENDY: You are. Yes. I agree with everything she says.

VIXEN: And I would love to be her, too. "Rachel, you've gone too far. You've stolen my car. My boyfriend. And now this...my baby." That's pretty close, don't you think?

WENDY: Yes, it's close. It's astounding to me how she comes up with so much to say, so many different topics. A sign of brilliance, I think. A sign of genius.

VIXEN: Oh no, is that the john? That is just too perfect. I'm gonna go in there and practice my audition piece. I love to practice in johns, don't you?

WENDY: Yeah, I guess.

VIXEN: I mean. People come in. They pee. They wash their hands. Then they, like, get a little show. And when you're done, they clap. And that is the reason I do it. For the clap.

WENDY: Right.

VIXEN: Every john is an itty bitty theatre. That's the way I think about it. So I'll be in there. *[VIXEN exits.]*

WENDY: Right. Truly amazing, don't you think? You're waiting around. And then life. It comes along and interrupts the flow of itself.

———

WAIT! is a full-length play commissioned by Salt Lake Acting Company, supported by NEA/TCG Residency Grant, recipient of the McKnight National Playwriting Fellowship from Playwrights' Center, Minneapolis, MN and workshopped at the Women's Theatre Festival, Seattle, WA.

The play premiered at Salt Lake Acting Company (Salt Lake City, UT) and subsequently produced by Cleveland Public Theatre (Cleveland, OH), Catalyst Theatre (Philadelphia, PA), and Perseverance Theatre (Juneau, AK) among dozens of others.

It is published by Dramatic Publishing Company.

Espiritu Santo

Marty Beaudet

Only gradually did he recognize that he was not lying on the cold, hard stone of a lightless dungeon. And his hands were not tied behind his back. He'd only dreamt that.

But the numbness in his right arm was not a dream. He'd been using it for a pillow and it had gone to sleep. When he raised his head, letting the blood flow once again into his unfeeling limb, the throbbing between his temples revealed itself to be every bit as real as the numbness. A lead weight seemed to roll from one side of his head to the other. He returned his head gently to the pillow and waited for the pounding to stop.

Early morning light stained the room's dark, heavy curtains, but failed to illuminate the interior. Only muted sounds stole through the windows from the awakening city outside. He was in his own apartment, in his own bed. The fetterdecke was partially thrown back and... he was naked! Was he still dreaming after all? He never slept in the nude.

Just then he thought he heard something—a shuffling in the dark. The creak of floorboards; footsteps coming closer. Before he could be certain a hand touched his shoulder and he started in fright.

"Sorry," whispered a voice. It was Jassim! To Kevin's astonishment the Kuwaiti, also naked, slipped into bed next to him. As Jassim wrapped his arms around him, a sudden mix of horror, bewilderment, and—most frightening of all—ecstasy washed over Kevin. This was no dream!

The memory of the previous evening came flooding back with a brutal clarity that paralyzed him with fear. *Did it really happen?*

They had gone to dinner together at a cozy local joint called *Espiritu Santo*. Jassim had quipped, "'Holy Spirit' seems like a good place for a little Mormon angel to fall from grace." Kevin thought the remark had been made only in jest, but it was all too accurate. The events that followed were as a fulfillment of prophecy.

Kevin had agreed to try his first alcoholic beverage last night. In Vienna, friends spent an inordinate amount of time—often an entire afternoon or evening—at either a bar or café, socializing over alcohol or coffee. He'd never thought about it before leaving his insular Mormon culture back home, but the world outside the Church seemed to run on caffeine and alcohol. When people got together after work, they went out for a drink. When they met for an afternoon chat, it was over a cup of coffee. How curious, he thought, that beverages played such a significant role in people's lives.

What was the Mormon alternative? Milk and cookies? The ubiquitous red punch that flowed at every church function? Pop, punch, cookies, ice cream, Jell-O, fudge, pie, cake, s'mores, Rice Krispie treats; no church social event was ever without these things. Maybe sugar was the Saints' drug of choice. And, he rationalized further, if the Word of Wisdom was meant to be a "health code," as the Church taught, how much unhealthier could an occasional beer or coffee be than a steady diet of sugar? Was it really such a big deal? Could Heaven or Hell really revolve around something as trivial as one's choice of beverage?

So, despite some lingering misgivings, he'd accepted the half-liter of beer that Jassim ordered for him. It was a *Weißbier*, because, Jassim said, wheat beer was smoother and more flavorful than a Pilsner. It would go down easier, he had assured him.

Jassim watched with an amused grin as Kevin braced himself for his first sip. Kevin couldn't deny that the wheat beer had "flavor" as Jassim had said. But he wasn't sure that was the same as tasting good. It took a little getting used to. Still, it was less bitter and did go down a heck of a lot easier than the sip of Budweiser he had stolen on a dare from classmates when he was twelve years old. At least he told himself it did. After all, that was nearly ten years ago.

What Kevin hadn't been prepared for was how quickly he began to feel lightheaded and giddy. By the time the half-liter glass was half empty, the noisy buzz of the tiny restaurant had already receded to a distant hum. Only Jassim's face was in focus; the rest was a blur. His features became curiously sharper, his voice warmer and more sincere. Even what he was saying became more earnest, more important, and rife with significance. Kevin wasn't sure if Jassim's drinking or his own was responsible for this phenomenon. He tried to assess the situation objectively, but found it difficult to keep his thoughts focused.

A second beer followed. It went down much more easily. In fact, it actually tasted good. Or at least he thought it did. It was like a warm, magical nectar that opened up his mind and made his thoughts clearer and more intense. And then there was wine with dinner. Kevin protested that, or did he? He'd meant to, anyway. One glass? Two? He had no idea really.

After that he was only vaguely aware of his surroundings. He thought he recalled two—or was it three—trips to a restroom behind some velvet curtains. By the time they finished dessert, he was completely dependent on Jassim to get him home.

He remembered now feeling a mix of guilt and exhilaration at his own decadence. He was researching an acting role, he had reminded himself, until it no longer mattered. Somehow this gave him the permission he needed to give himself over entirely to the new sensations he was experiencing. All of his strict Mormon inhibitions had floated away on a river of alcohol.

When they reached his apartment, he suddenly grew afraid. The warm fuzzies he'd reveled in earlier were beginning to subside, replaced by growing dizziness and lurking paranoia. He begged Jassim not to leave him there alone, insisting that he stay a while—at least until he was feeling better. It hadn't occurred to him that it was already past midnight and that Jassim might be needing sleep as well.

But Jassim agreed without hesitation. He was so kind, so caring. Kevin found his warm smile and boyish laughter comforting. As Jassim helped him up the stairs his touch seemed somehow electric, sending a tingling up and down Kevin's spine. Once inside, Jassim led Kevin to the edge of his bed, sat him down, and helped him out of his jacket.

Now Kevin remembered the night more clearly. It hadn't seemed real. His inebriated brain had processed the event in slow motion. A brush of soft, warm lips against his own. A warm breath of wine enveloping him. Was Jassim kissing him? Kevin had started to protest, but Jassim had put a finger to his lips hushing him, "*Ssss, Ruhe, mein Kleiner*"—Quiet, my little one.

Kevin had then closed his eyes and felt the backs of Jassim's fingers, still cold from the chill night air, stroke his cheek, the hand coming to rest at the back of his head, tousling his hair. Kevin remembered feeling a flood of tangled emotions, but in his drunken state he hadn't been sure just which ones they were.

Whatever he felt, it was not enough to compel him to move beyond Jassim's grasp. Before he knew it they were kissing and embracing again, this time with more fervor. Helpless, he felt his own tongue yield to Jassim's. Panic threatened as he realized that he was getting an erection.

After that Jassim laid Kevin back on the unmade bed, as his tongue began to gently probe the corners of Kevin's mouth. Kevin continued to yield to him, as though he hadn't an inhibition in the world. He was too confused, and drunk, to protest. He wanted to cry. Maybe he did. But he wasn't sure whether it was from fear or exhilaration. Jassim pulled back just inches from Kevin's face and the two stared into each other's eyes for several moments, not speaking. Then Jassim leaned forward, gave each of his drooping eyelids a soft kiss, and rolled onto the bed beside him.

By then Kevin's mind was awash with a torrent of muddy thoughts. Was it togetherness or abandonment that he feared? As if in answer to this unspoken question, Kevin felt a sudden, almost primal need to hold Jassim. He rolled onto his side and closed his eyes, pressing himself against Jassim's firm, compact body. It seemed a perfect fit, as though two pieces of a jigsaw puzzle had been happily reunited. He rested his head on Jassim's shoulder and... that was the last thing he could remember.

I Love You No Matter What

Emily January Petersen

"My dad's not gay! You're a liar!" I had never spoken to anybody with such violence, but I did so now to Jenny, a childhood friend.

We were settled in her bedroom, and the emptiness of the newly painted room echoed the grief that rang out in my voice. The walls seemed to be closing in on me. It was well past bedtime, and my two younger sisters were sprawled o on the carpet snoring in their sleeping bags.

We had arrived in California a few days earlier, just in time to visit our father for Christmas. My mother, step-father, and baby brother remained in Utah. We often spent Christmas at my dad's condo in San Jose; however, this year we drove to Fresno. Dad explained that his friend, Dale, and his daughter Jenny, had moved there and that's where we would be celebrating the holidays. Jenny and Dale had been part of our lives since my parents' divorce. Spending Christmas with them sounded fun to me. Jenny and I had spent the last few days bonding over music and boys. But now I was learning the most devastating news of my life at the age of nine.

I had needed a drink a few moments before, so Jenny and I had crept to the kitchen. We had passed the still-lit Christmas tree, then flooded the kitchen with light and raided the refrigerator. But tiptoeing back to bed, I noticed something I hadn't before. As we passed the master bedroom, I realized that both my dad and Dale were sleeping in the same bed. The door was wide open and the two of them lay snoring on their backs, unaware that Jenny and I were up way past our bedtime. We reached her bedroom and shut the door softly, thrilled that we hadn't been caught.

As we clambered back onto her bed overfull with pillows to talk, I giggled, "Our dads are having a sleep-over, too! They're sleeping in the same bed."

Jenny's smile vanished and she looked at me seriously. "Emily, it isn't a sleep-over."

"What do you mean?"

"Do you really want to know?" Her brown eyes were wide and full of concern. I wasn't sure if I did, but I said yes anyway.

"They're gay, Emily. That's why they're in the same bed."

And that's when my world exploded.

I have a few memories of my father before he left. My favorite is the one of him taking us to meet his coworkers or secretaries. Dad would say, "These are my daughters: Emily, Haley, and Afton." The coworker would inevitably say, "Oh, they're darling, Ron! This one looks just like you!" while pointing at me. I'd feel so proud to earn that distinction, the daughter who looked like Dad.

But the most vivid memory is of a Sunday morning, with my dad in bed while my mom, my two sisters, and I got dressed for church. My dad was a San Jose City police officer who often worked graveyard shifts, making this situation unremarkable. He could have been sick. He could have been tired.

When we arrived home after church, my mom's demeanor seemed to alter. Her hands shook slightly as she fit the silver key into the lock, her palm sweaty and struggling to grip the brass knob. Then, instead of entering the house, she poked her head in tentatively, her hot-rollered waves bouncing as she scanned the living room. She finally stepped over the threshold, her black open-toed heel getting slightly caught before she fully entered the house.

My sisters and I followed her, the three of us bumping into her legs and each other, pushing to enter the familiar territory that our mother was suddenly treating as unfamiliar. Mom seemed to get her senses back after entering, striding into the kitchen, setting down her bag.

"Ron?" she called down the hallway of our rambler. "Ronald? Are you still sleeping?" She paused to listen for a response, one that didn't come.

She lifted her leg, bending it at the knee, and removed one shoe, then the other. She took them in hand and walked slowly down the brown-carpeted hallway toward the master bedroom. We followed, tiptoeing so we wouldn't wake Dad. We knew the routine. We had to be quiet during the days; he needed to sleep.

We entered the bedroom behind our mother. The bed was neatly made and empty. The first thing that jumped out at me was an envelope lying against the pillows. At age five, it was just at my eye level. But Mom didn't see it because she was staring into the open closet. Half of it was empty, a stray tie dangling from a wire hanger like an exclamation point. Mom gasped as she stared into this void, not too loudly, but loudly enough. We all looked at up her.

But when she turned around she wore a tight smile, though her chin trembled slightly. "Let's find Daddy," she chirped. "He must be here somewhere."

She began calling his name, stumbling from room to room, finding the bathroom devoid of his toiletries and the linen closet missing its namesake. Her act worked on me. My dread subsided and I skipped gaily after her, calling for Dad and thinking that he had devised a new game of hide and seek, only removing his possessions to show that he wasn't hiding there.

After five desperate minutes of calling his name, my mother switched on a Strawberry Shortcake video and filled our hands with crackers. We sisters grinned at each other; watching cartoons was more exciting than our usual routine of changing our clothes and setting the table for dinner. But the change made me wary and dread began to pool in the bottom of my stomach. Usually Dad would be here too, just waking up or removing his tie if it hadn't been a late night.

Mom went to her bedroom and shut the door. Over the cheerful cartoon voices, I could hear her talking in a hushed yet frantic voice on the telephone. Haley wanted to pick up the kitchen extension to see if Dad was on the other line. I wouldn't let her. The dread in my stomach made me think that Dad wasn't on the line, that Dad wasn't coming home. Grandma was probably the one comforting my mother right now; doubtless the envelope was lying opened in my mother's lap.

While I yelled at her for being a liar, Jenny's face deepened with concern. She must have realized what she'd driven me, quiet and shy Emily, to do. "Yes, they are gay," she explained evenly. "My mom told me."

Jenny then told the story her mom had told her: how our dads had met, fallen in love and decided to leave their wives and children for each other. The news filled me with a sickness. I knew that what Jenny revealed was true. My heart knew it so violently that it tried to beat its way out of my chest. But I didn't want to accept it.

"No! No! NO!" I cried. "You're lying. You don't know what you're talking about! My dad's NOT gay!" Jenny relented. The tears pouring down my cheeks probably warned her against saying anything more.

"When you get home, you can ask your mom about it. Let's go to sleep now," she suggested. She turned out her bedroom light and we crawled into our sleeping bags.

Soon afterwards Jenny's breathing became even and rhythmic, but I laid there with my eyes open, my heart still smarting at the news. Everything Jenny had said to me made sense. I knew that Dad would never come back to Mom now, never come back to me. I had thought there was still hope. I had thought we would someday return to California to live with him again because he hadn't remarried the way my mom had. I imagined that he still pined for her, for his family. But all of those illusions now lay shattered around me. My stomach felt cold and empty. I didn't want what Jenny had said to be true, but I knew that it was.

I also realized that his gayness posed an enormous problem for me.

I remembered that I was a carbon copy of my father. So far in my life, I'd noticed that I had inherited his picky personality and perfectionist persona. I liked to organize and keep things clean. He had always been fastidious in everything, his dress, manners, and housekeeping. Dread crept into my heart. Did my similarity to him mean that I would turn out gay, too? My only knowledge of the homosexual orientation was that it was a sin and you would go to hell for it. The kids at school constantly teased one boy in our class because he enjoyed gymnastics and spent most of his time playing with girls. I did not want to be teased as he was. Being gay seemed so gross to me, so backward from everything I'd ever been taught. I began to sob, for I felt that my father would be eternally damned and me right along with him.

I returned home to Utah after the Christmas vacation, dejected and guilt-ridden. I had already become a worrier in my young life, worrying over my parents' divorce, my mother's emotional welfare, my school work, my sisters, my new baby brother, the many times I'd moved, not to mention life in general. Now, I added to that list my father's eternal welfare and burning questions about how much of my father was in me. Who was I? What would I become? It was something so horrible that I couldn't tell anybody, not even my mother. How could I talk to her about something so awful, so personal for us both?

I decided to lead a normal life. I resumed playing with my sisters, eating dinner with the family, loading the dishwasher, watching my favorite television show, practicing piano, returning to school, doing homework, and just being. However, each night I'd crawl into bed, turn out the light, and cry myself to sleep. The pain seemed to physically rip through my body; emotional pain and physical pain were one and the same.

One night my sobbing became uncontrollable, so loud, in fact, that my mother came in to check on me. As she opened the door I felt acutely embarrassed that I'd been caught, that my secret worry would now have to be revealed. But, I also felt a great sense of relief. I had wanted to tell my mother what I had learned, to ask if it was true, but I hadn't dared. Maybe my crying became loud on purpose. Maybe it was a cry for help.

As my mother stood in the doorway, the light from the hall surrounded her, creating a halo as if she were an angel of mercy. She asked with compassion what was wrong. Instead of breaking the news gently, as I had been plotting the last several days, I blurted out, "Is Dad really gay?" and then sobbed with renewed vengeance.

My mom immediately came to my bed and gently pushed my hair off of my forehead. She continued stroking my hair as I sobbed out pent up emotion. When I calmed slightly, she took my hand and led me into her room for a talk. I climbed into her bed beside her as I had many times before, and snuggled under the quilt. She handed me a box of tissue, then made me start from the beginning.

I explained to her through tearful hiccups how Jenny had told me about Dad and Dale. Mom sighed, but answered honestly. Everything Jenny had said was true. This prompted a new wave of tears, but Mom just kept her arms wrapped around me and waited. Which was good, because it gave me the bravery to ask my next question. Would I be gay like my father? Would I be damned? Would I follow him to hell because I was so much like him?

"We all have agency, Emily," Mom responded. "Yes, you look like your dad, but that doesn't mean you are the same person. You can choose who you want to be."

"I guess you're right," I said through a sob. I wiped my nose and rubbed my eyes. The salt left my skin red and raw. "It is just so horrible. I can't believe he's gay!"

At this Mom seemed to look far into the distance for a few moments. Then she spoke quietly.

"Your father spends a lot of money to fly you to see him. And he does it every chance he gets. Not all fathers do that, you know."

I nodded, but I wasn't quite listening.

"He is excellent at quilting and knows how to sew. How many other dads can do that?" She nudged me playfully.

I giggled a little. It was true; none of my friends could say their dads had made them a dress.

I sniffed hard, and said "Dad is good at French-braiding. *You* can't even do that!"

My mom threw up her hands in mock exasperation. "It's true. He's always been better at fixing yours and your sisters' hair than I have. But remember the time he ripped out his pants while chasing a suspect?"

I laughed. "I love his police stories!"

"He's also an excellent dancer," she sighed. "And ..." she leaned in close and whispered conspiratorially, "he speaks French!" We both squealed with delight.

What a man!

My tears were drying and the dark heavy feeling of guilt began to lift. After a few more minutes of "mommy-time" I went back to bed and slept soundly.

That experience with my mom was the beginning of my understanding of what true love is. My religion told me that my dad's sexual orientation was wrong, yet he remained my father. He was still a good person, still kind, still loving, still wonderful.

I sometimes think this next experience is silly and too comical to share, but it honestly changed me completely. The actress Sharon Stone, known for making borderline porn movies (e.g. *Sliver* and *Basic Instinct*), told Oprah about her near death experience after having a stroke. She explained that when she went to the next life, she felt an overwhelming presence of love and light.

At that moment, it hit me. God loves everybody. I laughed out loud and cried a little when I realized that even Sharon Stone, a woman who had not lived the way my religion teaches, felt the love of God when she died for a few minutes. His love is available to all, including my father. From, of all people, Sharon Stone, I learned not to judge. I learned that I could just love.

And that is why I finally talked to my dad about his orientation about a year ago. My husband and I had flown to California for my cousin's wedding. There we spent time with my dad eating out, visiting the Monterey Bay Aquarium, and shopping. But nothing really significant happened until we were sitting in the audience, my husband and daughter on one side of me, my dad on the other. All of the guests were dressed fabulously, and the scent of roses filled the air. The wedding had not yet started.

I don't know exactly how I started the conversation, but somehow, I called up the courage to ask my dad, "When did you know that you were gay?"

He cocked his head and nervously bounced his knees. "Well, right after my mission, at BYU all of my friends were dating girls and I realized that I didn't really want to date any girls."

"So, what did you do?" I asked eagerly, fascinated to finally get the story from him. I had no idea he had known before he had married.

"I went to my bishop. He told me to date anyway and get married. He said once I found the right girl and married her, everything would be okay."

"So sex would cure you, huh?" I laughed.

He chuckled. "Yes, that's what they told us in those days." He paused and stared ahead at nothing. He seemed far away, almost as if he were reliving the stress of his decision years ago. "It doesn't work," he finally said.

"Obviously. But, I think the Church is getting better at dealing with this," I said, hoping to comfort him.

"Yes, they are," my dad agreed.

I could see a longing in his blue-as-Paul-Newman's eyes. He seemed to be thinking that he wished the church he'd joined at fourteen, the one that had offered such love and acceptance to begin with, would accept him once again.

We continued to hold our quiet yet momentous conversation until the wedding procession began. We spent the rest of the evening laughing and talking. When the dance floor finally opened up, my dad took me in his arms and we floated around the room, waltzing and fox-trotting. We smiled more with each other because of our comfort. My dad now understood that my religion did not make me hate him. I understood that my dad still loved me despite my belief in a religion that shuns him.

We had finally said "I love you no matter what."

Excerpt from *Facing East*

Carol Lynn Pearson

(MEMORY SPOTLIGHT comes in. MARCUS "becomes" Andrew. This is the only time in the play we "see" Andrew; other times we have only heard him through the voices of his mother and father.) (SOUND OF CRICKETS AND FROGS.)

MARCUS as Andrew: Wanna catch frogs tomorrow, Marcus? That's what my dad and I always did when he brought me up here. Then we'd let them go.

(As Dad.) "Cause frogs, Son, frogs need to be in their frog home with other frogs. They need to be with their own kind." My dad is so great. Hey, Marcus—

(Sings.) "Have I told you lately that I love you?" You are the best frog and I am so happy I found a frog home with another frog, just like me.

(Laughs.) I did not say "fag," I said "frog," you faggy frog you.

(Deep, contented sigh.) So I'm lying here in this sleeping bag on planet earth wondering which of all those stars up there is Kolob. That's where God lives, did I ever tell you? Anyway, that's what Mormons believe. Kolob, Kolob, which one?

(Pause.) Whoa! Shooting star! Hope it wasn't Kolob.

(Deep voice.) Houston, we have a problem.

(Pause.) Maybe Mormons are wrong about God.

My Mom is totally certain that wishes on shooting stars come true. She believes in shooting stars about as much as she believes in the Book of Mormon.

My Mom. I love her so much. When I think about how much pain I cause her…Sometimes, if I think too much about that, I have to sing a hymn.

You know what I wished, every shooting star, every birthday cake, ever since I knew? I wished I wouldn't be gay anymore. I would wish that, and blow on those candles so hard. And I would still be gay. And I would see a shooting star and wish and wish and wish. And I would still be gay.

Whoa! There's another one!

No, Dork, I am wishing—now—that every person in the whole world could be as happy as I am right at this moment. No—this moment. No—this one. Because right now I feel sorry for everybody who is not me. Except maybe you.

Hey, Love, let's just stay here, okay? Let's not go back down the mountain. I'm afraid. Let's just stay in our sleeping bag here, and after we finish the Oreos we will die of starvation and they'll send helicopters and they won't find us for months and then finally they'll find two skeletons lying close to each other with their phalanges intertwined.

I want to play you something. No, it's not Shastakovich. I was driving my dad's car one time and heard this song on his CD. It sort of made my heart stop. I borrowed it and burned a copy. I would play it and dream and think—someday maybe I'll find someone and we'll listen to this song together and then we'll make love. Listen.

(SOUND: MANDY PATINKIN SINGING "GIVE ME A KISS TO BUILD A DREAM ON." Or possibly MARCUS sings it.)

Give me a kiss to build a dream on.
And my imagination will thrive upon that kiss.
Sweetheart, I ask no more than this—
A kiss to build a dream on.
Give me a kiss before you leave me.
And my imagination will feed my hungry heart.
(LIGHTS UP to GENERAL. MARCUS' eyes are closed, his head low.)
Leave me one thing before we part—
A kiss to build a dream on.
(MUSIC out.)

MARCUS: We should have stayed up in the mountains.
(Pause.) He'd hear the Tabernacle Choir sing, or he'd see a family walking by on their way to church, or he'd read in the paper the latest local push against gay marriage—all those things about your church that made him crazy. And of course, after the excommunication—every day, that look. That damned by the God that he loved look. That damned by the church that he loved look.
(Furious.) I'll tell you why your son died. He believed in your church more than he believed in himself. Sounds like an epitaph, doesn't it. Carve it in marble! Right there!

RUTH: He should have been one of those dads in white shirts, holding their babies. Not cast out. He should have married Karen.

MARCUS: Your bishop. No, the runner-up bishop—

ALEX: First counselor. Garth Taylor.

MARCUS: He came over that night—after the church court—with his wife. She brought this big plate of brownies.

RUTH: April Taylor?

Carol Lynn Pearson

MARCUS: He said he had loved Andrew since he was his cub scout master and that nothing would ever change that. And then he sort of gave us this talk about how a couple needs to behave toward each other, how they need to love each other and put each other first and never go to sleep on a quarrel, and how they should prepare sweet little surprises for each other. And forgive each other. Kind of like the talk they give before they do a marriage ceremony.

RUTH: He didn't—?

MARCUS: No. Nothing like that. He said he was sorry that he couldn't assign home teachers to visit us every month, but would we mind if he and April came over every now and then to see how we're doing. And we said we would like that. And then—he asked if we could kneel down and have a prayer.
(Moved.) He blessed our home, and he said we were very loved sons of God. Both of us. And it was...
(MEMORY SPOTLIGHT on MARCUS. Both PARENTS in turn speak as Andrew from the darkness.)
RUTH as Andrew: Marcus?

MARCUS: Yeah?

RUTH as Andrew: Something bad is coming.

MARCUS: What?

RUTH as Andrew: Something very bad.

MARCUS: Cut it out, Andy. Go to sleep.

ALEX as Andrew: You make me too happy.

MARCUS: Cut it out!

ALEX as Andrew: When I was ten and had bad thoughts, I would stick a pencil in the palm of my hand so Jesus wouldn't have to bear my sins alone.

MARCUS: Andy.

ALEX as Andrew: The summer I was thirteen I worked on my uncle's farm in Idaho. There was this boy. We didn't do anything, really, just touched. I knew it was bad, so I would do things.

RUTH as Andrew: One day when I was mowing this big lot I walked close to the fence, pushing my bare arm into the barbed wire. Because wickedness never was happiness.

MARCUS: You deserve to be happy!

RUTH as Andrew: I don't think so. Something bad is going to happen.

MARCUS: No! If there is a God—

ALEX as Andrew: Something very bad.

MARCUS:—He wants you to be happy.

ALEX as Andrew: Every other sin Jesus paid for.

MARCUS: Stop it, Andy. Now!

RUTH as Andrew: Maybe this one is the only one outside Jesus' power, it's that big.

MARCUS: Don't go back there, Andy. You're past that now.

ALEX as Andrew: Something bad...

MARCUS: Shh, Baby. Let me hold you. Shhh. That's it. *(MARCUS hums a moment, no special melody. LIGHTS up to GENERAL.)*
(*Furious.*) This should never have happened! No one has the right to tell another person what God thinks of him! I don't care if it's the Mormon Church or suicide bombers.

RUTH: Don't you dare compare us to—

MARCUS: (Laughs bitterly, indicates the grave) Lady, connect the dots!

ALEX: (Pause) Marcus, did he do it on temple grounds to make a statement against the church?

MARCUS: He told me that first day, "If I ever take my life I'm going to do it right by the temple, because kind angels will be hovering around that place and they will take care of me." *(RUTH and ALEX are stunned into a long silence.)*

ALEX: We thought he was doing better. Something happened.

MARCUS: After the letter...

ALEX: What letter?

MARCUS: That letter about your promotion. Your kids, your values.

RUTH: I am leaving, Alex.

ALEX: I never gave him a copy of that letter! *(RUTH has begun to leave. ALEX stops her.)* Ruth! You did that? You sent Andrew a copy of that letter?

RUTH: I made copies for all our children, so they could be proud of you, see how well regarded you are.

ALEX: You knew how it would make him feel!

RUTH: I thought it might be the final thing that would make him see the light. The thing that would bring him home!

ALEX: You play God with things you have no business in, Ruth! Just like my mother!

RUTH: I never thought—this! *(ALEX sinks to his knees by grave.)*

ALEX: He thought he was holding me back.

RUTH: It would have happened anyway, Alex! Wouldn't it, Marcus?

MARCUS: We'll never know.

RUTH: Yes, it would have! And it's a blessing in the long run. If you don't see it, Alex, then I will have to see it for both of us. He would have gotten deeper and deeper into the darkness. And where would our eternal family be then? A hole where Andrew should have been!
I worked to create a Celestial family, one that I could take back to heaven and say, Look, here is my family—and you can call the roll, Heavenly Father, and all my children, every single one of them, are here!
You've got your work, Alex, and millions of people listen to you and look up to you. You've got your priesthood. My calling, my one calling, the only thing to show that I have been a successful person on this earth, is my family! I gave up everything for my family. And God knows we did every possible thing. He is the only one who can help Andrew repair his broken temple covenants.

ALEX: Covenants? Do you know what covenants you and I have broken, Ruth? Covenants we made every Sunday as we sat on that bench and took the sacrament—

RUTH: No!

ALEX:—to bear one another's burdens—to comfort—

RUTH: We did that!

ALEX:—those that stand in need of comfort. Always to remember him—

RUTH: We did that! We never turned our backs on our son. He was always welcome in our home. Even afterward. I would clear the morning dishes and then I would pray for Andy. I would see what there was to fix for dinner and then I would pray for Andy. I would sweep the floor and then I would pray for Andy. I would be at the grocery store and the clerk would have to speak to me twice because I was praying for my son!

ALEX: We stand guilty, Ruth. I was the priest and you were the Levite, and we came upon the Jewish man who had been beaten and left by the side of the road. Our son.

RUTH: No!

ALEX: We were the thieves that stripped him of his raiment, and wounded him, and departed, leaving him half dead.

RUTH: I will not hear—

ALEX: The only binder of wounds I see standing here is this despicable, outcast, unclean, homosexual Samaritan—friend, who saw nothing but God in our son! We crossed the road and let him suffer. And the awful thing, the truly awful thing is—we are better than that!

RUTH: *(Sobbing)* There is nothing we didn't do for Andy. The encouragement, the therapists, the prayers, the family fasts, his name on the temple prayer rolls, every two weeks, seven different temples. He knew that I loved him. Didn't he know that, Marcus?

MARCUS: Yes. He knew that.

RUTH: *(To Marcus)* You tell me one thing that we did not do! *(To Alex.)* You tell me one thing!

ALEX: We did not hold our son in our arms, and look into his eyes, and say to him, "Andrew, what we want, more than anything, is for you to be happy."

RUTH: Wickedness never was—

ALEX: We trust you, Son, to follow the light inside your own soul—to find your own way home.

RUTH: We could not bless him in his sin! You know that was the one thing we could not do!

ALEX: His sin. That is a stone, Ruth, that I can no longer cast. What if we were very, very—wrong?

RUTH: *(Slowly, after a long silence)* If we were wrong, then my whole life is a waste and I would wish to be in that grave along with my son. And I would hope there is no resurrection morning.

Contributor Biographies

GERALD ARGETSINGER is Associate Professor of Cultural and Creative Studies at the National Technical Institute for the Deaf, a college of the Rochester Institute of Technology. He earned a B.A. in Theatre at Brigham Young University and a PhD in Dramaturgy at Bowling Green State University. He has published extensively on Scandinavian drama, theatre and magic. He served his LDS mission to Denmark and lives in Rochester, NY, with his wife Gail and their two sons. He is a member of the International Brotherhood of Magicians and has received both their top writing award and the Order of Merlin, Shield. His story "Lasting Impressions" was first place winner of the Sensations Literary Journal short story contest, "Sexuality in the Twenty-First Century." He is well known as a director of outdoor drama, including *The Hill Cumorah Pageant*, Palmyra, NY; *Utah! The Jacob Hamblin Story*, Tuacahn, St. George, UT; *Sword of Peace* and *Pathway to Freedom*, Snow Camp Outdoor Theatre, NC. His revision of *Trail of the Lonesome Pine*, the Virginia State Outdoor Drama, is produced annually at the Tolliver Theatre, Big Stone Gap, VA and his original play *Equality of Rights: The First Women's Rights Convention* at the Women's Rights National Historical Park, Seneca Falls, NY. He is founder of the Gay Mormon Literature Project.

DONNA BANTA is a former Mormon and author of the novel, *The Girls from Fourth Ward.* Her short fiction has appeared in the *Todd Point Review* as well as on various Mormon-themed blogs including *Ward Gossip, White and Delightsome, Ex-Mormon Mavens,* and *Main Street Plaza.* She is a graduate of Brigham Young University and was married in the Mormon temple in Oakland, California. For many years she tried to remain active in the LDS Church as a "Mormon feminist," an effort that led to her premature release from practically every ward position she was called to fill. Now she's just a feminist and her calling is writing. She also loves to garden, cook, travel, interact with the broader Mormon community, spend time with her family, and watch old episodes of *Columbo.* She lives in San Francisco with her husband.

MARTY BEAUDET is a freelance writer, graphic designer, communications consultant, and author of fiction. Originally from the San Francisco Bay Area, he has lived in Oregon since 1998 with his husband Chuck. He is fluent in three languages and can make educated errors in several more. He has traveled to 38 of the US states and 19 foreign countries. He has been a tea guest of Her Majesty Queen Elizabeth II, pursued by Hungarian security forces, and questioned by East German authorities (all for unrelated reasons). He also writes under the name Martin Bannon. Marty, who served an LDS mission in Puerto Rico, joined the Mormon

Church as a teenager in Switzerland. At BYU, he majored in Soviet Studies to pursue a career in Intelligence. When he discovered that there was no such thing, he became a writer instead. He has been living out cover legends ever since.

JOHN BENNION writes novels, essays, and short fiction about the western Utah desert and the people who inhabit that forbidding country. He has published a collection of short fiction, *Breeding Leah and Other Stories* (Signature Books, 1991) and a novel, *Falling Toward Heaven* (Signature Books, 2000). He has published short work in *Ascent, AWP Chronicle, English Journal, Utah Holiday, Journal of Experiential Education, Sunstone Magazine, Best of the West II, Black American Literature Forum, Journal of Mormon History, The Hardy Society Journal*, and others. An associate professor at Brigham Young University, Bennion teaches creative writing and the British novel.

JOHN CAMERON (AEA, SAG) received a BS degree in Psychology from Brigham Young University and an MA and PhD in Theatre from Kent State University. He is currently the Head of Acting at the University of Iowa and previously taught Theatre at Stony Brook University, the University of Dayton, and the University of Akron. As an actor he trained with Sanford Meisner and has performed on stage in Europe, Central America, Australia, and with numerous theatres throughout the United States; and in television and film. He is also a director and playwright. He has directed for the academic and professional stage and television, and his plays have been produced at a variety of academic and professional theatres.

BERNARD COOPER is an American novelist and short story writer, born on October 3, 1951 in Hollywood, California. His writing is in part autobiographical and influenced by his own experiences as a gay man. Bernard Cooper's fiction and essays have received several awards. He has both his BFA and MFA in art from California Institute of the Arts. Cooper has written five books, including *The Bill from My Father*, memoir; *Guess Again*, short stories; and *Truth Serum*, memoir.

STEVEN FALES is an actor/writer/producer whose work has been seen from Halifax to Houston. London to Los Angeles, Sao Paulo to San Francisco. He has worked at the Utah Shakespeare Festival and other regional theatres across the country. His first solo play, *Confessions of a Mormon Boy* (directed by Tony Award Winner Jack Hofsiss), received a NY Outer Critics Circle Award Nomination off-Broadway, Overall Excellence Award at New York International Fringe Festival, Oscar Wilde Award Nomination at the Dublin Gay International Fringe Festival, among others. He has played the prestigious Edinburgh Festival and has raised hundreds of thousands of dollars for charity including a benefit for the Point Foundation at Lincoln Center. The book of his play was a Lambda Literary Award Finalist. The original Utah version was published in *Sunstone Magazine. Confessions* is Part One in *The Mormon Boy Trilogy*, which includes the solo plays *Missionary Position* and *Prodigal Dad.* Other solo work includes his cabaret act *Mormon American Princess, Conversations with Heavenly Mother: An Uncommon Diva,* and other standup offerings. His adaptation of Everyman, Kate and Co., was commissioned by The Waterford School. He is a public speaker and has been a featured guest at the Philips Academy Andover, Affirmation, and Tyra Banks (GLAAD Media Award Nomination). Steven received his MFA from the University of Connecticut and his BFA from The Boston Conservatory/BYU. He has two children with actor/writer/producer Emily Pearson, daughter of celebrated Mormon poet Carol Lynn Pearson. Steven was recently featured in the book *The Creative Life* by Julia Cameron (*The Artist's Way*).

A native of southern California, MICHAEL FILLERUP is the author of numerous short stories, a short story collection (*Visions and Other Stories*), two novels (*Beyond the River* and *Go in Beauty*), and mounds of obscure, unpublished, illegible drafts. According to his son Benjamin: "My father is the best unread author I've never read." His three daughters are more complimentary about his writing career; they are also receiving a significantly larger portion of his estate, which means they will each get two sandpaintings instead of one. Michael attended Brigham Young University-Hawaii, Brigham Young University-Provo, and Arizona State University before moving to the Navajo Reservation in 1978 where he, his wife Rebecca, and their four children lived for six years. He started and directed two Navajo language revitalization programs and is the founder and former director of *Puente de Hozho Tri-lingual Magnet School.* Michael lives in Flagstaff, Arizona with Rebecca who doubles as his best friend and confidant, ruthless editor, and full-time Muse.

RIK ISENSEE has published three self-help books for gay men: *Love Between Men*, a book on resolving conflicts in gay relationships; *Reclaiming Your Life*, a guide to recovery from homophobic abuse; and *Are You Ready? The Gay Man's Guide to Thriving at Midlife*. He's also the author of *Spank the Monkey*, where his story "The Summer My Cousin Turned Mormon" first appeared; and *The God Squad—A Spoof on the Ex-Gay Movement*: "…brilliantly over the top…It's twisted, but it's getting funnier with each page…I couldn't help but enjoy this fine display of Rik Isensee's wicked humor. Honest!"—Jeffrey Jasper, *Lambda Book Report*. Rik is a Licensed Clinical Social Worker and specializes in psychotherapy with gay men in San Francisco. www.GayTherapist.com

JULIE JENSEN has been in the theatre all her life. Many of the experiences were wonderful, some were awful, almost all of them hopelessly funny. And for the last reason, she wrote this play. At this point, she's written 30-odd plays, all of which have been produced professionally, and a half-dozen of which have been published. Julie is the recipient of the Kennedy Center Award for New American Plays and many other awards. She lives now in Salt Lake City and works as a playwright and lecturer on playwriting around the country and abroad. She thinks it is a good life, providing you're always ready for public humiliation.

JONATHAN LANGFORD is a long-time reader, critic, and reviewer of Mormon literature. His novel *No Going Back*, about a same-sex attracted LDS teenager, was a finalist for the 2009 Whitney Award for best general fiction novel by an LDS writer. Married with three children, Langford is active in his LDS ward in western Wisconsin. He currently moderates *Dawning of a Brighter Day*, the Association for Mormon Letters blog, and is hard at work on several science fiction and fantasy stories in between freelance projects as an informational writer.

M. LARSEN was born and raised in the LDS Church. He served his two-year mission in Latin America.

JEFF LAVER grew up in a devout Mormon household in Salt Lake City. He served a mission in Colombia, earned a B.A. in Spanish literature from the University of Utah, and spent a year at BYU. He is the author of several short stories and the novel *Just Call Me Greg*. He likes gardening and antiques, and he lives in a 1920's era home in Salt Lake's Sugar House neighborhood. He is glad to be gay and would now choose to be queer if sexual orientation were a choice. Jeff has found a spiritual home in the Episcopal Church.

Born in Pittsburg, PA in 1961, DAVID LEAVITT is a graduate of Yale University and a professor at the University of Florida. He is the author of *Family Dancing* (finalist for the PEN/Faulkner Prize and the National Book Critics' Circle Award); *Equal Affections*; *The Page Turner*; *Martin Bauman, or A Sure Thing*; *The Lost Language of Cranes*; *While England Sleeps*, and numerous short stories. His most recent novel is *The Indian Clerk*. Leavitt is also co-editor of the anthologies *The Penguin Book of Gay Short Stories* and *Pages Passed from Hand to Hand*. At the University of Florida he is a member of the Creative Writing faculty and is also the editor of *Subtropics*, the University of Florida's literary review. He divides his time between Florida and Tuscany, Italy.

HUGO OLAIZ is a third generation Mormon from La Plata, Argentina, and has a degree in Letters from Universidad Nacional de La Plata and a Master's in Spanish from Brigham Young University. He served an LDS mission in Paraguay. Hugo has published both fiction and scholarly pieces in *Dialogue: A Journal of Mormon Thought*, and miscellaneous articles in *Sunstone* magazine. He is the current news editor for *Sunstone* and lives in Oxford, Ohio, with his husband John-Charles Duffy and a beagle-mix named Patches.

Canadian-born RON OLIVER's work has been twice nominated for the prestigious Director's Guild of America Award. Emmy-nominated director/writer/producer

Ron Oliver started his career with the cult hit *Prom Night II* (1987)—called "the *Blue Velvet* (1986) of high school horror movies" by the *Los Angeles Times*— and since then has directed and/or written award-winning theatrical feature films and television ratings hits for such studios as Warner Brothers, Fox and The Walt Disney Co. He is also a published author of award-winning short fiction as well as penning an acclaimed series of comic essays on filmmaking in the well-regarded *MovieScope* magazine. When asked to contribute to this anthology, he responded, "Um...you DO realize the Mormons in my story 'Nestle's Revenge' die horribly at the hands of a delusional, psychopathic homosexual?" We responded that it is in the tradition of Ray Bradbury's early horror fiction and that it demonstrates clearly that Mormons have become a part of the mainstream American culture.

CAROL LYNN PEARSON has been a professional writer, speaker, and performer for many years. Her autobiography, *Goodbye, I Love You*, tells the story of her marriage to a homosexual man, their divorce, ongoing friendship, and her caring for him as he died of AIDS. For many years, she has tirelessly worked to end the collision between religion and homosexuality. Among her contributions are a stage play, *Facing East*, the story of a Mormon couple dealing with the suicide of their gay son, and *No More Goodbyes: Circling the Wagons around Our Gay Loved Ones*, which examines the tragic and unnecessary goodbyes we continue to say around the issue of homosexuality, and also presents many inspiring stories of families finding new and positive ways to relate to their gay children. Ms. Pearson has an MA in theater, is the mother of four grown children, and lives in Walnut Creek, California. Learn more about her at www.clpearson.com

EMILY JANUARY PETERSEN holds a B.A. in English with an emphasis in editing and technical writing from Brigham Young University and an MA in English literary studies from Weber State University, where she taught composition courses for three years. She is currently working on her PhD in Theory and Practice of Professional Communication program at Utah State University, where she is a research fellow. Before pursuing a career in academia, she worked as an editor for the international section of a large non-profit corporation's security department. Her writing has previously been published in *Sunstone*, *Compendium2*, *The Atrium*, and *Indiana English*. Emily is an accomplished pianist and enjoys blogging about books at emilyjanuary.wordpress.com. She is married and lives in Kaysville, Utah, where she and her husband are raising two beautiful girls.

LEVI S. PETERSON is a retired professor of English at Weber State University, presently living in Issaquah, Washington, with his wife, Althea Sand Peterson. He is a former editor of *Dialogue: A Journal of Mormon Thought*. He is the author of two collections of short stories, *The Canyons of Grace* and *Night Soil*; two novels, *Aspen Marooney* and *The Backslider*; a biography, *Juanita Brooks: The Life Story of a Courageous Historian of the Mountain Meadows Massacre*; and an autobiography, *A Rascal By Nature, A Christian By Yearning*. He is also the compiler of an anthology, *Greening Wheat: Fifteen Mormon Short Stories*, and the author of many essays and articles on Mormon literature and culture.

ERIC SAMUELSEN was born in Provo, Utah on April 10, 1956, but spent most of his early life in Bloomington, Indiana. He received a bachelor's degree in theatre from BYU in 1983 and returned to Bloomington and earned a PhD from Indiana University in 1991. He taught at Wright State University in Dayton, Ohio before joining the faculty at BYU in 1992. Most of Samuelsen's early plays were produced at BYU, but more recently he has begun a relationship with Plan B Theatre Company, and many of his newer plays have been produced there. This may be due to a more controversial bent in later plays; *Borderlands* has a character who is an openly gay Mormon youth.

KEN SHAKIN is a writer of underground transgressive fiction and has been called the most flippant man in fiction. His irreverent books stain the shelves of the public library, including the highly acclaimed *Love Sucks* (1997), *Grandma Gets Laid* (2008), and most recently *Thrillerotica* (2010). Thrillerotica.com is home to his unique genre, "calculated to send a shiver down even the most desensitized spine" (Omnilit). The New York native is a graduate of the Juilliard School, with a degree in piano. He lives in Berlin. "Shakin's darkly humorous and perverse works have earned him an underground following, largely because he flaunts every standard of decency." -Contemporary Authors

SCOTT SINGER, see Gerald Argetsinger

TREVOR SOUTHEY was born in Rhodesia, Africa (now Zimbabwe) in 1940. He emigrated to the U.S. in 1965. Southey's formal training includes two years at the Brighton College of Art in Sussex, England, a year in Durban, South Africa, and two degrees obtained from Brigham Young University in 1967 and 1969. He taught at BYU through 1977 and has since pursued his career independently, although he remains deeply interested in art education, giving occasional workshops. In 1967, Southey married Elaine Fish, and together they had four children during their fifteen-year marriage. Environmental issues, especially relative to visual concerns such as urban planning, continue to command considerable attention from him. Many major commissions in various parts of the U.S. and Britain in painting and sculpture have dominated his production in the last few years. Southey's media also include drawing, printmaking, and stained glass. His work is included in many numerous private collections, ranging from that of actress Brooke Shields to Senator and Mrs. Orrin Hatch. His work is also included in a wide variety of institutional and corporate collections. He has been increasingly interested in writing and has collaborated with K. Mitchell Snow in the production of a major, lavishly illustrated volume about his work entitled *Trevor Southey: Reconciliation*.

JOHNNY TOWNSEND is a native of New Orleans who relocated to Seattle after Hurricane Katrina. He has designed and sewn over 25 quilts, some of which are housed at ONE Archives in Los Angeles. Townsend has earned three English degrees and a Biology degree. Voted "Most Courteous" in high school (along with a lesbian), he feels that it is essential to be kind to one another. He is the author of fourteen books, including *Mormon Underwear, Sex among the Saints*, and *Zombies for Jesus*. His book, *The Abominable Gayman*, about a gay Mormon missionary in Italy, was named to Kirkus Reviews' Best of 2011, and his book *Marginal Mormons* was named to Kirkus Reviews' Best of 2012. Townsend's research on the UpStairs Lounge fire, in which 32 people were killed in an arson attack at a French Quarter gay bar on Gay Pride Day in 1973, was published as *Let the Faggots Burn*. His partner is fellow ex-Mormon Gary Tolman.

"In the beginning was DIRK VANDEN…" His seven novels, written between 1969 and 1972, were among the very first literary assertions that "Gay is Good— (maybe better)" and help form part of the foundation of what has become Gay Literature. His "All Trilogy" was written in 1969, 1970, and 1971, republished as *All Together* and honored in 2012 with a "Lammy" as Best Gay Erotica of 2011 and is Dirk Vanden's acknowledged erotic masterpiece. Dirk's autobiography, *It Was Too Soon Before…*, written in 2010-2011, was the winner of the Rainbow Awards' Best Biography or Memoir of 2012, and it tied for 3rd place as Best Book or Novel of 2012.

ROBERT HODGSON VAN WAGONER's first novel, *Dancing Naked*, was awarded the Utah Center for the Book's Utah Book Award and the Utah Arts Council's Publication Prize. His short stories have appeared in literary periodicals, ezines, and anthologies, and have been selected for various awards, including *Carolina Quarterly's* Charles B. Wood Award for Distinguished Writing, *Shenandoah's* Jeanne Charpiot Goodheart Award for Fiction, *Sunstone's* Brookie and D.K. Brown Memorial Fiction Award, and *Weber Studies'* Dr. O. Marvin Lewis Award for Best Fiction, 1994-1997. Van Wagoner lives in Washington State.

ALAN MICHAEL WILLIAMS is working on a PhD in English/Cultural Studies at the University of Washington. His scholarly interests include queer religion, gender/sexuality, critical ethnic studies and transnational queer visual culture. His essay, "Mormon and Queer at the Crossroads," (2011) which is about the history of homosexuality in the LDS Church over the last 30 years, appeared in *Dialogue: A Journal of Mormon Thought*. Alan tries to balance his schooling with his other interests (speculative fiction writing, game design, martial arts and yaoi) with limited success. He lives in Seattle with his partner, Michael. Personal website: www.amwilliams.com

Genre Bibliography of Gay Mormon Fiction and Drama

1959—2012

Compiled by Gerald S. Argetsinger, PhD

While I have attempted to locate every conceivable work that fits the parameters of this study, I am not so naïve as to assume that other works do not exist. If the reader knows of *any* work which should be included, please forward bibliographic information to the author at gsanla@rit.edu.

Film

Advise and Consent. Directed by Otto Preminger; Script by Wendell Mayes, 1962.

Angels in America. Directed by Mike Nichols; Script by Al Pacino and Tony Kushner, 2003.

The Falls. Directed and Script by Jon Garcia, 2012.

The Laramie Project. Directed and Script by Moises Kaufman, 2002.

Latter Days. Directed and Script by C. Jay Cox, 2003

Plays

Cameron, John. "14." An original play produced by the University of Iowa Theatre Dept, Jan 31, 2008. Unpublished ms. Copyrighted by the author, 2007.

Fales, Steven. "Confessions of a Mormon Boy." (Utah version) Sunstone. Issue 130. December, 2003: 40-56. (Produced 2001).

Fales, Steven. "Confessions of a Mormon Boy: Behind the Scenes of the Off-Broadway Hit." (NYC version) Alyson Books, 2006. (Produced 2005).

Fales, Steven. "Missionary Position." An original play produced by Celebration Theater, Los Angeles, CA, January 9, 2009. Unpublished ms. Copyrighted by the author, 2009.

Fales, Steven. "Prodigal Dad." An original play produced in several workshop productions, 2010-13. Unpublished ms. Copyrighted by the author, 2010, 2013.

Feeser, Roman. "Missa Solemnis: the Play About Henry." An original play produced by the Manhattan Repertory Theatre, Feb 27-March 1, 2008. Unpublished ms. Copyrighted by the author, 2008.

Frost, Charles and Troy Williams. "The Passion of Sister Dottie S. Dixon." An original play produded in 2009 and 2010 at the Pygmalion Theatre, Salt Lake City, Utah. Unpublished ms. Copyrighted by the authors, 2009 & 2010.

Greene, Matthew. "Adam and Steve and the Empty Sea." An original play produced by Plan B Theatre, Salt Lake City, UT, January 31, 2013.

Hite, Devan Mark. "Ranging." An original play. Unpublished ms. 2010. US Copyright Case: 1-231868341

Hite, Devan Mark. "Since *Psychopathia Sexualis*." An original play produced by the Fresh Fruit Festival (The Seventh Annual International Festival of Lesbian, Gay, Bisexual, Transgender Arts & Culture), Hudson Guild Theatre, New York City, July 17, 2009. Unpublished ms. Copyrighted by the author, 2009.

Hunter, Samuel H. "The Whale." American Theatre. Vol. 30. No. 2. February, 2013.

Jensen, Julie. "Wait!" Woodstock, Illinois: Dramatic Publishing, 2005.

Kaufman, Moises. "The Laramie Project." NY: Vintage Books, 2001.

Kaufman, Moises, *et al.* "The Laramie Project, Ten Years Later." New York, NY: Dramatist's Play Service, 2012.

Kushner, Tony. "Angels in America, Part One: Millennium Approaches." NY: Theatre Communications Group, Inc., 1993.

Kushner, Tony. "Angels in America, Part Two: Perestroika." NY Theatre Communications Group, Inc., 1994.

LaBute, Neil. "A Gaggle of Saints." Bash: Latter-day Plays. Woodstock, NY: The Overlook Press, 1999.

Larson, Melissa Leilani. "Little Happy Secrets." *Out of the Mount: 19 From New Play Project.* El Cerrito, CA: Peculiar Pages, 2010.

O'Donnell, Mark. "Strangers in Town." An Elementary Education. NY: Alfred A. Knopf, 1985. reprinted. Strangers on Earth. NY: Dramatists Play Service, 1993: 105-114.

O'Donnell, Mark. Strangers on Earth. NY: Dramatists Play Service, 1993.

Parker, Trey, Robert Lopez and Matt Stone. "The Book of Mormon." An original play produced on Broadway at the Eugene O'Neill Theatre, March 24, 2011. New York: New Market Press, 2011.

Pearson, Carol Lynn. "Facing East." Walnut Creek, CA: Pivot Point Books, 2006.

Rogers, Laekin. "Hands of Sodom." An original play produced by Westminster College, Salt Lake City, UT, Oct. 8, 2008. Revised unpublished ms. Copyrighted by the author, 2008.

Rudnick, Paul. "The Most Fabulous Story Ever Told." New York City: Dramatists Play Service Inc., 1999.

Samuelsen, Eric. "Borderlanders." An original play to be produced by Plan B Theatre Company, Salt Lake City, March 30, 2011. Sunstone. Issue 162. March 31, 2011: 14-36.

Samuelsen, Eric. "Duets." An original play to be produced by Plan B Theatre Company, Salt Lake City, 2013.

Novels

Baker, Elna. *The New York Regional Mormon Singles Halloween Dance: A Memoir.* New York City: Plume. 2009.

Bills, Greg. *Consider This Home.* NY: Simon and Schuster, 1994.

Buchanan, James. *Hard Fall.* Albion, NY: MLR Press, 2009.

Buchanan, James. *Spin Out*. Albion, NY: MLR Press, 2011.

Drury, Alan. *Advise and Consent*. Garden City, NY: Doubleday and Company, Inc., 1959.

Ebershoff, David. *The 19th Wife*. NY: Random House, 2008.

Fabris, T. *Latter Days*. (novel adaptation of the screenplay by C. Jay Cox). Los Angeles: Alyson Books, 2004.

Jahns, Jason. *Gman: A Mormon Spy Story*. Phoenix, AZ: North Star Books, 2012.

Langford, Jonathan. *No Going Back*. Provo, UT: Zarahemla Press, 2009.

Leavitt, David. "The Term Paper Artist." *Arkansas*. NY: Houghton Mifflin, Co., 1997.

Maupin, Armistead. *Mary Ann in Autumn*. NY: Harper (An imprint of HarperCollins Publishers), 2010.

Mordden, Ethan. *How Long Has This Been Going On?* NY: St. Martin's Press, Stonewall Editions, 1995.

Pearson, Carol Lynn. *The Hero's Journey of the Gay & Lesbian Mormon*. Walnut Creek, CA: Pivot Point Books, 2012.

Peterson, Levi S. *The Backslider*. Salt Lake City, UT: Signature Books, 1990.

Smith, Emily Wing. *The Way He Lived*. Woodbury, MN: Flux - Llewellyn Publications, 2008.

Vanden, Dirk. (Richard Fullmer) *All is Well*. (Repbl. GLB Press, 2005) Frenchy's Gay Line, 1971.

Vanden, Dirk. (Richard Fullmer) *All of Me (Can You Take All of Me?)*. Pittsburgh, PA: RoseDog Books, 2010.

Vanden, Dirk. (Richard Fullmer) *All or Nothing*. (Repbl. GLB Press, 2005) Frenchy's Gay Line, 1970.

Vanden, Dirk. (Richard Fullmer) *All Together: The All Trilogy.* (Repbl. in one volume of *I Want It All, All or Nothing, and All Is Well)* Loveyoudevine Alterotica, 2011.

Vanden, Dirk. (Richard Fullmer) *I Want It All.* (Repbl. GLB Press, 2005) Frenchy's Gay Line, 1969.

van Wagoner, Robert Hodgson. *Dancing Naked.* Salt Lake City: Signature Books, 1999.

Novels—Self Published

Anthony, Garcia. *Raintree.* Lexington, KY: www.greatunpublished.com (Title No. 797), 2002.

Banta, Donna. *The Girls From Fourth Ward.* CreateSpace Independent Publishing Platform, 2012.

Beaudet, Marty. *By A Thread.* Lexington, KY: CreateSpace, 2010.

Beckstead, Brian D. *The Stallion Warriors.* Durham, CT: Strategic Book Group, 2011.

Diaconoff, Cara. *I'll Be A Stranger To You.* San Francisco: Outpost19. Kindle Edition, 2011.

Hawker, Libbie. *Baptism for the Dead.* Smashwords Edition, CreateSpace Independent Publishing Platform, 2012.

Jenkins, Cristi. *Execute This: Confessions of a Mormon Freak.* www.booksurge.com, 2009.

Killick, Jerod. *Without a Testimony.* Lexington, KY, 2012.

Laver, Jeff. *Just Call me Greg.* CreateSpace.com (an Amazon.com company), 2009.

Schabarum, Tom. *The Narrows, Miles Deep.* Lexington, KY: Cascadia Publishing, 2011.

Williams, Alan Michael. *Ockham's Razor.* Booksurge Publishing, 2009.

Short Stories

Banta, Donna. "The Call." *The Todd Point Review*. Summer 2010: 39-46.

Bennion, John. "The Interview." *Dialogue: A Journal of Mormon Thought* 18:2 (Summer, 1985): 167-176. Reprt. *Breeding Leah and Other Stories* by John Bennion, Salt Lake City: Signature Books, 1991.

Cooper, Bernard. "Hunters and Gatherers." *Guess Again*. NY: Simon & Schuster, 2000: 93-124.

Fillerup, Michael. "The Seduction of H. Lyman Winger." *Dialogue: A Journal of Mormon Thought*, 29 (2) Summer 1996, pp. 155-175.

Gullino, Derek. "Sleuths." *In Our Lovely Deseret: Mormon Fictions*, ed. by Robert Raleigh. Salt Lake City: Signature Books, 1998: 153-156.

Isensee, Rik. "The Summer My Cousin Turned Mormon." *Spank the Monkey: Reports from the Front Lines of Our Quirky Culture*. Bloomington, IN: Unlimited Publishing, 2003: 74-79.

Laver, Jeff. "Sharon." *Outfront Review* Vol. 1, No. 6, July 1-15, 1992:14-17.

Mortensen, Lee Ann. "Not Quite Peru." *In Our Lovely Deseret: Mormon Fictions*, ed. by Robert Raleigh. Salt Lake City: Signature Books, 1998: 157-178.

Olaiz, Hugo. "The Birth of Tragedy." *Dialogue: A Journal of Mormon Thought*. Vol. 44, No. 2. Summer, 2011: 157-160.

Oliver, Ron. "Nestle's Revenge." *Queer Fear*, ed. By Michael Rowe. Vancouver, BC, Canada: Arsenal Pulp Press, 2000.

Peterson, Emily January. "I Love You No Matter What" *Sunstone*. Issue 152. Dec., 2008:30-33.

Peterson, Levi S. "The Dream." *Dialogue: A Journal of Mormon Thought*. Vol. 44, No. 1, Spring, 2011: 131-143.

Peterson, Levi S. "Trinity." *Canyons of Grace*. Chicago: University of Illinois Press, 1982: 27-34.

Shoemaker, Ryan. "Richard Golightly: A Novel." *Dialogue: A Journal of Mormon Thought*. Vol. 44, No. 1, Spring, 2011: 144-161.

Shakin, Ken. "Strange Bedfellows." *Real Men Ride Horses*. London: GMP Publishers Ltd., 1999.

Singer, Scott. (Jerry Argetsinger) "Lasting Impressions." *Sensations Magazine*. Issue 22. Summer, 2001: 45-55.

Townsend, Johnny. "Almond Milk." *In Our Lovely Deseret: Mormon Fictions*, ed. by Robert Raleigh. Salt Lake City: Signature Books, 1998: 63-84. Reprt: *The Abominable Gayman* by Johnny Townsend, 2010.

Townsend, Johnny. "Bloodletting." *Christopher Street*. Issue 225. May, 1995. Reprt: *The Abominable Gayman* by Johnny Townsend, 2010.

Townsend, Johnny. "Bus Surfing." *Christopher Street*. Issue 174. March, 1992. Reprt: *The Abominable Gayman* by Johnny Townsend, 2010.

Townsend, Johnny. "The Buzzard Tree." *Dialogue: A Journal of Mormon Thought*. (4) Winter, 2007. Reprt: *The Circumcision of God* by Johnny Townsend, 2009.

Townsend, Johnny. "The Ditch." *Christopher Street*. Issue 220. December 1994. Reprt: *The Abominable Gayman* by Johnny Townsend, 2010.

Townsend, Johnny. "Killing Babies." *Backspace*. Vol. 4, No. 1. Fall/Winter, 1995/96. Reprt: *The Abominable Gayman* by Johnny Townsend, 2010.

Townsend, Johnny. "Moot." *Backspace*. Vol. 2, No. 3. Spring, 1994. Reprt: *Dinosaur Perversions* by Johnny Townsend, 2010.

Townsend, Johnny. "The 9:20 Express Train to Hell." *Backspace*. Vol. 2, No. 4. Summer, 1994. Reprt: *The Abominable Gayman* by Johnny Townsend, 2010.

Townsend, Johnny. "P-Day Man." *RFD*, Issue 66. Summer, 1991. Reprt: *The Abominable Gayman* by Johnny Townsend, 2010.

Townsend, Johnny. "Pissing in Peace." *Christopher Street*. Issue 201. May, 1993. Reprt: *The Abominable Gayman* by Johnny Townsend, 2010.

Townsend, Johnny. "Pronouncing the Apostrophe." *Glimmer Train*. (Issue 71) Summer, 2009. Reprt: *The Golem of Rabbi Loew* by Johnny Townsend, 2010.

Townsend, Johnny. "Rapture." *Dialogue: A Journal of Mormon Thought* (2) Summer, 1995: 153-160. Reprt: *The Circumcision of God* by Johnny Townsend, 2009.

Townsend, Johnny. "The Rift." *Massachusetts Review*, Vol. L, No. 3, Autumn 2009: 309-323. Reprt: *The Abominable Gayman* by Johnny Townsend, 2010.

Townsend, Johnny. "Shepherd Boy." *Christopher Street*. Issue 230. December, 1995. Reprt: *The Abominable Gayman* by Johnny Townsend, 2010.

Townsend, Johnny. "Transfer Cookies." *Harrington Gay Men's Literary Quarterly*. Vol. 9, Issue 3-4, 2007, pp. 5-21. Reprt: *The Abominable Gayman* by Johnny Townsend, 2010.

Townsend, Johnny. "Washing Dishes." *Christopher Street*. Issue 213, May, 1994. Reprt: *The Abominable Gayman* by Johnny Townsend, 2010.

van Wagoner, Robert Hodgson. "Staying Away From Blake." *In Our Lovely Deseret: Mormon Fictions*, ed. by Robert Raleigh. Salt Lake City: Signature Books, 1998: 1-36.

van Wagoner, Robert Hodgson. "Strong Like Water." *Dialogue: A Journal of Mormon Thought*, Vol. 27, No. 1. (Spring, 1994): 253-272.

Collections

Townsend, Johnny. *The Abominable Gayman*. BookLocker.com, Inc, 2010.
Gay Mormon Missionary Stories: The Abominable Gayman, The Napoletan Bump Syndrome, The Rift,* Coping With Camorra, The Letter,* The Shepherd Boy,* The Happiness Approach, The Ditch,* The 9:20 Express Train to Hell,* Let There Be Light, Being Bravo, Killing Babies,* Pissing in Peace,* As a Man Thinketh, Bus Surfing,* Washing Dishes,* A Wife of Whoredoms, Bloodletting,* Almond Milk,* P-Day Man,* Transfer Cookies*
*Reprints of published stories.

Townsend, Johnny. *The Circumcision of God*. BookLocker.com, Inc., 2009.
Gay theme stories: Rapture (reprt), The Removal of Debra, The Buzzard Tree (reprt), The Mission

Townsend, Johnny. *Dinosaur Perversions*. BookLocker.com, Inc., 2010.
All gay Mormon theme stories: Playing Around, Ambient Dreams, Moot, Dinosaur Perversions, Beauty All Around, Fostering Brotherhood, A Dildo for the United Order, Pot of Gold, Dual Diagnosis, Masturbating Loudly, Fucking an

Angel, God's Worry Beads, Becoming an Ammonite, The Opposite of Love, The Carrier.

Townsend, Johnny. *Flying Over Babel*. BookLocker.com,Inc., 2011.
Gay theme stories: The Disseminator of Seeds, A Breath of Fresh Air, To Open the Eyes of the Blind, Edited Out, Making Lemonade, Barricading the Emergency Exit, Sins of the Fathers, If You Asked Me To, Flying Over Babel.

Townsend, Johnny. *The Gay Mormon Quilter's Club*. Booklocker.com, 2010.
All gay Mormon theme stories: The Gay Mormon Quilter's Club, Sensitive Statues, Twinkell the Half-Elf and his Gold, The Face of a Missionary, Orange Trees in the Quarry, Empty Window Seats, The Inner Light of Outer Darkness, The Brother of Spotted Owls, Sob Story, Eunuch for the Blue Cross, The Hospitality of Sodom

Townsend, Johnny. *God's Gargoyles*. BookLocker.com, Inc., 2009.
All gay Mormon theme stories: God's Gargoyles, Swollen Testicles, Private Dick, Rocky Mountain Horror Show, Learning to Sing in Antwerp, Robbing People Blind, Ronnie and Clyde, The Sneakover Prince, Healing the Sick, Superman's Brain Tumor, A Light Going Out, Sex at Sunstone, African Queen Meets Alien, The Lithium Prophecies

Townsend, Johnny. *The Golem of Rabbi Loew*. BookLocker.com,In., 2010.
Stories with a Jewish bent; some with Mormon characters: Pronouncing the Apostrophe (reprt), The Convert's Mezuzah.

Townsend, Johnny. *Marginal Mormons*. BookLocker.com, Inc., 2012.
Gay theme stories: Drug of Choice, Partying with St. Roch, A Time to Die, The Occupiers, Playing the Card.

Townsend, Johnny. *Mormon Fairy Tales*. BookLocker.com, Inc., 2011.
Gay theme stories: The Three Nephites Get Syphilis, The Odds, Awkward Family Photos, Partying With God, A Grain of Mustard Seed, The Waters of Redemption, Death at the Temple of Inscriptions.

Townsend, Johnny. *Mormon Underwear*. BookLocker.com, Inc., 2009.
More extreme gay theme stories: Mormon Underwear, Splitting With Elder Tanner, The Pool Room, Revolt of the Morlocks, Verboten, Garbage Balls, Sex Organs, Dating the Homeless, Dirty Cock Sucker, Burning Love, Celestial Moving Vans, Alien Dick, The End of the World

Townsend, Johnny. *Sex Among the Saints*. Booklocker.com., Inc, 2009.

Gay theme stories: The Virgin Prostitute, The Pig Door, Making Hay, Drag
Queen Decoys, God's Prick, The Ass Man Cometh

Townsend, Johnny. *Zombies for Jesus*. Booklocker.com, Inc, 2010.
Gay theme stories: Betty's Dream Date, Twenty-Six Years, The Mark of Abel,
The Bishop's Confession, Tilly the Barbarian.

Books That Don't Really Fit the Study, But Seem To Be Significant

Fullmer, Richard F. *Why Me? Why Not? The Authorized Autobiography of
Dirk Vanden*, 2010.

Townsend, Johnny. *Let the Faggots Burn: The UpStairs Lounge Fire*.
Booklocker.com, Inc, 2011.
Interviews and a narrative description of the UpStairs Lounge Fire in New
Orleans, LA, June 24, 1973. Important research materials for reporters and writers.

Acknowledgments

Grateful acknowledgment is made for permission to reprint the following copyrighted works:

"The Interview" by John Bennion. Copyright ©1991 Signature Books. Used by permission of Signature Books and the author. Originally published in *Breeding Leah and Other Stories* by John Bennion, Signature Books, 1991.

"Hunters and Gatherers" by Bernard Cooper. Reprinted by permission of International Creative Management, Inc. Copyright ©2000 by Bernard Cooper.

"Lasting Impressions" by Scott Singer. Reprinted by permission of *Sensations Magazine*. Copyright ©2001, David Messineo, Publisher and by permission of Gerald S. Argetsinger.

Selection from *By a Thread* by Marty Beaudet. Copyright ©2010 by Marty Beaudet. Used by permission of the author.

Selection from "14" by John Cameron. An original play Copyright ©2008 by John Cameron. Used by permission of the author. Premier: University of Iowa Theatre Dept., January 2008.

Selection from "Missionary Position" by Steven Fales. An original play Copyright ©2009 by Steven Fales. Used by permission of the author. Premier: Celebration Theater, Los Angeles, CA, January 2009.

"The Seduction of H. Lyman Winger" by Michael Fillerup. Copyright ©1996 by Michael Fillerup. Used by permission of the author.

"The Summer My Cousin Turned Mormon" by Rik Isensee. Copyright ©2003 by Rik Isensee. Used by permission of the author.

Selection from "Wait!" by Julie Jensen. Copyright ©2005 by Julie Jensen. Used by permission of the author. Premier: Salt Lake Acting Company, Salt Lake City, UT, April 2003.

Selection from *No Going Back* by Jonathan Langford. Copyright ©2009 by Jonathan Langford. Used by permission of the author.

"The Term Paper Artist" by David Leavitt. Copyright ©1997 by David Leavitt. Used by permission of Houghton Mifflin Company.

"The Call" by Donna Banta. Copyright ©2010 by Donna Banta. Used by permission of the author.

"The Birth of Tragedy" by Hugo Olaiz. Copyright ©2011 by Hugo Olaiz. Used by permission of the author.

"Nestle's Revenge" by Ron Oliver. Copyright ©2000 by Ron Oliver. Used by permission of the author.

Selection from "Facing East" by Carol Lynn Pearson. Copyright ©2006 by Carol Lynn Pearson. Used by permission of the author. Premier: Plan B Theatre Company, Salt Lake City, UT, November 2006.

"I Love You No Matter What" by Emily January Petersen. Copyright ©2008. Used by permission of the author.

"The Dream" by Levi S. Peterson. Copyright ©2011 by Levi S. Peterson. Used by permission of the author.

"Duets" by Eric Samuelsen. Copyright © 2013 by Eric Samuelsen. Used by permission of the author. Premier: Plan B Theatre Company, Salt Lake City, UT, 2013/14 Season.

"Strange Bedfellows" by Ken Shakin. Copyright ©1999 by Ken Shakin. Used by permission of the author.

"Partying with St. Roch" by Johnny Townsend. Copyright ©2012 by Johnny Townsend. Used by permission of the author.

"Gay Messiah" by Dirk Vanden. Copyright ©2010 by Richard Fullmer. Used by permission of the author.

"Strong Like Water" by Robert Hodgson van Wagoner. Copyright ©1994 by Robert Hodgson van Wagoner. Used by permission of the author.

Selection from *Ockham's Razor* by Alan Michael Williams. Copyright ©2009 by Alan Michael Williams. Used by permission of the author.

In addition, the following stories are being published for the first time in *Latter-Gay Saints*. Copyrights are retained by the authors:

"MTC Interview" by M. Larsen. Copyright ©2013 by M. Larsen.

"Peter's Mirror" by Jeff Laver. Copyright ©2013 by Jeff Laver.

CPSIA information can be obtained at www.ICGtesting.com
Printed in the USA
LVOW07s0133130216

474949LV00004B/173/P